T0339783

# THE EMINENT DOMAIN REVOLT

# THE EMINENT DOMAIN REVOLT

## CHANGING PERCEPTIONS IN A NEW CONSTITUTIONAL EPOCH

## John Ryskamp

Algora Publishing
New York

ISBN-13: 978-0-87586-524-9 (trade paper)
ISBN-13: 978-0-87586-525-6 (hard cover)
ISBN-13: 978-0-87586-526-3 (ebook)

Library of Congress Cataloging-in-Publication Data —

Ryskamp, John.
    The eminent domain revolt : changing perceptions in a new constitutional epoch /
John Ryskamp.
        p. cm.
    Includes bibliographical references and index.
    ISBN 978-0-87586-524-9 (pbk.: alk. paper) — ISBN 978-0-87586-525-6 (hardcover:
alk. paper) — ISBN 978-0-87586-526-3 (ebook)  1. Eminent domain—United States.  I.
Title.

    KF5599.R97 2007
    343.73'0252—dc22

                        2006036483

Front Cover: USA - Eminent Domain Power Play
Image: © Jennifer Brown/Star Ledger/Corbis
Photographer: Jennifer Brown
Date Photographed: October 27, 2005
Location Information: Jersey City, NJ, USA

Printed in the United States

For
Michael Kasanoff
the most important of the attorneys who have begun
implementing the fourth Constitutional epoch.

*Carpe diem*

Glossary

Fact: a conclusion reached in litigation or legislation by evidentiary rules

Fact of the individual: an unchanging fact of human experience

Housing: a fact accorded minimum scrutiny by the United States Supreme Court in Lindsey v. Normet in 1973

Scrutiny: the review process by which the court determines whether a government action is Constitutional

Scrutiny regime: the entire Constitutional review process established by the United States Supreme Court in West Coast Hotel v. Parrish in 1937 and elaborated in later Supreme Court cases

# Table of Contents

# Foreword

On June 29, 2006, Susette Kelo simply gave up. She could no longer withstand the unrelenting pressure. A nurse in New London, Connecticut, and owner of a small house, she — along with some of her neighbors — had resisted, for five years, the attempt of New London to take her house by eminent domain as part of a plan to entice the pharmaceutical company, Pfizer, to expand operations in the city. She had taken her case to the United States Supreme Court, lost, and then continued to remain in possession although she had long since lost title to her house. But finally, on that day, she "agreed to have her pink cottage moved elsewhere in New London. 'Even though she lost her land, the little pink home that launched a national revolution is safe, and it's going to stand as a testament to her heroic struggle and the struggle against eminent domain abuse throughout the country,' said Scott Bullock, a spokesman for the Institute for Justice, which represented the homeowners."[1] Why had she fought a $100 million development project, even though no one felt she could win? Why did her loss in the Supreme Court spark a movement in every state and in Congress to restrict eminent domain laws? And why did the movement come as a surprise to the American political system? This book is the story behind those questions. The book has two unusual features. At the end of the book, the story has just begun. Also, you, the reader, are part of the story. Where are you in the political system, the public opinion polls, the resistance and the laws which tell the story of the eminent domain revolt?

---

1    *The Stamford Advocate*, June 29, 2006 (Stamford, Connecticut, archived at www.stamfordadvocate.com).

A profound change has begun in the government of the United States. It is the first reorientation of Constitutional policy since the Great Depression, and signals the beginning of the fourth epoch of the Constitution. In this struggle for Constitutional supremacy there are many battlefields, and we shall tour a few. This book is the first detailed report of the transition from one Constitutional epoch to another and the contest for control of that transition and of the emerging state. It is designed to give readers a working knowledge of parameters of the new state by providing a series of detailed fact situations as well as a series of discrete, interlocking mechanisms which take us beyond the current "minimum scrutiny" regime of the third epoch and into the new "facts of the individual" approach of the fourth epoch. In the midst of the political welter to be examined, the fourth epoch has managed to articulate its supreme doctrine: every law maintains an important fact. This is a change from the fundamental doctrine of the third epoch: every law has a rational relationship to a legitimate government purpose. The new political system operates through the terms "every," "maintain" and "important." Above all, this amounts to — in the anti-eminent-domain movement but also in every other facet of American life — the complete reallocation of resources to implement the new doctrine and maintain important facts.

At times, a view of the law becomes so entrenched that that view comes to seem inextricable from the law itself; it becomes impossible to believe that law was ever viewed differently, or that there is any alternative to these received ideas. The third Constitutional epoch was the "minimum scrutiny" regime, under which government obtained nearly absolute power over nearly all facts, including very important ones such as housing. And yet, if the eminent domain case to be examined here — *Kelo v. New London*[2] — stands for one proposition, it is the idea that public opinion will no longer tolerate a chief tenet of the regime: minimum scrutiny for housing. The idea that government policy with respect to housing need only bear a rational relationship to a legitimate government purpose — which is minimum scrutiny for housing — is based on the idea that government knows better than housing.

Public opinion — although haltingly and inconsistently expressed — has changed the policy to this one: housing knows better than government, and the Constitution exists to maintain the important fact of housing. This is the chief idea to emerge from the *Kelo* case, and it emerges from public opinion's understanding of the facts. Above all, public opinion concluded that the "minimum scrutiny" regime was inherently corrupt, that the regime was incapable of ridding itself of corruption, and that that corruption threatened housing. In short, suburbia pronounced a death sentence on the regime, and carried it out. This means the end of minimum scrutiny for housing, and the consequences of that spell the end of the third Constitutional epoch.[3]

---

2    545 US ___ (2005).

3    "Home mortgages have loomed continually larger in the financial situation of American households. In 1949, mortgage debt was equal to 20 percent of total household income; by 1979, it had risen to 46 percent of income; by 2001, 73 percent of income....Similarly, mortgage debt was 15 percent of household assets in 1949, but rose to 28 percent of household

In the wake of the *Kelo* decision, public opinion had many things to criticize about the "minimum scrutiny" regime, but chief among them was the complaint that minimum scrutiny for housing ignores the fact that housing *is* the Constitution. For public opinion, the data clearly showed that, as a factual matter, government is housing and *vice versa*. Therefore, it was nonsense to say that some policy intervened between the Constitution and housing. Worse, it was legerdemain, a corrupt game of ignoring either the Constitution, or housing, or both. In the transitional era between the "minimum scrutiny" regime and the new "facts of the individual" analysis, the Court, the political system and public opinion, play — willy-nilly — all three of these irrational "games." The import of their doing so, however, is just that: we are in a transitional era between Constitutional epochs.

As the "minimum scrutiny" regime founders on hard fact — and on public opinion's probes into the discrepancies between policy and fact — many other related policies inevitably change, and the view of the "minimum scrutiny" regime as an eternal monolith or an internally consistent argument has to be reexamined. When it is, we will find that far from embodying an eternal truth, it has been merely the third step on our endless Constitutional journey.

A commentator has summarized the three epochs of Constitutional law which are now giving way to the fourth epoch, which is the age of the New Bill of Rights and the "facts of the individual" analysis:

> At one point in its history American constitutional jurisprudence presumed that the distinction between "judicial" and "political" questions was intelligible; at another point it presumed that the boundary between public power and private rights could coherently be traced; at another it presumed that there was a clear difference between the sort of legislation that required heightened and the sort that only required minimal scrutiny. Those presumptions did not come from the Constitution or any other legal source. They came from a set of shared social and political attitudes that shaped conceptions of the role of the judiciary in American constitutionalism. As those attitudes changed, presumptions changed with them. A robust constitutional principle of departmental discretion gave way to judicial boundary tracing which gave way to judicially fashioned levels of scrutiny. None of those regimes of constitutional interpretation should be regarded as cast in stone. None should be regarded as intrinsically superior to the others. The scrutiny regime has been with us for approximately 70 years. It may have exhausted itself as a helpful technique of constitutional interpretation. If we understand its historical origins, perhaps we can understand its contingent status.[4]

One of the remarkable aspects of the story is the way in which ignorance played a role in bringing the fourth epoch of the Constitution into being. The po-

---

assets by 1979 and 41 percent of household assets by 2001." Richard K. Green and Susan M. Wachter, "The American Mortgage in Historical and International Context," http://ssrn.com/abstract=908976, at 93, 106-108 (citations omitted).

For an ad hoc "facts of the individual" analysis of housing from the other end of the spectrum — homelessness — and a discussion of the concept of maintenance in connection with housing, see Nestor M. Davidson, "'Housing First' for the Chronically Homeless: Challenges of a New Service Model," http://ssrn.com/abstract=898259.

4   G. Edward White, "Historicizing Judicial Scrutiny," http://law.bepress.com/uvalwps/uva publiclaw/art31, 142.

litical system was totally ignorant of legal history; even academics were unaware of fundamental legal historical issues. Knowledge of precedent masqueraded as historical knowledge — dangerously so, given that the expression of fundamental legal issues in precedent was immemorially problematic. Legal historical issues had often broken uncontrollably through doctrines and predictions, expressing themselves in bizarre ways. In the United States, precedent was superficial and shoddy across the board; professional legal knowledge in America turned out to be knowledge of nothing at all.

And so a lapse in the consensus on one method of proceeding implicated the whole legal structure. This created unlimited opportunity to sap the country of its vaunted power, so recently established as premier. The political system — moronic and corrupt — was at a loss to understand, much less combat, the phenomenon; every move it made only further tied it up in its own stupidity. None of the actors in this drama could identify, in the eminent domain revolt, a change in development with respect to fundamental legal issues. This allowed history — the uninvited, and indeed unidentified, guest at the eminent domain debate — to dictate every term of the debate and impose a new epoch.

The cast of characters is sadly robot-like. They exhibit a limited repertoire of actions and statements without the capacity for change in response to changed circumstances. History will evict many of them unceremoniously from the scene. The legacy of the Supreme Court is chiefly to blame. The Justices, political hacks (and operating glaringly as such in the *Kelo* case), are and have been unsophisticated and duplicitous and, as the history of Constitutional epochs suggests, have located their *ad hoc* responses by fishing around in a grab bag of bad traditions, hidden agendas and prejudices.

The eminent domain revolt is the judiciary's doing — and they know it. But they are not the only source. From the Justices to flunkeys on down, they are all cardboard characters and play out their role curiously unaware of the vast forces they are setting in motion. Their antics meant that the scrutiny regime, which its enforcers never understood even as they administered it, came to suffer cumulative disabilities: inevitably corruption, but also a failure to vindicate individual rights, unfairness, a rejection of the democratic process and internal inconsistency. As a result, the regime developed a reflexive deafness to the facts, and when the regime spoke, the facts stopped speaking. That, in turn, was the beginning of the process by which public opinion dislodged the scrutiny regime.

Both public opinion and the political system, including the Supreme Court, groped toward the new Constitutional synthesis. In the shadow of the crumbling "minimum scrutiny" regime, the grounds of the Constitution are being contested in an intense and sometimes violent struggle, a struggle which, moreover, is just beginning. The idea of the scrutiny regime that certain facts may be left to the political process, has provided the entrée for public opinion to extract facts from that process, and to stop the political system from acting on those facts — a tactic which progressively implicates more facts, and implies less power for the regime. This book is a survey of that Constitutional situation.

We are, all of us, in the very early stage of working out our destinies in the fourth epoch of the Constitution. Public opinion is progressively leaving the third Constitutional epoch behind by undermining health and welfare regulation; eminent domain is merely the point of entry of this attack. Public opinion has yet to articulate the Constitution of the fourth epoch or the disposition of facts in that articulation. It is above all this delay which is working to undermine health and welfare regulation.

This essay will chart the corrosive effects of the delay by presenting many detailed fact situations. These are included for several reasons:

1. The political system, oblivious to public opinion, greatly exacerbated tensions by racing ahead after the *Kelo* decision to increase the rate of eminent domain seizures: during "the year since the ruling, local governments threatened to use eminent domain against more than 5,429 homes, businesses, churches and filed 354 condemnation actions — more than half of the 10,282 threatened or condemned properties tallied over the five years between 1998 and 2002."[5] These do not include sales made under duress (the threat of formal eminent domain action). Readers need to examine representative actions afresh in light of the complex response to *Kelo*.

2. We have not previously had a revolt against the scrutiny regime — readers need to see the details of where and how this is occurring.

3. In the process of this revolt, issues are raised which have never been raised before — these need to be seen in context. And finally,

4. Readers will be called on to make political judgments, and need unfiltered reports in order to do that. I present my view, but that is only one view. I then step out of the way to allow readers to form their own views of the facts.

In these accounts, there will certainly be facts which some readers feel are dispositive and others feel are less important or even irrelevant. It is important, however, for readers to think of all their judgments as part of the formation of a new view of the Constitution, for it is a comprehensive process.

The Supreme Court has participated in this process, playing the same mixed role undertaken by all the other confused players. Recently, it has both undermined and reinforced the foundation of the third epoch. It doesn't know what it wants, what public opinion wants, or what the political system wants; this may also fairly be said of the other players. Not unpredictably, as a result the Court has extemporized and sent mixed signals — all the more reason for readers to get a complete grasp of the facts. Public opinion's response to a recent Court case was somewhat less mixed, and it is that response which has been most effective in putting an end to the third epoch.

*Kelo* launched the United States on a new era of its political development, in which the political system began to lose the power it had previously exercised. Public opinion removed health and welfare regulation from the political system. Public opinion decided that many facts, such as housing, are, for Constitutional purposes, now like "free speech" and "freedom of worship": "fundamental rights"

---

5   June 20, 2006 (archived at www.globest.com).

which have to be "withdrawn...from the vicissitudes of political controversy."[6] There is nothing to say about that. The question is, how is public opinion interpreting and implementing it? Enmeshed in a web of corruption and misrepresentation which ultimately ensnared the Supreme Court, the *Kelo* case has led to the demand for an increase in the individually enforceable Constitutional level of protection for housing. And that is just the beginning. There is a further demand for a change in the method by which the decision in the *Kelo* case was reached.

The response to *Kelo* revealed the pathology of the third epoch. Indeed, evaluating certain facts situations may cause readers to feel that they are at an unpleasant version of the Mad Hatter's tea party; for example, even natural — if unsavory — allies bared fangs at each other. Forty years into a political reaction, it was not a pretty sight. Strangely mixing threats and confrontation with dispassionate discourses about Founder intent, a surprise crisis no one anticipated, the eminent domain controversy has spread to every corner of the country.

But it is proving to be difficult. Eminent domain has become a sore on the body politic; public opinion and the political system can neither heal it nor cease intervening in it, and so the crisis spreads. At the heart of the crisis is ignorance: due to the "minimum scrutiny" straightjacket into which the Supreme Court has forced the law, neither public opinion nor the political system knows much about the facts involved in the crisis. The law has never provided a forum in which relevant facts could be evaluated — we are very ignorant about our own country. Overcoming that ignorance means changing Constitutional law,[7] and this work aims to be part of the educational process by showing some of the forces which are changing the law and the ways in which those forces are changing it, often in spite of themselves.

The response of public opinion to the *Kelo* case generated that unique set of historical circumstances during which, according to the Court, the nature of Constitutional interpretation must change if the Constitution is to survive: "facts [premising] a constitutional resolution of social controversy had proven to be untrue, and history's demonstration of their untruth not only justified but required the new choice of constitutional principle."[8] The true facts were "facts that the country could understand, or had come to understand already, but which the Court of an earlier day, as its own declarations disclosed, had not been able to perceive...[:] applications of constitutional principle to facts as they had not been seen by the Court before."[9] The Court, having given us a Constitutional epoch which led to an unprecedented legal crisis, shows us the way out of the crisis. Uncovering the history and doctrinal bases of the third epoch reveals the facts — many of which are disturbing — and when these are understood in light of the way in which the "minimum scrutiny" regime operates, it generates new Consti-

---

6    *West Virginia State Board of Education v. Barnette*, 319 US 624, 638 (1943).

7    The ongoing development of law in the European Union touches on some of the same dilemmas explored in this essay. See Neil Walker, "Legal Theory and the European Union," http://ssrn.com/abstract=891032.

8    *Planned Parenthood v. Casey*, 505 US 833, 862 (1992).

9    *Id.*, at 863-864.

tutional rights and transitional levels of Constitutional scrutiny in addition to the current three: a renovation of Constitutional law. This, in turn, points the way to an alternate and much more accurate Constitutional analysis, and a new bill of rights. The response of public opinion to the *Kelo* case, the resistance of the political system to that response, and problematic doctrine, have combined to force us to rewrite Constitutional law in its entirety.

As with so many issues in an individual rights-poor country such as America, eminent domain is about violence. If people won't leave, will law enforcement remove them? The law's relation to the outcome is problematic. This hitherto arcane issue has revealed startling and often secret details of government operations which touch everyone's lives. It has re-opened fundamental issues of power, law and right which go back to the founding of the nation — and before. Readers will have to deal with this controversy — it shows no sign of going away; indeed, it is implicating more and more of the policies and laws of the country.

The fourth Constitutional epoch has crept up on various players without their realizing what is happening. The bond market, for example, reacted in a presumptuous, corrupt and self-satisfied manner — and on stunningly bad advice. The attack on eminent domain revealed that, although the scrutiny regime comprehended all facts, it defended none — leaving a void successfully filled by opponents of the regime; the market failed to recognize that. The market also should have realized that the maintenance of facts — the only argument to which public opinion would now listen, and through which all policy now had to be filtered — was not in the ideological armory of the regime's defenders, including its legion of lawyers. The market failed to realize that the attack on eminent domain signaled the inevitable reallocation of resources as the fourth Constitutional epoch succeeded the third. Control of the money was shifting. The transition undermined all investment expectations; the market hadn't the slightest awareness of this development which was occurring under its nose. It remained to be seen who would round on whom — and with what consequences — when public opinion blithely, without significant obstruction, rearranged the economy.

At the right end of the political continuum, various shadow governments saw the revolt as their entry into the light. Who are these shadowy figures? What do they want? In between stand the hearts and minds of American homeowners — the true movers of the anti-eminent domain movement — as they stumble blindly into a position of control over the society. At the heart of the eminent domain debate was a simple but mighty principle which alone moved the transition to its fourth epoch: important facts, such as housing, are not fungible. This titanic change was the single greatest in the history of law.

To understand the eminent domain revolt, then, requires being briefed on the facts, appreciating the background of the nature and operation of eminent domain, insight into the Constitutional context in which the controversy is being played out, and a play-by-play review of the responses which have been developed by important political groups. Through this process we can identify the steps by which the third Constitutional epoch was removed by adherents of the fourth:

1. Identify an important fact, such as property.
2. Limit the activity of the scrutiny regime with respect to one of its power, such as eminent domain.
3. Extend the ban on power to similar powers, such as zoning and land use.
4. Generalize from one important fact to another.
5. Repeat the process.

Thus, fact by fact the scrutiny regime fell out of power. The regime's defenders — blustering, dictatorial, smug, corrupt — served the anti-eminent domain movement admirably. The dark side of the regime was revealed in all its seaminess; the regime's defensive antics appalled public opinion. The effect was irremediable.

What follows also attempts to provide what is largely absent among the actors: an understanding of the doctrines and applications of the fourth epoch of the Constitution as these pertain to the intent of the Founders, an understanding which incorporates the facts and public opinion rather than promoting deception, exacerbating tensions and provoking resistance. We have to act, and in the absence of knowledge of many facts. How to do it? My aim is to provide the Supreme Court with new standards and principles which are internally consistent, harmonize with retained doctrines, and allow the Court to smoothly take the system over into its own jurisprudence. From there, applications will reveal new facts, new rights and new progress in the endless process of vindicating individual rights. This is the classic interchange under the Constitution between the Court and the individual. The response to the *Kelo* decision has made it clear that there will be an increase in individually enforceable protections under a new interpretation of the Constitution. These increases should occur sooner rather than later, in ways which are clear cut rather than problematic, and peacefully rather than violently.

The *Kelo* case was supposed to resolve one issue of governmental power. It didn't. In *Kelo* the Court demanded that public opinion accept the idea that although the Court *could* vindicate for government an abuse of the rights of an individual, that same Court *could not* vindicate for the same individual the same rights against the same government. In the response to *Kelo* public opinion declined any longer to accept that idea, and instead embarked on a new Constitutional journey.

These are the conditions under one Constitutional epoch gives way to another. It's quite a story.

# THE EMINENT DOMAIN REVOLT

But the quietness lasted too long. The new forces did not emerge. The obsolete party did not mean to yield power. On the contrary, it gripped the nation's throat with a tenacity that was terrifying, for it pertained to another realm than life. For the grip of a living man must relax if he grows tired; it is only ghostly hands that, without term, can continue to clench.

— Rebecca West, *Black Lamb and Grey Falcon*

# Chapter 1. Individual Rights Before *Kelo v. New London*

## The Third Constitutional Epoch at Its Close

This section is part of the history of the revolt against the *Kelo* decision and part an exposition of the law involved in the case. Appearing here in somewhat revised form, it was published on the Social Science Research Network — a website for essays in various social science disciplines — shortly after the Supreme Court decided to hear the *Kelo* case in mid-2004. Along with many other comments, it predicted that the *Kelo* property owners would lose their case when the Court made its decision in June 2005. After you have read the later sections detailing the history of the revolt, consider whether the assumptions of this section were affirmed or contradicted by the revolt against the *Kelo* decision.

## Introduction

What are the facts of the individual?

This question is at the heart of the dispute in *Kelo* v. *City of New London*, which was accepted for review by the Supreme Court. You would never know it by looking at the Question Presented to the Court: What protection does the Fifth Amendment's public use requirement provide for individuals whose property is being condemned, not to eliminate slums or blight but for the sole purpose of "economic development" that will perhaps increase tax revenues[10] and improve

---

10   We are just beginning to subject taxation to an *ad hoc* "facts of the individual" analysis. See Robert W. McGee, "Taxation and Public Finance: A Philosophical and Ethical Approach," http://ssrn.com/abstract=461340.

the local economy? It is not mentioned here that the "property" involved is hous-ing. The real question is: Should there be elevated scrutiny for housing because James Madison says that the Constitution prevents "every assumption of power in the legislative or executive"? Attorneys have long sought elevated scrutiny for housing and similar facts, but have sought such scrutiny on the basis that such facts are important, even fundamental, in themselves or important to the exercise of other rights. They have always failed to convince the Court because they have been unable to see that these facts go to the essence of the Founders' intent re-specting the Constitution. Madison's statement turns out to be the place where every such analysis must begin. If it does begin there, and the analysis proceeds to carry out his intent, the *Kelo* petitioners — and many others dealing with similar facts — will find a Court newly willing to increase its scrutiny in these areas.

The Court has taken the case because conflicting results have been reached by different courts. Two courts had to decide whether eminent domain could be used to take housing and turn it over to private developers. The Connecticut Supreme Court, in *Kelo*, said it could. The Michigan Supreme Court, in *County of Wayne v. Hathcock*,[11] said that it could not.[12] Glossed over by the courts and ignored by the parties, housing is what is at stake in both cases; in fact, the homeowners will lose *Kelo* unless their counsel, the "property rights"-oriented Institute for Justice, stop harping on eminent domain and address the real issue. Since *Kelo* involves an action for eminent domain over housing, it provides the first opportu-nity to apply the New Bill of Rights to a case which the Court is about to decide. This is because the New Bill of Rights — proceeding from an understanding of Madison's statement — recognizes housing as a fact of the individual (which is a new formulation in our law), on a par with protected speech and freedom from an establishment of religion. Alternate scenarios for Supreme Court adjudication are provided, as is the theoretical background of the New Bill of Rights.

## DEVELOPING THE NEW BILL OF RIGHTS

The Constitution is the legal meaning of human experience. Since the Civil War, much adjudication of rights has involved clarification of textual Consti-tutional rights, and the extension of their application. Since the Founders expe-rienced deprivation of political rights, these rights figured prominently both in the original Constitution and in the Bill of Rights. Legal equality with respect to rights was the main goal of much Constitutional litigation over the past thirty years. But what rights? This has been the domain of thinking about social rights, and social rights have faced stern opposition from all courts. This does not mean that there has been no development of thinking regarding those rights. Quite the contrary. By 1944, it had developed to the point where Franklin Roosevelt could put his own "black letter law" version before Congress: "The right to a useful and remunerative job in the industries or shops or farms or mines of the nation; the

---

11    471 Mich. 445, 684 NW2d 765 (2004).

12    This seems to be the only palatable way to explain why the Court agreed to hear *Kelo*; the Court itself provides no explanation as to why it took the case.

right to earn enough to provide adequate food and clothing and recreation; the right of every farmer to raise and sell his products at a return which will give him and his family a decent living; the right of every businessman, large and small, to trade in an atmosphere of freedom from unfair competition and domination by monopolies at home or abroad; the right of every family to a decent home; the right to adequate medical care and the opportunity to achieve and enjoy good health; the right to adequate protection from the economic fears of old age, sickness, accident, and unemployment; the right to a good education."[13] This was some progress, since it took the matter out of the realm of vague aspiration and put it into words which could, if enacted, be litigated. However, notice that there is no enforcement mechanism in the "black-letter" language of these rights. FDR was able to finesse that issue by saying in his speech that "[w]e have accepted, so to speak, a second Bill of Rights...."

That turned out not to be the case, and the issue was revisited during the 1970s when the US Supreme Court considered various "affirmative rights." In this round, the mechanism was included, and it imposed a duty on government to provide for certain of these rights. The Courts rejected those formulations because they seemed to involve the Court in an executive branch function, a violation of the separation of powers. An affirmative duty on government to provide housing, for example, would involve the Court saying what, in fact, is housing, and forcing it into an executive, supervisory role of determining whether government was fulfilling its duty. *San Antonio School District v. Rodriguez* — in which the Court refused to examine school funding on the basis of a Constitutional right to education — is a good example of the Court's current view of "affirmative rights."[14] It has proved impossible to get any court or legislature to accord more than minimum scrutiny to housing — that is, to require that government action in relation to housing be anything more than rationally related to a legitimate government purpose. Not even a slight elevation has been permitted, to, say, threshold scrutiny, requiring that government action in relation to housing measurably effect a common government purpose. But this is not right. After all, the Court itself suggests threshold scrutiny. Intermediate scrutiny lies between strict and minimum scrutiny. Justice Ginsburg, as an attorney, herself argued for gender legal equality as existing at a higher level of scrutiny than minimum scrutiny — that's how intermediate scrutiny was established.[15] Today gender le-

---

13    Samuel Rosenman, ed., *The Public Papers & Addresses of Franklin D. Roosevelt* (Harper 1950) XIII at 40-42.

14    411 US 1 (1973).

15    She co-authored the briefs in *Reed v. Reed* (404 US 71 [1971]) and co-authored an amicus brief in *Craig v. Boren*, 429 U.S. 190 (1976). The method of analysis used here to raise the level of scrutiny for housing, is the method she employs in *Reed* and *Craig*. The battle over gender legal equality has now generated a level of scrutiny between intermediate and strict scrutiny: United States v. Virginia, 518 US 515 (1996). The facts of Virginia show us that gender legal equality now enjoys comprehensive scrutiny (infra). The move up in scrutiny to this level in particular is due to the difference between the facts in *Craig* and the facts in *Virginia*, just as the difference between the false and the true facts in *Kelo* accounts for the movement of housing from minimum to direct scrutiny. We now await a case in which, for Constitutional purposes, the facts are identical to those in Virginia, with

gal equality enjoys scrutiny beyond intermediate. Gender legal inequality must show an exceedingly persuasive justification.[16] Thus, facts (and only facts) not only establish the scrutiny continuum; they also move around within it. If a level of scrutiny is established by one fact, such as gender legal equality, and that fact moves out of that level, does the level still exist? Public opinion is now asking this question: What is the *factual* basis on which gender equality has moved up the scrutiny continuum while housing has *not*? Indeed, we shall see with respect to housing, public opinion appears to demand a level of scrutiny for housing between intermediate and strict scrutiny. It appears to demand fixed scrutiny, requiring that government action in relation to housing conclusively realize a preponderant government purpose.

Justice Scalia is a persistent critic of the scrutiny continuum, claiming that it is inherently vague. "[T]his Court [regards itself] as free to evaluate everything under the sun by applying one of three tests: "rational basis" scrutiny, intermediate scrutiny, or strict scrutiny. These tests are no more scientific than their names suggest, and a further element of randomness is added by the fact that it is largely up to us which test will be applied in each case."[17] This criticism is misplaced. It is properly directed toward the theoretical basis of the continuum, which the Court has never provided — that is the gravamen of Justice Scalia's complaint. The scrutiny continuum is simply an *ad hoc* "facts of the individual" analysis, and the basis of the continuum is the vindication of the individual in every case.[18] The Court has not yet been able to articulate the "facts of the individual" analysis, and so it labors on through the longstanding although outmoded concerns of the judi-

---

the exception that liberty is substituted for gender legal equality. This will elevate gender legal equality to strict scrutiny. The area between minimum and intermediate scrutiny has recently come into clearer focus in the concept of "rational basis-plus" scrutiny, the idea that the court should utilize heightened scrutiny when it is faced with an historical policy of animus against an important fact, in this case, bans on gay marriage. Government animus against a group is evidence of government animus against a fact: "['Rational basis-plus'] was developed by Pamela S. Karlan and William B. Rubenstein, law professors from Stanford and UCLA respectively....Karlan and Rubenstein wanted to ease the way for the Supreme Court's moderates to expand equal protection law, both for gay rights and more generally....[R]ational basis review shouldn't be a free pass for the state when the reasons for a law appear fishy, and when an important right is on the line....In effect, rational basis-plus neatly shifts the burden of challenging laws governing marriage and other basic rights from the plaintiff onto the state. In other words, judges employing rational basis-plus must think about whether the state's reasons for restricting marriage to opposite-sex couples are legitimate — meaning unrelated to prejudice — and about whether the law will really serve the purpose the state says it will." *The Boston Globe*, May 16, 2004 (Boston, Massachusetts, archived at www.globe.com).

16   *Mississippi University for Women v. Hogan*, 458 US 718 (1982).

17   *Virginia* at 567-568.

18   This is why the Court is constantly encroaching on its own categories of minimum, intermediate and strict scrutiny, with concepts such as "rational basis plus" scrutiny and "undue burden." The categories undermine themselves because they require the Court to extract more facts from them and group them under new steps along the continuum. The entire system tends toward the "facts of the individual" analysis. See David D. Meyer, "Lochner Redeemed: Family Privacy After Troxel and Carhart," http://ssrn.com/abstract=288816.

ciary: the developed state of the facts, the thoroughness of the achievement of the result, and the urgency of the government's claims — the Court as political actor, rather than as the Court. Since it has not articulated the "facts of the individual" analysis, the Court avoids the facts whenever it can, moving out toward them only when it feels it is necessary, and necessarily from a defensive concept of itself because it has no notion of itself in relation to the individual.

The threshold and fixed levels of scrutiny imply four more:

1. between minimum and threshold scrutiny;
2. between threshold and intermediate scrutiny;
3. between intermediate and fixed scrutiny; and
4. between fixed and strict scrutiny.

After forty years of reactionary politics, the Constitution has begun to function again.

What in *fact*, not in *law*, is the scrutiny continuum? It is the vindication of the individual in every case through the application of the "facts of the individual" analysis.

### Current Constitution of Scrutiny[19]

| Level | Development of Fact | Thoroughness of Achievement | Urgency of Government Claim |
|---|---|---|---|
| minimum | rationally | relates | legitimate |
| intermediate | substantially | furthers | important |
| strict | specifically | fulfills | overriding |

### New Constitution of Scrutiny

| Level | Development of Fact | Thoroughness of Achievement | Urgency of Government Claim |
|---|---|---|---|
| minimum | rationally | relates | legitimate |
| direct | articulately | facilitates | frequent |
| threshold | measurably | effects | common |
| relative | inherently | reflects | decisive |
| intermediate | substantially | furthers | important |
| comprehensive | essentially | determines | momentous |
| fixed | conclusively | achieves | preponderant |
| exclusive | urgently | implements | vital |
| strict | specifically | fulfills | overriding |

---

19 For some insight on enforcement of strict scrutiny, see Adam Winkler, "Fatal in Theory and Strict in Fact: An Empirical Analysis of Strict Scrutiny in the Federal Courts," http://ssrn.com/abstract=897360.

Now let's look at direct scrutiny, this new Constitutional test, more closely. It is a more focused inquiry by the Court.[20] Keep in mind that what prompts it is what is going on in the *Kelo* case. Government proposes 1) a policy of destroying housing; and 2) to destroy housing. Under minimum scrutiny the emphasis was ostensibly on hypothesis and policy. In fact, it is a standard which requires the Supreme Court to lie. As the Court has said, under minimum scrutiny it is only a policy's "purpose, and not its mechanics, that must pass scrutiny."[21] This does not mandate that the policy contain no facts, but it does mandate that the Court put the least rational construction on the facts. A lie is the least rational construction of the facts. The Supreme Court must lie. This dirty little secret was at work in the *Kelo* decision.

Once we stop lying about the facts — which is to say, once we remove a fact from minimum scrutiny — we begin to evaluate facts as they relate to each other. A fact is detached from minimum scrutiny by: (1) an historical policy of (2) animus against (3) an important fact.

In the *Kelo* case this test involves lies in the facts. Does policy which fails to pass this test always involve lies?

Why would lies trigger heightened scrutiny? Because policy is found to be an indicium of the fact: policy respecting housing and destruction of housing are indicia of housing. At this point housing and policy are adjudicated *equally*. Now the Court plays an unprecedented role; after a brief two hundred years, it is honest. "Equally," in this context, means limiting discretion by revealing and eliminating from permissible outcomes lies, prejudices, bluff, bluster, ruses, evasions, feints, dodges, kowtowing, avoidance, delays, conspiracies, inadequacy, and so on. These terms are the language of minimum scrutiny. Note that this allows the Fourteenth Amendment to be seen, for the first time, in a new light. The Fourteenth Amendment says that no state shall "deprive any person of life, liberty, or property, without due process of law; nor deny to any person within its jurisdiction the equal protection of the laws."[22] The new light is this: "equal" means truthful. The Fourteenth Amendment is about the truth. It vindicates the truth by mandating the truth. For example, the Court has never quite known where privacy is to be found in the Constitution. Now we do know. It is to be found in the word "equal." That is how direct scrutiny transforms the Fourteenth Amendment. It may seem a small advance — it is a small step out of minimum scrutiny. On the other hand, because it is a step out of minimum scrutiny, it has never before been the law.

For Abraham Lincoln, because the Declaration of Independence is a direct scrutiny analysis ("all men are created equal"),[23] so is the Constitution. This is his direct scrutiny analysis of involuntary servitude in the Constitution: Under

---

20  We have barely begun to understand what, in reality, is fact-finding on the part of the court. See Edward K. Cheng, "Independent Judicial Research in the Daubert Age," http://ssrn.com/abstract=885387.

21  *Hawaii Housing Authority v. Midkiff*, 467 US 229, 244 (1984).

22  U.S. const. amend. XIV, § 1.

23  *Declaration of Independence* [¶ 2] (1776).

the Constitution, "slavery is wrong"; and the Constitution is "a policy springing from that belief that looks to the *prevention* of the *enlargement* of that wrong, and that looks at some time to there *being* an *end* of that wrong"[24] (emphases added). Note that for Lincoln the Constitution is the proposition that no individual shall be involuntarily deprived of a fact of the individual; the Constitution proposes this by bringing involuntary deprivations to light (and, thereby, the facts themselves), and then eliminating them. The Constitution tends toward truth because it mandates fact, and the direct scrutiny analysis is this tendency; it is, above all, Abraham Lincoln who is the author of the level of direct scrutiny. He stands behind the opposition to the *Kelo* decision, and that is why the political system is having such difficulty defanging the opposition. Under direct scrutiny, involuntary servitude is a fact, but it is not the truth. Policy which does not survive direct scrutiny is unenforceable.

Like the opposition to slavery, the opposition to eminent domain was based on the "claim that the preservation of individual rights, and strict construction of the Constitution, demanded [its] restriction."[25] But what were the facts in the anti-eminent domain movement, and how did eminent domain, as government, vindicate them? Where to find the restriction in the Constitution — and where to find the rights in that restriction — these challenges were what turned the anti-eminent domain movement, like the anti-slavery movement, from a clear-cut opposition into an ambiguous struggle.

Under direct scrutiny we open the black box of government discretion and act only on the facts we find there; we do *not* get courts making statements, such as this one, in support of a use of eminent domain: "Evidence in the administrative record is slim....But that does not mean it falls beneath the standard of substantial evidence. It is not completely speculative."[26] In the *Kelo* case, when there are factual contradictions on the face of the pleadings — pleadings which don't even require a more in-depth factual investigation — the court is forced by the "minimum scrutiny" regime to sanction them. Statements such as this one, in turn, become code words telling us that violations of individual rights are involved. It is the court saying, "Watch out, the court is lying."

Statements such as this do not exist in a case of direct scrutiny. Note that the new layers of scrutiny also mean that minimum scrutiny is now a severely disfavored method of analysis, because whatever the discretion involved in it, that discretion does not involve determining the nature of the facts, which is what the Constitution mandates. This means that minimum scrutiny must specifically fulfill an overriding government purpose, i.e., it is conclusively presumed unenforceable. Simply put, no more lying — and we shall see that, over and over again, opposition to the *Kelo* decision was expressed by public opinion saying, You are lying. Obviously, minimum scrutiny cannot continue as a method of analysis in

---

24    Quoted in Allen C. Guelzo, *Abraham Lincoln: Redeemer President* at 224 (Eerdmans Publishing Co. 2003).

25    Sean Wilentz, *The Rise of American Democracy* (W.W. Norton & Co. 2005) at 225-226.

26    *Davis Enterprise*, December 1, 2005 (Davis, California, archived at www.davisenterprise.com).

the face of a consensus that it simply is not credible; it will be resisted — and that is exactly what happened in the *Kelo* case.

Under minimum scrutiny, "rationally" was evaluated in so lax a fashion that, initially, the Court did not in fact require that government have a policy; the Court would infer one if it could — a policy would be found, if it was "conceivable" to do so.[27] And yet, under pressure from public opinion, even the Court had to recognize that "conceivable" is still a question of fact for the trier of fact — a lie means not only that there is no government purpose, but also that the policy is not government. Government without purpose is one of Madison's assumptions of power in violation of *Marbury v. Madison*, a case which vindicates government as a fact of the individual.

"Articulately" means that there must in fact be a policy, which in turn means that the policy must incorporate facts because the policy is a fact. Which facts? The Court tests for these by determining that: 1) government can evaluate the policy in terms of facts; and 2) government does evaluate the policy in terms of facts. Then the Court evaluates 1 in relation to 2. Under minimum scrutiny, "relates" is not a means-ends test. It tests for a relation between hypothetical situations and an inferred purpose. Under direct scrutiny, "facilitates" means evaluating the fact the individual seeks to vindicate in terms of the factually articulated result. What happens to the fact in the process? Under minimum scrutiny, "legitimate" is defined negatively, by what the purpose cannot be. Under direct scrutiny, the "frequent" test looks at the process of change in the context of what government maintains already in fact exists. What is the factual connection between what is and what results? It is under these conditions, then, that New London has to justify factually its departure from such things as zoning for housing and intentionally substituting a private purpose for a government purpose, thereby abrogating government.

The thinking behind direct scrutiny comes from the Supreme Court itself, which engaged in an embryonic form of it in a case which predates by eleven years the establishment of the "minimum scrutiny" regime and the third Constitutional epoch in *West Coast Hotel v. Parrish.*[28] It is a case in which the Court found that zoning is Constitutional and is not a taking under the Fifth Amendment: *Village of Euclid, Ohio v. Ambler Realty Co.*[29] The question for the *Euclid* Court was whether zoning violates " 'the right of property...by attempted regulations under the guise of the police power, which are unreasonable and confiscatory'"?[30] The *Euclid* Court set up certain facts as important and then sustained the zoning law at issue (a single-family land use law) because it maintained the facts.

Maintenance — what it is and what it maintains — is what mattered to the Court. The Court saw housing as what was maintained in the case. "The serious question in the case arises over the provisions of the ordinance excluding from

---

27   *Hawaii Housing Authority* at 241.

28   300 US 379 (1937).

29   272 US 365 (1926).

30   *Id.*, at 386 (citation omitted).

residential districts apartment houses, business houses, retail stores and shops, and other like establishments. This question involves the validity of what is really the crux of the more recent zoning legislation, namely, the creation and maintenance of residential districts, from which business and trade of every sort, including hotels and apartment houses, are excluded."[31] Note that the Court finds zoning to be an indicium of the *creation* of housing. The Court finds that the zoning law at issue "bears a rational relation to the health and safety of the community"[32] — *not*, it bears pointing out, to a legitimate government purpose. The point that "rational relation" means maintenance — that government must show *results*, not *goals*, when it defends its policy — is shown when the Court approvingly cites another ruling sustaining zoning laws which preserve facts in the face of "changing conditions."[33] The law vindicates facts of abiding human experience.

How does government show this "rational relation?" By showing that the policy has *demonstrated* a "substantial relation to the public health, safety, morals, or general welfare."[34] For the Court, public health, safety, morals, and general welfare are not vague generalities, goals or even policies, and the anti-eminent domain movement is wrong when it feels it should take its cue from a Court concerned with "goals" or "ideals" such as property, freedom and so on. This test makes it clear that the Court feels that what others might feel are goals — public health, safety and so on — are, perhaps, important, but the Court is concerned with them as important *facts*. The Court's question for government is, How *has* the policy maintained those facts? (Not even how *might* it maintain those facts.) The Court does not decide on the basis of what *should be* done — it does not assume a legislative or executive role — but rather on the basis of what *has been* done.

And the Court sees this as a strict test, not a lax test. In short, the anti-eminent domain movement should argue the importance of *maintaining facts*. Note that the test is neither minimum scrutiny (rational relation to a legitimate government purpose) nor intermediate scrutiny (substantially advances an important government purpose). It takes one criterion from each test, and forms a test which is no part of the scrutiny regime. Note also that the *Euclid* Court imposes this test through the Due Process clause of the Fifth Amendment and *also* under the Due Process and Equal Protection clauses of the Fifth and Fourteenth Amendments.[35]

---

31  *Id.*, at 390.

32  *Id.*, at 391.

33  *Id.*, at 392.

34  *Id.*, at 395.

35  Has *Euclid* been implicitly overruled? If so, it was done in the takings case *Tahoe-Sierra Preservation Council v. Tahoe Regional Planning Agency*, 535 US 302 (2002), which concerned temporary moratoria on development in the Lake Tahoe basin. Property owners claimed that the period of the moratoria constituted a compensable taking. Instead of applying the *Euclid* test, the Court, to the contrary, asserted that it had always "'generally eschewed' any set formula for determining how far is too far, choosing instead to engage in 'essentially *ad hoc*, factual inquiries....'Indeed, we still resist the temptation to adopt *per se* rules in our cases involving partial regulatory takings, preferring to examine 'a number of factors'

When an historical policy of animus against, for example, housing is shown, animus triggers purpose as fact and housing triggers legitimacy as policy. Such facts as user behavior are seen as in *fact* policy, and *that* is why they are legally relevant and admissible.[36] **Government is no longer the sole source of policy.** The law is no longer afraid of the way individuals in fact live; the legal process no longer a matter of hiding and protecting itself — by jumping from one internally inconsistent doctrine to another — from the way individuals in fact live. The law becomes recognition of the way individuals in *fact* live. In turn, the recognition of law becomes the process of law. The facts flood in to the discovery process and American law is transformed. Given the enormous amount of pressing business, public opinion no longer allowed the Supreme Court to control the facts by holding back the flood. The Court was unceremoniously pushed aside.

* * *

One way to understand the current eminent domain controversy is to look at it from two opposing perspectives, one involving the concerns about "affirmative rights," the other demonstrating the profoundly important role of the Federal government in the exercise of eminent domain. We can understand something of the worldview which has stymied the development of individual rights by eavesdropping on a 1999 panel discussion on the possibility of "affirmative" rights: "[One question was] the apparent conflict between entitlement and affordability. On the one hand, a human rights perspective implied formal entitlement and claims by citizens; on the other hand, rights were expensive to fulfill....The health example [suggested] that difficult issues arose in connection with rationing — to what standard of care were people entitled? There was also conflict between individual rights (e.g. reproductive rights) and collective rights (e.g. a society's ability to feed and clothe its population)...."[37]

Keep in mind these concerns about restricting government powers and the resources available to government as you consider this instance of Federal power in an exercise of eminent domain:

> In *Kelo v. New London*...the US Supreme Court upheld the Connecticut city's use of eminent domain to take private property for local economic development. The *Kelo* decision is reminiscent of an infamous decision in the state courts. *Poletown Neighborhood Council v. Detroit*, 304 N.W.2d 455 (Mich. 1981), is widely re-

---

rather than a simple 'mathematically precise' formula." *Id.*, at 327 (citations omitted). This paves the way for the Court to sustain "permissible exercises of the police power" under the Takings Clause. *Id.*, at 335. That this is minimum scrutiny is confirmed when the Court indicates that it is done in "[t]he interest in facilitating informed decisionmaking by regulatory agencies." *Id.*, at 339. This is a nod to Justice Kennedy who, as we shall see, insists on minimum scrutiny as a factual inquiry as against the tendency of the "minimum scrutiny" regime to collapse the doctrines and branches of government.

36    Historically it has been a stumbling block for both courts and commentators that government policy can show both bias toward and animus against a fact, but if the fact is important, animus triggers scrutiny above minimum scrutiny irrespective of bias toward the fact. This new analytical alignment is starting to be made in equal protection analysis in its shift from an *ad hoc* "facts of the individual" analysis to a formal "facts of the individual" analysis. See Charles A. Sullivan, "Re-reviving Disparate Impact," http://ssrn.com/abstract=581503.

37    www.odi.org.uk/speeches/Eyben2.html.

garded as the nadir of public-use jurisprudence [this decision was overturned by the *Hathcock* decision, see below]. The Michigan Supreme Court approved the use of eminent domain to level a thickly-settled neighborhood in Detroit in order to build a General Motors assembly plant....[T]he supposed villain in *Poletown*, General Motors, was not the party most responsible for the project. The institution most responsible for the destruction of more than 1000 homes and the removal of over 4000 people was the United States government. It did not simply provide the funds to bulldoze Poletown; it provided them in such a way that Detroit had little choice but to demolish Poletown. The lesson to be drawn from this analysis of Poletown is that local governments are getting a bum rap for the abuse of eminent domain. They have been the front man, and now the fall guy, for state and federal policies that serve job-related interest-groups and fail to take into account local concerns about quality of life. Left to their own devices, local governments seldom use their own funds to take property for projects that have so little benefit to their citizens as those in *Poletown* and *Kelo*.[38]

The way to reconcile these two points of view is to focus the inquiry on what government in *fact* is doing, as opposed to what it says it is doing, should do, or cannot do. That was what public opinion determined to find out after being confronted, in *Kelo*, with a Supreme Court decision it simply would not accept and would not allow to be enforced.

Looking at facts works wonders for legal analysis. As one activist group learned in the course of its investigations, "today it can be demonstrated that economic and social rights are well-established in international and constitutional laws. They have been enforced through court action, and are no more costly to implement than traditional human rights such as the right to a fair trial."[39] All right, and just *how* are these rights being litigated? Recent developments in South Africa — the Constitution of which includes a right to housing — throw light on this question:

> Section 26 of the South African Constitution provides that: "(1) Everyone has the right of access to adequate housing[;] (2) The state must take reasonable legislative and other measures within its available resources, to achieve the progressive realization of this right." Section 28 provides that children have the right to shelter. Section 28 is not limited by internal qualifiers such as progressive realization nor is it made subject to available resources. First, the facts [surrounding a recent decision of the South African Constitutional Court] need brief explaining.
>
> A desperately poor community of 390 adults and 510 children had lived in the Wallacedene informal settlement, under appalling conditions, until they left and illegally occupied a site that had been earmarked for low cost housing. Following their eviction from that site, they settled on a sports field and an adjacent community hall. They applied to the High Court for an order requiring the state to provide them with adequate basic shelter or housing until they obtained permanent accommodation. Although the High Court refused to grant relief to the applicants under section 26, it granted relief under section 28 by ordering the state to provide the children and their parents (relief was therefore granted only

---

38   This is William Fischel's summary of his article, "The Political Economy of Public Use in Poletown," 2004 *Michigan State Law Review* 929 (Winter 2004).

39   See the Center's website at www.cesr.org.

to some of the applicants) with shelter in the form of tents and potable water, the "bare minimum." The High Court judgment concentrated on the differences between section 26 and 28 and uncritically adopted the approach taken by the Committee on Economic, Social and Cultural Rights (the ESCR Committee) in relation to the International Covenant on Economic, Social and Cultural Rights (ICESCR). The ESCR Committee defined with [sic] the substance of the right to adequate housing by reference to its "minimum core."

The state appealed from the High Court to the Constitutional Court, which took a very different perspective on the matter. The Constitutional Court defined the issue as one relating to the *reasonableness* of the measures taken by the state. The Court held that socio-economic rights can always be enforced in a negative manner, by preventing the state or other entities from impairing the right. The Constitutional Court noted that although the ESCR Committee had approached the enforcement of socio-economic rights with reference to the minimum core of the rights, it did not define the minimum core. The Constitutional Court held that the minimum core is only one consideration in determining whether the State has met its constitutional duty to implement reasonable legislative and other measures to progressively achieve the right of access to adequate housing. The Constitutional Court noted that the reasonableness standard did not call for it to consider whether the state could have used other more desirable measures or if public money could have been better spent. The only question is whether the measures that had been adopted by the state are reasonable. As the Constitutional Court pointed out[,] "It is necessary to recognize that a wide range of possible measures could be adopted by the state to meet its obligations." The Court declared that the state had breached its obligation to devise and implement within its available resources a *comprehensive and coordinated programme* progressively to realize the right of access to adequate housing. The existing program was inadequate because it failed to cater for homeless and desperately poor communities such as the one before the Constitutional Court. The Constitutional Court deferred to the political branches by declining to devise the content of the housing plan and by noting that sections 26 and 28 do not entitle anyone to claim shelter or housing immediately on demand. Nevertheless, the judgment reflected a shift forward for the realization of socio-economic rights in South Africa.[40]

As we shall see, this approach is similar to the way Texas and New Jersey are attempting to grapple with (longstanding) rights to education embodied in their state constitutions. Together, these developments mean that we are more or less backing into a new "affirmative rights" jurisprudence, with its own terms of art and contested doctrinal ground — the indicia of a new constitutional order replacing an old constitutional order.

We have moved beyond debate about "affirmative rights." They are here. The early terms in which they are being adjudicated — such terms as "minimum core" and "reasonableness" — are *factual* tests, and the discussion is focused on working out those tests in terms of their *criteria*. This means that legislatures invoking bugbears such as "progressive realization," "resources," and "legislative deference," are being put to the test: they are being instructed to show that they treat such concepts as facts and articulate criteria for enforcing them.

---

40  Reynaud Neil Daniels, "Counter-Majoritarian Difficulty in South African Constitutional Law," http://law.bepress.com/expresso/eps/1363, 19-20 (citations omitted).

"Affirmative rights" turn the tables on the legislatures; in fact, they turn the tables on everyone, calling "ghostly hand" doctrines into the light of fact. Individually enforceable rights presume that doctrines are simply attempts of the previous constitutional order — in any of its manifestations — to preserve itself in a new political situation in which that previous order has no place. The result is that courts increasingly distrust government's interpretation of the role of government; all political actors increasingly realize that government is looking to the old constitutional order for guidance. In the new political situation which followed the *Kelo* decision, looking to the old order simply proved impossible. Courts — not to mention public opinion — increasingly balked at government's contention that it was in possession of doctrinal black boxes into which government could dip in order to pull out unlimited discretion. That wouldn't work.

However, it became glaringly clear after *Kelo* that the new Constitutional order lacked many doctrines and criteria. Sixty years after the death of FDR, we had apparently learned nothing. When — as in the United States with the "minimum scrutiny" regime — judicial doctrine intentionally limits the facts as a virtue in itself, then that is an inducement to profound opposition. But it also induces ignorance.

History suggests that, since we are approaching individual rights again — this time through the unusual method of finding out what in fact they are — we need to answer three questions: What words? What rights? and, When?

**1. What words?** It seems clear by now that a flat statement of the right, or an affirmative mandate, is not the way to go. At least the judiciary doesn't seem to like such mandates as, "Government shall provide the housing of every individual." On the other hand, Texas and New Jersey have education affirmative mandates — and in their constitutions, no less. For Texas: "A general diffusion of knowledge being essential to the preservation of the liberties and rights of the people, it shall be the duty of the Legislature of the State to establish and make suitable provision for the support and maintenance of an efficient system of public free schools."[41] For New Jersey: "The Legislature shall provide for the maintenance and support of a thorough and efficient system of free public schools for the instruction of all the children in the State between the ages of five and eighteen years."[42] Consider these provisions in the housing context:

"Housing being essential to the preservation of the liberties and rights of the people, it shall be the duty of the Legislature of the State to establish and make suitable provision for the support and maintenance of an efficient system of housing."

"The Legislature shall provide for the maintenance and support of a thorough and efficient system of housing."

The education affirmative rights in Texas and New Jersey have led to much litigation over school financing. However, there has been no suggestion that the

---

41    Texas Constitution, Article 7, Section 1. The entire constitution is online at http://www.capitol.state.tx.us.

42    New Jersey Constitution, Article VII, Section IV, 1. The entire constitution is online at http://lis.njleg.state.nj.us.

education clauses have led to impermissible legislating by the judiciary. If anything, the legislatures have been unduly lax in carrying out their tax function in relation to education, thus preserving disparities in funding between school districts.

The legislatures take advantage of the fact that the courts fight shy of according to taxation the same level of scrutiny they accord education, which is something like strict scrutiny (the courts have not yet concluded that taxation is an individually enforceable right). Thus, current litigation in these states is in part about the level of scrutiny for taxation, but in no way about the justiciability of the education provisions, limited though they are. Indeed, the litigation suggests that justiciability questions arise when the level of scrutiny for a fact is *low*, not when it is *high*, because a low level of scrutiny for a fact tends to collapse the branches and doctrines of government.[43] The Supreme Court is slowly moving toward this point of view and toward the articulation of many new levels of scrutiny, based on its concern that government actions are tending toward the elimination of government, which is a fact of the individual under the Constitution.

- "Government shall provide the housing of all individuals."
- "No individual shall be involuntarily deprived of housing."

Would these provisions lead to identical outcomes in cases?

History suggests that prohibitions are easier to understand and enforce, and this is why the Founders use prohibitions using the word "no" in the Bill of Rights ("Congress shall make no law," "no warrants shall issue," "No person shall be held"). Why did they do that? For two reasons: prohibitions tend to avoid fact questions and they tend to be self-enforcing. For example, housing: if two parties are quarreling over whether one should be removed from housing, at least there isn't any question as to what is housing — they have agreed to that. So this minimizes the necessity for the Court to step in and answer the question: what, in fact, is housing? And, of course, there is no dispute between the parties in Kelo that housing is at issue. Second, a prohibition tends to minimize the affirmative need for government to make sure people aren't being forced out of housing. People tend to know when they're being forced out of housing. If they have an individually enforceable right, they'll squawk and take it to Court and get the threatened removal stopped. And, of course, the Kelo petitioners are not asking the court to supervise anything: they are asking to be left alone.

**2. What rights?** If facts are rights, which facts are they? Here is where Constitutional law actually turns out to be useful. Consider a statement by Founder James Madison (a non-lawyer) which was constantly cited in the later Fourth Amendment dissents of Justices Brennan and Marshall. As they moved steadily

---

43   For the history of litigation involving the Texas education provision, see the website of the Mexican American Legal Defense Fund, www.maldef.org. For the history of litigation involving the New Jersey education provision, see the website of the Education Law Center, www.edlawcenter.org.

into the minority, they came increasingly to cite this Madison statement.[44] Indeed, this statement is the supreme statement of Founder intent. Madison stated in Congress that the Bill of Rights would turn the judiciary and the state legislatures into "bulwark[s] against every assumption of power in the legislative or executive; they will be naturally led to resist every encroachment upon rights expressly stipulated for in the constitution by the declaration of rights. Besides this security, there is a great probability that such a declaration in the federal system would be enforced; because the State Legislatures will jealously and closely watch the operations of this Government, and be able to resist with more effect every assumption of power, than any other power on earth."[45] Although Madison uses "assumption of power" twice and "every" three times, the statement is somewhat anomalous. The Fourth Amendment guards against "unreasonable" searches and seizures. Reasonableness suggests a balancing approach (between the importance of what is sought and the individual's right to privacy) and not an absolutist approach, and the Court has adopted the balancing approach. However, Madison does not say every unreasonable assumption; he says EVERY assumption. Like everyone else, Brennan and Marshall saw that Constitutional litigation has always been over the meaning of this word, but they themselves never figured out what it meant. We have always seen applications of it. For example, there is no such thing as "reasonable" establishments of religion: even today, if the Court finds them, they are banned in EVERY case.[46] Again, EVERY act of

---

44   Brennan did not use this statement when he himself was making Fourth Amendment law for the Court: see *Schmerber v. California*, 384 US 757 (1966); *Warden v. Hayden* 387 US 294 (1967). But he became increasingly irate as the Court turned against him, and then he had recourse to Madison, and not only in Fourth Amendment cases; see *Davis v. Passman*, 442 U.S. 228, 241-42 (1979); *Valley Forge College v. Americans United*, 454 US 464 (1982). For good examples of the way Brennan and Marshall viewed Madison's statement see *United States v. Calandra*, 414 US 338 (1974); *United States v. Leon*, 468 US 897 (1984).

45   1 *Annals of Cong.* 439 (1789).

46   The "minimum scrutiny" regime provides a method for sustaining religious preferences without finding them to be establishments of religion. This has been severely criticized. The "minimum scrutiny" regime gets us in trouble when it comes to the religious clauses of the First Amendment: "Congress shall make no law respecting an establishment of religion, or prohibiting the free exercise thereof...."In the scrutiny regime, establishment becomes a test for applying — not finding — religion. Thus, establishment is assumed and the issue becomes one of preference. Too much, or improper, preference becomes state religion. Preference goes to establishment, dislike to prohibition. However, dislike also goes to establishment — it is a factual inquiry — so the distinction between an establishment and prohibition is discarded under the scrutiny regime, that is, the concepts of "no" and Madison's "every" are ignored. The scrutiny regime inevitably assumes that the religion clauses are addressed to two types of government action (which includes an assumption that state religion nevertheless implies that there is still, in fact, government). Thus, in *Everson v. Vitale*, 456 US 228 (1982), Justice Brennan mangles the distinctions: "Since *Everson v. Board of Education*, 330 U.S. 1 (1947), this Court has adhered to the principle, clearly manifested in the history and logic of the Establishment Clause, that no State can 'pass laws which aid one religion' or that 'prefer one religion over another.' *Id.*, at 15. This principle of denominational neutrality has been restated on many occasions. In *Zorach v. Clauson*, 343 U.S. 306 (1952), we said that '[t]he government must be neutral when it comes to competition between sects.' *Id.*, at 314. In *Epperson v. Arkansas*, 393 U.S. 97 (1968), we stated unambiguously: 'The First Amendment mandates governmental neutrality be-

protected speech is vindicated, no matter how hostile the crowd.[47] In fact, "strict scrutiny" is somewhat deceptive: it is difficult to imagine how any government could rationally allow — much less enforce — involuntary servitude, and yet it is supposedly allowable if it passes strict scrutiny. This is manifestly absurd, and here the "minimum scrutiny" regime loses one of its bulwarks: strict scrutiny. Certain facts simply prompt absolute vindication: they are vindicated in EVERY case. This aligns Supreme Court adjudication of these facts, more closely with what Madison intended: speech survives the heckler's veto, and now, for precisely the same reasons, housing survives the dispossessor's veto.

Those, then, are applications. But what does the word mean? Why do certain facts determine the result of every case in which they appear? This is the question the Court cannot yet answer. The history of English constitutional law is one of long-term efforts by government to, for example, impose a state religion or violations of what today are regarded by the Court as instances of protected speech. These efforts were made over thousands of years, so there is a long history to look at. It is simply a history of failure. In the end, governments don't succeed in imposing state religion or in violating protected speech — they simply distort the facts and cause all kinds of grotesque situations.[48] This is the sort of inquiry in which the Court engaged when, in *West Virginia v. Barnette*, it removed freedom of religion from the political system in the case of a student who did not wish to be compelled to recite the Pledge of Allegiance:

> Struggles to coerce uniformity of sentiment in support of some end thought essential to their time and country have been waged by many good as well as by evil men. Nationalism is a relatively recent phenomenon but at other times and

tween religion and religion....The State may not adopt programs or practices...which 'aid or oppose' any religion....This prohibition is absolute.' *Id.*, at 104, 106, citing *Abington School District v. Schempp*, 374 U.S. 203, 225 (1963). And Justice Goldberg cogently articulated the relationship between the Establishment Clause and the Free Exercise Clause when he said that '[t]he fullest realization of true religious liberty requires that government...effect no favoritism among sects...and that it work deterrence of no religious belief.' *Abington School District, supra*, at 305. In short, when we are presented with a state law granting a denominational preference, our precedents demand that we treat the law as suspect and that we apply strict scrutiny in adjudging its constitutionality." At 245.

Predictably, the scrutiny regime itself came to replace religion and to be sustained for that reason: the Court would decide if there was some sort of residual and amorphous religious content to legislation, and sustain the legislation under minimum scrutiny. See *Oregon* v. *Smith*, 494 U.S. 872 (1990). Which, in turn, put government at issue. Then, and just as predictably, the "minimum scrutiny" regime provoked legislation raising the level of scrutiny for religion as a fact — and in the context of eminent domain! This was the beginning of a "facts of the individual" analysis of religion, overturning the distinctly odd religious manifestation of the "minimum scrutiny" regime. However, the guise is no surprise: the "minimum scrutiny" regime assumes all facts, including religion.

47   Although the insinuation of the "minimum scrutiny" regime into protected speech, is proceeding apace, along the same lines as its insinuation into the religion clauses, as described in the footnote above. See Avinash Ashutosh Bhagwat, "The Test That Ate Everything: Intermediate Scrutiny in First Amendment Jurisprudence," http://ssrn.com/abstract=887566.

48   For two examples of past reactions to attempts to violate individual rights, see Margaret Judson, *The Crisis of the Constitution* (Rutgers University Press 1949) and Pauline Maier, *From Resistance to Revolution* (Norton 1992).

places the ends have been racial or territorial security, support of a dynasty or regime, and particular plans for saving souls. As first and moderate methods to attain unity have failed, those bent on its accomplishment must resort to an ever-increasing severity. As governmental pressure toward unity becomes greater, so strife becomes more bitter as to whose unity it shall be. Probably no deeper division of our people could proceed from any provocation than from finding it necessary to choose what doctrine and whose program public educational officials shall compel youth to unite in embracing. Ultimate futility of such attempts to compel coherence is the lesson of every such effort from the Roman drive to stamp out Christianity as a disturber of its pagan unity, the Inquisition, as a means to religious and dynastic unity, the Siberian exiles as a means to Russian unity, down to the fast failing efforts of our present totalitarian enemies. Those who begin coercive elimination of dissent soon find themselves exterminating dissenters. Compulsory unification of opinion achieves only the unanimity of the graveyard. It seems trite but necessary to say that the First Amendment to our Constitution was designed to avoid these ends by avoiding these beginnings. There is no mysticism in the American concept of the State or of the nature or origin of its authority. We set up government by consent of the governed, and the Bill of Rights denies those in power any legal opportunity to coerce that consent. Authority here is to be controlled by public opinion, not public opinion by authority.[49]

In short, the process of deciding which facts are vindicated in every case is a speculative process, not a normative one. This is why the result — the Constitution — is not pre- or proscriptive, but rather, descriptive.[50] Note that for the Court, it is the Constitution which is the result of the historical investigation, not the historical investigation which is the result of the Constitution. That is, the Court is not removing freedom of speech from the political system because freedom of speech is part of the Constitution; it is removing freedom of speech from the political system because the Constitution is part of freedom of speech. Thus, the question is not, What fact does history tell us is part of the Constitution? but rather, What fact does the Constitution tell us is part of history? Much is made of abiding by the "original intent" of the Founders in applying the Constitution, but the intent of the Founders is to make the sort of historical investigation undertaken by the Court in *Barnette*. In response to *Kelo*, but above all in response to the mandate of the Court in *Barnette*, public opinion continued its immemorial inquiry into facts. Public opinion was proceeding to answer the momentous question, whether — like freedom of speech — housing, maintenance, education, medical care and liberty should be removed from the political system. And much to the consternation of the political system — which exercised absolute power over all those facts — the answer was, yes. Hence the revolt which is the subject of this essay. Finally, it was not so much that public opinion was proceeding with an historical investigation of the facts of the New Bill of Rights. Rather, the *Kelo* revolt revealed an immemorial function of public opinion. The *Barnette* Court is saying that public opinion *always* conducts historical investigations of facts and *always* reaches conclusions about facts and *always* resists attempts to destroy

---

49  *Barnette* at 640-641.

50  *Barnette* is sometimes seen as a moral endorsement of freedom of religion. See, for example, Steven Douglas Smith, "*Barnette*'s Big Blunder," http://ssrn.com/abstract=417480.

facts. The Constitution is merely part of that process, and with respect to some matters it is not the most important one, or even a relevant one. Indeed, when the Constitution becomes a bone of contention, it is probably a sign of its unimportance in the context in which that contest takes place. Public opinion's process had simply been hijacked by *West Coast Hotel* as the Court attempted to turn the process over to the political system. That simply hadn't worked, and now the process had to be returned to its normal channel.

Although not all of the following criteria need be met, and although they are not ranked or accorded different weights, historically, a fact of the individual is usually involved — on a par with protected speech or freedom from an establishment of religion — if the government (or a private party):

1. seeks to eliminate the fact;

2. at best only succeeds or would, if allowed, only succeed, in eliminating incarnations of it;

3. in the process violates other rights;

4. brings to bear a disproportionate effort; and

5. does not consider alternatives which could achieve the goal.

This is the "facts of the individual" analysis. Facts of the individual inhere in the individual and are never violated.[51] "Never" goes to "incarnation"; when the Founders could not exercise the protected speech they had chosen to exercise, they exercised it otherwise — but they exercised it.[52] People forced out of housing simply seek other housing. **"Every" means this: what people do over and over again, no matter what obstacles are put in their way.** It is clinical, dispassionate, but it tells us both why and how the Constitution exists. On the other hand, the disproportionate effort to be shown is something like an Office of the Inquisition: whether formal or informal, it is in fact an integrated operation the function of which is to deprive individuals involuntarily of a fact. Part of the way

---

51    Alan Dershowitz, like most commentators, still sees these facts through the lens of jurisprudence, and so, not clearly. See his *Rights from Wrongs* (New York 2005). See also Avi Ben-Bassat and Momi Dahan, "Social Rights in the Constitution and in Practice," http://ssrn.com/abstraction=407260.

52    Speech as a fact of the individual has been described as "a spirit that demands self-expression" or "the basic human desire for recognition." *Procunier v. Martinez*, 416 US 396, 427 (1974). Constitutionally, religion is the process of truth. Madison, in his "Memorial and Remonstrance Against Religious Assessments" (1785), described freedom of religion as a fact of the individual, as that which is "inalienable." Nevertheless, it is difficult to tease out of Madison's comment what, in FACT, he believes religion, the exercise of religion, or the free exercise of religion, to be. They appear to have in common: 1) facts which exist only in the mind, 2) creating a feeling of duty in the individual, 3) leading to "homage," which is undefined. Since this has remained undefined, it has been "approached" negatively, that is, it has been looked at through the lens of the facts "Civil Society" generates. The most moving thing about the Founders is that we don't seem to understand facts much, if at all, better than they did. Two hundred years of Constitutional jurisprudence have been designed to keep us in complete ignorance as to what "homage" — the central fact of the First Amendment — is; this is an example of our almost complete ignorance of the individual. Madison's text is widely available, most widely on many internet sites, including www.law.ou.edu/hist/remon.html.

it works, historically, is by depriving individuals with respect to other, protected facts.

Indeed, one of the major arguments of the *Kelo* petitioners is that there is a burgeoning industry in using eminent domain to turn housing over to private developers — government is being stolen. But that is merely one part of the whole establishment devoted to depriving individuals involuntarily of their housing. The Court will want to see everything which falls under the heading, "Depriving Individuals Involuntarily of Their Housing." What they will find is a state within a state, one not within the jurisdiction of the Constitution because housing itself is not currently within the jurisdiction of the Constitution. In the case of housing, the Court will find an immemorial policy of depriving individuals involuntarily of housing.

This qualifies housing for a level of scrutiny higher than minimum scrutiny under the new analysis because it shows an historical policy of animus against an important fact. At that point, the Court requires under the new scrutiny that the policy at least articulately facilitate a frequent government purpose. In order to arrive at the proper level of scrutiny, the Court will look at the congruity of facts with policy, policy with enforcement and enforcement with outcome — an *ad hoc* "facts of the individual" analysis. The Declaration of Independence raises the question, what in fact is revolution? It is the conjunction of this new analysis and scrutiny.[53] But revolution is a thing of naught compared to the canonical "facts of the individual" analysis. Nevertheless it means that housing and many other facts have now detached themselves from minimum scrutiny and begun their rise through the scrutiny continuum. The tyranny of a century is over, the door to the new Constitution has opened.

Our very subject shows historical use of eminent domain to destroy what the Court has already acknowledged to be an important fact: housing.[54] However, it was the policy of the "minimum scrutiny" regime to keep us ignorant of the regime's enforcement by way of involuntary deprivations of housing; we only know that it is ongoing. When there was only minimum scrutiny for housing, none of this evidence was relevant and therefore none of it was admissible. Now there will, I suspect, be a lot of special masters appointed by the courts when they have, for the first time, to take an organized look at various ministates — those devoted to depriving individuals involuntarily of housing, medical care

---

53   On the little-studied factual indicia for legal regime change, see Michael Steven Green, "Legal Revolutions: Six Mistakes about Discontinuity in the Legal Order," http://ssrn.com/abstract=881073.

54   "We do not denigrate the importance of decent, safe, and sanitary housing. But the Constitution does not provide judicial remedies for every social and economic ill. We are unable to perceive in that document any constitutional guarantee of access to dwellings of a particular quality, or any recognition of the right of a tenant to occupy the real property of his landlord beyond the term of his lease without the payment of rent or otherwise contrary to the terms of the relevant agreement. Absent constitutional mandate, the assurance of adequate housing and the definition of landlord-tenant relationships are legislative, not judicial, functions. Nor should we forget that the Constitution expressly protects against confiscation of private property or the income therefrom." *Lindsey v. Normet*, 405 US 56, 74 (1972).

and other facts. A "facts of the individual" analysis has, after two hundred years, finally unlocked the Constitution. Despite strenuous efforts, the Founders and their successors were not able to effect the synthesis. This inability explains how the Constitution could recognize both freedom from an establishment of religion — and slavery. The "facts of the individual" analysis does not explain why we will never know all the facts of the individual, but it does mean that the Constitution has entered its maturity. Indeed, it means that the Constitution is vestigial, constitutionalism itself problematic. We have moved on. What is the successor fact of the Constitution? of the individual? What are their indicia?

The human race not being particularly perceptive, it took thousands of years to conclude that protected speech, freedom from state religion, freedom from involuntary servitude, and so on, are facts of the individual. It is not a walk in the park to identify such facts — never mind to vindicate them in law. Nevertheless, such facts do tend over time to be identified; it is neither here nor there that they have tended to be "political"-type facts, since the people who make the laws are politicians, and they are most interested in facts which relate to their work as politicians. But politicians are not the only individuals. Even Roosevelt understood that. Look at his list again. It is really an attempt to say: these are facts of the individual, they are what we mean when we say the word, "individual." But his little essay is just the tip of the iceberg. There is an ongoing debate as to what, if any, are facts of the individual. However, one thing is certainly clear. In our jurisprudence, the burden falls on the violated to assert that they have been violated with respect to a fact of the individual. The courts do not assume it, and the wrongdoers will never raise it, but it sits there, on the record, if an individual claims a violation of fact of the individual because even benighted American courts realize that if it is in one, it must be vindicated in EVERY case. The problem in the *Kelo* case is that no one previously had raised the issue of housing as a fact of the individual, and it hasn't been raised by anyone, at any level, in the *Kelo* case itself — so far.

A consensus very likely could be found that five new facts of the individual meet the test given above. However, there is no political consensus. These facts are housing, education, maintenance, liberty and medical care. Running them through the criteria listed above, they are probably in the Constitution as follows:

- no individual shall be involuntarily deprived of housing;
- no individual shall be involuntarily deprived of education;
- no individual shall be deprived of maintenance;
- no individual shall be involuntarily deprived of liberty;
- no individual shall be involuntarily deprived of medical care.

This is the New Bill of Rights.[55] Advocates for each of these facts should begin to think about the cases they will bring once the New Bill of Rights is law

---

55  Sadly, after two hundred years under the Constitution we have just begun to examine the ways in which one fact of the individual helps us to understand another, for example, what the fact of medical care tells us about the fact of liberty, and *vice versa*. See, for ex-

because, as we shall see, it has already begun to be enforced. I am moving as quickly as I can to enforce it in situations in which public opinion demands it immediately, and even the political system is beginning to come to terms with it; comparative analysis will speed enforcement of the rest of it. Following are my suggestions, in this case to the Ohio task force charged with evaluating changes to eminent domain laws:

> I think that the consensus is that you should not attempt to restrict eminent domain with respect to generalities. For example, stating that eminent domain shall not be used for economic development does not prevent confrontation over the facts. The reason is that the terms...are simply too vague. No one can agree on the meaning of blight, no one can agree on the meaning of economic development, and so on. The result is that however the political system resolves cases, the facts underlying those cases still lead to physical confrontations over the facts....Physical resistance to removal is where the rubber meets the road in eminent domain reform....No matter what you feel about this, you should not ignore it. In fact, you should keep that scenario always in your minds as you deliberate. Will the police go in if your legislation ultimately demands it, and will they succeed? I also think you should have someone representing law enforcement on your task force. It is a big mistake to leave them out. They are the ones who are going to have to decide, in the end, if orders promulgated pursuant to your legislation are legal orders. They have to make that determination and they can only follow legal orders. Public opinion is undergoing a sea change and you should not assume that simply because a legislature passes a law and a judge orders that it be enforced, that law enforcement will regard the order as legal. Watch out for this. It is a very important consideration. It also seems that public opinion demands that the level of scrutiny for housing be raised...[,] whether intermediate or strict is unclear. But it cannot remain at minimum scrutiny any longer. If it does, this too will lead to physical confrontation over the facts in eminent domain cases. Thus, you should compare what you come up with, with this formulation:
>
>> "Eminent domain shall not be exercised unless it substantially furthers an important government interest, and with respect to housing unless it specifically fulfills an overriding government purpose."
>
> That is, this is intermediate scrutiny for ALL facts in the eminent domain context, and strict scrutiny for HOUSING in the eminent domain context. From what I can tell, this is the current state of public opinion on this question. But as you evaluate public opinion, make sure you are asking: what does public opinion want in terms of FACTS? One thing is certain about public opinion: it demands restriction of eminent domain in terms of FACTS. The legislation must contain FACTS (housing, business, churches, and so on). If legislation restricts eminent domain only with generalities, public opinion will reject it, and you will ultimately see physical confrontation over the facts you have failed to put in your legislation....Outcomes have to change, and your legislation must change outcomes.

ample, Eric S. Janus and Wayne A. Logan, "Substantive Due Process and the Involuntary Confinement of Sexually Violent Predators," 35 *Connecticut Law Review* No. 2 (Winter 2003); Thomas L. Hafemeister, "Parameters and Implementation of a Right to Mental Health Treatment of Juvenile Offenders," 12 *Virginia Journal of Social Policy and the Law* No. 1 (2004).

Now let's take a look at the New Bill of Rights in detail: these are
1. prohibitions with respect to
2. facts
3. as to the existence of which the parties would agree; they
4. tend to be self-enforcing, and
5. neither the Government nor the Court would tend to be dragged into fact-finding or supervisory roles.

There is thus no jurisprudential problem with recognizing them as facts of the individual IF they are facts of the individual. Of course, there is always SOME role for the different branches with respect to facts of the individual. The Court is constantly hearing cases on establishments of religion and legislatures are constantly legislating with respect to them one way or another. The central issue in these actions is: are the facts under review, for example, protected speech, or an establishment of religion? We know what to do if that's what we are dealing with, but are we in fact dealing with it?

**3. When?** How on earth do you bring new rights into law? We are currently living in a political reaction which has lasted longer than the reaction which succeeded the fall of Napoleon. What if we signed off only on my right to housing? Look at it. What about eminent domain? There is, of course, a huge and swelling legal movement aimed at exposing the egregious human rights abuses carried out in the name of eminent domain. But remember that "economic development" and "enhanced tax revenue" — the government goals in *Kelo* — are not the only ends for which eminent domain is the means. What, no road which would benefit all humanity because Grandma won't take the buyout? And is now standing on her right to housing? I sense the bulldozers waiting, purring....And what, "Squillionaire Defaults On Mortgage, Squats in Mansion?" What if we all stop paying? And no forced evacuations due to natural disasters?

Eminent domain has been used throughout human history for a wide variety of reasons. To suddenly impose housing as an objection means rethinking policy and procedure to a degree which would daunt a Pharaoh. On the other hand, slavery has been endemic throughout most of human history, and we got over that. More generally, which prongs of the "facts of the individual" test get what degree of emphasis? What if a fact fails one or more of the prongs? How do we treat facts depending on our degree of certainty that they are facts of the individual? And what do we do with our current extensively articulated scrutiny continuum? Are the prongs unrelated to balancing, balancing in disguise, or a logical development from balancing? And by the way, is privacy a fact of the individual? Remarkably, as Daniel Solove notes, although the right is upwards of a hundred years old, we still have only a primitive idea of what, in fact, privacy is.[56]

---

56  Whatever privacy turns out, in fact, to be, "[t]his does not mean that privacy is an individualistic right." Daniel J. Solove, "A Taxonomy of Privacy," http://ssrn.com/abstract=667622 at 7. For a discussion of the factual nature of privacy in the context of recent jurisprudence, see Lois L. Shepherd, "Looking Forward With The Right Of Privacy," http://ssrn.com/abstract=225040.

Is property a fact of the individual?[57] Intellectual property?[58] Democracy?[59] Is old age?[60]

Is death?[61] Is freedom?[62] Violence?[63] Dignity?[64] Self-defense?[65] A park, or a road?[66] The environment?[67] Voting?[68] Water?[69] During the third Constitutional epoch, these debates took place within the political system. In the fourth epoch, they take place within the "facts of the individual" analysis. For its part, the New Bill of Rights does not ask what in *law* is a fact of the individual. It asks what in *fact* is a fact of the individual. Find out: that is the mandate of the New Bill of Rights, because it is the mandate of the Constitution, because it is the mandate

---

57   Gregory S. Alexander, "Property As a Fundamental Right? The German Example," http://ssrn.com/abstract=384161.

58   Laurence R. Helfer, "Toward a Human Rights Framework for Intellectual Property," http://ssrn.com/abstract=891303.

59   Although the literature grants democracy independent status as a fact, we know virtually nothing about democracy as a fact of the individual. It is almost always discussed in terms of other facts, not on its own terms. The result is that, apart from the notion that it is bound up with the degree of control over other facts, we have virtually no idea what democracy is, much less what are its indicia in a "facts of the individual" analysis. See Michael J. Perry, "Protecting Human Rights in a Democracy: What Role for the Courts?" http://ssrn.com/abstract=380283.

60   Marshall Kapp, "Geriatric Depression: Do Older Persons Have a Right to be Unhappy?" http://ssrn.com/abstract=310581.

61   Michael Patrick Allen, "The Constitution at the Threshold of Life and Death: A Suggested Approach to Accommodate an Interest in Life and a Right to Die," http://ssrn.com/abstract=595763; Abhik Majumdar, "The Right to Die: The Indian Experience," http://ssrn.com/abstract=902875. For a discussion of *Lawrence* as establishing a right to physician-assisted suicide, see Diana Hassel, "Sex and Death: Lawrence's Liberty and Physician-Assisted Suicide," http://ssrn.com/abstract=902429.

62   Clifford G. Holderness, Michael C. Jensen and William H. Meckling, "The Logic of the First Amendment," http://ssrn.com/abstract=215468.

63   Susan S. Kuo, "Bringing in the State: Toward a Constitutional Duty to Protect from Mob Violence," http://ssrn.com/abstract=910554.

64   Christopher McCrudden, "Human Dignity," http://ssrn.com/abstract=899687.

65   Nelson Robert Lund, "A Constitutional Right to Self Defense?" http://ssrn.com/abstract=912277.

66   Peter L. Strauss, "Citizens to Preserve Overton Park v. Volpe," http://ssrn.com/abstract=650482.

67   Robin Kundis Craig, "Should there be a Constitutional Right to a Clean and Healthy Environment?" http://ssrn.com/abstract=877286.

68   Jeffrey C. O'Neill, "Everything that can be Counted Does not Necessarily Count: The Right to Vote and the Choice of a Voting System," http://ssrn.com/abstract=889466.

69   William L. Andreen, "The Evolving Contours of Water Law in the United States: Bridging the Gap between Water Rights, Land Use and the Protection of the Aquatic Environment," http://ssrn.com/abstract=889744; Marca Weinberg, "Assessing a Policy Grab Bag: Federal Water Policy Reform," http://ssrn.com/abstract=320420.

of the individual. Finding out, is what the "facts of the individual" analysis allows us to do.[70]

But don't forget the fear really lurking behind the denial of a right to housing. The housing right certainly implies the right to liberty, because it is hard to see how you can have a ban on involuntarily deprivations of housing (and remember, Madison says it's in "every" case) and still put people in prison. I think it is pretty clear that that would involve an involuntarily deprivation of housing. Imagine the test case: the sheriff enforcing an arrest warrant by going up to the door of a building in which both the defendant and the sheriff concede the defendant is housed. And what about all the nasty characters currently in prison? Are they simply to be let out? On the other hand, that prison is their housing: could you kick them out? How about an equitable action to prevent government from removing a prisoner from the prison after the prisoner's sentence has been served?

It is embarrassing, but we caused it. Every individual right is a perfect storm of extremes, reflecting the pathology of attempts to destroy facts of the individual. These grotesque situations must be analyzed directly. Here is a classic rights problem: the majority will not currently allow the right, that is, an end to incarceration — and yet it is a necessary implication of the right to housing. Support for incarceration remains strong — particularly for certain crimes and all violent crimes — and even opposition to it never reflects the idea that liberty is a fact of the individual.[71] There are obvious reasons we don't have a right to housing, but there is also a hidden one that has escaped our notice: it's because we don't have the right to liberty, or, as we shall see after the *Lawrence* case, the right to be free from incarceration.

Instead of proceeding as usual — linking liberty to due process — the Supreme Court recently *conflated* liberty and due process (as we shall see, in doing so it also conflated the Due Process Clauses of the Fifth and Fourteenth Amendments). The Court did so in Justice Kennedy's opinion in the 2003 case *Lawrence v. Texas*, which found laws against sodomy unconstitutional. Ordinarily housing is considered an aspect of privacy under minimum scrutiny. However, in *Lawrence*, Kennedy doesn't evaluate the sodomy law using the scrutiny continuum. He evaluates the law exclusively with respect to liberty. And yet, although housing figures in that liberty analysis, Kennedy doesn't apply the scrutiny continuum to housing either. Again, he uses liberty. So where is housing?

As is well known to commentators today, the question *Lawrence* left in its wake is, what level of scrutiny does liberty now enjoy? strict scrutiny? intermediate scrutiny? The commentators are unclear about the level of scrutiny. However,

---

70 We might begin with equality, a term which is hardly known in the law outside very traditional contexts, such as equal protection. We have only begun the task of examining equality using an *ad hoc* "facts of the individual" analysis. See Matthew D. Adler and Chris William Sanchirico, "Inequality and Uncertainty: Theory and Legal Applications," http://ssrn.com/abstract=886571.

71 A 2001 poll by the American Civil Liberties Union concluded that a majority of Americans favors imprisonment for *all* drug dealers. The ACLU regularly takes the public pulse regarding incarceration, and maintains an online library of its studies at www.aclu.org.

several things are clear. First, Kennedy applied at *least* direct scrutiny; in fact, *Lawrence* is the first case to use the level explicitly detached from minimum scrutiny. Liberty is detached from all facts, and in particular from any facts which enjoy minimum scrutiny. The decision is based on the idea "that it was necessary to invalidate a discriminatory law as if it applied to all persons in order to prevent the aftereffects of discrimination that would linger if it were not."[72] The state law in question was an historical policy (which means individuals evaded the law) of animus against an important fact (which means government promoted it), liberty.[73]

The case permits us to articulate, for the first time, not the "liberty interest" of the "minimum scrutiny" regime, but rather, and at a minimum,

**THE RIGHT TO LIBERTY.**

To sustain an involuntary deprivation of liberty, government must articulately facilitate a frequent government purpose. An involuntary deprivation of liberty must

1. construct liberty and policy;
2. facilitate liberty and policy; and
3. sustain liberty and policy.

The second thing which is clear is that under *Lawrence* crime is exclusively a policy which fails direct scrutiny. It's a modest elevation of liberty after two hundred years, but it has substantial consequences; for example, it mandates re-

---

72  Kathleen M. Sullivan and Pamela S. Karlan, summarizing their article, "The Elysian Fields of the Law," http://ssrn.com/abstract=630805.

73  Justice Scalia misread the Court's holding. In his dissent, he claimed to have found the "ground on which the Court squarely rests its holding: the contention that there is no rational basis for the law here under attack." The sodomy law should have been upheld under this standard. *Lawrence v. Texas*, 539 US 558, 599 (2003). However, what the Court actually said is that the Texas sodomy law "furthers no legitimate state interest." *Id.*, at 560. A glance at the scrutiny chart shows what the Court has done: it has taken the "furthers" prong from intermediate scrutiny and the "legitimate" from minimum scrutiny. This hybrid is not a scrutiny regime test, nor does the Court claim that it is. Nor does the Court ever refer to liberty as an "interest." Under the "minimum scrutiny" regime, when the Court says something is an interest, that means it is adjudicated only under minimum scrutiny. The absence of the use of "interest" in connection with liberty in *Lawrence*, is the strongest signal of all that the Court is not viewing, or establishing tests for, liberty under the "minimum scrutiny" regime. The hybrid is an *ad hoc* "facts of the individual" test in which policy is treated as a fact. The Court thus continues the line of analysis in *Euclid*: straight through, from the pre-*West Coast Hotel* era to the present, the Court has had its own method for identifying and vindicating important facts — but somehow the rest of us are stuck with the scrutiny regime. The Court makes it clear that the test is not its last word on liberty adjudication: "Had those who drew and ratified the Due Process Clauses of the Fifth Amendment or the Fourteenth Amendment known the components of liberty in its manifold possibilities, they might have been more specific. They did not presume to have this insight. They knew times can blind us to certain truths and later generations can see that laws once thought necessary and proper in fact serve only to oppress. As the Constitution endures, persons in every generation can invoke its principles in their own search for greater freedom." *Id.*, at 578-579.

consideration of health and welfare regulation and criminal law and procedure.[74] In turn, the new right to liberty generates two new doctrines:

1. any policy which does *not* articulately facilitate a frequent government purpose, is an indicium of a fact of the individual; and

2. the scrutiny continuum is a fact continuum with respect to every indicium of a fact of the individual.

Health and welfare regulation is a fact continuum, criminal law is a fact continuum, criminal procedure is a fact continuum, and so on. The Court transforms the scrutiny continuum into a fact continuum by locating liberty in an analysis of the sodomy policy as a *fact*. We are finally able to analyze according to one theory, for example, marriage with respect to contemporaneous policies which both display bias *toward* marriage and animus *against* marriage; in fact, that is encountered as a matter of course under direct scrutiny. These policies are evidence going to the question, what is marriage? Are the facts of *Lawrence* marriage?[75]

The third thing to notice is that, although the scrutiny regime exercises vast power over all our lives, the supporters of the anti-sodomy law did not argue that the scrutiny regime is a right. It is the Constitution as far as the third epoch is concerned, and there is a right to government, but it is never argued that the scrutiny regime is itself a right. The result is that supporters of the scrutiny regime are forced to argue against the notion of important facts. But that is clearly at odds with Supreme Court jurisprudence throughout all the Constitutional epochs.

And there are other consequences. Under *Lawrence* we apply direct scrutiny to the indicia of liberty, and Kennedy is careful to enumerate them: "In Houston, Texas, officers of the Harris County Police Department were dispatched to a *private residence* in response to a reported weapons disturbance. They entered an *apartment* where one of the petitioners, John Geddes Lawrence, *resided*. The right of the police to enter does not seem to have been questioned. The officers observed Lawrence and another man, Tyron Garner, engaging in a sexual act [there was no warrant]. The two petitioners were arrested, held in custody overnight, and charged and convicted before a Justice of the Peace"[76] (emphases added). Note that in these facts not only is housing an indicium of liberty, but also, involuntary deprivation of housing is an indicium of liberty. Under direct scrutiny we watch housing move, after two hundred years, directly into the Constitution. This or-

---

74  The first analysis — a landmark essay — of the implications of *Lawrence* for the concept of crime, is Catherine L. Carpenter, "On Statutory Rape, Strict Liability, and the Public Welfare Offense Model," http://ssrn.com/abstract=907682. It implicates the scrutiny regime by suggesting that the "public welfare offense" doctrine — the application to minimum scrutiny to government proscription of acts — does not survive the vindication of liberty. What doctrine — and by implication, does the scrutiny regime itself — survive *Lawrence*, and if any does — under what internally consistent theory? For more on the transition from concern with privacy to concern with liberty, see Helen J. Knowles, "From a Value to a Right: The Supreme Court's Oh-So-Conscious Move from 'Privacy' to 'Liberty,'" *http://ssrn.com/abstract=921916*.

75  Analysis of fact as policy has recently been done by subjecting adjudication itself to an *ad hoc* "facts of the individual" analysis. See Lawrence B. Solum, "Procedural Justice," http://ssrn.com/abstract=508282.

76  *Lawrence* at 562-563.

dering of facts is the Court *sua sponte* taking the first, halting steps to displace the "minimum scrutiny" regime. In doing so, it moves away from *both* public opinion *and* the political system. Nevertheless, it also moves *toward* the Constitution, and it had laid the groundwork for doing so. A decade before *Lawrence*, in an opinion co-authored by Justice Kennedy, the Court unsuccessfully tried to add the concept of truth to minimum scrutiny — actually, it was giving notice of a shift in doctrine. In that opinion it said that minimum scrutiny is invoked when there is

1. an historical demonstration of
2. untruth respecting
3. a social controversy.

Compare that to what invokes direct scrutiny:

1. an historical policy of
2. animus against
3. an important fact.

That is, according to the Court, minimum scrutiny was invoked when "facts [premising] a constitutional resolution of social controversy had proven to be untrue, and history's demonstration of their untruth not only justified but required the new choice of constitutional principle."[77] But that is not minimum scrutiny. Minimum scrutiny does not treat policy as a fact. Thus, the Court's new minimum scrutiny "formulation," invoking truth, left a gap between fact and truth. Kennedy realized this, and, in *Lawrence*, filled that gap the only way it could be filled, by using the concept of equality. And what "required" the new principle? "[F]acts that the country could understand, or had come to understand already, but which the Court of an earlier day, as its own declarations disclosed, had not been able to perceive...[:] applications of constitutional principle to facts as they had not been seen by the Court before."[78] Note that the Court under these circumstances sees the change in the Constitution as being made by the country *first* and that the change is "truth." It is what Madison means when he says "every." The response to *Kelo* revealed precisely this change, prompting public opinion to raise the level of scrutiny for housing from minimum scrutiny (the level the Court gave housing in the case of *Lindsey v. Normet*) to direct scrutiny. Public opinion was now demanding that *Lindsey* be overruled, and was itself overruling the case.

We know just when fact was removed from the Constitution by the Supreme Court. It was in 1937, when the "minimum scrutiny" regime was established by the *West Coast Hotel* decision, which sustained a minimum wage law for women and minors. With this decision, the third Constitutional epoch began. In sustaining the law, the Court stated that "the Constitution does not recognize an absolute and uncontrollable liberty. Liberty in each of its phases has its history and connotation. But the liberty safeguarded is liberty in a social organization which requires the protection of law against the evils which menace the health, safety, morals, and welfare of the people. Liberty under the Constitution is thus necessarily subject to the restraints of due process, and regulation which is reasonable in relation to its subject and is adopted in the interests of the community is due

---

77   *Planned Parenthood* at 862.

78   *Id.*, at 863-864.

process."[79] The claimed authority for the law was merely that "the statute is a reasonable exercise of the police power of the state."[80] Nevertheless, the Court went on to assume, without deciding, that minimum wage laws were an aspect of due process and that due process conflicted with liberty. It further assumed, again without deciding, that indicia of liberty are

1. absoluteness combined with uncontrollability;
2. "phases;"
3. "history and connotation;" and
4. "evils which menace the health, safety, morals, and welfare of the people."

Among other charming features, this characterization both insulated and contradicted the Founders, who thought sufficiently highly of liberty to vindicate it in the Constitution. But not according to the *West Coast Hotel* Court which, while adept at describing liberty, concludes that the Constitution "does not recognize" it, that is, the Constitution does not recognize fact. This nonrecognition is also the recognition of "liberty," the indicia of which are

1. regulation
2. reasonably relating to
3. a subject.

That is, the subject is the same one the Constitution "does not recognize." The regime — the "social organization" — is the subject, that is what is recognized. This is a view of the Constitution as pre- or proscriptive, rather than descriptive. It assumes, without deciding, that either liberty or due process is "subject" to the other and assigns the definition of "subject" to another term which is undefined, the "social organization." By far the most damaging assumption, however, was that, prior to the vindication of the minimum wage law, liberty had somehow been an individually enforceable right.

By "demoting" it to an "interest," the Court constructed for itself a place to put all facts with which its limited understanding made it incapable of coping; the history of the "minimum scrutiny" regime is the history of the Court's progressive refusal to let anyone else deal with them, either. Government purpose died in that place, and the response to the *Kelo* decision was the fraught process of restoring it on a new basis.

Clearly the Court was using an *ad hoc* "facts of the individual" analysis, with government as a fact of the individual, in allowing minimum wage laws to go forward: "The importance of the question, in which many states having similar laws are concerned, the close division by which the decision in the Adkins Case [the earlier Supreme Court case finding minimum wage laws unconstitutional][81] was reached, and the economic conditions which have supervened, and in the light of which the reasonableness of the exercise of the protective power of the state must be considered, make it not only appropriate, but we think imperative,

---

79   *West Coast Hotel* at 391. Both the origins and the subsequent history of the "minimum scrutiny" regime are — to put it generously — ramshackle. See Barry Cushman, "Some Varieties and Vicissitudes of Lochnerism," http://ssrn.com/abstract=754190.

80   *West Coast Hotel* at 389.

81   *Adkins v. Children's Hospital*, 261 US 525 (1923).

that in deciding the present case the subject should receive fresh consideration."[82] In short, wages were important. The ban on minimum wage laws was unenforceable. Unenforceability was an indicium of government. So the Supreme Court lifted the ban in order to vindicate government as a fact of the individual.[83]

Fair enough. However, the *West Coast Hotel* Court was incapable of a formal "facts of the individual" analysis of maintenance, even though the minimum wage law the Court upheld expressly stated as *fact* that wages lower than the new law allowed, "were not adequate for...maintenance," and research serving as the basis of the law, had shown as *fact*, the need for wages "sufficient for...decent maintenance...."[84] The issue the Court ducked was not government in relation to maintenance — that was not considered relevant — but rather, the fact of maintenance, which *was* considered relevant, and evaded. On the one hand, the Court did not discuss its use of maintenance in the context of *Euclid*. On the other, the Court did not address the fact that in the *Adkins* case, the basis of the minimum wage law it had found unconstitutional was that the law would "maintain decent standards of living."[85] The third Constitutional epoch was born in the chaotic *West Coast Hotel* decision.

However, the factual discussion in the response to *Kelo* includes maintenance (especially as it relates to eminent domain with respect to businesses affected by eminent domain). We are finally beginning to discuss maintenance using the "facts of the individual" analysis which *West Coast Hotel* refused to engage in seventy years ago — and in which, thereafter, the political system of the third Con-

---

82  *West Coast Hotel* at 390.

83  In doing so, it felt the need of a fact it considered important, one it considered an indicium of government: the community. "[R]egulation which is reasonable in relation to its subject and is adopted in the interests of the community is due process" — apparently community is also an indicium of Due Process under both the Fifth and Fourteenth Amendments. *Id.*, at 391. "Liberty implies the absence of arbitrary restraint, not immunity from reasonable regulations and prohibitions imposed in the interests of the community." Quoted in *id.*, at 392. Minimum wage laws "will enure to the benefit of the general class of employees in whose interest the law is passed, and so to that of the community at large." Quoted in *id.*, at 397. "[T]he denial of a living wage is not only detrimental to [workers'] health and well being, but [also] casts a direct burden for their support upon the community." *Id.*, at 399. "The community is not bound to provide what is in effect a subsidy for unconscionable employers. The community may direct its law-making power to correct the abuse which springs from their selfish disregard of the public interest." *Id.*, at 399-400. Apparently, the political system is not the community, although the political system and maintenance are reconciled through the community. The Court never answers the question, what is the community?
Earlier cases establish that "the community" is characterized by "safety, health, peace, good order, and morals," is, for Constitutional purposes, "civilized and Christian," and is subject to "danger," although there are also facts which are "useful" to it. *Crowley v. Christensen*, 137 US 86, 89, 91, 94 (1890). "The community" vindicates "self-defense, of paramount necessity...." which facts can be "legally enforced...;" it has "persons" who are "residing" in it and "enjoying the benefits of its local government...." *Jacobson v. Massachusetts*, 197 US 11, 27, 37, 38 (1911). The concept itself is ancient; see Steven J. Heyman, "Ideological Conflict and the First Amendment," http://ssrn.com/ abstract=436985.

84  Quoted in *West Coast Hotel* at 386.

85  Quoted in *Adkins* at 542.

stitutional epoch refused to engage. The consensus was that maintenance as a fact was not an issue for the third Constitutional epoch, that it was an issue to be put over for the next Constitutional epoch, the fourth.

The Court established the "minimum scrutiny" regime in the only way it could be established: by eliminating fact from the Constitution. The vast array of health and welfare regulation — with its attendant contradictions, inefficiencies and pervasive corruption — proceeds under a minimum scrutiny which has so undermined the country that minimum scrutiny is laxly enforced even by those who stand to lose under such a feeble enforcement. From the point of view of the interaction of law and politics, however, the most important thing to note about minimum scrutiny is the "demotion" of liberty which brought it about. Remarkably, that "demotion" of liberty is the **sole** justification the *West Coast Hotel* Court provides for the "minimum scrutiny" regime. This justification was never taken seriously because there is no logical content to take seriously — the justification is, simply, ridiculous. On the other hand, it took seventy years for public opinion to decide that liberty did have factual content — a good example of the slow-motion decision-making process in which public opinion engages when it considers facts of the individual.

It is time someone told the truth about *West Coast Hotel*: it's junk law.[86] It would not earn a first-year Constitutional law student a passing grade. It has been a dreadful law joke for seventy years, leading, as we shall see, more than one legal doctrine into a dangerous swamp.[87] Nor is its most important implication anti-democratic, although it certainly is that since the political process it envisions for the facts was the pre-Revolutionary situation: "[O]nce the electors had chosen their representatives, they ceded power, reserving none for themselves until the next election....The people, as a political entity, existed only on election days. If the unelected had any other political voice, it came in the form of extralegal mob violence and crowd disturbances....[T]he mass of ordinary citizens had no regular, legal, permanent involvement in the making of decisions, the actual stuff of government and politics. [Such actions also reinforced the traditional image of the people as the rowdy multitude, not to be entrusted with formal pow-

---

86   In 2005 John Roberts, unaware of the changes going on with respect to the scrutiny regime, was required to subscribe *in writing* to the regime, as a condition of his confirmation as Chief Justice: "In 1923, the Supreme Court in the *Adkins* case ruled that the liberty clause outlawed Congress from providing women a minimum wage. In 1937, the Court in *West Coast Hotel* v. *Parrish* overruled *Adkins*....Judge Roberts, do you agree with the decision in *Parrish* to overrule *Adkins*....? If so, what justified not following precedent in that 1937 case?" Although *Lawrence v. Texas*—throwing the scrutiny regime into doubt—was already two years old, Roberts dutifully, and ignorantly, complied: "I agree that *West Coast Hotel Co. v. Parrish* correctly overruled *Adkins*....The Court in *West Coast Hotel* found several additional reasons for reexamining the prior decision in *Adkins*, including '[t]he importance of the question, in which many states having similar laws are concerned, the close division by which the decision in the *Adkins* Case was reached, and the economic conditions which have supervened.'" The entire document is online at http://www.washingtonpost.com/wp-srv/nation/documents/roberts/biden_responses.pdf (citations omitted).

87   Also, the justification barely made it into the law: *West Coast Hotel* was a 5-4 decision.

er."[88] The main problem with *West Coast Hotel* was that it subtracted government from the facts of the individual, and in doing so implicitly overruled *Marbury*, for which government is one of the facts of the individual. The Court presumed to change the *Marbury* question, what is the difference between government and the individual? The Court's substitute question was, what is the distinction between government and the individual? *West Coast Hotel*'s answer to the latter question was, the political system. Rather than exculpate the Court, this bit of legerdemain promptly inculpated the Court, which inevitably set the stage for the crisis of its legitimacy. By its narrow majority, its subversion of democracy, its encouragement of corruption, its exceedingly poor reasoning, its contradictions, its abandonment of fact and history, and its cavalier dismissal of explicit Constitutional terms, *West Coast Hotel* laid well the groundwork for its own undoing. Like all previous Constitutional compromises which had sought to buy off disputes, it could not in the end prevent the surfacing of the points at issue, when public opinion would no longer defer to its failure to resolve them.

The *Lawrence* decision, with its re-elevation of scrutiny for liberty from an "interest" to an individually enforceable right, signaled — both from the point of view of public opinion, and from the point of view of the law — an end to the third Constitutional epoch. However it managed to stagger along, the "minimum scrutiny" regime was doomed. From the point of view of *Lawrence*, the response to *Kelo* was inevitable, as yet another assertion of opposition to the regime but this time the fatal one, because it contemplated physical resistance on the one hand and, on the other, the police and the military in politics. The engines of the third epoch could not function in such an environment. After *Kelo*, public opinion knew it had inaugurated the new Constitution and was now, step by step, enforcing it throughout American life. *Lawrence* opened up liberty — and other facts — to inquiry in terms of each other in the context of the "facts of the individual" analysis. And that, at least, is indisputably where we are now. There is no going back. Under *Lawrence*, health and welfare regulation becomes an indicium of liberty — exactly what the *West Coast Hotel* Court most feared, but which the Court's fear brought about. It means not only that "rational" means "liberty;" so do "relationship" and "legitimate." In a "facts of the individual" analysis, laws are sustained as the facts relate to each other. The *Lawrence* Court implicitly overruled *West Coast Hotel*. Indeed, since there is no reasoned discussion by the Court of liberty in its pre-*West Coast Hotel* state, and since *West Coast Hotel* is itself such a poorly reasoned opinion, it is entirely unclear that *West Coast Hotel* "demoted" liberty in the first place. Nor do we have any idea how the Court has, in fact, treated liberty during the past seventy years.

Nevertheless, before *West Coast Hotel* is formally overruled, we probably need to see several things happen:

1. the Court enumerates other criteria and indicia of liberty than those attached to it by the scrutiny regime; and

2. the *Lawrence* liberty right is adjudicated by the Court outside the privacy/sexuality context.

---

88  Wilentz at 7-8.

Above all, the Court needs to show how the meanings it gives such terms as "furthers" and "legitimate" in *Lawrence*, differ from the meanings of those terms in the scrutiny regime. This involves reconciling them through the *Euclid* concept of "maintenance," which in turn sheds light on the role of housing in *Lawrence*. Maintenance characterizes the role housing plays in *Lawrence* as an indicium of liberty: housing facilitates liberty. Therefore, as facilitation, housing is raised to direct scrutiny in *Lawrence*: *Lawrence* stands for the proposition that no individual shall be involuntarily deprived of housing unless it articulately facilitates a frequent government purpose.

This shows facts of the individual forcing themselves through the "minimum scrutiny" regime and displacing it. Once the Court makes the "maintenance" connection between "furthers" and "legitimate," we will see the Court beginning to play its role in the fourth Constitutional epoch. It will do so by making the New Bill of Rights the mediator between the Constitution and the Court's own tradition of identifying and vindicating facts it considers important — *Euclid* will survive. But not *West Coast Hotel*.

On to the warrant as a fact of the individual. *Lawrence* also allows us for the first time to understand why the Founders pick out "houses" to illustrate their intent with respect to the Fourth Amendment, which provides: "The right of the people to be secure in their persons, houses, papers, and effects, against unreasonable searches and seizures, shall not be violated, and no warrants shall issue, but upon probable cause, supported by oath or affirmation, and particularly describing the place to be searched, and the persons or things to be seized."[89] *Lawrence* allows us to see that the Founders use "houses" because housing is an indicium of liberty. *Lawrence* establishes by way of example, a test to be used in other contexts:

1. the warrant is an indicium of liberty;
2. liberty enjoys direct scrutiny because the warrant is an indicium of liberty;
3. the warrant enjoys direct scrutiny.

The *Lawrence* Court reveals the warrant to be, not a power of government, but rather, an individual right.[90] A warrant under direct scrutiny comprises fact, which is why there are no warrants under minimum scrutiny:

---

89  U.S. Const. amend. IV.

90  Under the facts of *Lawrence*, the warrant enjoys intermediate scrutiny. We now await a case in which, for Constitutional purposes, the facts are identical to those in *Lawrence*, with the exception that housing is substituted for liberty. This will elevate the warrant to strict scrutiny. Manifestly one of the meanings of direct scrutiny, is that we have our work cut out for us. For the thoroughly alarming manner in which a predatory "minimum scrutiny" regime took over the Fourth Amendment, see Morgan Cloud, "A Liberal House Divided: How the Warren Court Dismantled the Fourth Amendment," http://ssrn.com/abstract=885669: "The impact of Justice Brennan's opinions is perhaps the most unexpected. Although Justice Brennan has been one of the twentieth-century justices most revered by civil libertarians, his most important Fourth Amendment opinions during the 1960s were central to the revolution in constitutional theory that led to the...constriction of individual rights and the concomitant expansion of government power....According to Brennan, the procedural devices embodied in the warrant process supplied adequate protection of Fourth Amendment privacy. As the Court's subsequent decisions have demonstrated, he was wrong." At 35-36 (citations omitted).

## THE RIGHT TO WARRANT.

Every warrant articulately facilitates a frequent government purpose. A warrant

1. constructs liberty and housing;
2. facilitates liberty and housing; and
3. sustains liberty and housing.

We apply direct scrutiny to warrants with these consequences:

1. any policy which does *not* articulately facilitate a frequent government purpose, is a not a warrant; and
2. the scrutiny continuum is a warrant with respect to every fact.

Where do we locate these doctrines in the Fourth Amendment? It is the word "unreasonable." We need not wander into the didactic, preaching to the Constitution in terms of "privacy" and "balancing;" the Constitution provides us with the words we need. This is the beginning of the analysis of the warrant as a fact of the individual.[91] The warrant is an indicium of housing and liberty, and we are shown this by such words as "searches," "seizures," "probable cause," and so on. Finally, note that it is the involuntary deprivation of housing by which the policy in *Lawrence* fails direct scrutiny (there is no warrant in *Lawrence*). This conjunction moves both housing and liberty above direct scrutiny. We have moved on.

We are now ready to formulate, for the first time, the right to housing. *Lawrence* says that, in the contexts of housing and without a warrant, "[t]he petitioners are entitled to respect for their private lives. The State cannot demean their existence or control their destiny by making their private sexual conduct a crime. Their right to liberty under the Due Process Clause gives them the full right to engage in their conduct without intervention of the government. It is a promise of the Constitution that there is a realm of personal liberty which the government may not enter."[92] Under *Lawrence*

1. housing is an indicium of liberty;
2. liberty enjoys direct scrutiny because housing is an indicium of liberty;
3. housing enjoys direct scrutiny.

And so to:

## THE RIGHT TO HOUSING.

To sustain an involuntary deprivation of housing, government must articulately facilitate a frequent government purpose. An involuntary deprivation of housing must

1. construct housing and policy;
2. facilitate housing and policy; and
3. sustain housing and policy.

---

91    The literature has just begun coping with the idea of the warrant as a fact of the individual. See Erik Luna, "Sovereignty and Suspicion," 48 *Duke Law Journal* 787 (No. 4, 1999); Thomas Y. Davies, "Recovering the Original Fourth Amendment," http://ssrn.com/abstract=220868.

92    *Lawrence* at 578. Does Kennedy's formulation mean that liberty is visible, like race, hence subject to heightened scrutiny under substantive due process?

In establishing the right to housing in *Lawrence*, the Court is merely taking another step in articulating the "scheme" of the Court when it applies to the states certain rights of the Bill of Rights (Fifth Amendment Due Process) through the Fourteenth Amendment (Fourteenth Amendment Due Process) by way of a "scheme of ordered liberty."[93] But these new rights also tell us that the "scheme of ordered liberty" is itself a process, and every case which does not further articulate the "scheme of ordered liberty," degrades it. After two hundred years, health and welfare regulation in its entirety enters the "scheme of ordered liberty." The *Lawrence* Court is saying: it's time.[94]

Finally, it is important to note the various contexts in which facts serve as indicia of each other. This allows us to see more clearly than anything else, that the scrutiny continuum is an *ad hoc* "facts of the individual analysis," and one of the important things about that analysis: it is a process. Thus, housing is an indicium of liberty in the due process context, but liberty is an indicium of housing in the warrant context. In this way, legal terminology ceases to be an area in which the facts can hide. It becomes the method by which the facts are brought to light and are used.[95]

We can clearly see the Court using an *ad hoc* "facts of the individual" analysis in *Lawrence*, in which the state of Texas

1. seeks to eliminate the fact.

Here the government is attempting to prosecute consensual sodomy in a private home, conduct accidentally discovered during a warrantless search.

2. at best only succeeds or would, if allowed, only succeed, in eliminating incarnations of it.

---

93   *Palko v. Connecticut*, 302 US 319, 325 (1937). We now await a case in which, for Constitutional purposes, the facts are identical to those in *Kelo*, with the exception that protected speech is substituted for housing. This will elevate housing to strict scrutiny.

94   The incorporation of the new right to housing effected by *Lawrence*, has already begun with the discussion of liberty and housing in the context of zoning. See Sara L. Dunski, "May Way for the New Kid on the Block: The Possible Zoning Implications of *Lawrence v. Texas*," 2005 *University of Illinois Law Review* 847 (No. 3, 2005). The *ad hoc* "facts of the individual" analysis of zoning is already well developed, especially in the context of housing. See Michael Lewyn, "How Overregulation Creates Sprawl (Even in a City without Zoning)," http://ssrn.com/abstract=837244. Prior to the enactment of Federal environmental law, the Supreme Court developed a common law of nuisance through its control over disputes between the states. Is there a Federal common law of housing? See Robert V. Percival, "The Frictions of Federalism: The Rise and Fall of the Federal Common Law of Interstate Nuisance," http://ssrn.com/abstract=452922.

95   The facts of *Lawrence* show us that liberty now enjoys relative scrutiny. The move up in scrutiny to this level in particular is due to the difference between the facts in *Griswold* and the facts in *Lawrence*, just as the difference between the facts in *Craig* and *Virginia* accounts for the movement of gender legal equality from intermediate to comprehensive scrutiny. We now await a case in which, for Constitutional purposes, the facts are identical to those in *Lawrence*, with the exception that gender legal equality is substituted for liberty. This will elevate liberty to intermediate scrutiny.

Here the activity is one of those recurring decisions "regarding sexual conduct extend[ing] beyond the marital relationship."[96] Note that the Court begins its historical analysis with the year 1533.[97]

3. in the process violates other rights.

"Equality of treatment and the due process right to demand respect for conduct protected by the substantive guarantee of liberty are linked in important respects, and a decision on the latter point advances both interests."[98]

4. brings to bear a disproportionate effort.

"If protected conduct is made criminal and the law which does so remains unexamined for its substantive validity, its stigma might remain even if it were not enforceable as drawn for equal protection reasons. When homosexual conduct is made criminal by the law of the State, that declaration in and of itself is an invitation to subject homosexual persons to discrimination both in the public and in the private spheres."[99]

5. does not consider alternatives which could achieve the goal.

"[O]ur laws and traditions in the past half century are of most relevance here. These references show an emerging awareness that liberty gives substantial protection to adult persons in deciding how to conduct their private lives in matters pertaining to sex [and in]...those States where sodomy is still proscribed, whether for same-sex or heterosexual conduct, there is a pattern of nonenforcement with respect to consenting adults acting in private. The State of Texas admitted in 1994 that as of that date it had not prosecuted anyone under those circumstances."[100]

How important is "a pattern of nonenforcement" to the Court's analysis? Does nonenforcement mean unenforceability? Is nonenforcement an indicium of a fact of the individual, that is, is it evidence of an incarnation of a recurring fact?[101]

Note the grotesque situation in which this *ad hoc* "facts of the individual" analysis — instead of a direct "facts of the individual" analysis — places the Court. It

---

96  *Lawrence* at 565.

97  *Id.* at 568. The Court ranged through history as well as through other countries' laws, in its *ad hoc* "facts of the individual analysis." This is consistent with the method of the Founders, who, in writing the Constitution itself, freely borrowed not only from other law, but also, from other foreign writers on the law.

98  *Lawrence* at 575.

99  *Id.*, at 575.

100  *Id.*, at 571-573. Of course, when every case has had to be decided by the Supreme Court using an *ad hoc* "facts of the individual analysis" — that is, when the Court has had to undertake the analysis not knowing what it was doing — it was bound to create confusion, even in the minds of the justices, as to its intentions; even the Founders were unclear about the judiciary because they *themselves* were capable only of an *ad hoc* "facts of the individual" analysis. This anomalous situation has generated two hundred years of bad tradition on the "role" of judges: should they apply the law or interpret it?

101  On nonenforcement, and the problem of understanding *Lawrence* as a product of the "minimum scrutiny" regime, see Cass R. Sunstein, "What Did *Lawrence* Hold? Of Autonomy, Desuetude, Sexuality, and Marriage," http://ssrn.com/abstract=450160.

looks to life — another fact of the individual in the Constitution — to illuminate liberty, rather than treating them as equals for purposes of analysis; somehow, there can be liberty without life. "[C]hoices a person may make in a lifetime" are an indicium of liberty.[102] So are defining "one's own concept of...the mystery of *human* life,"[103] "sexual practices common to a homosexual life*style*,"[104] and "the *personal* and *private* life of the individual."[105] But life *qua* life never puts in a direct appearance, so the Court must harken back to its old "minimum scrutiny" regime bad habits, lie, and say that *Lawrence* is not about life, in the same breath telling us quite a bit about what the Court believes are factual indicia of life: time, humanity, style, the personal and the private. What keeps life below liberty? The bizarre emphasis on the power of government over all under the "minimum scrutiny" regime — that is what intervenes to turn logic on its head and force us into the topsy turvy world of the "minimum scrutiny" regime. The facts of *Lawrence* show that liberty now enjoys relative scrutiny. However, the upshot of the Court's analysis is that life enjoys a lower level of scrutiny than liberty, threshold scrutiny. At the same time, since life is not distinguished from property — which has enjoyed the same level of scrutiny as life — property moves up with life to threshold scrutiny. However long they remain in their weirdly dependent position, it is worth arraying life and property in their new legal clothes simply to see them, for the first time, as individually enforceable rights rather than, under the "minimum scrutiny" regime, as unenforceable "interests:"

### THE RIGHT TO LIFE

To sustain an involuntary deprivation of life, government must measurably effect a common government purpose.

### THE RIGHT TO PROPERTY

To sustain an involuntary deprivation of property, government must measurably effect a common government purpose.

It was hitherto inconceivable to distinguish health and welfare regulation from involuntary deprivations of liberty; the former implied the latter. Amusingly (and appropriately?) it took sex to pry apart these mutually enamored ideas. *Lawrence* is a coded message from the Court: the "facts of the individual" analysis has reasserted itself, replacing the "balancing" analysis — argue accordingly. Will our benighted lawyers get the message? In the post-*Kelo* welter of conflicting claims in the political system, *Lawrence* also affords us a glimpse into the Court as, itself, a participant in a struggle with the political system.

The source of Justice Kennedy's "facts of the individual" analysis is the case on which all American law depends, *Marbury v. Madison. Marbury* is a "facts of the individual" analysis, in which government is the fact of the individual. It voids an act giving the Supreme Court the power to order delivery of a confirmed, signed commission for justice of the peace, where the Constitution does not allow it.

---

102 *Lawrence* at 574.

103 *Id.*, at 574.

104 *Id.*, at 578.

105 *Id.*, at 578.

Neither could this act could be enforced: "If [the Court] upheld *Marbury* and ordered delivery of the commission [of a nominee put forward by outgoing Federalist President John Adams], the order would surely be ignored by [opposition Republican Secretary of State James] Madison, [and] the Court would be exposed as impotent...."[106] This was Alexander Hamilton's scenario in *The Federalist*, No. 78, come to life: "The judiciary...has no influence over either the sword or the purse; no direction either of the strength or of the wealth of the society; and can take no active resolution whatever. It may truly be said to have neither force nor will, but merely judgment; and must ultimately depend upon the aid of the executive arm even for the efficacy of its judgments." *Lawrence* voids a law which cannot be enforced. *Kelo* sustains a law which cannot be enforced. What, in *fact*, not in *law*, is enforcement?

For the *Marbury* Court, unenforceability was an indicium of a fact of the individual, reflecting an approach to "natural law" (the idea that there are laws unrelated to any body of "laws") as speculative, not normative. Marshall's *ad hoc* "facts of the individual" analysis proceeds as follows (this is the first time Marshall's analysis has been published):

1. seeks to eliminate the fact.

The act contradicted "principles...most conducive to [the people's] own happiness."[107]

2. at best only succeeds or would, if allowed, only succeed, in eliminating incarnations of it.

The "principles" would be "repeated."[108]

3. in the process violates other rights.

As to "a rule as operative as if it was a law," "[t]here are many other parts of the constitution which serve to illustrate" it.[109]

4. brings to bear a disproportionate effort.

---

106 Quoted in Bruce Ackerman, *The Failures of the Founding Fathers: Jefferson, Marshall and the Rise of Presidential Democracy* (Harvard University Press 2005) at 193. Louise Weinberg disagrees, finding no evidence to support the conclusion that a writ could not have been enforced and stating that, in any event, "[n]o likely recalcitrance of the administration would matter to Chief Justice Marshall." Why not? Because in *Marbury* he is "shaping to great, uniquely American uses, both Court and Constitution." She does not consider whether Marshall may have felt that, even if the Jefferson Administration obeyed a writ, future administrations would not. Why would future administrations not obey a writ? Because the act is unconstitutional. Louise Weinberg, "Our *Marbury*," 89 *Virginia Law Review* 1235, 1295 (2003).

107 *Marbury v. Madison*, 5 US (1 Cranch) 137, 176 (1803).

108 *Id.*, at 176. It is worth nothing that Justice Powell, although he concurred in the result in *Craig*, voiced his dissatisfaction with intermediate scrutiny: "I would not endorse that characterization and would not welcome a further subdividing of equal protection analysis, [although] candor compels the recognition that the relatively deferential 'rational basis' standard of review normally applied takes on a sharper focus when we address a gender-based classification." *Craig* at 211. Justice Marshall's statement here is the reconciliation of Justice Powell's conflicting positions: it is the finding of facts of the individual, and that alone, which is the Constitution. Would Powell support or oppose the six new levels of Constitutional scrutiny?

109 *Id.*, at 177, 179.

The act was an "extravagant" assertion that "the constitution should not be looked into."[110]

5. does not consider alternatives which could achieve the goal.

The act has "mistaken or forgotten" that "[t]he powers of the legislature are defined and limited."[111]

The "facts of the individual" analysis is canonical, long predating the "minimum scrutiny" regime which is a usurper analysis; the "facts of the individual" analysis is always operative.[112] Indeed, for the *Marbury* Court, it is simply the way the individual thinks — it is analysis, or more precisely, it is Constitutional process. *Marbury* is a case from 1803, *Lawrence* a case from 2003. The "facts of the individual" analysis is the only Constitutional analysis which, when applied, has

---

110  *Id.*, at 179.

111  *Id.*, at 176.

112  The methods by which it became the usurper analysis are explored in John C. Yoo and Saikrishna Prakash, "The Origins of Judicial Review," http://ssrn.com/abstract=426860. One author claims that an *ad hoc* "facts of the individual" analysis was used prior to the imposition of the "minimum scrutiny" regime, which regime had to scramble to rescue such vindication of facts of the individual as had existed under the pre-"minimum scrutiny" regime: "Substantive Due Process rights during the *Lochner* period went beyond economic liberties, however, and included freedom of speech, press and parental autonomy. [In *Lochner v. New York*, 198 US 45 (1905), the Court voided a New York maximum work hours law for bakers, as a violation of the Due Process clause of the Fourteenth Amendment; the Court called it an impermissible interference with the right to contract implicit in that Amendment. The dissent of Oliver Wendell Holmes laid out the tenets of the "minimum scrutiny" regime.] Under the common law methodology of *Lochner*...the fact that speech and press were listed in the text of the Bill of Rights was irrelevant to their enforcement as fundamental Due Process liberties....Lacking a textual amendment, the Court [which imposed the "minimum scrutiny" regime] embarked on a revolution of jurisprudence — the construction of a new and more legitimate approach to judicial review. The core principle of this jurisprudential revolution was the embrace of textual originalism. Regardless of its history as a common law right, liberty of contract was nowhere mentioned in the text of the Constitution and, therefore, could not be a legitimate ground for interfering in the political process....At the same time the Court abandoned common law liberty of contract, it also abandoned judicial construction of state common law....Moreover, if the error of Lochnerian liberty of contract was its lack of textual foundation, then Lochnerian parental autonomy shared the same error....[Parental autonomy]...would have to be recharacterized to represent judicial protection of textual rights like religious freedom and equal protection under the law....[Under the pre-"minimum scrutiny" regime]...there had been no reason to speak of incorporating the 'texts' of the First Amendment because liberties like speech and press were protected as fundamental liberties under the common law. The fact they were (or were not) mentioned in the Bill of Rights was irrelevant. The abandonment of common law methodology and the new emphasis on textual originalism required a new justification for the enforcement of individual rights, including those of speech and press. Ultimately, consensus formed around [the idea that]...some, but not all, of the texts of the Bill of Rights were incorporated into the Fourteenth Amendment. This 'selective incorporation' approach, however, echoed the selective approach of the *Lochner* Court....[T]he New Deal emphasis on textual originalism conflicts with the modern embrace of non-textual common law rights like privacy and parental autonomy, and with the increasing use of federalism principles as a substantive limit on the otherwise plenary powers of Congress. If one embraces the New Deal as a 'constitutional moment,' it appears one must reject both non-textual due process liberties and non-textual federalist restraints on federal power." Kurt Lash, summarizing his article, "The Constitutional Convention of 1937: The Original Meaning of the New Jurisprudential Deal," http://ssrn.com/abstract=264214.

produced consistent results over two hundred years. The "facts of the individual" analysis is process; in the "minimum scrutiny" regime, process is the evasion of facts.

In particular, Marshall's idea of the "principles" being "repeated" is a process. This is at odds with the consensus of the "minimum scrutiny" regime that government is an object of some sort; we shall see repeated use, by advocates of eminent domain, of the term "tool" to describe eminent domain as it works on government as a machine or object. As we shall also see, eminent domain works, among other ways, by breaking down the branches or doctrines of government; this was also attempted in *Marbury*. In short, the "minimum scrutiny" regime thwarts Marshall — precisely what had been attempted in *Marbury*. It appears even the Supreme Court is beginning to sense this. How then does the case vindicate Marbury, who lost?[113] By voiding "a rule as operative as if it was a law."

So much for *Marbury*. Justice Ginsburg — who will hear *Kelo* — has said that the law is won by slow wooing.[114] But slowness is not the reason it is won. The real reason human rights progress has stalled is that we have indeed reached something like a logical consensus on new facts, but this awareness has to confront very high institutional and political barriers. Given all this, let's see how the Court might decide *Kelo*.

---

113 And would lose today. Marshall takes pains to point out that under the Constitution Marbury has a right to his commission: "[I]f [Marbury] conceives that by virtue of his appointment he has a legal right either to the commission which has been made out for him or to a copy of that commission, it is equally a question examinable in a court, and the decision of the court upon it must depend on the opinion entertained of his appointment. That question has been discussed, and the opinion is, that the latest point of time which can be taken as that at which the appointment was complete, and evidenced, was when, after the signature of the president, the seal of the United States was affixed to the commission. It is then the opinion of the court, 1. That by signing the commission of Mr. Marbury, the president of the United States appointed him a justice of peace for the county of Washington in the district of Columbia; and that the seal of the United States, affixed thereto by the secretary of state, is conclusive testimony of the verity of the signature, and of the completion of the appointment; and that the appointment conferred on him a legal right to the office for the space of five years. 2. That, having this legal title to the office, he has a consequent right to the commission; a refusal to deliver which is a plain violation of that right, for which the laws of his country afford him a remedy," *Marbury* at 167-168. However, "the laws" are not any particular law. There is no specific remedy in the law. Marshall doesn't point to any, isn't obliged to point to any, says it's Marbury who "conceives" of such a law and says the question is, not examined in the case, but rather, "examinable" whenever Marbury may happen to find such a law. The law Marbury would need doesn't exist. Why not? Again, because a writ to deliver the commission is unenforceable. Modernly, Marshall's hypothetical *Marbury* lawsuit is nonjusticiable. See *Baker v. Carr*, 369 US 186 (1962); Guy-Uriel E. Charles, "Constitutional Pluralism and Democratic Politics: Reflections on the Interpretive Approach of *Baker v. Carr*," http://ssrn.com/abstract=312402. It turns out that *Baker*'s analysis of justiciability is an *ad hoc* "facts of the individual" analysis: if it's a fact of the individual (in *Marbury*, the fact of the individual is government, and that is why the Court agreed to take the case) it's justiciable, not otherwise. On the writ as a fact of the individual, see Steven Semeraro, "A Critical Perspective on Habeas Corpus History," http://ssrn.com/abstract=599141.

114 Quoting Benjamin Cardozo. *Nomination of Ruth Bader Ginsburg, to be Associate Justice of the Supreme Court of the United States*, Hearings before the Committee on the Judiciary, United States Senate, 103rd Congress, U.S. Government Printing Office, 1994, 53.

## DECIDING *KELO V. NEW LONDON* UNDER THE NEW BILL OF RIGHTS

Three scenarios suggest themselves for adjudication of the *Kelo* case. The first involves the Court not recognizing housing in deciding the case. The second involves recognizing housing and developing a test which falls short of the housing provision of the New Bill of Rights. The third involves adoption of the housing provision and applying it to the case.

*First Scenario: The Court Doesn't Recognize Housing*

> It is important to note that *Kelo* is not posed as a question of housing. It is brought under the Fifth Amendment, which reads: "No...private property [shall] be taken for public use, without just compensation." The question for the Court is whether the proposed taking is for a public use. As the Supreme Court put it, in the *Kelo* case, the city of New London, Connecticut, claimed it sought to target New London, and particularly its Fort Trumbull area, for economic revitalization. To this end,...New London Development Corporation (NLDC), a private nonprofit entity established some years earlier to assist the City in planning economic development, was reactivated. In January 1998, the State authorized a $5.35 million bond issue to support the NLDC's planning activities and a $10 million bond issue toward the creation of a Fort Trumbull State Park. In February, the pharmaceutical company Pfizer Inc. announced that it would build a $300 million research facility on a site immediately adjacent to Fort Trumbull; local planners hoped that Pfizer would draw new business to the area, thereby serving as a catalyst to the area's rejuvenation....Parcel 1 is designated for a waterfront conference hotel at the center of a "small urban village" that will include restaurants and shopping. This parcel will also have marinas for both recreational and commercial uses. A pedestrian "riverwalk" will originate here and continue down the coast, connecting the waterfront areas of the development. Parcel 2 will be the site of approximately 80 new residences organized into an urban neighborhood and linked by public walkway to the remainder of the development, including the state park. This parcel also includes space reserved for a new US Coast Guard Museum. Parcel 3, which is located immediately north of the Pfizer facility, will contain at least 90,000 square feet of research and development office space. Parcel 4A [the site of Susette Kelo's home] is a 2.4-acre site that will be used either to support the adjacent state park, by providing parking or retail services for visitors, or to support the nearby marina. Parcel 4B will include a renovated marina, as well as the final stretch of the riverwalk. Parcels 5, 6, and 7 will provide land for office and retail space, parking, and water-dependent commercial uses. The NLDC intended the development plan to capitalize on the arrival of the Pfizer facility and the new commerce it was expected to attract.[115]

It was the false statements in this statement — and the realization that the Court knew it was making false statements — which enraged public opinion and ended public opinion's tolerance of the third Constitutional epoch. The homeowners claimed that proposed transfers of their property to private owners in connection with New London's plan had no government purpose and so violated minimum scrutiny and was not a public use. The city claims that the mechanism is not consequential; what matters is that the city proposes to take the housing

---

115  *Kelo* at 2-4.

for development in order to raise tax revenue, and raising taxes is a public use protected by the Fifth Amendment.

Currently, housing is not recognized by the Constitution. What do we mean by "recognize?" Perhaps the best way to understand it is, again, to pose the question in a negative way. Under the current law of searches and seizures, the "houses" of the Fourth Amendment are recognized only as a dependent of the concept of privacy.[116] Privacy is recognized by the Constitution; housing is not, and even privacy is subject to balancing. Is it anomalous to recognize a fact of the individual but not to vindicate the individual with respect to that fact in every case? It leads one to wonder whether a fact is not subject to balancing because it is a fact of the individual, or is a fact of the individual because it is not subject to balancing. The anomaly arises because of political considerations. The courts are worried, above all, about what is politically possible.

This first scenario contemplates the Court NEVER using the word "housing" in its opinion. It should be clear by now that that is, politically, the easiest option for the Court, and that's why even the *Kelo* counsel embraced it even though it meant losing the case for their clients. The case is decided as if anything might have been seized by the city under its eminent domain power: what was seized can be left a blank space in the opinion. What matters, under this scenario, is whether the city had a public use in seizing whatever it seized. In this, the Court is following the text of the Fourth Amendment itself. Housing there does NOT appear as it does in Roosevelt's bill of rights: there is no bald fact of housing in the Constitution. It only appears dependent on, and as an application of, the search and seizure test established. The Court itself has followed the Fourth Amendment approach through two hundred years of adjudication of proposed new facts of the individual: such facts are either so close to explicitly stated facts as to be "penumbral" to the rights vindicated with respect to those facts, or so subject to explicitly stated discretion as to be unrecognizable under the Constitution. This is in conformity with the Court's Fourth Amendment treatment of housing: there, it has no existence apart from the balancing to which it is subject. The Court will often talk about its unsuitability for deciding where certain facts fall under the Constitution, but it only finds itself unsuitable for doing so with respect to "social" or "affirmative" facts, and we now see the reason: housing, which is one of those facts, is buried deep within Fourth Amendment jurisprudence — so that is where the Court has buried similar facts! But this does not explain why the Court has never laid down a test for treating in different ways, facts which it feels do fall under the Constitution, that is, we are never told directly why one fact gets intermediate scrutiny, in relation to another which gets strict scrutiny, in relation to another which gets minimum scrutiny. This area of Constitutional law remains completely undeveloped; it is in a primitive state. The courts have simply never thought about it.[117] Why? Because no one has ever insisted they pass the facts through Madison's statement, and that is because no one previously knew what

---

116 See, for example, *Alderman v. United States*, 394 US 165 (1969).

117 For an examination of the manner in which the Court squirms in its own "minimum scrutiny" regime, see Pamela S. Karlan's amusing essay, "Exit Strategies in Constitutional

Madison meant when he used the word "every." Let's begin by considering that "unreasonable" does not refer to process, conclusion, policy or judgment of any kind: it refers to a fact. This new point of view does not depend on circumstance, and so it eliminates balancing. What, in *fact*, not in *law*, is unreasonable? This is a new question in our history. It regards the Fourth Amendment as neither proscriptive nor prescriptive, but rather, descriptive.[118]

It is most likely that the Court will not consider (indeed, counsel themselves will not consider) that the word "houses" in the Fourth Amendment has anything to do with the *Kelo* facts (although they involve houses). Indeed, the Fourth Amendment will not be mentioned at all, and housing as a separate issue will have no bearing whatsoever on the case — a grotesque result which will be the subject of much scorn. If this is the case, the *Kelo* homeowners will lose, as they lost in Connecticut, because the Court will state that there is no difference when the city seizes housing and then turns it over to a developer, or when it seizes housing to, for example, build a publicly owned park. In short, the taking was for a public use. In fact, the Court is very likely to come up with a very broad holding — that there is unbridled discretion to use eminent domain — in order clear up the conflict between the courts. *Hathcock* turns on the word "necessity," a word which has developed in Michigan jurisprudence as a limitation on eminent domain. There, Michigan law said that government could not use eminent domain to take private property and turn it over to private owners except in certain circumstances. The Michigan Supreme Court did not find these circumstances in the *Hathcock* facts. The circumstances are: (1) where "public necessity of the extreme sort" requires collective action; (2) where the property remains subject to public oversight after transfer to a private entity; and (3) where the property is selected because of "facts of independent public significance," rather than the interests of the private entity to which the property is eventually transferred. Note that no specific facts — like protected speech or freedom from an establishment of religion — are mentioned.

This is where the US Supreme Court will intervene, to state that Michigan law, and the *Kelo* petitioners, are basing their argument on a false premise. They are looking at the words "public use" in the Fifth Amendment, and concluding that if there is "public use" in the Fifth Amendment, there must be "private use." This is plausible, but it by no means necessarily follows. Historically, if the Founders had anything like a "private use" concept, it was merely a very traditional idea that eminent domain could not be used if it conflicted with other laws,

---

Law: Lessons for Getting the Least Dangerous Branch out of the Political Thicket," http://ssrn.com/abstract=295163.

118  Scholars are just barely beginning to examine the notion that the Founders did go through — and necessarily must have gone through — an *ad hoc* "facts of the individual" analysis, and that is why housing is mentioned at all in the Fourth Amendment. And, indeed, that is why there is a Fourth Amendment at all. Then what is the *ad hoc* "facts of the individual" analysis in the Fourth Amendment itself? See David E. Steinberg, "Restoring the Fourth Amendment: The Original Understanding Revisited," http://ssrn.com/abstract=822267. Is your analysis changed by contemplating the contemporaneous existence of slavery in the Constitution?

or if it was used by a public official simply to transfer property to that official's private account, *i.e.*, there was some fraud or other criminal activity involved in its use — we don't reach "private use," we simply find that a case for public use has not been made out. Practically, the Court will not allow eminent domain to be restricted. After all, it is one of the powers reserved to the states by the Constitution because it was part of the law of the states when they entered the Union, and it has been used throughout recorded history.[119] To the extent that Michigan's restriction on the use of eminent domain goes beyond the conflict or fraud bars mentioned above, Michigan's law will be stricken down as an unconstitutional restraint on the powers of the state. The *Kelo* petitioners may think that *Hathcock* means they will face an amenable Court because the Court has decided to hear *Kelo*. In reality, they will face a Mack truck which will smack down the growing anti-eminent domain movement and destroy all their hopes. I doubt it will even allow the states to cut back on eminent domain, although it normally allow states to provide more protection than is required by the US Constitution; it won't see this as a matter of granting more freedoms or protecting individuals more — it will see these restrictions on eminent domain as undermining the role of the states in the Federal system. Nasty! How do we avoid this wreck?

The Court is not amused by petitioners hiding their real motives behind "private use" and "eminent domain." It doesn't like petitioners trying to sneak a Constitutional right in through the back door — it is very suspicious of those who are not willing to use the front door. It knows that what the homeowners want is to protect housing. So don't be surprised if one of the Justices leans over the bench and says: "Don't hide behind the chimera of 'private use.' Don't use the subterfuge of eminent domain. If you feel your housing shouldn't be taken because it is housing, then be up front with us. Tell us why." Of course, the reason the *Kelo* petitioners don't want to talk about housing directly is because petitioners have been burned in the past when they tried to talk about housing as an "affirmative right." Not only in *San Antonio School District v. Rodriguez*, but also in *Lindsey* and *Dandridge v. Williams*.[120]

---

119 "The recognition of eminent domain as an inherent right of the sovereign predates the Constitution, and was described at least as early as the seventeenth-century jurist Hugo Grotius. See *Welch v. Tennessee Valley Auth.*, 108 F.2d 95, 98 (6th Cir. 1939) (noting that '[t]he phrase "eminent domain" appears to have originated with Grotius who carefully described its nature, and the power is universal and as old as political society. The American Constitution did not change its scope or nature, but simply embodied it in the fundamental law') (citations omitted). Zoning laws, on the other hand, are a relatively modern invention, and were generally unknown prior to the turn of the twentieth century." *Faith Temple Church v. Town of Brighton*, No. 0-4-CV6355L (U.S. Dist. Court, Western District of New York) December 19, 2005, at 7, n. 3. This decision is online at www.wdny.uscourts. gov.

120 397 US 471 (1970). See also *DeShaney v. Winnebago County*, 489 US 189 (1989). This case involves an involuntary deprivation of liberty and its concealment by the Court; Dena S. David, "Moral Ambition: The Sermons of Harry A. Blackmun," http://ssrn.com/abstract=839405. As Justice Blackmun pointed out in his dissent, the Court employed the same bad faith analysis the Court had used in *Dred Scott* — particularly egregious lying, if there is such a "lying continuum" under the "minimum scrutiny" regime. Probably not, because it implies the Court indulges in "lesser" lies. In any event, for Constitutional pur-

However, the real reason the Court refused to elevate scrutiny of the facts in those cases is because the facts had not been given proper Constitutional expression. If the parties make a mess of things, the Court will make a mess of things when using the parties' assertions to come to a conclusion. Look at how Justice Powell messed up *San Antonio School District*, when he fumbled around, trying to explain why education is not "fundamental" in keeping with the scrutiny regime's approach to Equal Protection in the Fourteenth Amendment (minimum scrutiny for all facts with respect to a state's discrimination unless a "fundamental" right is at issue): "[T]he key to discovering whether education is 'fundamental' is not to be found in comparisons of the relative societal significance of education as opposed to subsistence or housing. Nor is it to be found by weighing whether education is as important as the right to travel. Rather, the answer lies in assessing whether there is a right to education explicitly or implicitly guaranteed by the Constitution. [Appellees] insist that education is itself a fundamental personal right because it is essential to the effective exercise of First Amendment freedoms and to intelligent utilization of the right to vote, [but effective exercise of First Amendment freedoms is not a value] to be implemented by judicial intrusion into otherwise legitimate state activities."[121] Never mind that minimum, intermediate and strict scrutiny are comparisons arrived at by weighing what the Court has previously and informally decided are important facts, or that strict scrutiny operates to vindicate facts in the face of what the Court considers to be legitimate state activities. Note also that requiring that a fact and its protection be "explicitly or implicitly guaranteed by the Constitution" is a method of drawing attention away from the Court's own anomalous scrutiny continuum for facts.[122] It is also the way the Supreme Court has, for two hundred years, imposed ignorance about what, in fact, is education, so that, today, the Court is

poses the difference between *DeShaney* and Kelo is the difference between the truth and false facts in *Kelo*. Maintenance is thereby elevated to threshold scrutiny. We now await a case in which, for Constitutional purposes, the facts are identical to those in *DeShaney*, with the exception that housing is substituted for maintenance. This will elevate maintenance to comprehensive scrutiny, that is, an involuntary deprivation of maintenance will have to essentially determine a momentous government purpose.

121  *San Antonio* at 11-12. Obviously, what is important to the Court is maintenance, because that concept is found even in the Court's minimum scrutiny jurisprudence: maintenance is found in the Constitution, according to the Court. That is, the Court has no difficulty granting the importance of a wide variety of facts. The question it needs answered is: how are those facts *maintained*, such that the disposition of maintenance at issue in *fact* fails at the task of maintenance? Maintenance is what is at issue for the Court, and above all the ability of counsel to articulate factual criteria for maintenance with respect to the facts (we shall see Justice Kennedy's attempt to provide this in the context of eminent domain in his *Kelo* concurrence). Maintenance is the concept the *San Antonio* counsel needed, and it was and is right there, in *Euclid*. Why didn't counsel find it? Because the "minimum scrutiny" regime deforms the ability of the individual to articulate individually enforceable rights — and counsel (although their cravenness suggests otherwise) are individuals, too.

122  And of the highly anomalous discretion it grants under "minimum scrutiny." We have just begun to analyse minimum scrutiny discretion using the "facts of the individual" analysis. See Lisa Schultz Bressman, "Judicial Review of Agency Inaction: An Arbitrariness Approach," http://ssrn.com/abstract=569821; Sidney A. Shapiro and Richard E. Levy,

completely ignorant about it. If it was ever "useful," this ignorance does seem to have outlived its "usefulness,"[123] even as far as the Court is concerned. After

---

*Marbury's* Unfulfilled Promise: Government Benefits and the Rule of Law," http://ssrn.com/abstract=324500.

123 All along, the Court has been engaging in an alternative jurisprudence based on "importance," which incorporates a standard of review. *San Antonio* is, above all, the story of the failure of the litigants to argue that taxation is identical, for purposes of importance, to education, and that is why a factual inquiry needed to be undertaken: to show whether taxation is in fact playing its "maintenance" role in education. It is important to note that the Court never analyzes education under the scrutiny regime. It gives two reasons: first, "based on decisions of this Court affirming the undeniable importance of education." *San Antonio* at 18. Second, the Texas Constitution itself found education to be important: "A general diffusion of knowledge being essential to the preservation of the rights and liberties of the people, it shall be the duty of the Legislature of this State to make suitable provision for the support and maintenance of public schools....The Legislature shall as early as practicable establish free schools throughout the State, and shall furnish means for their support, by taxation on property...." Quoted in *id.*, at 7 (footnote 8). Scrutiny analysis is the *disfavored* analysis when it comes to education, and the litigants should never have bothered with it. The Court made it clear, in addition, that property taxes were never regarded as the only means of school funding. It opened the door to the litigants to argue the importance of other facts: taxation; government spending; government; and freedom. The litigants never bothered to go through that door. They stopped at the threshold: the scrutiny regime, which was irrelevant.
The Court made it clear that school funding had gone forward "relying on *mutual* participation by the local school districts and the State. As early as 1883, the state constitution was amended to provide for the creation of local school districts *empowered* to levy ad valorem taxes with the consent of local taxpayers for the 'erection...of school buildings' and for the 'further *maintenance* of public free schools....'Such local funds as were raised were *supplemented* by funds distributed to each district from the State's Permanent and Available School Funds. The Permanent School Fund, its predecessor established in 1854 with $2,000,000 realized from an annexation settlement, was thereafter *endowed* with millions of acres of public land *set aside* to assure a *continued* source of income for school *support.*" *Id.*, at 7-8 (citations omitted, emphases added). The Court also pointed out relevant facts to be used to argue for the importance of the four facts named above, as well as their relevance to deciding if the tax structure met its maintenance role: "Sizable differences in the value of assessable property between local school districts became increasingly evident as the State became more industrialized and as rural-to-urban population shifts became more pronounced. The location of commercial and industrial property began to play a significant role in determining the amount of tax resources available to each school district. These growing disparities in population and taxable property between districts were responsible in part for increasingly notable differences in levels of local expenditure for education." *Id.*, at 8 (citations omitted). The litigants argued as if these were hurdles to be overcome in their argument: for the Court, they are resources to be used to vindicate important facts.
    For the Court, the suspect class and fundamental rights arguments were simply irrelevant. If taxation had been argued as an important fact, rather than poverty as a suspect class, then it would have been relevant to inquire whether taxation was in fact playing a role in maintenance, that is, whether the litigants, "because of their impecunity...were completely unable to pay for some desired benefit, and as a consequence, they sustained an absolute deprivation of a meaningful opportunity to enjoy that benefit." *Id.*, at 20. Note that this sheds light on education as a fact: it is, in fact, desired; it is, in fact, a benefit; consequence is a fact; ability is a fact; meaningfulness and opportunity are indicia of education; enjoyment is an indicium of education. All these could have been litigated if the litigants had argued that taxation was an important fact. They did not.
    The Court also makes it clear exactly where the above facts should be litigated in connection with education in its relation to taxation. It does so in its comments on the

*Lawrence*, the right to education in Texas must be seen as a Federal Equal Protection right, overruling *San Antonio School District*. "Fundamental" analysis under the scrutiny regime, is used by the Court in the latter case. Under *Lawrence*, however, the scrutiny regime is not used to adjudicate any part of the Constitution, so we do not ask, with respect to education under Equal Protection, whether there is a "fundamental" right to education. Instead, we ask, what is the education right under Equal Protection? We know that Texas has found that education is essential to liberty. Since liberty is an Equal Protection right, the question becomes, under Federal Equal Protection, whether the Texas school finance system is essential to education? It is the Equal Protection liberty right which now allows the finance question to be adjudicated on the Federal level, requiring that the finance plan be essential to education. Justice Powell, of course, is spinning in his jurisprudential grave. But in advancing the "minimum scrutiny" regime, he dug that grave.

Nevertheless, looking back, can the Court be blamed that the appellees did not use the "fundamental" statement of Constitutional law available to them, which is Madison's statement? Obviously, if your concept is what is "fundamental," you should start your analysis with Madison's words. They did not. It is obvious that appellees knew nothing more about the facts of the individual than did the Court. If they had, they wouldn't have fumbled around with the notion of a "fundamental" fact: a fact is a fact of the individual, or it is not. Nor were the appellees correct in arguing that a fact of the individual has to do with its degree, extent or quality. Because they could not assert that education is a fact of the individual, because they didn't start their analysis at the beginning, they were in no position to shift the burden to the other side to justify the disparity in spending on education, which is at the heart of *San Antonio*. The terms were those of the appellees, not the terms of the Court. The Court sees with the eyes the parties give it. The Court is not afraid of a fact, if it can see the fact in the Constitution, but

---

argument that education is a fundamental right. The role of the above facts is in showing that education is an indicium of taxation. Remember that, for the Court, one of the indicia of maintenance is that it both acts and is acted upon. If taxation had been argued as an important fact, rather than education as a fundamental right, then it would have been relevant to inquire whether education was in fact playing a role in taxation, that is, whether education was "among the rights and liberties protected by the Constitution" because taxation was. *Id.*, at 29. It did not occur to the litigants to argue that taxation is "among the rights and liberties protected by the Constitution." And how to show it is? By pointing to the presence of both maintenance and education in the Texas Constitution. And what do the facts of maintenance and education show us about taxation? That taxation is, in fact, desired; taxation is, in fact, a benefit; consequence is an indicium of taxation, as is taxation of the fact of consequence; ability is an indicium of taxation and taxation is an indicium of ability; taxation is an indicium of meaningfulness and opportunity; enjoyment is an indicium of taxation.

This is an invitation, not taken up by litigants, to argue that taxation is important by arguing that education is an indicium of taxation. When the Court states that "social importance is not the critical determinant for subjecting state legislation to strict scrutiny," it is saying that the scrutiny regime must be relevant in the first instance. *Id.*, at 32. If, as in the case of education, it is not, then it is not relevant to invoke it in order to say that education is important. We know education is important. The question is: is taxation factually relevant to education, that is, does education maintain taxation? The scrutiny analysis does not in any way assist us in answering that question: that is what the Court is saying.

the Constitution is words, so if the Court is to see it, it must see the words. "Affirmative rights" and "fundamental facts" were then, this is now, and the proper words exist.

It's worth noting that developments show a progression toward a crisis on eminent domain: earlier instances involved marginal plaintiffs, in poor housing. Moving up the socioeconomic ladder, the *Kelo* plaintiffs are owners of freestanding housing which sits in an area so desirable that the government wants to kick them out — not a marginalized group of plaintiffs. This suggests that one day we will get a group of plaintiffs living in mansions in an area the government very much wants. Can they also be swept aside? These homeowners' political network may be activated to prevent it. And what if they simply refuse to go? The police and the military in politics? Since the Court, although it sometimes accommodates weakness, always obeys power,[124] we may then actually get a right to housing. It will have been brought to us by the elite, just as leadership of the American Revolution was brought to us by an elite.

In any event, *San Antonio* seems to have been implicitly overruled by the finding of the liberty right in *Lawrence*. Recall the provision of the Texas Constitution concerning liberty and education: "A general diffusion of knowledge being essential to the preservation of the liberties and rights of the people, it shall be the duty of the Legislature of the State to establish and make suitable provision for the support and maintenance of an efficient system of public free schools." *San Antonio* held that the provision was not justiciable at the Federal level. However, although in *Lawrence* a state law was found unconstitutional under Due Process and in *San Antonio* a state law was found constitutional under Equal Protection, the issue in both is justiciability of state law at the Federal level. In *Lawrence* the same liberty operates at both state and Federal levels — that was the basis on which the Texas sodomy law was found unconstitutional. Education is a textual indicium of liberty in the Texas Constitution (indeed, the Texas Constitution finds multiple incarnations of liberty, not just one as in the Federal Constitution). Thus, *Lawrence* makes the Texas educational right, justiciable at the Federal level.

*Second Scenario: The Court Recognizes Housing*

Even if the Court doesn't express impatience with fiddling around with "private use" and eminent domain, a Justice (but which one?) may still have the bad taste to lean over the bench and ask: "What's so special about housing?" — that is, in the midst of a basically arcane discussion of the history of eminent domain since the Roman Empire, the big gorilla in the room — housing — may be noticed. This is another reason to make an issue of housing: the Court may be waiting for

---

124  As one writer puts it: "We know that the Supreme Court necessarily reflects — at least in part — the felt necessities of its time. The difference between *Bowers v. Hardwick* [487 US 186 (1986), upholding sodomy laws] and *Lawrence v. Texas*, is one of a changing national consensus in which the Court can hardly fail to join. No Supreme Court doctrine is likely to succeed for long if it strays too far from what a majority of Americans desires." Suzanna Sherry, "The Intellectual Background of *Marbury v. Madison*," in Mark Tushnet, ed., *Arguing* Marbury v. Madison (Stanford University Press 2005), 50. See also Jack M. Balkin, "What Brown Teaches Us about Constitutional Theory," http://ssrn.com/abstract=555685.

petitioner counsel to do so. Indeed, the homeowners have been jurisprudentially rude enough to state publicly that one of the reasons they feel they should be allowed to remain in their housing, is the extraordinary proposition that it is their housing. If the Court is prepared to say that, to a degree, the Constitution recognizes housing, then there will have to be some application of the standards enunciated above. Whatever else "recognition" of a fact may mean, it will mean that the Court finds the individual in that fact. However, the Court doubtless will NOT conclude from that that no individual shall be involuntarily deprived of housing. It will find that that does not inexorably follow. Probably, the Court will instead find that a right to housing is penumbral to other rights of the Constitution: not merely those in the Fifth Amendment (not under the "public use" section, but where it belongs: under the due process section — "nor be deprived of life, liberty, or property, without due process of law"); also, in the Fourteenth Amendment...and perhaps even under the poor Fourth Amendment. Perhaps, if it is playing for time against the momentous political consequences of taking Constitutional cognizance of housing, it may say something like: a penumbral right is subject to other tests for vindication than explicitly articulated facts of the Constitution. Indeed, it may restrict its holding to actions involving eminent domain over housing; this would be politically prudent, and buy it (and the rest of the political system) time.

There will then follow the conclusion that a proposed eminent domain action is first subject to a test to see whether it involves HOUSING. If it does involve housing, the Court will not even reach the "public-private use" issue and there's an end to that foolishness. If the Court does recognize the individual in housing, it will then go on to inquire into the degree to which already-recognized facts of the individual (such as freedom from an establishment of religion) are vindicated by the Constitution. It will find that it is to a very high degree. Indeed, even the poor "houses" of the Fourth Amendment are balanced. You can see that, under this scenario, we have traveled far from the first scenario under which housing is not even mentioned in a discussion of eminent domain, which itself is not subject to any balancing whatever. This is one reason why, under the second scenario, there will probably be a remand. Once housing is recognized as a fact of the individual, it becomes very clear that — despite its longevity — the concept of eminent domain is quite undeveloped in our law, as it relates to housing. The Court has to have this cleared up by the parties. This also buys the Court time.

The Court will then develop standards to determine if an action for eminent domain for housing is allowable. Note that the Court, in *San Antonio*, was perfectly prepared to impose a higher level of scrutiny of actions involving housing, if it could see such a mandate in the Constitution. Under a "facts of the individual" analysis, it finally sees its way clear to doing so. Considering that housing is involved, and is a fact of the individual, and that facts of the individual are given a high priority by other Constitutional provisions which mention them, the Court will insist that an overriding government purpose be served by taking housing. It will also insist that the city show why it is specifically housing which must be taken in order to fulfill the government's purpose. That is, the city must show that it has no practical alternative to taking housing in order to carry out its purpose. This finally — after two hundred years! — brings the enormous housing plant of the United States under the jurisdiction of the Constitution. When you think of in that way, it's hard not to ask: what took so long? And the answer is: stupidity.

Under this second scenario, unlike the first scenario, the petitioners remain in their housing unless the government can meet stiff tests and articulate previously unarticulated legal concepts. This is because of what the city wants. Its purpose is to raise tax revenue. Is this an important government purpose? Yes. However, is taking housing the only practical way to achieve this? Of course not. If the city's purpose is to raise revenue, then raise it: raise taxes. What is so uniquely desirable about eminent domain as a means to this end? Who knows? Previously, it was not a question allowable under the Constitution — it is legally irrelevant if the standard is minimum scrutiny and the Court would not admit a proffer of evidence on the point. Under this scenario, it becomes a central question. Now the city must justify itself about public use, about eminent domain, about tax policy — frankly, about a lot of embarrassing things. This buys the system time. By the way, it is also a perfect example of the way in which a failure to recognize a fact of the individual, has deformed law — through presumptuous neglect — and how the simple recognition of a fact of the individual, mandates an exploration of old legal concepts.[125] The option is foreclosed, however, if housing is not recognized as a fact of the individual.

*Third Scenario: The Court Finds a Right to Housing*

Under this scenario, the plaintiffs win, but not because the city cannot meet its burden under a test which recognizes housing as a fact of the individual. Here, the Court does not see the individual through housing. It simply sees the individual, and housing is a fact of the individual. The distinction is important, because it means that there is no test a governmental entity can pass, because the individual is vindicated in EVERY case and housing is a case of the individual. This is the scenario from which the Court will shy away, for two reasons: it invites other facts to immediately receive the same treatment as housing, and it invites peremptory rejection of procedures, such as eminent domain, which have always operated on housing. Even strict scrutiny is highly disruptive of police states, and severely disfavored by them — reactionary revolts have been provoked by developments far less important than a right to housing. Thus, although the second scenario is not without its logical problems, if the Court deals with housing at all in *Kelo*, the second approach is the approach it probably will take. Again, it will permit government to adjust to a new reality, its massive though unexamined programs and laws involving housing. Consider that if government must pass a

---

125  The making and coordination of categories and distinctions — well suited to the "balancing" inquiry but ill-suited to a "facts of the individual" analysis — is earliest recorded in Egypt, but seems to be an adoption of a memorialized legal ideology of long standing and a high degree of development. See Russ VerSteeg, *Law in Ancient Egypt* (Carolina Academic Press 2002); Francesco Parisi, "The Genesis of Liability in Ancient Law," http://ssrn.com/abstract=874179.

stern test in order to remove individuals from housing through eminent domain in order to raise tax revenue, then how important is it to remove individuals from housing because they don't pay their rent or mortgage? There's a strong interest there, but is execution of a writ of possession the only practical way to vindicate that interest? But does this imply the immediate availability of injunctive relief against the execution of all writs of possession for housing throughout the United States? Perhaps not, but then again, what about the numerous tax provisions and other government programs, the purpose of which is to put people in housing and keep people in housing? Currently, government seems to be of two minds, whether it wants people in housing or not, and whether it "allows" them to be housed or not. Is this a rational situation? No. It is a mess. And yet, it must be faced.[126]

There is no question that, should the Court decide to recognize housing, government will have to rethink every general welfare purpose relating to housing. This is nothing new: government had to rethink every general welfare purpose when it could no longer attempt to violate protected speech, or establish religion, or impose involuntary servitude. There is no need to waste sympathy on government. But such adjustments do take time, and I suspect that even if the Court contemplates something like the second scenario, it will put its ruling in a form that puts government "on notice" that in the future it will no longer allow involuntary deprivations of housing — again, a remand which nevertheless keeps the homeowners in their housing. That is, a compromise. Intelligent bureaucrats see this coming already, simply because so many eminent domain actions are over housing (as well as businesses which are the sole source of their owners' incomes — maintenance?).[127]

The idea that the individual is vindicated in every case, implies a conclusion which alarmed even the Founders: the Constitution is neither more, nor less, nor other, than the individual and manifestly we never know exactly what that is, because amendments have kept adding new facts to the Constitution. Even the Founders felt that the Constitution is prescriptive or proscriptive — this is the reason Madison finds a role for the courts and the state legislatures under the Bill of Rights. It's not because they are the courts and the state legislatures or even because he was courting the states in order to obtain ratification of the Bill of

---

126 Through a technical explication, Stephanie Bell explores the mirage of "taxes" and "bonds," finding the reality to be "policy," an *ad hoc* "facts of the individual" analysis: "Can Taxes and Bonds Finance Government Spending?" http://ssrn.com/abstract=115128. On partisanship as a factual indicium of maintenance see Bruno Amable *et al.*, "Welfare State Retrenchment: The Partisan Effect Revisited," http://ssrn.com/abstract=889041.

127 The Founders had their own *ad hoc* "facts of the individual" analysis of maintenance, and it is bound up with the contemporary notion of lawful trades in the speculative context of natural rights. A *very* great deal of work has to be done to disentangle maintenance from those terms, as well as to rescue it from the partisan debate which surrounds it: some conservative commentators see maintenance as a right to be protected against regulation, that is, they see maintenance as a defining component of much minimum scrutiny health and welfare regulation. See James W. Ely, "'To Pursue any Lawful Trade or Avocation:' The Evolution of Unenumerated Economic Rights in the Nineteenth Century," http://ssrn.com/abstract=881833.

Rights. Rather, it is because he is alarmed at the idea that the Constitution does not have an enforcement mechanism. And yet, he dislikes enforcement mechanisms, because an enforcement mechanism implies failure and discretion, and in his statement he is clearly worried about these things. If the Constitution can fail or if there is discretion in enforcement, are the alleged facts really inherent in the individual, is it true that they operate in every case? Though, through their writings, it is unambiguously clear that they felt that the Constitution was descriptive, this idea frightened them. In this way, Roosevelt's bill of rights is bolder than the Constitution's. Perhaps there is no enforcement mechanism in his bill of rights because he felt enforcement would suggest that there are no individuals — that they must somehow be created, maintained or defended, by law. Under the New Bill of Rights this is not a problem: it simply asks whether a fact is a fact of the individual.

In fact, the Founders' fears were in defiance of their own experience. In the event the Revolution was lost, all of the Founders would have been executed, probably without further process. And yet the fact is that throughout that experience they were free from an establishment of religion, and engaged in protected speech — AND WERE HOUSED. It seems not to have occurred to them that they were enacting what they were defending, and defending what they were enacting, and that the "difference" between enforcement and enactment is a distinction without a difference.

The Constitution is not *about* anything: it *is*. When John Marshall said that it is "the province and the duty of the judicial department to say what the law is," he meant that the individual is vindicated in every case.[128] The Constitution is not mentioned. For him the rule of law is the individual: "The very essence of civil liberty certainly consists in the right of every individual to claim the protection of the laws, whenever he receives an injury."[129] Again the Constitution is not mentioned. The individual both pre- and post-dates the institution of the Constitution, and will survive the Constitution itself.[130] Marshall's statements *originate* in Thomas Jefferson's statement that "all men are created equal," and Jefferson's statement is later *applied* by Abraham Lincoln. Indeed, understanding that Jefferson's statement does apply, was the great intellectual accomplishment of Lincoln's career;[131] the Union could not have been maintained without it. The law, the rule *of* law, the Declaration of Independence, the Constitution and the Union, all are problematic in contemplation of the individual.

---

128  *Marbury* at 177.

129  *Id.*, at 163.

130  Marshall's analysis was also implemented pre-*Marbury*. See Michael William Treanor, "Judicial Review before *Marbury*," http://ssrn.com/abstract=722443.

131  Allen C. Guelzo, *Abraham Lincoln: Redeemer President* (Eerdmans Publishing Co. 2003).

And so to the subject of this book, the interesting case in which facts of the Constitution violate the law.[132] What to do about them?[133] They violate the law

132  The manner in which such facts drift in and out of the Constitution, is itself now subject to an *ad hoc* "facts of the individual" analysis. See Christopher Bryant, "Stopping Time: The Pro-Slavery and 'Irrevocable' Thirteenth Amendment," http://ssrn.com/abstract=467280.

133  In Lincoln's view, this situation was the mutual exclusivity of law and enforcement. Here is how he expressed it in the context of slavery: "[N]either the word 'slave' nor 'slavery' is to be found in the Constitution, nor the word 'property' even, in any connection with language alluding to...slavery,...and...wherever in that instrument the slave is alluded to, he is called a 'person'...and wherever his master's legal right in relation to him, is alluded to, it is spoken of as 'service or labor which may be due' — as a debt payable in service or labor. [This allusion]...was employed on purpose to exclude from the Constitution the idea that there could be property in man" (quoted in Harold Holzer, *Lincoln at Cooper Union* [Simon & Schuster 2004], 278).
This again is "natural law" as speculative not normative (it is also factually incorrect: the Founders did not believe there was any contract between master and slave out of which a "debt" arose). It carried over from Lincoln's attitude to *Dred Scott v. Sandford*, 60 US 393 (1857). *Dred Scott* had voided the so-called "Missouri Compromise," by which legislation, (1) Missouri was admitted as a slave state and Maine (formerly part of Massachusetts) as free, and (2) except for Missouri, slavery was to be excluded from the Louisiana Purchase lands north of latitude 36°30; the decision also completely deprived African-Americans of any rights. The *Dred Scott* decision was also unconstitutional because it was unenforceable. This was proved, in general, by the Civil War, and in particular, by Lincoln himself once he became President: "In office, Lincoln...[consistently refused] to treat the *Dred Scott* decision as creating a rule of law binding on the executive branch. His administration issued passports and other documents to free blacks, thus treating them as citizens of the United States in despite the Court's denial of their status as citizens. He signed legislation that plainly placed restrictions on slavery in the western territories in defiance of [Chief Justice Roger] Taney's ruling" (Robert P. George, "Lincoln on Judicial Supremacy," archived at www.aclj.org). For that matter, the "Missouri Compromise" and similar further territorial compromises were also proved unenforceable by the War, and Lincoln had both pointed to and foreseen their unenforceability in his famous "house divided" speech of 1858, even before the War broke out: "We are now far into the fifth year since a policy [the Kansas-Nebraska Act of 1854, dealing with territories and slavery] was initiated with the avowed object, and confident promise, of putting an end to slavery agitation. Under the operation of that policy, that agitation has not only not ceased, but has constantly augmented. In my opinion, it will not cease, until a crisis shall have been reached and passed. 'A house divided against itself cannot stand.' I believe this government cannot endure permanently half slave and half free. I do not expect the Union to be dissolved — I do not expect the house to fall — but I do expect it will cease to be divided. It will become all one thing, or all the other. Either the opponents of slavery will arrest the further spread of it, and place it where the public mind shall rest in the belief that it is in the course of ultimate extinction; or its advocates will push it forward, till it shall become alike lawful in all the States, old as well as new — North as well as South." This comment is also a statement that involuntary deprivation of a fact of the individual collapses the doctrines and branches of government: this is the meaning of the Civil War. The speech is widely available, particularly on the internet, including www.historyplace.com. Lincoln never commented directly on *Marbury*.
Madison was well aware of the danger of the collapse of the branches of government, but he was not quite on point as to the meaning of the danger. He said in *The Federalist*, No. 47: "The accumulation of all powers, legislative, executive, and judiciary, in the same hands, whether of one, a few, or many, and whether hereditary, self-appointed, or elective, may justly be pronounced the very definition of tyranny....[W]here the whole power of one department is exercised by the same hands which possess the whole power of another department, the fundamental principles of a free constitution are subverted. This would

because they do not survive the "facts of the individual" analysis. For Marshall, such violative facts define "the province and the duty" of the Court. For Lincoln, they are the limiting case of the Constitution. Is "public use" such a fact?[134] For what it's worth, here is how Lincoln tried to step over the problem of illegal facts in the Constitution: "[a]lthough the Constitution gave some measure of legal sanction to slavery, this was only because the choice in 1787 was between making those concessions and getting a national Constitution, or a descent into national anarchy and misrule; and because the authors who made those concessions made them in the expectation that slavery would gradually die out anyway on its own."[135] As we know, slavery did not "gradually die out anyway on its own," any more than FDR's second bill of rights came to pass. For "slavery" substitute "public use" as applied to an exercise of eminent domain over housing: there is the dilemma. It was also Lincoln's dilemma. It is the immemorial dilemma of the mutual exclusion of fact and law. What are the indicia of this "choice?"

The implication of Lincoln's phrase, "dedicated to the proposition that all men are created equal," is the Union *as* individuals through vindication *of* the individual in *every* case, with power and the subversion of power in endless dynamic

---

have been the case in the [British] constitution...if the king, who is the sole executive magistrate, had possessed also the complete legislative power, or the supreme administration of justice; or if the entire legislative body had possessed the supreme judiciary, or the supreme executive authority. This, however, is not among the vices of that constitution. The magistrate in whom the whole executive power resides cannot of himself make a law, though he can put a negative on every law; nor administer justice in person, though he has the appointment of those who do administer it. The judges can exercise no executive prerogative, though they are shoots from the executive stock; nor any legislative function, though they may be advised with by the legislative councils. The entire legislature can perform no judiciary act, though by the joint act of two of its branches the judges may be removed from their offices, and though one of its branches is possessed of the judicial power in the last resort. The entire legislature, again, can exercise no executive prerogative, though one of its branches constitutes the supreme executive magistracy, and another, on the impeachment of a third, can try and condemn all the subordinate officers in the executive department" (emphases omitted). But what does the "definition of tyranny," define? This is the same question as was raised with respect to Barnett's comment on *Lawrence*: what does the presumption of liberty, presume? In the case of government, it was left for Marshall to elucidate: the collapse of the branches of government eliminates government as a fact of the individual.

134 For an interesting discussion of eminent domain as an *ad hoc* "facts of the individual" maintenance analysis, see Hanoch Dagan, "Takings and Distributive Justice," http://ssrn.com/abstract=158194; Howard C. Klemme, "Takings and the Regulatory Roles of Government (Introduction and Overview)," http://ssrn.com/abstract=348400.

135 Guelzo at 198. And Madison of "every" fame? "He took so many positions on the clause extending the slave trade...that determining which, if any, [principles] he actually believed is impossible." Lawrence Goldstone, *Dark Bargain: Slavery, Profits, and the Struggle for the Constitution* (Walker & Company 2005) at 189. "The Migration or Importation of such Persons as any of the States now existing shall think proper to admit, shall not be prohibited by the Congress prior to the Year one thousand eight hundred and eight, but a Tax or duty may be imposed on such Importation, not exceeding ten dollars for each Person." U.S. Const., art. I, § 9. "This obsolete provision was designed to protect the slave trade from congressional restriction for a period of time." http://www.senate.gov/civics/constitution_item/constitution.htm#a1_sec9.

tension.[136] In this view, the Constitution is only facts, of two types: a seizure of power or an assumption of power. Are any facts both? Neither? If either, is it because they are not the Constitution? "Is," "all" and "every," are the vindication of the individual in every case. The individual is NEVER the Constitution, but the Constitution is ALWAYS the individual — that, according to Marshall, is what the law is. The individual is all. What is the Constitution? What is "public use?" What are the facts of the individual?

---

136 "Gettysburg Address" (November 19, 1863) in Janet Podell and Steven Anzovin, eds., *Speeches of the American Presidents* (H.W. Wilson Co. 1988) at 193.

# Chapter 2. *Kelo* and Its Discontents

## The Consensus Evaporates and the Doctrines Unravel

> Was our society, which had always been so assured of its humil-
> ity and rectitude, so confident of its unexamined premises, assembled
> round any thing more permanent than a congeries of banks, insurance
> companies and industries, and had it any beliefs more essential than a
> belief in compound interest and the maintenance of dividends?

> — T. S. Eliot, *The Idea of a Christian Society*

The lessons of *Kelo* are straightforward: first, only housing is housing; no generalities — not "private use," not "property rights," not "economic development"
— nothing substitutes for it. Second, if you don't understand how the law (in this
case, the Constitution) got to be the law, you probably don't understand the law
and will have a tough time vindicating your rights. Those who cannot describe
a writ of assistance, or arbitrary power, or ship money, or decide whether James
Madison means housing when he says "every," don't stand a good chance of per-
suading the Court of anything.

The Institute for Justice, representing the *Kelo* homeowners, never did make
the argument that there was a right to housing, and the Court never asked about
it.[137] Instead, the IJ advanced its losing argument — and lost. As the Court noted

---

137 Neither did commentators pay any attention to the housing involved in the facts:
avoidance of the facts is endemic to — and mandated by — the "minimum scrutiny" regime. What concerned the commentators was the *goal* or *process* of eminent domain, not
the Constitutional ramifications of *what* is taken; for example, 119 *Harvard Law Review* 287

in *Kelo*, the IJ contended "that using eminent domain for economic development impermissibly blurs the boundary between public and private takings." It asked the Court to raise the level of scrutiny for all facts in the context of eminent domain because eminent domain should not be invoked in cases of economic development. However, "our cases foreclose this objection. Quite simply, the government's pursuit of a public purpose will often benefit individual private parties."[138] The IJ maintained "that for takings of this kind we should require a 'reasonable certainty' that the expected public benefits will actually accrue." As the Court noted, such a rule "would represent an even greater departure from our precedent. 'When the legislature's purpose is legitimate and its means are not irrational, our cases make clear that empirical debates over the wisdom of takings — no less than debates over the wisdom of other kinds of socioeconomic legislation — are not to be carried out in the federal courts.'"[139] In short, the Court was not about to undo Holmes[140] in favor of legally empty phrases.

On the other hand, consider the following:

1. the *ad hoc* "facts of the individual" analyses in *Marbury* and *Lawrence* suggest the presence of that analysis in *Kelo*;

2. the collapse of doctrines and branches of government in the scrutiny analysis suggests that it fails to distinguish facts.

These considerations together suggest that when, as in *Kelo*, the Court does not vindicate a fact of the individual, it is because the scrutiny analysis assumes what is to be proved, that is, the scrutiny analysis does not analyze facts. It is irrational:

1. seeks to eliminate the fact.

The New London redevelopment plan, the Court said, "was projected to create in excess of 1,000 jobs, to increase tax and other revenues, and to redevelop an economically distressed city...."[141] This assumes creation, whereas creation is what is at issue. In fact, the only project is the plan.

---

(No. 1, November 2005). The failure of this case note — and so much other commentary — to take account of housing as it relates to Madison's use of the word "every," led to theory giving false predictions. Again like much other commentary, this note provides recourse to the "democratic process" in the case of disputes over the use of eminent domain; indeed, the political system provided this for itself. This was another formulation of minimum scrutiny: a method of avoiding dealing with facts. It was wishful thinking — or was it? In the event the "democratic process" did not produce the result predicted for it — it didn't produce any result at all. It produced stalemate, with the parlous result of eliminating the "democratic process," just as the response to *Kelo* had eliminated the Court. What now?

138 *Kelo*, slip op., at 17.

139 *Kelo*, slip op., at 17-18, citing *Midkiff* at 242.

140 For more on Holmes' role in establishing the "minimum scrutiny" regime — including discussion of the *ad hoc* "minimum scrutiny" regime (operating alongside a *Lochner* era *ad hoc* "facts of the individual" analysis) — see Brian R. Leiter, "Holmes, Nietzsche & Classical Realism," http://ssrn.com/abstract=215193; Louise Weinberg, "Holmes' Failure," http://ssrn.com/abstract=729906; Patrick J. Kelley, "Holmes, Langdell and Formalism," *http://ssrn.com/abstract=312841*; Gerald Leonard, "Holmes on the Lochner Court," http://ssrn.com/abstract=933603.

141 *Id.*, slip op., at 1.

2. at best only succeeds or would, if allowed, only succeed, in eliminating incarnations of it.

"[I]t is clear that a State may transfer property from one private party to another if future 'use by the public' is the purpose of the taking...."[142] This assumes the future, whereas the future is at issue. In fact, the private party is excluded from the future "use by the public."

3. in the process violates other rights.

"[The Court] embraced the broader and more natural interpretation of public use as public purpose."[143] This assumes the "embrace," whereas the "embrace" is at issue. The Court does not engage in the "embrace."

4. brings to bear a disproportionate effort.

"[T]he city's development agent has purchased property from willing sellers."[144] This assumes the sales, whereas the sales are at issue. In fact, the city's development agent seeks the sales.

5. does not consider alternatives which could achieve the goal.

"In 2000, the City of New London approved a development plan...."[145] This assumes the development plan, whereas the development plan is at issue. In fact, the plan seeks to eliminate housing.

This shows the Court taking the vital step in enforcing the "minimum scrutiny" regime: hiding the facts. The housing, the sales, the "embrace," the exclusion, the creation — the "facts of the individual" analysis reveals the absence of *every* fact in the scrutiny analysis, including *Marbury*'s fact: what the law is.[146]

The Court's shabby fabric of lies is so transparent that it raises the question, who did the Court expect to be fooled? Not public opinion, which promptly rejected and resisted it. Not the political system, which did not dare send in the police. Only the "minimum scrutiny" regime, which existed largely in the minds of the Justices. The "facts of the individual analysis" is a method for examining *every* decision of *every* court. This is how Constitutional law is conformed to Madison's statement. And the purpose of the "minimum scrutiny" regime? To make the facts uncontestable — to make the entire political system uncontest-

---

142 *Id.*, slip op., at 6.

143 *Id.*, slip op., at 8.

144 *Id.*, slip op., at 1.

145 *Id.*, slip op., at 1.

146 As the Court noted, "the State authorized a $5.35 million bond issue to support the NLDC's planning activities and a $10 million bond issue toward the creation of a Fort Trumbull State Park." *Id.*, slip op., at 1. However, this use of finance was passed over silently. It putatively created no rights in Kelo, even though finance is subject to a "facts of the individual" analysis. Although the bond market is supposed to come under minimum scrutiny health and welfare regulation, bonds themselves are now considered facts of the individual and other facts of the individual persistently assert themselves through the finance state within a state, to the consternation of the Court. The Court is having to revisit facts in yet another area, whereas it felt it had relieved itself of that duty by setting up the "minimum scrutiny" regime — it hasn't worked out that way. See W. Bartley Hildreth and C. Kurt, "The Evolution of the State and Local Government Municipal Debt Market over the Past Quarter Century," http://ssrn.com/abstract=857750; Andrei Shleifer, "Will the Sovereign Debt Market Survive," http://ssrn.com/abstract=373980.

able. However, as in the case of resistance to *Kelo*, a system which makes the facts uncontestable, marks the end of the system. The move to make the facts incontestable, means that the connection has been broken between the political system and the Constitution.

Under direct scrutiny, the Court no longer hustles its shabby lies and its automatic corruption. Honesty relieves tension in the political system. Under minimum scrutiny, missing facts are true facts, present facts are false facts. Worse and worse. Following is a portion of the testimony of Susan Kniep, President of the Federation of Connecticut Taxpayer Organizations, given before a Connecticut legislative committee investigating eminent domain in the wake of the *Kelo* decision. It is typical of suspicions about the arrangements behind many decisions to exercise eminent domain:

> As the State legislature contemplates protecting the public from eminent domain abuse, consideration should be given to conducting a full scale investigation of those involved in the [New London Development Corporation's] takeover of private property, the victimization of private citizens and their rights, and the funneling of millions of state taxpayer dollars for contracts and to the politically influential. A forensic audit should immediately be initiated by the State and all funds on this project should be frozen until such an audit and investigation is conducted and concluded. The players in this land grab deal are either in jail, are awaiting trial, or are under federal scrutiny for their roles in other state funded development projects. Why, therefore, would the state legislature sit quietly and not begin their own inquiry into former Governor [John] Rowland and Peter Ellef's involvement in the NLDC deal....We understand the properties acquired by the NLDC are all in its name, not that of the City. Yet, State statutes stipulate that "title to land taken or acquired pursuant to a development plan shall be solely in the name of the municipality." Were the 90 homeowners who have left intimidated into leaving their homes prior to the NLDC or their agents having legal authority to even approach them to purchase their homes?....Were the contracts bid or no bid? Did [the general contractor or subcontractors] contribute to [former Connecticut Governor] Rowland's election campaign? Another registered lobbyist, [attorney] Jay Levin, was hired to write the Fort Trumbull neighborhood Municipal Development Plan. What has he been paid to date? Philip Michalowski, who testified before you during the last hearing, was also an NLDC contractor responsible for many people losing their homes. What has he been paid? The NLDC has paid millions to consultants, planners, marketing firms and other advisors. Who at the State is monitoring these funds?[147]

Her suspicions were confirmed when the true facts emerged from the eminent domain underworld to show how this particular piece of chicanery went forward:

> In mid-July [of 2004, after the Supreme Court had accepted the *Kelo* case], as commentators and politicians around the country decried [New London's] attempt to seize private homes for economic development on the Fort Trumbull peninsula, a press release appeared on the Web site of Pfizer Inc. The pharmaceutical company, whose $300 million research complex sits adjacent to what remains of the neighborhood, announced that it wanted to set the record straight

---

147 The testimony is available online at the Federation's website, www.ctact.org. See also http://www.cottagecoalition.org/rowland.htm.

on its involvement in the Fort Trumbull development project. The project, the statement said, wasn't Pfizer's idea. "We at Pfizer have been dismayed to see false and misleading claims appear in the media that suggest Pfizer is somehow involved in this matter," the statement said. The writers said the company "has no requirements nor interest in the development of the land that is the subject of the case." But a recent, months-long review of state records and correspondence from 1997 and 1998 — when officials from the administration of then-Gov. John G. Rowland were helping convince the pharmaceutical giant to build in New London — shows that statement is misleading, at best. In fact, the company has been intimately involved in the project since its inception, consulting with state and city officials about the plans for the peninsula and helping to shape the vision of how the faded neighborhood might eventually be transformed into a complex of high-end housing and office space, anchored by a luxury hotel. The records — obtained by *The Day* through the state Freedom of Information Act — show that, at least as early as the fall of 1997, Pfizer executives and state economic development officials were discussing the company's plans, not just for a new research facility but for the surrounding neighborhood as well. And, after several requests, the state Department of Economic and Community Development [DECD] produced a document that both the state and Pfizer had at first said did not exist: a 1997 sketch, prepared by CUH2A, Pfizer's design firm for its new facility. Labeled as a "vision statement," it suggested various ways the existing neighborhood and nearby vacant Navy facility could be replaced with a "high end residential district," offices and retail businesses, expanded parking and a marina. Those interactions took place months before Pfizer announced that it would build in the city, on the site of the former New London Mills linoleum factory, and months before the New London Development Corp. announced its redevelopment plans for the neighborhood and the former Naval Undersea Warfare Center next door.[148] The NLDC's plans, while

---

148  In an email to me, Scott Bullock defended himself against my contention that he had failed to make the argument that New London had failed minimum scrutiny because the city had failed the government purpose factual inquiry of minimum scrutiny: "Of course, this is utter nonsense. We proved at trial that the redevelopment of the Fort Trumbull neighborhood was part of the agreement with Pfizer to move to New London and that Pfizer had a major role in directing the municipal development plan. Indeed, as we demonstrated, everything that Pfizer wanted in the plan it got. All of the supposed new revelations in *The Day* article...were in fact set forth at the trial (including the production of an internal Pfizer email that *The Day* did not have access to but that we obtained in discovery). That is why Justice Thomas noted in his dissent that based on the evidence produced at trial that the plan was 'suspiciously agreeable to the Pfizer Corporation.' But none of it mattered to the majority of the justices. They ruled that because the intent of the government officials in New London was not only to benefit Pfizer but all of New London, then these facts did not matter. Once a court rules that a party must show a specific intent to benefit only a particular private party to raise any concerns about a private use, it becomes virtually impossible to separate out public and private benefits and the government is going to win." Of course, arguing that the development was "part" of an agreement with Pfizer misses point: the development was *all* Pfizer, not "part." If the IJ had argued the correct chronology, the result would have been more than suspicious. But the IJ conceded the chronology, agreeing with New London that the chronology was the one which favored New London. Here is the chronology presented by the IJ in its Petitioner's Brief (at 3): "In February 1998, Pfizer, Inc. announced that it was developing a global research facility on a site adjacent to the Fort Trumbull neighborhood where Petitioners live....In April 1998, the city council of Respondent City of New London...gave initial approval to Respondent New London Development Corporation...to prepare a development plan for the Fort Trumbull area....The NLDC prepared the Fort Trumbull Municipal Development Plan...that sought to create economic development complementing the facility that Pfizer was planning to

different in many respects from the hand-drawn 1997 plan, maintain the vision statement's core purpose — a total replacement of the existing stock of modest homes, apartment houses and businesses, and the development of upscale housing and office space to jibe with the new Pfizer complex. NLDC and city officials have long characterized their efforts to recast the working-class neighborhood as a response to Pfizer's decision to build on the peninsula, rather than a move made as a condition of Pfizer's involvement in the project. And in the state and federal court rulings that upheld the city's takings of homes for the private development project, judges at every level of the judiciary have assumed the same. Even in a blistering dissent, which warned that the NLDC's plan left all private property under the "specter of condemnation," US Supreme Court Justice Sandra Day O'Connor sets the beginning of the case in February 1998, when Pfizer announced its plans to build its facility. While challenging the constitutionality of the eminent domain project, O'Connor and the other justices accept that it was an independent effort to "complement" the construction of a research complex next door. But in a series of recent interviews, several former high-ranking state officials confirmed what opponents of the project have long insisted and what the company continues to deny: the state's agreement to replace the existing neighborhood was a condition of Pfizer's move here....Any attempt to clarify the origins of the development project is hindered both by the passage of time and by the fact that many of the participants in the earliest discussions with the company will not, or cannot talk about their efforts. Peter N. Ellef, who as DECD commissioner and later [former Governor] Rowland's co-chief of staff oversaw the state's involvement, is awaiting trial on federal corruption charges stemming from his years in the governor's office....Rowland, who publicly embraced this and other urban development projects and poured in state bond funds, sits in federal prison in Pennsylvania after pleading guilty to a corruption charge.... But some former members of the Rowland administration with knowledge of the state's negotiations with Pfizer, speaking on the condition of anonymity because they wished to spare their relationships with current and former colleagues, confirmed Pfizer's involvement in the planning of the Fort Trumbull project. The company's formal assistance agreements with the state, which lay out more than $118 million in financial incentives and other amenities that were offered by the state and the city to convince Pfizer to build in New London, [do] not specifically offer to redevelop the neighborhood. But the redevelopment project, largely paid for with an additional $73 million in bonded funds, was an integral part of the state's deal with Pfizer, the officials said, and the company would not have built its headquarters in New London without being assured that the surroundings would undergo a radical change. "They would not have done the deal without the commitment to make the surrounding area more livable," said a high-ranking official who was privy to negotiations between Pfizer and the state. "They were trying to attract people with Ph.D.s who make $150,000 to $200,000 a year to eastern Connecticut...and they were not going to tell them they had to drive to work through a blighted community....I'm not going to tell you it was a difficult decision," the official said. "It wasn't, because of the number of jobs...."But for years, executives at Pfizer, along with the state and the NLDC, have disputed that view. Instead, they have maintained that the effort to redevelop the neighborhood came only in response to Pfizer's announcement that it would locate its headquarters here, and they have insisted that the company never directed the state or city to overhaul the surrounding area in ex-

build....On January18, 2000, the City adopted the development plan as prepared by the NLDC." The IJ never made the case, either orally or in writing, that New London had failed to meet the government purpose prong of minimum scrutiny. It is evident that IJ did not realize there was such a prong.

change for that construction....In interviews, however, the state officials made clear that the difference between a demand by Pfizer and a statement of preference about what it would like to see next door was a small one, especially when the city and state had already committed to invest, according to figures from the DECD, a total of $118 million in other incentives. "This wasn't like convincing a bank in Norwalk to move to Stamford," a former NLDC employee said. "This was a major league deal. This was 2,000 jobs, et cetera. They know what that means. DECD knows what that means....What do we need to make this happen?"....In retrospect, the company's interest in the Fort Trumbull project does not seem to have been much of a secret at the state level, where the project seems largely to have been treated as part of the package of incentives prepared for Pfizer. For instance, on Dec. 11, 1997, DECD Commissioner James F. Abromaitis wrote...[that the state would help] by "defraying the cost of that development and improving its value through a comprehensive, state-funded waterfront improvement and development project," seemingly a reference to the Fort Trumbull neighborhood....In the meantime, the NLDC and the city — not the state, and not Pfizer — have absorbed the sharpest criticism since the Supreme Court decision brought the New London case to the public eye. And that, one of the state officials said, was no accident. "They have taken all the missile attacks," the official said, referring to the development corporation. "That's the beauty of distance."[149]

Minimum scrutiny mandates that New London show that its exercise of eminent domain is rationally related to a legitimate government purpose. Whether New London has a government purpose is a question of fact. These revelations show that New London does not, in fact, have a government purpose. In fact, it has Pfizer's purpose.[150]

---

149 *The Day*, October 16, 2005 (New London, Connecticut, archived at www.theday.com). False facts were also alleged in the massive Riviera Beach, Florida, eminent domain controversy: "In what has been called the largest eminent-domain case in the nation, the mayor and other elected leaders want to move about 6,000 residents, tear down their houses and use the emptied 400-acre site to build a waterfront yachting and residential complex for the well-to-do. The goal, Mayor Michael D. Brown said during a public meeting in September, is to 'forever change the landscape' in this municipality of about 32,500 [located near Palm Beach]. The $1 billion plan should generate jobs and move Riviera Beach's economy out of the doldrums, local leaders have said....'What they mean is that the view I have is too good for me and should go to some millionaire,' said Martha Babson, 60, a house painter who lives near the Intracoastal Waterway....In Florida, the law allows local officials to take private land for redevelopment if they deem it 'blighted.' In May 2001, a study conducted for the city found that 'slum and blighted conditions' existed in about a third of Riviera Beach and that redevelopment was necessary 'in the interest of public health, safety, morals and welfare.' A skeptical Babson, who lives in a single-story, concrete-block home painted aqua that she shares with parrots and a dog, did her own survey. For three months, she walked the streets of Riviera Beach photographing houses classified as 'dilapidated' or 'deteriorated' by specialists hired by the city. The official study, she said, was riddled with errors and misclassifications. Lots inventoried as 'vacant' (one of 14 [sic!] criteria that allow Florida cities or counties to declare a neighborhood blighted) actually had homes on them built in 1997, she said. One house deemed 'dilapidated,' she found, was two years old. Mayor Brown and Floyd T. Johnson, executive director of the Riviera Beach Community Redevelopment Agency, did not respond to repeated requests from the Los Angeles Times for an interview." *Minneapolis Star Tribune*, December 6, 2005 (Minneapolis, Minnesota, archived at www.startribune.com).

150 This substitution of purposes is well known in public choice theory. It is called "interest group capture." See Peter Kulick, "Rolling the Dice: Determining Public Use in

So what? In *United States v. Virginia*, which ended gender discrimination in state higher education, the Court silently added an additional test for intermediate scrutiny, under which government policy must substantially further an important government interest. The new test had the effect of creating a level of scrutiny between intermediate and strict scrutiny. Justice Ginsburg, writing for the Court, said: "The justification must be genuine, not hypothesized or invented *post hoc* in response to litigation."[151] Justice Ginsburg's proposition is that there must in *fact* be a justification. Note that this proposition is not restricted by the Court to intermediate scrutiny: at *all* levels of scrutiny, there must in *fact* be a purpose. Unnoticed, this put an end to the casual assumption that the justification could be merely "conceivable." *Virginia* was the first case in which the Court had addressed the issue of purpose as a *fact*, as opposed to a contrived, inadequate, false — or even "conceivable" — justification. As we shall see, *government* purpose as an issue, follows inexorably from it. Justice Ginsburg's proposition was so obvious that no authority was cited for it.[152] At the same time, it was equally obvious that if *government* purpose was not specified, it was a standing invitation to "government" to substitute a private purpose. The invitation was cordially accepted in *Kelo* — but for reasons we shall examine, New London was not called on it.

Since Justice Ginsburg had not made clear, in *Virginia*, the "government purpose" factual prong of scrutiny, Justice Kennedy fumbled with it in *Kelo*. In his concurring opinion, he said that "[t]here may be private transfers in which the risk of undetected impermissible favoritism of private parties is so acute that a presumption (rebuttable or otherwise) of invalidity is warranted under the Public Use Clause."[153] What is not clear in this statement, is what is being transferred: a private purpose is being substituted for a government purpose via a transfer of government to a private entity. It is the abrogation of government, in defiance of *Marbury*.

However, Justice Kennedy does take a very useful step: he articulates *chronology* of the facts as being the determining factor in government purpose, although after seventy years this is both an insultingly meager step forward and only occurs in a concurring opinion. For Kennedy, it is chronology which will bring the truth to light. This is his contribution to the Court's ongoing development of "government purpose" minimum scrutiny jurisprudence. He lays out a civil discovery program for lawyers whose clients stand to lose because government has invoked minimum scrutiny. He says, in the context of eminent domain use relying on minimum scrutiny, that lawyers should ask for evidence on the following

---

Order to Effectuate a 'Public-Private' Taking — A Proposal to Redefine 'Public Use,'" http://ssrn.com/abstract=262585. Consider capture as a form of corruption in the bond market: Alexander W. Butler, "Corruption and Municipal Finance," http://ssrn.com/abstract=576601.

151  *Virginia* at 533.

152  And neither of the cases cited after it stand for the Court's proposition with regard to justification. See *Weinberger v. Wiesenfeld*, 420 U. S. 636, (1975) and *Califano v. Goldfarb*, 430 U. S. 199 (1977).

153  *Kelo*, slip op. (Kennedy, J., concurring), at 4.

issues in order to determine whether government has met its burden of proof. He says the Court needs to know if, in *fact*, there is a government purpose and he says that the Court can only know that after the Court has seen facts relating to specific criteria:

> A court confronted with a plausible accusation of impermissible favoritism to private parties should [conduct]....a careful and extensive inquiry into 'whether, in fact, the development plan [chronology]

> [1.] is of primary benefit to . . . the developer..., and private businesses which may eventually locate in the plan area...,

> [2.] and in that regard, only of incidental benefit to the city...[.]'

Kennedy is also interested in facts of the chronology which show, with respect to government,

> [3.] awareness of...depressed economic condition and evidence corroborating the validity of this concern...,

> [4.] the substantial commitment of public funds...before most of the private beneficiaries were known...,

> [5.] evidence that [government] reviewed a variety of development plans...[,]

> [6.] [government] chose a private developer from a group of applicants rather than picking out a particular transferee beforehand and...

> [7.] other private beneficiaries of the project [were]...unknown [to government] because the...space proposed to be built [had] not yet been rented....[154]

Why does Kennedy go to these extraordinary lengths? He is trying to find a point at which to intervene in a factless minimum scrutiny downward spiral.[155]

---

154 Id., at 2-3. Laurence Tribe, who had argued *Midkiff*, says: "In arguing *Midkiff*, at the level of formal doctrine I urged a standard identical to that for substantive due process challenges; but fearing precisely the kinds of identity-attacking and/or [sic] community-disintegrating moves that some think New London made in *Kelo*, I emphasized both in my brief and in oral argument the strong support in historical tradition and in economic utility for the state's comprehensive scheme for transforming oligopolies with respect to residential property in key areas of the state into well-functioning real estate markets — thereby arguing that the state law at issue would survive not only rationality review but any plausibly heightened standard, as well. Although Justice O'Connor's opinion for the Court in *Midkiff* recited some of that material, her opinion was painted with a surprisingly broad brush — and I was only mildly surprised in *Kelo* to see her retrace some of her steps from *Midkiff* and retract the most sweeping of the statements to be found there. Adding the Kennedy *Kelo* concurrence to the O'Connor *Kelo* dissent yields a 5-4 majority for at least trying to develop workable criteria for ferreting out corrupt or otherwise pretextual takings." Quoted in www.scotusblog.com (June 26, 2005).

155 Kennedy had earlier tried out both his *Lawrence* and his *Kelo* approaches in *Romer v. Evans*, 517 US 620 (1996), which voided a Colorado Constitutional amendment barring any state governmental entity from taking any action to protect homosexuals from discrimination based on their sexual orientation. The fact that this case was decided at the same time as *Virginia*, shows a Court alarmed at a political system acting on minimum scrutiny as if it is not a fact-based test. In his opinion for the Court, Kennedy in *Romer* tried out both articulating factual criteria for government purpose, and evaluating facts not based on the "minimum scrutiny" regime at all. He said that striking down the Colorado amendment served two purposes: "By requiring that the classification bear a rational relationship to an

He understands that the government's presentation, in *Virginia*, of purpose as a false fact, illuminates a corner of the "minimum scrutiny" regime. The scrutiny regime purports to have jurisdiction over all facts; this in turn means that the regime arises in every component of the Constitution, including the component of the Fifth Amendment involved in *Kelo*: "nor shall private property be taken for public use, without just compensation." This is how Kennedy brings Madison's "every" back into the Constitution. It allows Kennedy to reveal an aspect of the meaning of "public" in "public use." After two hundred years under the Constitution, we are prepared to say that "public" means true, and that, in the first instance, means a fully articulated scrutiny continuum.[156] Thus does Kennedy smooth the path for direct scrutiny and all the other new layers of Constitutional scrutiny.

He also sees true as meaning the maintenance of importance facts. His *Kelo* criteria are concurrence is his silent protest that housing — a fact of importance to the Court since zoning was upheld in the 1926 *Euclid* case which sustained residential zoning — is not being maintained by the New London eminent domain use, it is being destroyed. These are results-oriented criteria. He wants to see a change in the facts and a correlation between the facts and the projections. When we read these criteria against the backdrop of the liberty test in *Lawrence*, we understand that Kennedy here is articulating the idea that every law maintains an important fact, because his concern is the same concern in *Euclid*. This is an advance over *Lawrence*, when he simply abandoned the "minimum scrutiny" regime. It is an invitation to use scrutiny criteria to effect a transfer to the dominant doctrine of the fourth Constitutional epoch.

Kennedy's criteria also reflect his sense that there were false facts in the *Kelo* case — his criteria are his message to his colleagues that he thinks they are enforcing lies. He was right. His fundamental concern with the Court adopting false facts, was that New London eliminated government by its lies. But never mind New London: that act had implications for the *Court*. By signing off on lies, the Court finds itself formulating a government position and then enforcing it. In short, Kennedy is concerned that unless minimum scrutiny is a well-articulated fact-based standard, the Court is *legislating*, in clear violation of the separation of powers and to the destruction of government. Even Kennedy, signing off on *Kelo*, apparently draws the line at this. What does it say about the Court that he could

---

independent and legitimate legislative end, we ensure that classifications are not drawn for the purpose of disadvantaging the group burdened by the law." *Id.*, at 633. He also said that striking down the Colorado amendment keeps the political system within the jurisdiction of the Constitution: "the disadvantage imposed is born of animosity toward the class of persons affected...A State cannot so deem a class of persons a stranger to its laws." *Id.*, at 634-635. Of course, he adds "independent" to "legitimate" and subtracts "stranger" from it. That is, either minimum scrutiny must be subject to factual criteria, or the fact at issue must be evaluated outside the "minimum scrutiny" regime. In either case, he is pointing out that under the Constitution, minimum scrutiny is related to fact. The next step was to evaluate the Constitution as a fact. What sort of fact?

156 This is the beginning of an *ad hoc* "facts of the individual" analysis of "public use." See also Abraham Bell and Gideon Parchomovsky, "The Uselessness of Public Use," http://ssrn.com/abstract=903805.

not get his colleagues to sign off on his idea, and had to put it in a concurring opinion?

It turns out that the IJ — instead of pursuing power-grabbing legal "theories" — should have stuck to the minimum scrutiny test available to them, linking it to a Racketeer Influenced and Corrupt Organizations claim. This statute[157] provides penalties for defendants engaging in an enterprise which commits two or more of a variety of crimes (such as fraud or conspiracy), within a ten-year period as part of an enterprise, using an instrumentality of interstate commerce (such as the telephone or mail). One commentator describes its use in eminent domain actions:

> To predicate a RICO (Racketeer Influenced and Corrupt Organizations Act) claim simply on the wrongful use of a city's eminent domain power is a difficult task. Two reported decisions in the case of *Pelfresne v. Village of Rosemont*, 22 F. Supp.2d 756 (N.D. Ill. 1998) and 35 F. Supp.2d 1064 (N.D. Ill. 1999) shed light on some of the hurdles an ousted property owner is likely to confront. In *Plefresne*, the plaintiff alleged that city officials had been trying to acquire plaintiff's property since 1979 by condemning it as "blighted" and by raising the real estate taxes to confiscatory levels. The city, plaintiffs claimed, initiated fraudulent tax proceedings against the property, supported by false affidavits from tax officials, all in an effort to further raise plaintiff's property taxes. It was also alleged that city officials breached a previous settlement agreement with plaintiff, requiring the plaintiff to obtain a zoning permit to open a restaurant on the property, even though the property was zoned for commercial use and, therefore, no such permit was required. When the plaintiff applied for the permit, the application was denied. Plaintiff claimed that Defendants' actions were doubly motivated: 1) the defendant city officials wanted to use the property for facilities or businesses owned or operated by the Village and award themselves lucrative concessions; and 2) the city officials wanted to put the property into the hands of a few favored developers who, aided by improper real estate tax exemptions, have the ability to compete unfairly with private business. Coincidentally, some of the city officials' businesses benefited from sweet-heart leases with these favored developers. Plaintiff asserted that the sham eminent domain proceedings constituted a pattern in that almost all of the industrial and commercial real estate in the city had been acquired by condemnation or eminent domain, or by the threat thereof, and was controlled by the defendant city officials. The first hurdle the Plaintiff in *Plefresne* had to overcome was legislative immunity. The city officials argued they could not be held liable because the exercise of their eminent domain authority was a legislative function. 35 F. Supp. 2d at 1070. The court held that even if the zoning resolutions constituted legislative functions, the city officials' other allegedly wrongful behavior (*e.g.*, refusing the grant permits and initiating tax proceedings) were administrative functions that were not immune. Defendants also argued that, although plaintiff named individual city officials as defendants, the actual defendant was the city, and a city cannot constitute a defendant person under RICO section 1964(c). 22 F. Supp. 2d at 760. The court was not persuaded by the defendants' effort to recast plaintiff's complaint. Because the Defendants were the city officials, not the city, the allegations were sound. Plaintiff initially named the Office of the Mayor as the enterprise, which the court held to be improper, since it was the city not the Office of the Mayor that had authority to condemn property. The court, however, gave Plaintiff leave to amend its complaint to name the city as the enterprise. *Id.* at 762. Plaintiff based its pattern of racketeering activity allegations on two letters

---

157 18 U.S.C. §§ 1961-68.

mailed by the city officials: one letter denying Plaintiff's restaurant permit and another letter informing Plaintiff of the eminent domain action. Plaintiff alleged that these letters constituted acts of mail fraud. Defendants argued that the letters were not acts of mail fraud because they contained no fraudulent statements. The court sided with Plaintiff and held that a mailing need only further a scheme to defraud and need not contain any actual fraudulent statements itself. If, in fact, the city officials were engaged in a scheme to defraud plaintiff through sham eminent domain proceedings, then the letters furthered that scheme and were sufficient to constitute mail fraud. *Id.* at 764. The court also held that Plaintiff had sufficiently alleged a "pattern" on the basis of the two mailings, because Plaintiff alleged an ongoing scheme to use the eminent domain process for wrongful purposes and the mailings were part of that ongoing scheme. *Id.* at 763. The court's conclusion on pattern is thinly supported. A defendant is only liable for engaging in a pattern of racketeering activity, *i.e.*, mail fraud or some other criminal conduct enumerated in section 1961(1). If other actions engaged in by the city officials were not subject to sanction under RICO, then it is questionable whether the two instances of mail fraud were sufficient to constitute a pattern. Finally, with regard to injury, Plaintiff claimed lost rent on the restaurant and lost property value by reason of the eminent domain proceedings. The court held that Plaintiff's lost rent and present lost property value was compensable, but damages based on the future reduced value of the property were too speculative. *Id.* at 765. As *Plefresne* demonstrates, the largest impediment to a RICO claim arising out of eminent domain proceedings is alleging and proving a pattern of racketeering activity. If a city only once condemns property in favor of another business, then obviously a pattern will be difficult to establish. Ideally, the city officials should have a history of engaging in this type of behavior. In addition, a RICO claim would be aided by acts beyond mail or wire fraud. Some clients have complained about city officials threatening to reduce city services unless they cooperated with the condemnation proceedings and other clients relate threats of increased traffic enforcement around their business (*i.e.*, the city threatening to ticket customers for little or no reason unless the business cooperates). Arguably, such activity could constitute extortion under 18 U.S.C. §1951. The more blatant such extortion, the better the basis of a RICO claim. In short, the strongest RICO claims based on eminent domain would arise out of a long pattern of wrongful eminent domain proceedings, which included acts of extortion by city officials.[158]

This scenario does not include inquiry into bond deals which, as we shall see, play a prominent role in economic development/eminent domain activities.

As for the new criteria for government purpose, Kennedy's minimum scrutiny criteria are all prospective; government purpose is shown *ab initio*, not *post hoc*. The record must show that government established rationality, relation and government purpose before the exercise of eminent domain. And these are shown by *facts*. Which facts? Important facts, and note that under *Marbury*, government and

---

158 Jeffrey E. Grell, "RICO and Eminent Domain: Condemnation or Crime?" November 15, 2000 (archived at www.ricoact.com). Also, watch out for *sua sponte*, irrational impositions on RICO by lower courts which attempt to make it more difficult to claim a government entity itself as a RICO "enterprise." See Michael Goldsmith, Michael, "Judicial Immunity for White-Collar Crime: The Ironic Demise of Civil Rico," http://ssrn.com/abstract=891520; Michael Goldsmith, "Resurrecting Rico: Removing Immunity for White-Collar Crime," http://ssrn.com/abstract=892431. These impositions are themselves violation of government purpose under minimum scrutiny; they are examples of corruption of the judiciary under the "minimum scrutiny" regime.

all its concepts are important facts. Note that this showing involves doing discovery on the question, did government in fact consider using eminent domain and decide not to do so? What in fact were its policy alternatives? Curiously, in mandating a factual inquiry, Kennedy places the burden on government to show that any of its actions do *not* fall under minimum scrutiny; he also sweeps *all* facts into minimum scrutiny. Under his formulation, all facts are proximately related to minimum scrutiny. This is what drives the articulation of new levels of scrutiny.

We need only begin to generalize Kennedy's formulation — for example, substituting health care — to see how much emphasis the Court now places on factual showings with respect to minimum scrutiny. The outlines become much clearer:

To show whether the health care purpose chronology:

1. is of primary benefit to another purpose than health care,

2. and in that regard, only of incidental benefit to health care,

and whether the facts of the chronology show

3. awareness of deficiencies in health care and evidence corroborating the validity of this concern,

4. a substantial government health care policy...before another purpose is known,

5. evidence that government reviewed a variety of health care policies,

6. government chose a policy from a range of choices rather than picking out a particular policy beforehand and

7. other policy implications were unknown to government.

*Kelo* counsel were too obsessed with publicity to present a chronology of facts on government purpose. They were much more interested in ideology than in doing their homework and preparing their case carefully. If they had done so, they would have seen that there was no need to invoke the logically empty notion of "economic development." Much more effective defenses lay much closer to home.

Lest we forget: Kennedy came to bury the scrutiny regime, not to praise it. He does so by turning the tables on the Court. Irrespective of the front the Court imposes at any given time, the Court reserves to itself judgment over all facts — it ranks them according to their importance, and imposes another standard on everyone else. Fine. Kennedy simply made the scrutiny regime itself one of those facts, and thereby forced the regime to articulate the facts it feels are important and — something the Court has never really done even with the facts it feels are important — *why* it feels those facts are important.

Notice those facts for which Kennedy does *not* provide criteria: use and public use. These are the terms to which his criteria are laying siege. Kennedy's factual criteria are deceptive. To be sure, they comprise government purpose *in its entirety*: when government meets these criteria, there is no further showing it has to make on government purpose — for eminent domain or for any other policy. His criteria *are* government policy. Nevertheless, the criteria deliver endless revisiting of policy — stalemate. This is because *every* policy lays claim to justification on the basis of minimum scrutiny, and minimum scrutiny implicates *every* fact of policy.

Note that his criteria are not restricted to any branch of government — they are a factual inquiry into the doctrines and branches of government, but unmoored. This turns on its head the idea that the political process sustains — by determining the hierarchy for — important facts. For example, when two uses of eminent domain come into conflict, that is merely two successful invocations of minimum scrutiny, nevertheless coming into conflict. They now become Lear's daughters — orphan daughters. Resolution cannot be had by lifting the facts of one above minimum scrutiny, nor does any branch or level of government have the last word. And what about the other direction in minimum scrutiny — policies which fall out of minimum scrutiny because the facts change? Then what policy to pursue? For the implication of government purpose as a factual inquiry is that a "passing grade" on minimum scrutiny is never final; the court always retains jurisdiction, precisely what the "minimum scrutiny" regime intended to avoid (or did it?).

Valuation in eminent domain is a good example. "Fair market value" begs the minimum scrutiny questions, what is the internally consistent basis for distinguishing one noncompensable health and welfare regulation from another? one compensable health and welfare regulation from another? any compensable regulation from any noncompensable regulation? To answer, we have to go over the facts, but one of them is *always* government purpose, which is a factual inquiry. It is like the rule of witness credibility in the law of evidence: credibility is *always* at issue. For Kennedy, government purpose is *always* at issue. This means there never was a "fair market value" determination to dispute in the first place — it was always about government purpose, the Constitutional ranking of facts, government itself. There is no subsidiary debate: every issue — no matter how small — goes instantly to the heart of the Constitution and stays there. So valuation must be gone over again — and again, and again. And if the new result does not suit one of the parties? There is no synthesis to which competing claims can be referred. There is only more litigation and failure, either to deliver possession on the one hand, or on the other, to deliver government services.

Note how minimum scrutiny as a factual inquiry, resembles the "facts of the individual" analysis of facts. With this difference. Under the "facts of the individual" analysis, facts shed light on each other. Under minimum scrutiny as a factual inquiry, facts foreclose each other. Despite the tendency of the criteria to allow us to rummage around in the various ragbags of the branches of government in order to see what they consider important facts, there is no such thing, under minimum scrutiny, as either stipulating to or finding a fact — stipulating as to housing, for example, ends in disputing housing. This follows inexorably from litigating chronology: *when* eminent domain is invoked, is an indicium of *why* it is invoked. Which means that past, present and future are litigated factually under minimum scrutiny, which means that the court never loses jurisdiction over the matter. In eminent domain, government purpose pops up again when government takes property for one purpose (say, open space) and then later shifts the purpose (for example, zoning it commercial). Or government takes property after laying out a plan for its use, and then never uses it, or winds up only using part of it. In these scenarios — to name just two — government purpose comes back into play as a litigable claim. Thus, even as a fact-based test, the "minimum scrutiny" regime stood Madison on his head. Under the regime, every fact became an assumption of power, and that was the doctrine — and that doctrine was a fact. There was no way to escape, and no way to be included. Decisions could only be irrational — that, for reasons we are only beginning to understand, was no longer acceptable to public opinion and so facts were forcing their way to the fore of the regime. This helps to explain why the judiciary can't get rid of cases even when — as in the case of the education right in the New Jersey Constitution — the facts are accorded elevated scrutiny. Government purpose is a factual inquiry at all levels of scrutiny, and its circular argument traps the Court and turns it into the sort of administrative agency it dreads becoming.

For example, the New Jersey right to education supposedly enjoys strict scrutiny, but because government purpose is part of that test as well, the New Jersey Supreme Court has turned time and time again to the legislative branch to come up with a way to implement the right (the Court has also consistently framed the right in terms of equal protection in the context of financing; the Court claims that financing brings the legislature into the picture). Nor do the claimants assert either that there is a right to education apart from a relation to financing — one which is vindicated in *every* case (Madison has never been invoked) — or that the basis of the "minimum scrutiny" regime is dubious to begin with, and that the Court should severely disfavor looking to the legislative branch (no Court looks to the legislature for any policy to maintain freedom from an establishment of religion). To assert that the education provision is subject to *both* legislative deference *and* equal protection, is simply to raise the question, what is education? and the further question, what is maintenance? without ever allowing the indicia of these to be found. The result is that the New Jersey Supreme Court has had jurisdiction over the financing claim since 1973. It *still* retains jurisdiction over the case.[159] This situation was the result of all parties agreeing that the political

---

159  The well-nigh endless series of cases can be read at www.edlawcenter.org. The conceptual problems inherent in according legislatures some deference with respect to the right to education, are well summarized by Richard Briffault: "The law of school finance reform is conventionally described as consisting of three waves, each associated with a distinctive legal theory — a first wave based on federal equal protection arguments, a second equity wave based on state equal protection clauses, and a third adequacy wave based on state constitutional education articles. The asserted shift from equity to adequacy has been credited with the increasing success of school finance reform plaintiffs. The wave metaphor and especially the differences between the second and third waves, however, have been sharply overstated — temporally, textually, in terms of litigation success, and as a matter of legal theory. State courts have repeatedly blurred adequacy and equity arguments and judicial analysis of adequacy often reflects equity concerns. Nor is there a clear or consistent judicial approach to the idea of adequacy. Rather, state courts have treated adequacy and the adequacy-equity relationship in three different ways. In one set of cases, courts have cited the adequacy of the educational system to mitigate or excuse a judicial finding that school financing does not violate equality. In a second set of equity minus cases, courts have used the concept of adequacy to require states to equalize the resources of the poorest districts to an adequate level without requiring that the poor be brought up to the level of the rich. Finally, some courts have held that adequacy actually requires more than simple interdistrict tax-base or per-pupil spending equalization. In these equity plus cases, that more can be more-than-equal resources for the poorest districts, or an

system had all power — a situation which could only be brought about if there was also agreement that education had none.

Government purpose as a factual inquiry, the prospect of endless litigation, and the equality of facts under minimum scrutiny — with the miasma of corruption pervading all three — are perfectly illustrated in the following example (one of many) of the phenomenon — increasingly bizarre in the post-*Kelo* era — of "housing v. housing:"

> The city [of Camden, New Jersey] will abandon a $1.2 billion Cramer Hill redevelopment plan that would have used the government's powers of eminent domain to displace more than 1,000 families, officials announced Thursday. The project, which also called for construction of 6,000 houses, has been entangled in legal battles for more than two years because 211 residents filed a lawsuit, saying they did not want to surrender their homes. Instead of continuing to fight for the plan in court, Camden will go back to the beginning, holding neighborhood meetings to ask residents what they want, and taking as few homes as possible, said Randy Primas, the city's chief operating officer....When the new plan is finished, Primas said he still hopes thousands of new houses will be built and "a substantial number" of residents will be allowed to keep their existing homes...."They're still going to have to take a lot of homes for the developer to make his money," said lifelong Cramer Hill resident Vinnie St. John, 53. He is willing to surrender his home "if it would improve the neighborhood," but the city had appraised his house for only $85,000. "Where would I be able to buy another home for that kind of money?" he asked. The city is also discussing whether it also wants to start over on another billion-dollar redevelopment plan in the Bergen Square neighborhood, Primas said. That plan would take 479 homes and 82 businesses. The Bergen plan was ruled invalid in April by state Superior Court Judge Michael Kassel for the same technicality that caused legal troubles for Cramer Hill: Experts were not sworn in before they gave testimony. The city will serve notice today in state Superior Court that it will not continue with the Cramer Hill project, Primas said. He said he hopes a new plan can be adopted before the end of this year. Cherokee Investment Partners, a North Carolina firm, will remain involved with the Cramer Hill project, Primas said....Even though hundreds of homes will be saved, Cramer Hill activist Jose Santiago said he wanted to know which homes were still on the chopping block. No one should be forced to sell their homes to benefit a private developer like Cherokee, he said. "As far as I'm concerned," he said, "eminent domain is out of the question." Continuing to fight in court for the old plan would have wasted at least another year, Primas said, so the city will save time by taking this new course. He said he hopes a revamped plan, embraced by the neighborhood, will be in place before the end of this year. While many of the 450 homeowners in the largely Hispanic Cramer Hill neighborhood will keep their homes, residents in more than 500

across-the-board increase in state funding. The more can also mean greater state definition of the components and costs of an adequate education, and more state oversight of, and responsibility for improving, local performance. Some of these equity plus concepts have crossed over into equality litigation, further contributing to the blurring of adequacy and equity concerns. Although adequacy gives reformers another legal theory, it has not been a panacea. A number of state supreme courts have concluded that adequacy is nonjusticiable, and others have been locked in long-term conflicts with their legislatures, over remedies. Still, some state courts have been relatively successful in forcing the adoption of significant financial and administrative changes, and adequacy has contributed to a growing concern with education governance as part of the project of school finance reform." This is his summary of his article, "Adding Adequacy to Equity: The Evolving Legal Theory of School Finance Reform," http://ssrn.com/abstract=906145.

public housing units in Centennial and Ablett villages will still be required to relocate. "Where are they going to put all of the people who are living here?" asked Mark Smith, a 38-year-old Ablett Village resident. Primas has promised that places will be found for those living in subsidized public housing. The city also wants to move forward with plans for the Michaels Development Co. to build affordable housing on River Avenue, near 20th Street in Cramer Hill. The number of homes Michaels could build has fluctuated between 72 and 162. Some plans call for 17 residents to lose their homes to make room for the new homes that Michaels wants to build. Olga Pomar of South Jersey Legal Services said she has opposed the Michaels plan because she does not want 17 residents to be forced to surrender their homes. In general, Pomar said, she found the city's announcement to be "good news" but said she still had "serious concerns" because too many details remain unknown. City Council President Angel Fuentes said he has resolved questions about a conflict of interest and will vote on the new Cramer Hill plans. A longtime Cramer Hill resident, Fuentes purchased a home in the neighborhood only weeks before the original plan was made public. He said Cherokee's development plan, which would increase property values in the area, had nothing to do with his decision to buy the home. He bought a house in Cramer Hill to be near his family, Fuentes said. Recently he received a legal opinion from the state Local Finance Board, saying he had no conflict of interest and should be permitted to vote in the future.[160]

Obviously, this situation no longer stands for the tenet of the "minimum scrutiny" regime that government knows better than housing. It stands for the tenet of the New Bill of Rights that housing knows better than government. But how to enforce that? Any change in government plans implicated government purpose and invited relitigation not only of government purpose, but also of other facts involved in minimum scrutiny, such as valuation. This in turn promised further revelations of substitution of private for government purpose. In lieu of political consensus, the boundary dissolves between public opinion and the political system. For example, in *Kelo* the Constitutional status of housing was never raised during any phase of the litigation. Lo and behold, it takes center stage when Susette Kelo loses and still refuses to give up possession of...her housing. The decision could not be enforced; the branches and doctrines of government collapsed, the facts along with them, and the judiciary found itself once again called on to intervene. But who would enforce what it decided? Housing as fact becomes housing as policy; in turn, the policy comes with factual criteria attached, and these criteria are then subject to a relevance inquiry in a counter assertion of housing as policy — all of this takes place without any internally consistent distinctions between judicial and political processes, and without granting housing any more importance than any other fact even though it is at the center of the dispute. It is the blind leading the blind. But it is willful blindness.

Minimum scrutiny as a factual inquiry, only reveals conflicts — then the process stops. The factual criteria for minimum scrutiny do not allow for ranking policies, but they do provide the opportunity for conflicting political actors to attack each others' policies and wait like vultures to see when one of Kennedy's criteria open up the prospect of initiating or stalling a policy. The new factual

---

160 *The Courier Post*, May 26, 2006 (Camden, New Jersey, archived at www.courierpostonline.com).

criteria and the new levels of scrutiny are thus facts themselves: new facts of life for the political system. The scrutiny regime was increasingly forced to articulate itself factually under the pressure of an eroding political consensus. Nevertheless, as it did so it opened itself up to further attack on the issue of internal consistency. That meant decreasing deference — again, enforceability was a problem. Now the regime became simply the decision-maker, but arbitrarily, and coercion became the basis of enforcement — when coercion worked. When facts could not be ranked, only articulated, a new "process" emerged: judicial decision-making all over the map, followed by new trips to the legislature for guidance — which guidance also proved to be all over the map — and finally to renewed conflict with recourse to the court. However, that brings the judiciary into the legislative branch and also causes it to revisit its own decisions, since there is no internal consistency. This was government?

What had happened? Predictably, the scrutiny regime itself had become problematic. It had self-confessedly prevailed on the basis of political, not internal, consistency. Once the political situation turned, there was manifestly no basis for finality in any policy. Every policy was contested at all times, in all branches, and at all levels — that was the legacy of the scrutiny regime. This not only left the individual to theorize from stalemate, it also failed to distinguish those in government, or in policy-making positions, or decision-makers, from those who were not. When property owners refused to cede possession, they were claiming to pick up the fallen mantle of government.

The process began once lawyers put the true facts of *Kelo* together with Kennedy's government purpose factual criteria. They contradicted each other, which meant that the government purpose factual prong of minimum scrutiny suddenly became an attractive litigation target. It could stop even ongoing eminent actions without recourse to argument for a raising of the level of scrutiny for facts, and without recourse to changes in eminent domain laws. The first lawsuit specifically claiming a right to discovery based on Justice Kennedy's criteria, occurred in a New Jersey eminent domain action in which the attorney, Michael Kasanoff, argued: "In his *Kelo* concurrence, Justice Kennedy commented that the evidence showed that New London, 'reviewed a variety of development plans and chose a private developer from a group of applicants rather than picking out a particular transferee beforehand.' Plaintiffs contend that did not happen here. Long Branch [New Jersey city government] promised the area to the [private development business] principals before the [private development business] was even created, and then everything — the designation of the area in need of redevelopment, the creation of [the private development business], the designation of [the private development business] as the developer, the passing of the Ordinance authorizing eminent domain — all were implemented to seal the deal." Indeed, this action reached back into the actions of the principals, pointing out their acquisition of properties and running them down purposely, in order to provide the government finding of "blight" which was legally necessary to proclaim a plan for rede-velopment and the invoking of the eminent domain power.[161]

In another case, conflicts of interest alleged in the eminent domain use auto-matically raised government purpose as a fact because it contested chronology in the decision-making process:

> According to the answers [and motion for discovery, of property owners in response to the city's eminent domain condemnation lawsuit], when the city retained [attorney Arthur] Greenbaum's firm as counsel in connection with the redevelopment project for which the properties were being condemned, Green-baum was, and still is, a member of the board of Hovnanian Enterprises, parent company of Matzel and Mumford, one of the city's designated redevelopers.... Greenbaum's firm, the answer charges, represented Hovnanian Enterprises when it acquired Matzel and Mumford. The Greenbaum firm stands to gain fi-nancially from its representation of Hovnanian Enterprises, Arthur Greenbaum stands to gain financially from any investment he has or had in Hovnanian En-terprises as a result of the subject property's redevelopment," the brief [in sup-port of a discovery motion made in connection with the answer to the condem-nation complaint] states....[The property owners are] also claiming that [city attorney James] Aaron's firm...has a conflict of interest because the firm repre-sents Hovnanian Enterprises and "has an actual conflict and/or an appearance of impropriety in representing the plaintiff in connection with the redevelopment of the subject property. This continued involvement further taints this action and therefore should be void." [Another defense of the property owners is] that the designated developer was involved in dictating what properties should be condemned...."Probably because the developers were doing so well with Phase I of Beachfront North [the first phase of the redevelopment plan]...they wanted more properties and improperly designated this area as condemned," [property owners' attorney William] Ward said in an earlier interview last week.[162]

To which of Kennedy's criteria go which facts alleged by the property own-ers? What would be the basis for deciding that any of the above-alleged facts are *not* relevant to the minimum scrutiny inquiry?

And then, how are the criteria ranked and what weight do we assign to each criterion? The criteria inevitably broaden the scope of the factual inquiry beyond what government would like it to be — which is, no facts at all. On the other hand, there is no limit to the facts at all, because all facts circulate equally within minimum scrutiny. And yet criteria imply ranking of facts — some decision must be made, and these are the criteria for that decision. Round and round it goes. Conceptually, Kennedy's criteria so heavily weigh on the minimum scrutiny in-quiry that they call into question restricted levels of scrutiny — indeed, they are an implied critique of the scrutiny continuum itself. Most importantly, they lead us to conduct that inquiry by articulating the factual criteria of *each* term of *each* level of scrutiny. The scrutiny regime looks to be, either imploding by exploding, or exploding by imploding — driven in either case by an erosion of the political consensus. Indeed, attorney Ward, with thirty-five years' experience in eminent

---

161 Complaint at 6. This complaint is online at www.kevinbrownformayor.com. I have a hand in this and other cases which, in a somewhat haphazard yet continuous fashion, are effecting the transition from the third to the fourth Constitutional epoch.

162 February 16, 2006 (archived at www.atlanticville.gmnews.com).

domain law, makes it clear below, how, employing Kennedy's criteria creatively, he can make these criteria weigh even more heavily on the scrutiny regime so that the government purpose test becomes all factual inquiry and no regime. Result? Endless stalemate. The usual chronology in eminent domain actions was to allow for possession by government, and *then* argue about any remaining issues, such as compensation. But government purpose as a factual inquiry to be carried out through discovery at the *outset* of litigation, mandated enjoining possession until discovery provided the Court with enough evidence to make a preliminary determination as to government purpose. The possession "club" was placed further and further out of reach of the political system as Ward laid out the ramifications of the chronology:

> New Jersey has 1,000 redevelopment projects planned or under way. The deck is stacked against the residential property owner, the small business owner, and even industry....Bruce MacCloud, whose property was seized in 2002 for the Beachfront North Phase I in Long Branch, cannot claim that his 10,000-square-foot property could be used for condominiums like the ones that now stand on his former lot and sell for $630,000 to $1.2 million. He's stuck in the residential zone that existed at the time his property was taken. Long Branch changed the zone to C-6 with a minimum lot size of 80,000 square feet, effectively zoning MacCloud and his neighbors into non-utility. Nothing could be developed unless you owned approximately eight to 12 lots. Who owns or can assemble lots of that size except real estate developers? Certainly not the residents of the bungalows and oceanfront cottages that exist on small lots in the MTOTSA (Marine Terrace, Ocean Terrace, Seaview Avenue) area. These residents were denied permits to improve or develop their properties, or forced to sign waivers they would not claim the value of their improvements in an ensuing condemnation trial. The requested waivers were illegal, but that didn't stop the city from trying to obtain them. Relocation regulations need to further reflect compensation for businesses, business discontinuance and business loss resulting from acquisitions and temporary takings. Battista Auto Body, a business that will be taken for the arena project in Newark, recently lost the beneficial use of its business because access to the property was obstructed for more than one month prior to the taking itself. While the owner waits for his property to be condemned, he has already lost his livelihood and the ability to carry the property and pay employees and related expenses....The law must be balanced so local officials can't just designate whole neighborhoods areas in need of redevelopment, then seize and condemn them for another vague standard, economic benefit....Looking at the enormous profits the developers stand to gain at the expense of senior citizens and families in Long Branch, the concept of public use remains questionable.[163]

---

163 *Asbury Park Press*, May 7, 2006 (Long Branch, New Jersey, archived at www.app.com). And yet the court, citing *Kelo*, declined to halt the eminent domain action: "The court finds that it cannot overturn the city's decision merely because the decision was debatable. No further evidence or testimony is required, as the court is satisfied that the 'area in need of redevelopment' designation was supported by substantial evidence, and therefore was not 'arbitrary, capricious or unreasonable,' according to Lawson's opinion." It appears counsel did not focus on the government purpose test of minimum scrutiny. Quoted in *The Hub*, June 29, 2006 (Red Bank, New Jersey, archived at www.hub.gmnews.com). On appeal, the MTOTSA attorneys brought in the Institute for Justice, which soon had to fight a charge it also faced in the *Kelo* matter: selling out. It wrote the *Asbury Park Press*: "The Oct. 12 [2006] article 'Eminent domain litigants in talks' stated that the Institute for Justice engaging in discussios with city officials and developers about settling the Long Branch

This was the direct result of the Court bringing in an *ad hoc* "facts of the individual" through the back door, instead of opening the front door of the Court to it. What now? The claim of the "minimum scrutiny" regime was that fact had been removed from the Constitution so that public opinion could make its own determination of fact. But public opinion had to find its way back into the Constitution once public opinion became aware that the regime was merely a ruse to allow the Court to impose its own social policy without any interference whatsoever. Buried somewhere deep in the archives is evidence of how long members of the Court felt this particular gambit would last. We will find it one day. One answer certainly is, as long as public opinion would tolerate it. But longer? If so, by what new ruse?

The elaboration — *via* civil discovery in the context of a lawsuit — of the factual inquiry into government purpose, is no surprise: litigants are discovering the power the Court always felt free to exercise quietly. After all, the Court only restricted levels of scrutiny for *other* actors in the political system. The Court itself has always, and freely, made a preliminary judgment — according to hidden, but apparently unrestricted criteria — about the importance of the facts of a case and about how the society should treat them.[164] Only then has the Court turned to the

eminent domain controversy was a 'significant departure' from our earlier claim that the case was ground zero in the fight against eminent domain abuse nationwide. Nothing could be further from the truth. Until eminent domain is taken off the table and the homes in the MTOTSA neighborhood are saved, the Long Branch case will remain at the forefront of our nationwide efforts to stop the abuse of eminent domain for private parties. If the city and the developers wish to discuss ways of keeping people in their homes that would not require the parties to exhaust the appeals process, we are certainly willing to listen and discuss those options. But nothing will shake our resolve and commitment to the MTOTSA homeowners to stop the city and the developers from taking their homes against their will."

164 This is one scholar's account of continuity in pre- and post-*West Coast Hotel* Supreme Court jurisprudence, in which account we discover that the Court never claimed that any of its approaches made any sense: "From the opening of the twentieth century to the 1930s, the Court adopted a particular doctrinal approach to cases in which state police power legislation, or federal legislation based on the commerce power but designed to promote public health, safety, or morals, was challenged as a violation of the due process clauses. The approach, as Chief Justice William Howard Taft described it in his dissent in the 1923 case of *Adkins v. Children's Hospital*, anticipated that judges would be 'pricking out ... [t]he boundary of the police power beyond which its exercise becomes an invasion of the guaranty of liberty under the Fifth and Fourteenth Amendments.' The approach assumed that the Court would regularly be determining the content of 'liberty' in due process cases, and thereby establishing categories of permissible and impermissible legislation. The 'liberty of contract' doctrine that characterized many of the Court's early-twentieth-century decisions was a product of the approach. It was a device to help judges trace out the boundary. The Court's boundary-tracing approach thus assumed that it was appropriate for judges to give content to open-ended provisions in the Constitution such as 'liberty' in the due process clauses. In an 1877 decision, *Munn v. Illinois*, the Court had intimated that the scope of the police power in due process cases was a legislative rather than a judicial question, so that if legislation could be justified on police power grounds, it necessarily met the requirements of due process. By the early twentieth century, that view of the Court's role in due process cases had been replaced with the one Taft described. The emergence of the latter approach meant that any early-twentieth-century justice confronted with a due process challenge to police power or commerce power legislation would be making an

rest of the political system with the Court's will. The "minimum scrutiny" regime is not a method of adjudication, and so it is not the law — it is a veil behind which the real adjudication takes place. The only thing the Court has not done is to tell us why the Court retains total control over this process. That is, the Court is doing an *ad hoc* "facts of the individual" analysis of every element of every case, but the Court winds up assuming power. That violates Madison's rule, and the Court won't tell us why it has committed that violation. Public opinion was no longer satisfied to jump through the — now proliferating — hoops of the scrutiny regime, because there was obviously some sort inscrutable behavior at work in the Court. The proof was the *Kelo* decision itself — the first Supreme Court decision opposed by a flat-out consensus. Evidently the Court could no longer be trusted to give orders.

The fact of government purpose is first invoked in *Marbury*. In *Marbury*, there is in *fact* no government unless there is in *fact* government purpose because lack of government purpose at one fell swoop deprives the Constitutional government of its only two characteristics: its republic form and its democratic content. What now? Ginsburg voted with the majority in *Kelo*. Her own new test, therefore, provides the basis for overturning *Kelo*. *Virginia* also tells us that government *lying* about its "purpose" is an historical policy of animus against an important fact, that is, it is the absence of government purpose which lifts the level of scrutiny for facts — such as the housing in *Kelo* — out of minimum scrutiny to direct scrutiny, or of gender equality above intermediate scrutiny. Why the housing,

---

independent appraisal of the scope of legislative power. That appraisal was incumbent in the technique of 'boundary pricking.' In the 1905 police power–due process case of *Lochner v. New York*, Justice Oliver Wendell Holmes declined to adopt the boundary-pricking approach. He concluded that the doctrine of 'liberty of contract' represented a judicial engrafting of a 'particular economic theory' onto the Constitution, which was illegitimate. As a judge, he maintained, he felt bound to defer to legislative efforts to regulate economic activity if they appeared to be reasonably grounded on protecting public health, safety, or morals. Holmes was alone among the justices who decided *Lochner* in rejecting boundary pricking, and his opinion was not singled out by commentators for several years. Thirty years after the *Lochner* case, the Court continued to use the boundary-pricking approach in police power cases. The boundary-pricking approach adopted by the majority opinion in *Lochner*, which invalidated a New York statute regulating the number of hours that employees could work in the baking industry, was subsequently given the pejorative characterization of 'substantive due process' by commentators, and assailed as a judicial effort to equate 'liberty' in the due process clauses with the ideology of laissez-faire. But it was not invariably solicitous of free markets, or of the interests of employers in labor cases. Court majorities using the approach concluded that states could limit the hours of miners or women, and regulate stockyards, oil pipelines, fire insurance premiums, and the prices of residential leases, coal, and grain futures. Three justices used boundary pricking to conclude that the statute in *Lochner* was a reasonable public health measure. The primary significance of the Court's dominant early-twentieth-century approach to due process cases was thus not that it tended to favor employers over employees, or private interests over public regulators. It was that it decisively affected the way in which justices, whatever their ideological point of view, justified the decisions they reached. A justice such as Holmes, who chose to reject the approach altogether, did so with the realization that he was not engaging his colleagues on their common doctrinal terms." G. Edward White, "Constitutional Change and the New Deal: The Internalist/Externalist Debate," 110 *American Historical Review* 1046, 10-14 (No. 4, October 2005), www.historycooperative. org 10-14 (citations omitted).

which was not raised directly in *Kelo*? Because in *Marbury* the unconstitutional law is not *government*. Since *Marbury* uses an *ad hoc* "facts of the individual" analysis with government as a fact of the individual, the Court must use the facts in order to "say what the law is" — it is reestablishing government, which the unconstitutional law took away. Otherwise, the Court simply connives at the shift from government purpose to private purpose to the elimination of government, which is exactly what the Court did in *Kelo*. Kennedy attempts to correct this by saying that under the "minimum scrutiny" regime, the Court must fully articulate the scrutiny continuum.

The same observation which created a level of scrutiny between intermediate and strict scrutiny, put downward pressure on the scrutiny continuum itself. Since it is the lie which has made the scrutiny continuum a severely disfavored analysis, the *lie* is an indicium of a fact which enjoys *strict* scrutiny. Government lied in *Virginia*; it lied again in *Kelo*. Had Ginsburg been up on her Constitution, she would, in *Virginia*, have been able to establish strict scrutiny for gender legal equality. But then she would not have voted with the majority in *Kelo*.

She can make amends and begin to rehabilitate herself by reversing herself on *Kelo*. In order to prepare herself for that arduous *volte face*, she can study what Justice Kennedy did in *Lawrence*. He has been criticized for discussing *Lawrence* as a liberty issue, not as an issue of government purpose. But he *does* discuss the case as a government purpose. He says, extending Ginsburg's test, that whatever the purpose, it is not a *government* purpose — and that goes to liberty. Why to liberty? Because, according to *Marbury*, government is a fact of the individual. For Kennedy, this means that government is an indicium of liberty, and that is his great contribution in *Lawrence*: the Court had not, prior to *Lawrence*, said what is the *factual* relationship between government and liberty. He is using an *ad hoc* "facts of the individual" analysis to tell us what liberty says government in fact is, what government says liberty in fact is, and so on: this is the Constitution as discovery, and he adds the idea to Due Process. The commentators have remarked on the absence, in *Lawrence*, of any discussion of the level of scrutiny for sexual orientation. But Justice Kennedy *does* tell us what the level is for sexual orientation. If there is no government with respect to liberty, the Court must address directly the *facts* of the case: for Justice Kennedy, whatever Justice Ginsburg's new test implies about a new level of scrutiny between intermediate and strict scrutiny, the new test at *least* stands for intermediate scrutiny. Sexual orientation is a fact of *Lawrence*. So what does liberty tell us government is? It tells us that sexual orientation enjoys intermediate scrutiny. And what does government tell us liberty is? Justice Kennedy is saying that the Court awaits a case in which, for Constitutional purposes, the facts are identical to those in *Virginia*, with the exception that housing is substituted for education. That case will elevate sexual orientation to strict scrutiny.[165]

---

165 *Lawrence* again demonstrates the internal inconsistency of the "minimum scrutiny" regime, and the need for replacing it with the "facts of the individual" analysis: under *Lawrence*, sexual orientation, an indicium of liberty, enjoys intermediate scrutiny, but liberty itself only enjoys relative scrutiny.

Nothing about gender legal equality had changed before Ginsburg elevated it above intermediate scrutiny in *Virginia* — except that it had come more clearly to be seen as a fact of the individual. That alone accounted for its rise in the scrutiny continuum. Since an *ad hoc* "facts of the individual" analysis had brought gender legal equality out of minimum scrutiny in the first place, and then moved it steadily up the scrutiny continuum, other facts would make the same journey, too. It was inevitable. *Reed v. Reed* (1971) brought gender legal equality out of minimum scrutiny by striking down a law giving men preference as administrators of estates. The analysis was apparently minimum scrutiny, but actually the Court used an *ad hoc* direct scrutiny analysis. It said that minimum scrutiny excluded any policy which did not function articulately, by which it meant any that displayed an "arbitrary preference," a rationale not based on any fact.[166] The Court showed that the policy failed the facilitation prong by pointing out that the "probate judge gave no indication that he had attempted to determine the relative capabilities of the competing applicants to perform the functions incident to the administration of an estate."[167] That is, there were no facts showing that women would do a worse job as estate administrators or men a better job. The policy failed the frequency prong because there was no way provided to connect the "arbitrary preference" to establishing "degrees of entitlement [to administer estates] of various classes of persons in accordance with their varying degrees and kinds of relationship to the intestate."[168] The preference was an historical policy of animus against an important fact. But note the Court's summation of what direct scrutiny is: it is a *factual inquiry* into "whether a difference in the sex of competing applicants for letters of administration bears a rational relationship to a state objective that is sought to be advanced by the operation."[169] That is, there is no predisposition on the part of the Court to regard the factual relationship as rational, which is the government's assertion. The Court simply treats that assertion of rationality as another fact which the Court then considers in a *process* of factual examination. In that process, *all* assertions are approached as *facts*, and then subjected to a "facts of the individual" examination by the Court.

A scant five years later, *Craig v. Boren* (1976) lifted gender legal equality to intermediate scrutiny by striking down a statutory scheme prohibiting the sale of 3.2% beer to males under the age of 21 but allowing it to females 18 or older. The Court was able to come up with the black-letter law of that level because between 1971 and 1976 it had continued its examination of the fact of gender legal equality. It emphasized "old notions" and "archaic generalizations" which marked the distance that factual inquiry had traveled. The Court also made it quite clear that other branches of government must also engage in this ongoing factual inquiry as the basis for sustaining levels of scrutiny: it is "necessary that the legislatures choose either to realign their substantive laws in a gender-neutral fashion, or to

---

166  *Reed* at 74.

167  *Id.*, at 73.

168  *Id.*, at 77.

169  *Id.*, at 76.

adopt procedures for identifying those instances where the sex-centered generalization actually comported with fact."[170] The scrutiny continuum was not stable, and the reason was that factual inquiry was a *continuing* process. It is this continuing factual inquiry which required that the Court look at what government policy was in *operation*.

*Virginia* ratified *continuing* examination of the facts as the force which moves facts within the scrutiny continuum, when it looked at gender legal equality again and moved it above intermediate scrutiny. Finally, *Lawrence* treated housing as a continuing process *assumed to be such* by government. This assertion left the Court no room but to find that housing was an indicium of liberty. That was why housing lifted liberty out of minimum scrutiny. Public opinion sensed — even if it could not articulate — this shift, and acted to elevate housing to direct scrutiny at the first opportunity. That opportunity was *Kelo*.

Incidentally, Chief Justice Warren Burger had written the opinion in *Reed* for a unanimous Court. But by the time of *Craig* he had lost the thread of his own argument — he dissented in *Craig*. He had overlooked the most obvious implication of the direct scrutiny analysis: the continuing analysis of one fact could only take place with respect to an expanding number of facts: all facts were subject to evaluation under the "facts of the individual" analysis. He had a clear premonition that elevated scrutiny for gender legal equality would lead to the Court finding an increase in the levels of scrutiny for at *least* education and housing: "[W]e have only recently recognized that our duty is not 'to create substantive constitutional rights in the name of guaranteeing equal protection of the laws.' San Antonio School Dist. v. Rodriguez....Thus, even interests of such importance in our society as public education and housing do not qualify as 'fundamental rights' for equal protection purposes because they have no textually independent constitutional status....[San Antonio] (education); Lindsey v. Normet...(housing)....[S]ince...the Court think the means not irrational, I see no basis for striking down the statute as violative of the Constitution simply because we find it unwise, unneeded, or possibly even a bit foolish."[171] However, *Craig* did not stand for the proposition of lifting housing and education to intermediate scrutiny, merely the *Reed* proposition — Burger's own proposition — of considering government assertions as facts and testing their validity with respect to other facts. It remained for Justice Kennedy to point out that "equal" in "equal protection" meant "truthful" — it meant the *whole* truth, with respect to *all* the facts. Ironically, the implication of Burger's dissent is that he has in fact carried out his own tests, and finds that housing and education do enjoy intermediate scrutiny.

What in *fact*, not in *law*, are the indicia of the shift from government to private purpose? In part, we look to the redevelopment agency to see the facts of the shift. It is to the redevelopment agency state within a state that we must turn, both for the facts and for further elucidation of the collapse of the branches and doctrines of government under the "minimum scrutiny" regime. What, in *fact*, not in *law*, is a redevelopment agency? Since Justice Stevens pointed out that economic

---

170  *Craig* at 198-199.

171  *Id.*, at 216-217.

development — a component of redevelopment — does not distinguish one use of eminent domain from another, what other aspects of redevelopment fail to distinguish it from eminent domain, and fail to satisfy the public purpose requirement? How far does the redevelopment agency as a *fact*, extend? For example, is the Federal Reserve Board in *fact* a redevelopment agency? The Federal Government moved with unseemly haste to take advantage of the sanction the Supreme Court provided for the redevelopment agency: the Federal Government's District of Columbia Redevelopment Act was passed in 1945. The "minimum scrutiny" regime came into effect in 1937, with *West Coast Hotel*. The case which found the Act constitutional, *Berman v. Parker*, provided such blanket authority that there was no substance — only affirmation — for the Court to provide in *Kelo*.[172] Are Fannie Mae and Freddie Mac in *fact*, not in *law*, redevelopment agencies? Are indicia of redevelopment, indicia of redevelopment "agency?" In short, is the supposed government entity, in *fact* a collapse of the doctrines and branches of government?

In part, the opposition of public opinion to *Kelo* was the recognition on the part of public opinion that the *Kelo* opinion was delivered in bad faith.[173] The Court simply lied, and it promulgated a thoroughly discreditable statement behind which it could hide its lies: "The trial judge and all the members of the Supreme Court of Connecticut agreed that there was no evidence of an illegitimate purpose in this case."[174] This statement — part of the "minimum scrutiny" regime of dirty little secrets and lies — makes one ashamed to be an American.[175] And consider the signal it sends! The Court is saying that minimum scrutiny itself is a lie — this flagrant lie is the source of the decline in the Court's credibility. Ste-

---

172  Peter J. Kulick suggests that pure economic analysis may be conclusively presumptive on the issue of private purpose. See Kulick, *op. cit.* Tax increment financing and enforceability may also provide evidence going to a conclusive presumption on the issue. In what ways is the Federal Reserve Board in *fact* (not in *law*) a redevelopment agency — indeed, a precursor or model of the "minimum scrutiny" regime? See Henry W. Chappell, and Rob Roy McGregor, "Fed Chat: FOMC Transcripts and the Politics of Monetary Policymaking," http://ssrn.com/abstract=235882; Gauti B. Eggertsson, and Eric Le Borgne, "The Politics of Central Bank Independence: A Theory of Pandering and Learning in Government," http://ssrn.com/abstract=699481; Cynthia Crawford Lichtenstein, "The FED's New Model of Supervision for 'Large Complex Banking Organizations': Coordinated Risk-Based Supervision of Financial Multinationals for International Financial Stability," http://ssrn.com/abstract=882474; Anthony B. Sanders, "Measuring the Benefits of Fannie Mae and Freddie Mac to Consumers: Between De Minimis and Small?" http://ssrn.com/abstract=830926. See also William Greider, *Secrets of the Temple: How the Federal Reserve Runs the Country* (Simon & Schuster 1989).

173  Bad faith is also studied with respect to legislation: see Richard L. Hasen, "Bad Legislative Intent," http://ssrn.com/abstract=883678.

174  *Kelo*, slip op., at 7-8.

175  We can evaluate the Supreme Court as a fact of the individual by examining the idea of bad faith. We have examples of good faith Supreme Court adjudication, *Marbury* and *Lawrence*. We can compare them to two examples of bad faith Supreme Court adjudication, *Dred Scott* and *Kelo*. In addition, *Dred Scott* and *Kelo* were unenforceable. What, then, are the indicia of bad faith Supreme Court adjudication such that we can say that bad faith Supreme Court adjudication is unenforceable? What are the indicia of bad faith Supreme Court denial of certiorari? See Lynn A. Stout, "Judges as Altruistic Hierarchs," http://ssrn.com/abstract=287458..

vens is attempting to set up a little code in this statement, one which can only be deciphered by those who know minimum scrutiny is a lie; the Court hopes that most will not know that minimum scrutiny is a lie. Decoded, the statement is saying: watch out, the "minimum scrutiny" regime is making us lie here; there are violations of individual rights being committed in the decision in which you are reading this statement. But after *Kelo*, public opinion no longer found acceptable the idea of Constitution as gambit.

Note that Stevens — vain, presumptuous, foolish, as well as mendacious and conniving[176] — never for a moment considers that public opinion might resist the Court's decision, or that the political system might hesitate to enforce it. Neither, for that matter, do any of the dissenting justices. The Court was a set of ninnies, and public opinion would simply not tolerate bad faith on the part of the Supreme Court. No more games.

When we re-litigate *Kelo* under direct scrutiny — using the facts, this time including the lies, not as the truth, but rather, as simple facts — we see how the lies array themselves in the analysis:

### A. Articulately

*1) government can evaluate the rationale in terms of facts;*

Actually, we don't even get to square one on this one, since New London did not have a rationale. However, that is revealing. Absence of a rationale means, not beginning with Parcel 4A [the location of Susette Kelo's house] of the Fort Trumbull neighborhood of New London. The process proceeded *toward* the facts at issue, not *from* them: "The city of New London (hereinafter City) sits at the junction of the Thames River and the Long Island Sound in southeastern Connecticut. Decades of economic decline led a state agency in 1990 to designate the

---

176 Hypocritical, too. It turns out that Justice Stevens, too, has his own method of determining which facts are important. In the Equal Protection context, at least, he expresses his dissatisfaction with the scrutiny regime and doesn't use it in his analysis. This suggests that the reason he found for New London in the *Kelo* case is that he simply doesn't think housing is very important: "The flexibility of Justice Stevens's [Equal Protection] inquiry is not accidental. To the contrary, Justice Stevens expressly views evidentiary eclecticism and case specificity as virtues in the equal protection context. While the Justice will frequently express the meaning of the Equal Protection Clause in broad terms, he is famously unsympathetic to attempts to frame the rules for applying that meaning to cases in a similarly broad fashion. He is skeptical of the utility of 'an attempt to articulate [an equal protection standard] in all-encompassing terms' and dismissive of decisions that turn on the rote application of 'glittering generalities.' For three decades, Justice Stevens has consistently argued for the proposition that the answer to the toughest equal protection cases lies not in broad rules but in the details of the statutory scheme and the accompanying legislative and historical record. As Justice Stevens has endeavored to demonstrate the virtues of his approach, he has consistently used the approach of his colleagues as a foil....[H]e has sharpened the affirmative case for his eclectic and free-form methodology by demonstrating the drawbacks — and on occasion the absurdities — of the standard tiered approach. In critiquing the work of the other Justices, Justice Stevens has shown particular passion and frustration in cases where he believes his colleagues have simply failed to take into account salient pockets of evidence because of the ostensible requirements of their doctrinal rules." This last criticism, in particular, can be made of Justice Stevens in relation to the facial contradictions in the *Kelo* record. Andrew M. Siegel, "Equal Protection Unmodified: Justice John Paul Stevens and the Case for Unmediated Constitutional Interpretation," http://ssrn.com/abstract=9-6624 at 2358.

City a 'distressed municipality.' In 1996, the Federal Government closed the Naval Undersea Warfare Center, which had been located in the Fort Trumbull area of the City and had employed over 1,500 people. In 1998, the City's unemployment rate was nearly double that of the State, and its population of just under 24,000 residents was at its lowest since 1920. These conditions prompted state and local officials to target New London, and particularly its Fort Trumbull area, for economic revitalization."[177] The 4A parcel as an indicium of a "distressed municipality" is speculative and, sure enough, there were no facts to support it.

*2) government does evaluate the rationale in terms of facts;*

This is the point at which the *Kelo* decision has aroused the most ire. However, direct scrutiny transforms this moral outrage into an analysis of fact. New London did not evaluate a rationale in terms of the Parcel 4A properties:

"There is no allegation that any of these properties is blighted or otherwise in poor condition; rather, they were condemned only because they happen to be located in the development area."[178]

"Parcel 4A is slated, mysteriously, for 'park support.' At oral argument, counsel for [New London] conceded the vagueness of this proposed use, and offered that the parcel might eventually be used for parking."[179]

*3) the Court evaluates 1 in relation to 2.*

This is the runner-up for point arousing the most ire. Here are the Court's indicia for the evaluation, as well as the Court's evaluation:

"There is no allegation that any of these properties is blighted or otherwise in poor condition; rather, they were condemned only because they happen to be located in the development area."

### B. facilitates

Evaluate the fact the individual seeks to vindicate in terms of the factually articulated result. What happens to the fact in the process?

This means relating the facts at issue to the proposed "economic revitalization." However, on the one hand there is no fact "that any of these properties is blighted or in poor," and on the other there are no factual indicia of what "might" be done with the properties. That is, there are no facts to support the Parcel 4A as an indicium of "economic revitalization." This came in (a close) third for point arousing the most ire.

### C. a frequent government purpose.

Look at the process of change in the context of what government maintains already in fact exists. What is the factual connection between what is and what results?

The problem here is that "[t]here is no allegation that any of these properties is blighted or otherwise in poor condition...."Thus the 4A parcel is not an indicium of any factual link between a "distressed municipality" and "economic revitalization."

---

177  *Kelo*, slip op., at 1.

178  *Id.*, at 4-5.

179  *Id.*, at 3 (O'Connor, J., dissenting, citations omitted).

That is how direct scrutiny analysis is carried out with respect to a policy regarding housing. In this case, it revealed the total absence of indicia for all factual criteria. The result is this:

Every government purpose analysis is a direct scrutiny analysis.

"Every" in this context means exactly what we have been led to believe it means: the Bill of Rights prevents "every assumption of power in the legislative or executive."

Why did the Court find for New London? Because it "mandated" itself to lie. And what keeps housing from being evaluated under direct scrutiny, rather than minimum scrutiny? That same lie. One lie leads to another — it filters down from the Court to the lowest level of government, and back up again. Once public opinion realized this, resistance began, thereby establishing that realization as an indicium of resistance.

Two issues remain to be cleared up. The first issue concerns Justice Kennedy. How could Justice Kennedy, who found the right to housing in *Lawrence* (not to mention the right to liberty and warrant), sign off on a shoddy lie like *Kelo*, albeit by way of a concurring opinion? The answer is that he uses an *ad hoc* "facts of the individual" analysis instead of a formal facts of the individual analysis. Kennedy, in his jurisprudence, is most often seen peeking out from behind some other Justice's robe, but he seems to be *trying* to understand that the Constitutional climate has changed and he obviously smells a rat in *Kelo*. He says that "[a] court applying rational-basis review under the Public Use Clause should strike down a taking that, by a clear showing, is intended to favor a particular private party, with only incidental or pretextual public benefits, just as a court applying rational-basis review under the Equal Protection Clause must strike down a government classification that is clearly intended to injure a particular class of private parties, with only incidental or pretextual public justifications."[180] However, then he backs off, noting that "[t]he trial court concluded...that benefiting Pfizer was not 'the primary motivation or effect of this development plan'; instead, 'the primary motivation...was to take advantage of Pfizer's presence.'"[181] He signs off on Stevens' lies.

Kennedy's befuddlement lies elsewhere. He does allow for a higher level of scrutiny for facts with respect to eminent domain: "a more stringent standard of review...might be appropriate for a more narrowly drawn category of takings. There may be private transfers in which the risk of undetected impermissible favoritism of private parties is so acute that a presumption...of invalidity is warranted under the Public Use Clause."[182] But what are his indicia of bias toward private parties? He points to a test in which a policy is found to be a taking: it is where the policy "imposes severe retroactive liability on a limited class of parties that could not have anticipated the liability, and the extent of that liability is

---

180  *Id.*, at 1-2 (concurring, citations omitted).

181  *Id.*, at 3.

182  *Id.*, at 4.

substantially disproportionate to the parties' experience."[183] What does he see in such a situation? Animus "against unpopular groups or individuals" with respect to an important fact. From which it follows that the policy cannot be evaluated under minimum scrutiny because it can bear "no legitimate relation" to the policy.[184] That is, Due Process is direct scrutiny. Then why doesn't he sustain the homeowners in *Kelo*? Because *Kelo* was brought under the Public Use Clause of the Fifth Amendment, not under the Due Process Clause of the Fifth Amendment. What is inconsistent about Kennedy's reaction to it? It is the fact that, for Kennedy, a Public Use inquiry embodies and is preceded by a Due Process analysis. Whether reflecting befuddlement or prevarication, Kennedy's concurring opinion in *Kelo* does imply that compensation is subject to direct scrutiny:

## THE RIGHT TO COMPENSATION

Every compensation articulately facilitates a frequent government purpose. A compensation

    1. constructs private property and public use;

    2. facilitates private property and public use; and

    3. sustains private property and public use.

We apply direct scrutiny to compensation with these consequences:

    1. any policy which does *not* articulately facilitate a frequent government purpose, is not a compensation; and

    2. the scrutiny continuum is private property with respect to every public use.

Here we begin to enforce the maintenance right of the New Bill of Rights.[185]

The second issue concerns Justice Ginsburg. How could Justice Ginsburg, who so insisted on the *fact* of purpose in *Virginia* that she invented a new layer of Constitutional scrutiny to bring it off, bolt down the contradictions of a mess like *Kelo* without gagging on them? For it is clear now that not only Ginsburg, but also other Justices, knew the case was fishy. Indeed, as Justice Souter revealed in oral argument,[186] he clearly understood the lie: New London neither could, nor did, evaluate the rationale in terms of the facts, because there was no rationale — it was all a lie. His problem was that he didn't direct his questions to Wesley Horton, the New London attorney, but instead to the Institute for Justice lawyer, Scott Bullock, who for his part was, as we shall see, interested in a political

183  *Eastern Enterprises v. Apfel*, 524 US 498, 529-530 (1998). *Eastern* involves a mining company subject to a new Federal benefits policy for a mining business Eastern sold before enactment of the policy. The Court found the policy an unconstitutional taking.

184  *Id.*, at 548, 549 (citation omitted). Kennedy finds the Federal program unconstitutional on the basis of the Fifth Amendment Due Process clause, without specifically finding that mining companies are "unpopular."

185  The facts of *Kelo* show us that compensation enjoys fixed scrutiny, that is, an involuntary deprivation of compensation must conclusively achieve a preponderant government purpose. The move up in scrutiny to this level in particular is due to the difference between the facts in *Lawrence* (in which there was no warrant) and the facts in *Kelo*. We now await a case in which, for Constitutional purposes, the facts are identical to those in *Kelo*, with the exception that the warrant (there is no warrant in *Kelo*) is substituted for housing. This will elevate compensation to exclusive scrutiny.

186  The entire transcript of oral argument is available online at www.supremecourtus.gov/oral_arguments.

agenda, not in conducting pointed discovery with the goal of aiding his client. In short, a zoo at the Supreme Court. (What a crew!)

> JUSTICE SOUTER: I take it there isn't, but maybe there is, there isn't any question in this case that the city was acting in good faith and did — and I presume still does — intend to convey it to developers who will, will actually proceed to develop a project. Is there a question about that?

> MR. BULLOCK: A question of whether or not the procedure —

> JUSTICE SOUTER: Yeah, in other words, I can understand perfectly well, why we would want to draw a distinction between the use of the eminent domain power that takes a parcel of property from private person A and simply then reconveys it to private person B without any particular object in mind except that the city likes B, you know, the mayor is the Democrat and B is the Democrat. That kind of thing here. The question is when you say there have to be minimum standards, I guess, is do we have a problem historically or in this case about the good faith of the taking so that we need the minimum standards to make sure that we are not getting into the first example?

> MR. BULLOCK: Yes, Your Honor. And there is a number of reasons why there has to be reasonably foreseeable uses —

> JUSTICE SOUTER: Is there a reason in this case? Is there some doubt here?

> MR. BULLOCK: Well, it goes to the doubt about whether or not the public benefits will actually come about in this case. The takings here are really for speculative purposes, pure speculative purposes. And that's where the minimum standards come into play to ensure —

At this very moment, Justice O'Connor interrupts to steer the Court away from this dangerous area (oddly, since she dissented from *Kelo*).

> JUSTICE O'CONNOR: But do you really want courts to be in the business of trying to weigh the evidence to see if the utility will be successful or the hospital will be successful or the road will be well constructed? I mean, what kind of a test are you proposing?[187]

However, it is Justice Ginsburg who takes it on herself to do the enforcing. As we can see in her questioning during the *Kelo* oral argument, she knows exactly what "connivance" means under the "minimum scrutiny" regime — exactly what has to be nailed down. And she nails it down, and makes sure counsel play their role, too. She orchestrates this song and dance to make sure all roles are correctly played:

## A. Articulately

*1) Government can evaluate the rationale in terms of facts;*

> JUSTICE GINSBURG: Mr. Bullock, you are leaving out that New London was in a depressed economic condition, so this is distinguished from the case where the state has no particular reason for wanting this, but the critical fact on

---

187 Transcript of oral argument at 19-20.

the city side, at least, is that this was a depressed community and they wanted to build it up, get more jobs.[188]

JUSTICE GINSBURG: But you concede that on the facts, more than tax revenue was at stake. The community had gone down and down and the town wanted to build it up.[189]

*2) Government does evaluate the rationale in terms of facts;*

JUSTICE GINSBURG: So it's not the area development but this house, will there be — is it reasonably likely that there will be development in that particular plot.[190]

*3) The Court evaluates 1 in relation to 2.*

JUSTICE GINSBURG: Even though in *Berman*, there was a department store that was not blighted, and it was permissible because the whole area was to be improved to raze that department store, even though it wasn't contributing in any way to blight.[191]

## B. facilitates

Evaluate the fact the individual seeks to vindicate in terms of the factually articulated result. What happens to the fact in the process?

JUSTICE GINSBURG: [Most of the property for the "development"]...was voluntarily sold....[192]

## C. a frequent government purpose.

Look at the process of change in the context of what government maintains already in fact exists. What is the factual connection between what is and what results?

JUSTICE GINSBURG: It was a finding, a finding before to be a fact in the trial court that this development was going to be primarily for the benefit of the citizens of New London, and not for the benefit of Pfizer or the private developer.[193]

In fact, so desperate is she to keep the case from going off the rails that at one point she has to rein in her natural ally, Wesley Horton. He seems dangerously prone to wander from the lies into the facts — because, of course, even as he defends the "minimum scrutiny" regime before the Court, he knows each and every fact revealed by *The Day* which you have just read. He *knows* it's all a lie. It must

---

188  *Id.,* at 3-4.

189  *Id.,* at 4.

190  *Id.,* at 25.

191  *Id.,* at 15.

192  *Id.,* at 40.

193  *Id.,* at 33.

have been difficult for him to toe the line. Never mind: Justice Ginsburg is there. And she marches him right back into line:

> MR. HORTON: Your Honor, my position is that purely taking from one person to give to another that shows no public benefit other than just giving from — taking from one person to another would not be a public use....An excellent example of that is the case the other side has cited...where the Trump Association just wanted a parking lot that was next door. There was no assembly problem. No problem putting small parcels together. There was no talk in the case about taxes or more taxes or more jobs or anything....[A]s long as you get over —
>
> JUSTICE GINSBURG: Is that what the Connecticut Supreme Court that we are reviewing said, you — you are arguing, it seems to me, for something that goes beyond what was adjudicated in this case. I mean —
>
> MR. HORTON: Yes.
>
> JUSTICE GINSBURG: It was a finding, a finding before to be a fact in the trial court that this development was going to be primarily for the benefit of the citizens of New London, and not for the benefit of Pfizer or the private developer.
>
> MR. HORTON: Yes, Your Honor. I agree with that and that is why I say my back-up position is you don't need to determine whether you go beyond economic depression of a city in this particular case.[194]

In short, his "back-up" position — to be used in case the true facts inadvertently slipped out — is that "economic depression" is to be assumed without needing to be proved. And why not? Again, under the "minimum scrutiny" regime, the law is that a lie is the least rational construction of the facts. The logical consequence — and here he adds a new minimum scrutiny test — is that the lie is a threshold test for invoking minimum scrutiny. You must lie or else the Court won't give you what you want.

But why was it so important that he be marched back into line? Because unless the ruse was maintained, the regime itself was directly threatened. The lies went directly to the heart of the "minimum scrutiny" regime. This was not a case about eminent domain — eminent domain merely implicated the "minimum scrutiny" regime itself through its founder, Oliver Wendell Holmes:

> MR. HORTON: But as I say, Your Honor, if public use and public purpose are the same thing, which they are unless you're going to overrule Holmes' decisions from 1905 and 1906....
>
> JUSTICE GINSBURG: Well, I think you'd have to take some substantial chunks of language out of Berman as well, because Justice Douglas spoke very expansively in that case.
>
> MR. HORTON: Plus I think Holmes was right when he said that to say that the public actually has to use the property is not an appropriate meaning of the

---

194 *Id.*, at 32-33.

phrase, so I would not think you'd want to revisit that case, even if you want to revisit some other of Holmes' decisions.[195]

They did not scruple to go over the bald terms of this connivance, even with Susette Kelo — the victim of it — sitting in the courtroom as it was gone over. This chiding and cajoling — all in the service of pure graft — saw the Supreme Court at its lowest ebb, groveling abjectly before a dirty deal, groveling precisely because they knew it was dirty. When the Court acts as browbeating thug, things have to change: this was the message of public opinion in response to the *Kelo* decision.

But to revert to Ginsburg's motivation. How could she bring herself to participate in this unholy alliance? How could she fail to open up the argument to confront the facial contradictions? Since the "minimum scrutiny" regime is founded on lies, facts of the individual constantly reveal this foundation: try as they might, the regime's minions can't quite keep the truth from coming out. She purposely turns a blind eye to the facial contradictions right there on the pleadings and in the testimony:

1. redevelopment in the face of housing;
2. destruction of housing without purpose.

But these are simply the facts reported in *The Day*: they are the lies. Which, of course, is why Ginsburg must hustle the Court — and everyone else (but not, as it turned out, the country) — past them: no dawdling, no second thoughts, above all no hesitation. This is public works and payola: it's going down. The "minimum scrutiny" regime forces the Court to stipulate to lies as law — this from a Court whose duty, according to John Marshall, is to say what the law is. Ginsburg reveals the place of the Supreme Court in the "minimum scrutiny" regime: the Supreme Court imposes false facts on itself, on lower courts, on the trier of fact. Note that that is precisely what Justice Stevens said in his opinion for the Court. It is entirely in line with traditional implementation of the "minimum scrutiny" regime, as one commentator noted:

> [The *Kelo* decision reveals] a marked preference for preserving and furthering [the Court's] vision of an institutional system of governance — a jurisprudence that is focused on the question of who should decide rather than on the substantive issue of what should be decided, and that is committed to the passive virtue of deference. In short, the Rehnquist Court explicitly chose to adopt a "legal process" approach to takings. Because it privileges structure and process over explicit considerations of substantive legal and normative issues, this approach is unsatisfactory to property and constitutional theorists; because it defers to government decisions, it is maddening to property rights advocates; and because it is technocratic and abstract, it is unsatisfactory to the public. Given the prominence of the legal process approach to constitutional review of state regulatory action in the post-New Deal era, however, judicial passivity remains attractive, if unromantic, to judicial actors. [196]

---

195 *Id.*, at 50-51.

196 Mark Fenster, summarizing his article, "The Takings Clause, Version 2005: The Legal Process of Constitutional Property Rights," http://ssrn.com/abstract=888755.

If the Court feels free to lie about the facts, then what *is* it doing? Process — balancing, allocating between the branches of government — is the means by which the Court attempts to prevent public opinion from breaking into the political system. The hodgepodge of doctrines which constitute the Court's scrutiny jurisprudence, are the (apparently) disorganized points, times and ways in which public opinion has done so. How then do we square what Hamilton said about the impotence of the Court, with what Marshall says is its duty? By the Court dealing with facts, as everyone else does. After the *Kelo* decision, and it part in reaction to it, a referendum was placed on the South Dakota ballot:

> The South Dakota Judicial Accountability Initiative Law [JAIL] is a ballot measure that would establish a process to allow litigants to sue judges for various kinds of misconduct....The proposed amendment to the state's constitution would create a special grand jury that would have the power to set aside a judge's judicial immunity and allow a petitioner to sue a judge for either civil or criminal misconduct. JAIL is intended to address a laundry list of alleged judicial abuses, including eminent domain abuse, probate fraud, falsification of court records, and family court misconduct, says Gary Zerman, a Valencia, Calif., lawyer who is both a consultant and spokesman for JAIL. The text of the amendment, posted on the Web site [www.jail4judges.org], says judges shall not have immunity for
>
> - Deliberate violations of the law, or of the state or federal constitutions.
> - Fraud or conspiracy.
> - Intentional violations of due process.
> - Deliberate disregard of material facts.
> - Judicial acts without jurisdiction.
> - Acts that impede the lawful conclusion of a case, including unreasonable delay and willful rendering of an unlawful judgment or order.[197]

Rebecca Love-Kourlis, formerly of the Colorado Supreme Court, tried to explain the reason this initiative found its way onto the ballot, and in doing so revealed the unreal world into which the scrutiny regime had forced the judiciary:

> "My sense is it falls into two general categories. One of them is dissatisfaction with the court system itself, based on personal experience or the stories of neighbors and friends. People believe the system is inefficient, extraordinarily costly, unpredictable and slow. I think the other general cause is a pretty widespread lack of understanding about what courts are supposed to do. There was an American Bar Association poll taken last year in which most people agreed that courts routinely overruled the will of the majority. Courts are not supposed to be enforcing the will of the majority, except that they are charged with enforcing laws as written. They are also charged with safeguarding constitutional rights and those can be at odds with the views of the majority. But that's the beauty of our system of government. The courts serve as a check and balance in our system, and many people don't understand that. There is actually a third reason. I think there is a foam along the top of the wave that I'd attribute to

---

197 Quoted on the American Homeowners Resource Center (June 20, 2006, archived at www.ahrc.com).

people who believe the courts are too activist. I do think that happens on oc-casion, but far less than the media would suggest to the average reader. When you look at the millions of cases around the country each year, the number that bubble up to the appellate system where the result could be political is really de minimis."[198]

Missing from this analysis is the idea that public opinion had concluded that the scrutiny regime is inherently corrupt, and that therefore the judiciary enforc-ing it is inherently corrupt and has to have its power removed as part of the de-struction of the scrutiny regime. Her sense of the facts has been so deformed by the scrutiny regime, that she cannot even isolate the facts alleged by the refer-endum. It never occurs to her that the referendum is, in fact, an indictment—so she never feels obliged to defend the judiciary in terms of the allegations. This decadence doomed the scrutiny regime.

The *Kelo* counsel were besotted by politics, but even they couldn't help pro-posing a "reasonableness" test. They stumbled toward a demand that the Court look through the lies to the truth:

> JUSTICE O'CONNOR: What is your test?
>
> MR. BULLOCK: Well, the test, Your Honor, for —
>
> JUSTICE O'CONNOR: Is it no economic development purpose?
>
> MR. BULLOCK: Yes. Yes. When it's only justified in order to gain the sec-ondary benefits from ordinary private uses of land, and the way that businesses always make use of their land to try to make money or to try to make a profit. That's our bright line rule. But for our second test, if this Court accepts that eco-nomic development can be a public use, then we advocate a test of reasonably foreseeable uses and minimum standards in order to counter the dangers posed by such private involvement in the use of eminent domain power....Those could be such things as a commencement date for the project, a construction schedule, financial eligibility for the developers, there's a number of different things.[199]

The disruptive nature of the "minimum scrutiny" regime is why the Court itself couldn't help asking if the housing was being destroyed to any purpose:

> JUSTICE O'CONNOR: And there's some — to be developed first, you say that your clients lived in parcels that are not likely to be developed soon, if at all. So when making this determination, is development reasonably likely, do you have to do it parcel by parcel or can it be with the whole —
>
> MR. BULLOCK: No, Your Honor. We believe it should be done where the property is actually being conveyed.[200]

But why Ginsburg's collusion? She did it because she was still suffering from WCHS, West Coast Hotel Syndrome. One of the characteristics of this disease is severe impairment of acknowledgment of facts. Also, like everyone who signs off on the "minimum scrutiny" regime — and as we see blatantly displayed in her

---

198 *Newsweek*, October 24, 2006.

199 Transcript at 15-18.

200 *Id.*, at 25.

line of "questioning" — she thinks it's about public works, giving people jobs, the money, and so she's duly bringing home the bacon for the "minimum scrutiny" regime. Things only get done by lying. By the way, is she still suffering from WCHS?

We also clearly see how close the *Kelo* property owners came to winning their case. The vote was 5-4, and both Kennedy and Ginsburg voted with the majority. However, the *Kelo* property owners' counsel — instead of confronting the contradictions — decided to throw it all away. For what? As we shall see, it was so counsel could broadcast fascism. What do the *Kelo* property owners think of that legal strategy now? They were betrayed on every hand, not least by a public opinion which did not want a right to housing. Like Justice Kennedy, the *Kelo* property owners were trapped and reduced to sad shifts in an attempt to get out of a dreadfully stupid policy.

In *Kelo* the Court was being asked to return to the time when the Court DID exercise something like strict scrutiny — and for most legislation. Then, with the advent of the Progressive era, protest developed over the sort of scrutiny the Court was exercising under the guise of strict scrutiny: it was voiding most reform legislation. This led to the Court-packing crisis, when Franklin Roosevelt threatened to attempt to expand the Court in order appoint enough justices to overturn decisions voiding New Deal legislation. At that point, the Court adopted, in *West Coast Hotel*, what Oliver Wendell Holmes had long suggested: barring violation of some other provision of the Constitution, legislation should be found Constitutional if it was rationally related to a legitimate government purpose.[201] Note, however, that as government grew larger — as the number of rules increased — it also became importance for corruption to find expression as formal rules. As we shall see, "minimum scrutiny" became one of those rules.

"Economic development" has always been an important bugbear of the "property rights" legal movement. The movement, like the IJ argument, views "property rights" as the foundation of all other liberties, and feels that the recognition of "property rights" protects other freedoms. Indeed, "property rights" advocates view this recognition as the barrier against a police state. Curiously, the "property rights" movement also often finds itself opposing restrictions on new development. It maintains that the erosion in liberties principally results from community restrictions on new development. Local zoning measures, for instance, restrict where new buildings can be constructed and their size. Environmental statutes set limits on development in natural areas. The "property rights" movement's concern is that government asserts a measure of control that infringes on fundamental freedoms. This reveals the hidden agenda of the IJ argument in *Kelo*: not that there is an insufficient reason for the eminent domain action in *Kelo*, but rather, that there is no good reason for any government action at all.

Predictably after *Kelo*, a rash of legislation was proposed, eliminating the right of government entities to use eminent domain for "economic development." The problem with these proposals is that there is no logical content in the concept of

---

201 Marian McKenna, *Franklin Roosevelt and the Great Constitutional War* (Fordham University Press 2002).

"economic development," just as there is none in "private use" or "property rights." Justice Stevens, in his *Kelo* opinion, revealed the intellectual bankruptcy of the "property rights" movement when he noted that "[t]here is...no principled way of distinguishing economic development from the other public purposes that we have recognized." He said that "neither precedent nor logic supports" the IJ position — a damning indictment.[202]

Nor were these virtues in evidence in the proposals to "overturn" *Kelo*. From the point of view of Madison's statement regarding the Bill of Rights, the problem with the "property rights" argument is that these rights are not defined in terms of facts. Because "property rights" are not defined factually, they cannot limit "economic development" — they don't tell you what a "property right," in fact, *is*; therefore they cannot tell you what "economic development," in law, should *not be*. The old rule applies: you can't beat something with nothing. It should also be noted that, even if the IJ had succeeded in its claim, it would still have left housing vulnerable to an eminent domain action which met the IJ standard. This again points up the fact that although the *Kelo* case was about housing, the IJ supported neither a right to housing nor housing itself, only a rule which did not increase rights in housing and still, under circumstances the IJ specified, made housing fair game.

The Court did not overrule the Michigan law or *Hathcock*, but since that law and the holding do not relate to specific facts either, they can hardly be considered substantive restraints on the use of eminent domain. Instead, they invite creative ways of maintaining title or "oversight" in the public entity while effective control passes to private parties.[203] Note that the IJ never made another argu-

---

202 545 US ___ (slip op., at 14).

203 Here is an easy way to evade the *Hathcock* ruling: "In planning to move Ace Hardware to a central downtown location, the City of Beloit's [Wisconsin] Community Development Authority (CDA) will acquire properties in the 400 block of Broad Street and 200 block of Pleasant Street through eminent domain. The CDA voted Wednesday night to utilize eminent domain after declaring several properties blighted. Ace Hardware will move from its Pleasant Street location to Broad Street by 2007 following action taken by the Beloit City Council Sept. 6. The city council approved a development agreement between Harris Ace Hardware and the City of Beloit, approving the city's purchase of the Ace Hardware property. The planned use for the property is to extend park property along the shores of the Rock River. Both the City Council and the City Plan Commission recommended the project and the council authorized the CDA to acquire the properties on Broad Street through eminent domain for occupation by the new Ace store. Stateline Properties, LLC — a Ken Hendricks company — owns the parcels at 210 and 214 Pleasant Street and 440 and 448 Broad Street. Martin Kades owns parcels at 430 and 434 Broad Street and 441 St. Paul. Roger Bryden's RVB Partnership owns the land at 426 Broad Street. The City Council does not have jurisdiction to give land to a private company. The CDA can do so through eminent domain if it determines the properties are blighted. The CDA held a public hearing Wednesday, deciding that the properties are blighted. According to 66.1333(2m)(3)(bm) State Statutes, an area may be designated as blighted due to a number of structural and conditional characteristics such as unsafe structures, obsolete platting, fire hazards or diversity of ownership — anything that 'substantially impairs or arrests the sound growth of the community.' Labeling a property as blighted does not mean the structure is ready to collapse, Assistant City Manager Steve Gregg said, rather the city looks for any factors to qualify it for such a designation. Gregg said obtaining the land by eminent domain as opposed to traditional means is preferred as it safeguards against any landowner refusing

ment which was available to it: that eminent domain over housing — destroying
it — simply is not "economic development." Nor, of course, could it argue that a
housed individual *is* "economic development" — *i.e.*, the argument it was looking
for was right before its eyes (and the eyes of Justice Stevens too, for that matter).[204] Under the New Bill of Rights, the formulation is: with respect to housing eminent domain is never a "public use." That is a slight change of policy. It
immediately raises the question, whether any involuntary deprivation of hous-

---

to sell and preventing the entire block from coming into the CDA's possession. Despite
a 'scary' connotation, Gregg said eminent domain does protect landowners by ensuring
them the market value for their property. Law requires the city to provide alternative sites
for business owners displaced through eminent domain. The city will hire an appraiser to
assess the land but must also pay for a second appraiser if the owner requests a second
opinion. The city also will hire a relocation specialist to plan the move of the existing tenants....Oscar Roman, owner of La Belle Boutique on Broad Street, said....he will be sorry to
leave his downtown spot where his clothing and accessories store has been for the past
nine months. 'Most of these businesses are so big they can find customers anywhere,' he
said. 'It's the smaller businesses that suffer.'" *Beloit Daily News*, September 30, 2005 (Beloit,
Wisconsin, archived at www.beloitdailynews.com).

As Adam Mossoff notes: "*In Kelo v. City of New London*, the Supreme Court held that economic development is a public use under the Fifth Amendment, but offered property
owners some solace in federalism. Justice Stevens noted that many States already impose
'public use' requirements that are stricter than the federal baseline, citing the Michigan
Supreme Court's July 29, 2004, decision in *County of Wayne v. Hathcock*. In *Hathcock*, the
Michigan Supreme Court unanimously reversed its famous 1981 *Poletown* decision, holding
that economic development is not a public use under the eminent domain provision in
Michigan's constitution. But was Justice Stevens justified in citing *Hathcock* as an example
of a stricter limitation on the use of a state's eminent domain power? This essay suggests
that he may not have been....[B]right-line rules typically become nullified in practice by alternative standards-based regimes....Something similar may occur under *Hathcock*, because
the Michigan Supreme Court identified a standards-based exception to its bright-line rule
prohibiting economic development in the use of eminent domain power-blight removal.
As a standards-based legal regime, blight doctrine provides substantial discretion to local
authorities in determining if property is blighted. Courts routinely defer to these policy
judgments by public authorities. The result is that this standards-based exception may
ultimately swamp the bright-line rule — economic development may continue with the
aid of the state's eminent domain power under the rubric of blight removal. If this occurs,
then Justice Stevens's paean to stricter state rules is mistaken, and property owners in
Michigan and in the other states that have adopted blight exceptions to prohibitions on
economic development are no more safe under their state constitutions than under the federal constitution." This is his summary of his paper, "The Death of Poletown: The Future
of Eminent Domain and Urban Development after *County of Wayne v. Hathcock*," http://ssrn.
com/abstract=775885.

204 We have only recently begun to study the idea that facts of the individual are not policy desiderata but, rather, are in *fact*, the economy and economic growth. See Fabio Sabatini,
"Social Capital, Public Spending and the Quality of Economic Development: The Case of
Italy," 2006 (archived at http://www.feem.it/Feem/default.htm); Helje Kaldaru and Eve
Parts, "The Effect of Macro-level Social Capital on Sustainable Economic Development,"
http://ssrn.com/abstract=875435; Henry Saffer, "The Demand for Social Interaction," http://
ssrn.com/abstract=875732; Nan Lin, *Social Capital* (Cambridge 2001). Given the enormous
role of zoning in facilitating and protecting housing, and that facts enjoy only minimum
scrutiny with respect to zoning, is zoning in fact housing? Is minimum scrutiny in fact
housing? See William A. Fischel, "Municipal Corporations, Homeowners, and the Benefit
View of the Property Tax," http://ssrn.com/abstract=233210; Peter H. Schuck, "Subsidizing
and Mandating Diversity: Residential Neighborhoods," http://ssrn.com/abstract=305819.

ing is due process? Finally, the IJ couldn't argue that "economic development" is coterminous with eminent domain — that is, that all facts receive strict scrutiny with respect to eminent domain — because it reserved the right to use eminent domain in some situations. The IJ couldn't make these arguments because the concept of "economic development" has no distinguishing factual characteristics. Unfortunately for the "property rights" argument, however, that leads us to the conclusion that "property rights" allow eminent domain over housing (and indeed is contemplated in the "property rights" eminent domain model legislation). Do supporters of "property rights" know this? Would they care?

"Property rights" advocates fight shy of defining exactly what rights those are in terms of facts. Housing, for them, is not a "property right:" that wasn't argued by the IJ in *Kelo*, either. Why not? Because, as the IJ lawyers explained to me, they do not believe there is a Constitutional right to housing — something which might surprise the *Kelo* homeowners. Again, this foreclosed an option to limit "economic development." In the end, the Court found the distinction meaningless; it was without factual content, a distinction without a difference: drivel.

It strangely turns out that the "property rights" movement avoids facts precisely because dealing with them would involve demanding rights, although rights are ostensibly what the movement is demanding. Conclusion? It is not a rights movement at all. What is it, then? It is simply a power movement — by means of power, for the end of power. Period. It resembles the movement to return to gold as the sole store of value: those who have value are those who have gold. Those survive who have power: power is the only thing which survives. Power is all — legally, conceptually, politically.[205] The similarity of the "property rights" movement to fascism should not be underestimated. Fascism has two ideas: power and the leader. The "property rights" movement has the idea of power; it lacks only the leader, and the pathological inability of public opinion to articulate rights provides an *entrée* for such a leader because it brings on the situation that tends to produce such leaders: the spreading paralysis of the political system, with corruption as its last surviving reflex.[206]

Far from being an argument which implies controls over eminent domain, the point of view of the "property rights" movement implies no controls over eminent domain: "In....the months since the *Kelo* decision, several municipalities have moved to take property from small businesses in hopes of boosting tax revenue. Many of the cases are of the replace-the-corner-butcher-with-a-Wal-Mart variety, but others fit less neatly into a David vs. Goliath story line: [by] 2007, Baltimore officials hope that their research park will be home to several bootstrapping biotech entrepreneurs....[and] Freeport's [Louisiana] redevelopment plan seems like a great opportunity for small business along the Texas Gulf Coast....

205 Indeed, the views of the "property rights" movement extend back in time at least to the *Legal Tender Cases*, 79 US 457 (1870).

206 The most recent—and by far the most sophisticated—attempt to distill the essence of fascism, is Gregor, A. James, *Mussolini's Intellectuals: Fascist Social and Political Thought* (Princeton University Press 2006). Although it traces out several more dimensions of fascism, these tend to collapse back into the notions of power and the leader.

Wright Gore III's family shrimp-packing operation, Western Seafood, owns one of the plots that Freeport officials are condemning for the marina. 'We would understand if the city wanted our land for a bridge, a road, or a tunnel,' says Gore, whose company is challenging the seizures in federal court. 'But we feel it's un-American to take our property to enrich our next-door neighbor.' That's a common sentiment among property-rights advocates in the wake of the *Kelo* decision....Yet eminent domain disputes are about market competition as much as property rights. From a Darwinian perspective, as opposed to a legal or moral one, eminent domain is simply a mechanism that allows more capable (read: wealthy and politically connected) entrepreneurs to exploit market opportunities at the expense of their less capable brethren...."[207] The inconsistencies of the "property rights" movement are the successful result of undermining individual rights. Undermining individual rights has led to an infirm understanding of individual rights and this facilitates facile "property rights" notions. Note also that no anti-eminent domain group actually advocates eliminating the Takings Clause of the Fifth Amendment. They want the power — but they want it to be used the way *they* want it to be used.

There was no fact sought to be advanced by the IJ in *Kelo* — that was why it lost. What then was sought to be advanced? The people who are involved in the "property rights" movement. And it is a movement. Stripping out the partisanship from the following account, what is the ideological mechanism by which the "property rights" movement extends the definition of eminent domain? Does this signal the need for a corresponding elevation of facts of the individual on the part of groups — such as environmental protection groups — which have simply relied on a combination of public opinion and the Federal Government's tax and spend power?

> Cattle rancher, dairy farmer and Chairman of the House Resources Committee, 42-year-old Rep. Richard Pombo ([Republican]-CA) recently accomplished one of the top priorities of the nation's resource extraction industries. On September 29, Pombo, along with co-sponsor Rep. Dennis Cardoza ([Democrat]-CA) and considerable help from Rep. Greg Walden ([Republican]-OR), was able to push a gutting of the 1973 Endangered Species Act (ESA) called the Threatened and Endangered Species Recovery Act (TESRA) through the House on a 229-193 vote. Here is what TESRA accomplishes:
>
> - Full compensation for "takings" which has often meant merely denying landowners the ability to pollute or threaten species. Under TESRA, any disputes over value of such "takings" "are to be resolved in the favor of the property owner." (Of course, if a government entity actually does take your property to build a Wal-Mart or some other economic development scheme, as allowed by the recent Supreme Court *Kelo v. New London* decision, no such resolution in favor of the homeowner is available.)
> - No more Critical Habitat designations. Instead, calling habitat designation "irrelevant to recovery," Pombo gained a switch to required "recovery plans" when a species is listed as threatened or endangered;

---

207 *Fortune Magazine*, October 2005 (archived at www.fortune.com).

- Much more power will be vested in the states in determining such "Recovery Plans;"
- "No surprises protection." Property owners are protected against any future changes to "Recovery Plans" forever, no matter what changed conditions may require;
- Invasive Species (a huge problem with cattle ranching) are not addressed at all. Clearly the ESA has not been working. Out of almost 1300 species listed, only 10 have recovered and been de-listed. Obviously, with a less than 1% recovery rate, the protection provisions have not been tough enough! Yet, Pombo has achieved this extraction wet dream of lessening those meager protections, while selling it as protection for private property owners.

Rep. Dennis Cardoza notes: "I am confident that this bi-partisan bill will strengthen the ability of ESA to recover species, while reducing the burden on local economies and landowners." TESRA supporter Rep. Joe Baca ([Democrat]-CA) adds: "Passing the new legislation will remove burdens that have hampered job creation, community development and other improvements for the Inland Empire." However, when one looks past the veneer of property rights, economic development and, of course, species recovery (wink, wink), it doesn't take much to find corporate fingerprints all over TESRA. Industry's main ally in this is something called the International Foundation for the Conservation of Natural Resources (IFCNR). This Mother of all Astroturf groups claims in its website that "IFCNR takes a holistic view of protecting wildlife and wild places that includes preserving human cultures. Conservation & preservation of wild resources requires a measured degree of sustainable use."[208]

But note that the "property rights" movement is not at all democratically oriented. At the point the "property rights" movement came to prominence, public opinion had retreated into itself — become a detached entity — in the process of forming a new view of facts. Of this motive the movement knew little and cared not at all. There was no evidence that public opinion supported the "power" argument of the movement, but neither did the movement ever seek such support. Indeed, as its opponents pointed out, the movement hid its point of view behind public opinion's concern with such facts as housing — it never moved beyond that to come to grips with public opinion's complicated understanding of the facts.

The "power" argument would simply have to be foisted on public opinion — revealed at a later date, when it came into force and there was no countervailing force. What the "property rights" movement is not, then, is a legal argument. The longer the "property rights" movement refuses to identify the facts with respect to which there are rights (and, by the way, what rights those are), the more clearly it reveals itself, not as a lobby, movement or even a political party, but rather as something surprising: an *extra*-legal movement. "This cause lacks nothing but a cause."[209]

---

208 *Counterpunch*, October 21, 2005 (archived at www.counterpunch.org).

209 Cicero, quoted in Christian Meier, *Caesar* (Basic Books 1996) at 5.

The "property rights" movement is fond of court cases, but only because the court is a public forum — the court is propaganda in the form of litigation. To lose because you have *no facts* to assert, *either* against precedent *or* with respect to the new rule you would establish, is to believe that litigation is a useful form of self-advertisement. Indeed, unbeknownst to the *Kelo* property owners, propaganda was the agenda when the Institute for Justice took the case. They had simply been used: "Paul Farmer, executive director of the American Planning Association[, said that the opposition to eminent domain]....was not so much a popular revolt as a well-financed attack by the Institute for Justice and its affiliate, the Castle Coalition. He said the organization is substantially financed by Richard Mellon Scaife, a Pittsburgh billionaire and supporter of ultraconservative causes. 'The Institute for Justice was prepared to spend $3 million in a public relations campaign regardless of how the court ruled,' Farmer said."[210] The "property rights" underworld turned out to be just as murky and lurid as the eminent domain underworld. This was not a battle of ideas: it was a battle of anacondas, a debate within the quasifascist camp. What was there to decide in such a debate?

Currently the "property rights" movement is exactly that "assumption of power" against which Madison vindicates "every" fact of the individual. Note, however, that the "property rights" movement only loses because it lacks facts. They day it gets them, the situation changes. Then the movement finds itself in the same position as everyone else: no one ever knows all the facts. Then we must look at it again. In addition, to be fair, it's not as if the political system made any attempt whatever to justify *Kelo* in terms of individual rights. If anything, it engaged in exuberant acclamation. According to Representative Nancy Pelosi of California, *Kelo* "is a decision of the Supreme Court. If Congress wants to change it, it will require legislation of a level of a constitutional amendment. So this is almost as if God has spoken. It's an elementary discussion now. They have made

---

210 *Kansas City Star*, November 1, 2005 (Kansas City, Missouri, archived at www.kansascity.com). A list of grants to the Institute for Justice can be found at www.mediatransparency.org. More on the Scaife Foundation can be found at www.scaife.com. More on Scaife can be found at the People for the American Way website: www.pfaw.org. It gets worse: "The public face of the Institute is Clint Bolick, the right's favorite media talking head and a protégé of Clarence Thomas since their days together at Reagan's Equal Employment Opportunity Commission. Bolick's Institute for Justice was started with hundreds of thousands of dollars in grants supplied by the three Koch family foundations. In 1993 the Kochs gave $700,000 to the Institute, 70% of its budget. The Kochs continue to play a major role in financing the Institute, while a representative of the Charles Koch Foundation has one of the five seats on its board. The quiet workings of the right's foundation and think tank apparatus in the planning and nurturing of the assault on the public infrastructure have been a mostly behind-the-scenes operation. State-financed school vouchers, attacks on public television and radio, privatizing welfare, indeed the whole privatization movement, can be traced to the agenda and funding pattern of the richest, in-your-face, hard right foundations....The John M. Olin, Lynde and Harry Bradley, and Sarah Scaife foundations, along with the three right libertarian foundations run by David and Charles Koch, have been the primary sponsors of this agenda....The think tanks with innocuous sounding names create the experts with their papers and reports, while the far right laissez-fairest foundations and their money men keep the cash flowing. They are, in reality, a tightly knit and mutually supported network working in close concert." Archived online at the website of The Progressive Populist, www.populist.com.

the decision."[211] The *Minneapolis Star Tribune* even exulted in the threat of eminent domain: the "real value [of eminent domain] lies not in its execution but in its leverage. Just having the *authority* to condemn blighted land has been enough...."[212] The National League of Cities was vociferous in its support of the decision in *Kelo*. Nominally a liberal group, it suddenly became an advocate of states' rights when it became a matter of reforming eminent domain:

> [It claimed that Congress] appears to have shifted land use controls from the local and state level to the federal level, assuming a self-appointed role as the nation's zoning board, according to NLC officials. "The practical effects from this bill [a proposal in Congress to restrict eminent domain] — should it ever become law — could be to freeze the process of public-private economic development projects across the country," said NLC Executive Director Don Borut, citing vague and confusing definitions of economic development contained in the bill....[The League] also stressed that the use of eminent domain is already closely governed through state statute and local ordinances, and any changes should be made at the state level. "Each state should have the opportunity to assess its individual needs, economic requirements, geographic and demographic changes, as well as the age of its communities to determine to what extent eminent domain should and can be used and under what circumstances," Borut said.... "This bill expressly preserves the right of power companies, gas and oil companies, and railroad and utility companies to exercise the power of eminent domain for their business purposes," wrote Hartford, Conn., Mayor Eddie Perez in a letter to several Members of Congress. "Apparently, states, cities and towns can't be trusted with eminent domain, but large private corporations will be allowed to use this power as they see fit.'"[213]

God and states' rights: these were the slogans of a doomed political system. Not a word was said about raising the level of scrutiny for facts which — the opposition to *Kelo* had revealed — were of great importance to public opinion. Seemingly fallen victim to a cunning plot, the liberal elite had wedded themselves to — and thus been trapped by — the scrutiny regime. It surprised everyone that in the event they had no policy alternatives. It shouldn't have. Corruption of the entire political system, on a massive scale, had intervened between *West Coast Hotel* and *Kelo*. Savvy liberals would have foreseen the revolt against *Kelo* and laid the groundwork for expanded individually enforceable rights. They did no such thing. Why not? Because corruption overtakes even the savvy. Liberals found they had been disarmed when facts with respect to which they putatively held the high ground — such as housing — migrated, under cover of eminent domain, to the murky right-wing "ideologies" of the "property rights" movement. What could liberals say? They supported the most important policy of the "property rights" movement: opposition to increased individually enforceable rights. On that there was an iron consensus across the spectrum of political system ideologies. And so liberals stood by helplessly as their consensus came to be marooned on the right-wing ideological fringes. Power had abandoned them.

---

211  Transcript of a June 30, 2005, press conference (archived at www.usnewswire.com).

212  *Minneapolis Star Tribune*, December 9, 2005.

213  November 4, 2005 (archived at www.usnewswire.com).

The liberals' policy — the "minimum scrutiny" regime — had laid such a stranglehold on the political system that the system could not be reformed. Indeed, propaganda had so thoroughly fulfilled its mission that there was no conception of what reform might be with respect to the regime. The regime seemed to be reality itself — this alone was symptomatic of a serious pathology. And the logical conclusion of the lack of alternatives was political stalemate. This in turn raised the accusation liberals had always dreaded: they cannot govern because they are agents of disorder. That rebounded on the political system: if the liberals failed, the alternative was no advocacy of order. What now?

It turned out that there was only discretion, pure power — and not policy — with respect to facts; that way, for example, housing could be asserted as a goal without having to take account of extant housing. Forbidden judicial interference in the other branches of government, was the excuse for this approach — transparently, flimsily so. It was an excuse which — through passive resistance, violence or otherwise — was bound to collapse. Such remoteness from reality in the political system suggested an imminent loss of power — and that is exactly what happened. No organ of the political system ever even asked why the system had been surprised by the opposition to *Kelo*.[214]

---

214 Once it became clear that simple resistance to eminent domain decisions was delaying the use of eminent domain, the political system tried in vain to come up formulations which would allow it to continue its usage of eminent domain while convincing resisters to stop resisting. Justice Stevens' comment that "economic development" had no logical content, suddenly cut across the political system's reliance on that concept as an explanation to public opinion for using eminent domain. Caught unawares, the system's theoreticians attempted a rush to the rescue. Here is an example of this "death throes" mentality: "Although California's redevelopment law is among the strictest in the nation, from a layperson's perspective, redevelopment agencies (RDAs) appear to be no more obstructed from their projects in California as they would be in, say, Connecticut....If redevelopment powers are 'over-harvested' such as to instigate serious political revolt against them, they will become barren and useless, and will no longer be available for the purposes for which they were intended and for which they are still needed. Even assuming that redevelopment is efficacious and necessary, redevelopment law ought not be made impotent. In a post-*Kelo* society, redevelopment finds itself in danger of being neutered of its ability to do what it is truly meant to do: to overcome market failure in urban areas and restore and preserve the vitality of our communities. If redevelopment agencies abuse their powers by manipulating the market rather than facilitating it, they expose themselves to political attack in an already volatile property rights climate. We are in need of reform that reminds RDAs why they exist in the first place: as market-facilitators, not revenue-generators. The problem cannot be properly addressed at the local level....[U]nscrupulous businesses will employ hostage-taker strategies to capture the RDA's eminent domain power. Cities are left resorting to economically-cogent-yet-legally-pathetic claims such as 'future blight' in order to appease '800 pound gorillas' like Costco or Wal-Mart. Thus it is not enough for local governments to self-regulate their use of eminent domain; the regulation must come from without. Because an ill-conceived redevelopment regime allows rent-seekers to blackmail cities, and because it entices cities to use coercive bargaining and offend landowners' sensibilities, RDAs are in danger of ruining the tools it needs to achieve their true purpose of blight removal. Thus without careful review, RDAs threaten to kill the golden goose. The solution lies in removing the blight from our redevelopment law, and in redeveloping the motivation that drives our redevelopment agencies." Tim Kowal, summarizing his article, "Who Will Redevelop Redevelopment?" http://law.bepress.com/expresso/eps/1396.

Nor is it fair to ignore the fact that not only did the "property rights" move-ment and supporters of *Kelo* depend on minimum scrutiny to sanction their pro-posals, but also, "grassroots" political organizations depended on it. It turns out that no one along the political spectrum, wanted to raise the level of scrutiny for facts. This demonstrates how well minimum scrutiny had succeeded in retarding the discussion of individual rights. The "New Rules Project" of the Institute for Local Self-Reliance, was an awkward mix of felt wrongs and hazy rights:

> The rules call for:
> - Decisions made by those who will feel the impact of those decisions.
> - Communities accepting responsibility for the welfare of their mem-bers and for the next generation.
> - Households and communities possessing or owning sufficient pro-ductive capacity to generate real wealth.
>
> These are the principles of "new localism." They call upon us to begin view-ing our communities and our regions not only as places of residence, recreation and retail but as places that nurture active and informed citizens with the skills and productive capacity to generate real wealth and the authority to govern their own lives.
>
> All human societies are governed by rules. We make the rules and the rules make us. Thus, the heart of this web site is a growing storehouse of community and local economy-building rules — laws, regulations, and ordinances — be-cause these are the concrete expression of our values. They channel entrepre-neurial energy and investment capital and scientific genius. The New Rules Project identifies rules that honor a sense of place and prize rootedness, conti-nuity and stability as well as innovation and enterprise....
>
> **Doesn't localism pose a threat to those who are not in the majority? Doesn't it allow those with means, or power, to secede from responsibility for the whole, leaving the powerless behind?**
>
> If localism were absolute, yes, it would do that. But it is not. Localism is an approach that allows us to sort out which roles are appropriate for which lev-els of government. Guarantees of basic rights must come from the federal level. Higher levels of government appropriately should set floors — *e.g.*, a minimum wage or a minimum level of environmental compliance or minimum guarantees of political rights — but not ceilings. They should not pre-empt lower levels of government from exceeding those minimums (as international trade agree-ments do, for instance).
>
> **Why would localism guarantee efficient, environmentally benign development?**
>
> It doesn't. There are no guarantees in a true democracy, because power rests with the citizens. But it does create the possibility. And without local-ism, we are guaranteed the opposite: rootless corporations with no allegiance to place, other than to the place with the lowest wages and least environmental restrictions; long lines of transportation, which are inherently polluting; and out-of-scale development that wrecks neighborhoods and destroys habitat. By its very nature, localism would shorten transportation lines, encourage rooted businesses, demand an active citizenry. Localism is a development concept that

would enable humanly-scaled, environmentally healthy, politically active, economically robust communities.[215]

This, too, is an argument for power as power, just as in the case of the Institute for Justice. Not a word is said about the individual enforceability of any of the facts set forth. The "facts" themselves are desiderata. The discussion proceeds, not from what is, but rather, from what ought to be. Minimum scrutiny for decisions by localities is taken for granted. "Local" is as vague as "property rights." Its logical content is problematic when its advocates grant that "[g]uarantees of basic rights must come from the federal level." Assuming that the higher the level of government, the more important the right protected by it, can backfire. When California put an "inverse condemnation" clause in its eminent domain ballot initiative, critics complained about "taxpayer requirements any time a local or state agency enacts a law or regulation that a property owner claims 'devalues' his or her property. For instance, if voters or a city or county conclude that 50 homes can be built on a piece of property and the developer contends that the property could hold 200 homes — this measure allows the developer to sue the local government (ultimately taxpayers) to demand a payout for the value of the land as if the other 150 homes could be built. 'It essentially guts local communities' ability to make decisions in the best interest of all residents and gives that power to a few large, wealthy landowners,' said Chris McKenzie, executive director of the League of California Cities."[216] But if the right was sufficiently important for it to be protected by state law, then what could localism argue against it? That "localism" is important? What kind of importance does it have? The same importance as freedom from an establishment of religion? But localism does not claim localism as a fact, much less a fact of the individual. There is thus no difference, here, from the program of the Institute for Justice, because there is no program. There is only power. Yet another shadow government in the shadow world of minimum scrutiny. Localism could not prevent the further removal of facts from the control of public opinion — it did not advocate any facts.

Even a group as corrupt as the Supreme Court rejected the "property rights" movement. But why? It was the logical implication of the "minimum scrutiny" regime. Still, it was too clearly a jostle for power. It was too overt, a premature show of the hand. Not now, the Court was saying: perhaps later, perhaps the society will deteriorate sufficiently so that your gang will get the call. Have the right-wing think tanks go back, recrunch the numbers, conspire to better effect. In the meantime, the "minimum scrutiny" regime was quite corrupt enough for the Court's purposes. And then there was that glaring *faux pas*: suggesting in open court that the Justices end the regime. In case the IJ hadn't noticed, the Justices were part of the regime. Very distressing. Clearly, a reconstituted police state would need to present a better front than the oafish "property rights" clowns.

---

215 See the "New Rules Project" on the Institute for Local Self-Reliance website, www. ilsr.org. Links to a wide-ranging group of grassroots organizations are provided at www. grassroots.org.

216 Press release of the Coalition to Protect California, June 27, 2006 (archived at www. prnewswire.com).

In short, no case for a coup having been made, why change thieves mid-theft? Justice Stevens said in *Kelo* that "nothing in our opinion precludes any State from placing further restrictions on its exercise of the takings power,"[217] but he is saying that the States have the power to restrict eminent domain by raising the level of scrutiny for the fact underlying the case, which in *Kelo* is housing. Clearly not by any other means, because restricting it by generalities will lead only to stalemate. This has two implications: first, for the Court, attempts to restrict eminent domain with generalities, alters the role of the states in the Federal system, a gambit the Court will not undertake. Will we now see a spate of cases advocating facts? Probably not, if *Kelo* is any indication, because in these cases it is clear that there is no focus yet on facts — detectable in them is an inability or unwillingness to focus on facts. Second, and more importantly, if "economic development" does not distinguish "types" of eminent domain, the implication is not that eminent domain is subject to minimum scrutiny; instead, the implication is that eminent domain is a fact, and whatever else are the indicia of that fact, housing is one of them.

Thus, without facts of some sort, the "property rights" movement is simply another government-in-waiting, a shadow cabinet lacking the facts to make itself a power.[218] In all this is the missed opportunity to make the case. The IJ could easily have done so even after it lost. It could have petitioned for a rehearing "on the merits" (Rule 44). The Court will grant rehearings to consider historical evidence bearing on the Framers' intent.[219] Using Madison's statement, it could have argued that housing is what Madison means when he says "every." Using the tests laid out for a fact of the individual, it could have claimed that

1. New London seeks to destroy the housing at issue in the case;
2. New London itself has granted that these homeowners will have to, and will, seek other housing, so there is no dispute the eminent domain action would simply destroy an incarnation of a fact which would be replicated;
3. association, speech and several other protected facts are sought to be destroyed by the eminent domain action;
4. the *Kelo* eminent domain action is part of a nationwide, well thought-out plan between developers and politicians to use eminent domain to turn housing over to private developers (here the IJ has done its homework and documented fully, what is a truly insidious process); and
5. the *Kelo* eminent domain action does not specifically fulfill an overriding government purpose.

Now that argument awaits another day and another case.[220]

---

217 Slip op., at 19.

218 On the Constitutional politics of opposition to Kelo, see Marcilynn A. Burke, "Much Ado About Nothing: *Kelo v. City of New London, Sweet Home v. Babbitt*, and other Tales from the Supreme Court," http://ssrn.com/abstract=895008.

219 *Reid v. Covert*, 352 US 901 (1956).

220 An exceedingly unreflective and uninformed petition for rehearing — rejected by the Court on August 22, 2005 — was submitted by the IJ. The Court had suggested what the article above also suggests: that transfers of property to private owners might mean

Will that day arrive? Probably — but in the distant future. The proposals to "overturn" *Kelo* are logically empty and feckless. They are not, however, without significance. In the article I suggested that it takes a long time for a consensus to form, that a particular fact is a fact of the individual. When that consensus occurs it tends to do so rapidly and to be embodied swiftly in legislation, but in the meantime the law does not change even slightly to elevate the fact. The change tends to be all or nothing. American opposition to involuntary servitude, for example, was strong and articulate long before the Thirteenth Amendment was ratified banning involuntary servitude. Before the Civil War and contemporaneous ratification, however, involuntary servitude was firmly embedded in law and practice in this country. In fact, the *Dred Scott* decision of 1857 actually *increased* the rights of slave owners. And yet involuntary servitude completely disappeared during the Civil War; in a few years it went from being a doctrine enshrined and strengthened in the Constitution, to being removed entirely from the Constitution.

Before the legal change occurs, two processes are at work: perfecting the "black letter" law to express the desired new situation and what, for lack of a better term, might be called "informing" the consensus. A good example of the first process is the formation of the Equal Rights Amendment, which hasn't changed since it was written in 1923 (it still isn't in the Constitution).[221] The second process involves education, both by persuasion and example: articulating the reasoning behind the proposed change and publicizing extreme examples of why the change needs to occur and the benefits of the change. Eminent domain was exercised over housing long before *Kelo*. Suddenly that is a horror story. The significance of the opposition to *Kelo* — as opposed to its legal meaning — is that it reflects a change in the attitude of Americans toward housing. It should be noted that the *Kelo* decision changes nothing — it simply allows to continue happening what has always happened. What has changed is the attitude toward what

a criminal or Constitutionally prohibited motive was at work. It referred to these "hypothetical cases posited by petitioners" and said that they "can be confronted if and when they arise." 545 US ___ (slip op., at 16-17). Actually, the IJ never said that such cases as it posited involved either situation, merely that they involved transfers for economic development.

Nevertheless, in its petition for rehearing, the IJ ignored the Court's qualification, paraded a list of eminent domain actions going forward subsequent to the Court's decision, and indicated that the "abuses" had already begun; it requested a rehearing based on the notion that "eminent domain for economic development purposes" discriminated against those who could not afford to litigate "on public use grounds." Petitioner's Brief at 7; this and other briefs in the case are available online at www.ij.org. Apparently a stab at a Fourteenth Amendment "suspect class" argument, the brief did not cite that Amendment, nor did it take cognizance of the Court's holding, in *San Antonio*, that poverty does not create a suspect class. The IJ also forfeited the opportunity afforded by the petition, to rebut the Court's finding that "economic development" has no logical or factual content. The IJ claimed that the Court, which was merely restating standards of eminent domain misuse, had instead promulgated "a new standard for examination of public use claims in economic development." It requested a remand to examine possible misuse, without presenting any evidence of misuse in the *Kelo* case itself. *Id.*, at 7, 8. Not a word was said about any right to housing.

221 See, for example, www.ratifyeraflorida.net. Also www.ERAcampaign.net.

is happening. Is it is enough of a change? Obviously not, at least for increasing scrutiny for housing. The change in attitude doesn't even necessarily bode well for increasing rights in housing; *Kelo* may be part of a movement of an altogether different tendency.

When their principles fail to deliver results, organizations like the IJ lose supporters, who reformulate the principles.[222] What are those principles? Not surprisingly, much of the change in attitude with respect to facts, occurs first among those with a stake in the facts. Giving more rights to housing — even if it means restricting eminent domain — is not a new idea. Perhaps (and this is also suggested in the article) eminent domain over housing is starting to creep up the socioeconomic ladder: it is becoming more "noticeable" because the individuals affected are more powerful and articulate. And yet even among those homeowners fighting eminent domain actions — even among their advocates — there is still no evidence of a belief in *any* right to housing. There is, perhaps, a sense that there is something wrong, but no clear articulation of a right. This suggests that current eminent domain actions over housing are politically marginal. By themselves they simply don't affect a large enough number of people — directly, or indirectly as a stimulus to rethink individual rights — to change the consensus on housing. Most people don't lose their housing to eminent domain — ever. Is "more" what is "needed?"

On the other hand, most people are not involuntarily deprived of medical care, education, maintenance or liberty, but that does not determine whether they are or are not facts of the individual. As with every fact of the individual, the New Bill of Rights is an individually enforceable right to survive, but it has not always been clear that a fact of the individual is an individually enforceable right to survive; in the meantime, the ambiguity of public opinion is bound to result in ambiguous — transitional — legal concepts. For example, the theoretical foundations of the right to privacy and penumbral rights are clearly embryonic formulations of the idea of a fact of the individual. The unending search for such facts is well put by Samuel Warren and Louis Brandeis at the very beginning of their landmark essay on privacy: "That the individual shall have full protection in person and in property is a principle as old as the common law; but it has been found necessary from

---

222 For a revealing look at Justice Scalia's bungling of the "property rights" agenda, see Richard James Lazarus, "The Measure of a Justice: Justice Scalia and the Faltering of the Property Rights Movement within the U.S. Supreme Court," http://ssrn.com/abstract=847666. Scalia's penchant for shooting from the lip has been the undoing of his jurisprudence. If ever other than a clown, he is certainly one now, as Justice Blackmun's papers amply reveal. His papers also starkly reveal that Blackmum felt Sandra Day O'Connor was an idiot. See also Laura Underkuffler, "*Tahoe*'s Requiem: The Death of the Scalian View of Property and Justice," http://ssrn.com/abstract=820266. For the opposite point of view — that Scalia actually has ideas — see Bradford R. Clark, "The Constitutional Structure and the Jurisprudence of Justice Scalia," *http://ssrn.com/abstract=453521*.

time to time to define anew the exact nature and extent of such protection."[223] It is worth noting that throughout the essay it is the "individual" who enjoys the right to privacy.

Warren and Brandeis see the right to privacy arising from patently inappropriate extensions of existing doctrine in order to make room for newly recognized remedies: some new law is obviously called for. In developing the right of an individual to be — in the homely phrasing of the right to privacy — let alone, the problem the authors needed to solve and could not, was, determining what "let alone" meant. That needed an explanation of what is an individual, which explanation they could not provide, and so the argument tended to assume what it was trying to establish. The unrecognized flaw was the individual as an assumption, rather than as enumerable results, of the law. The authors were trying to serve two masters, and ended up giving precedence to the law over the individual; they looked at the law as a repository rather than as a process. This obviously reflected perceived constraints within the Constitution — but those are only constraints of an understanding of the individual. Giving precedence to the law over the individual was not a mistake the Founders made, although as we have seen, they were uncertain and fearful, and tempted to do so.

There is something of a reverse problem with penumbral rights. Supposedly they "help give...life and substance" to "specific guarantees in the Bill of Rights,"[224] as Justice Douglas put it in *Griswold v. Connecticut*, which found unconstitutional, bans on the sale of contraceptives to adults. However, the notion of penumbra immediately begins to swallow the rights themselves: they become all penumbra, and no rights. Defending the formulation by pointing out that the words of the rights themselves are in the Constitution, progressively begs the question as the penumbra progressively swallow the definitions of the words. Again, the law is looked on as a repository, rather than as the process it is; if you don't know what process that is, you tend to restrict it, even though you are being led on irresistibly to expand it — the irresistibility itself comes to be seen as justification for restricting it. Note that in asserting the Constitutionality of both privacy and penumbral rights, forthright resort is had by the authors, to a concept of the individual which is *apart from* the Constitution. A dual struggle is going on: these writers are struggling both to articulate the idea of a fact of the individual, and to identify the fact itself. It is remarkable that neither Douglas nor Brandeis and Warren, take any account of Founder intent. No statement by any Founder is mentioned, or for that matter, any Founder — not Madison, not Jefferson, none; in the name of expediency, Founder intent has been balanced off the scale. Both concepts — privacy and "penumbral" rights — are, clearly, revoltingly meager and reveal how little progress has been made in understanding the individual since the ratification of the Constitution.

With this going on in the political system, it is not clear that "more" — some other ingredient added to the legal-political mix — is a good point of view of

---

223 Samuel Warren and Louis D. Brandeis, "The Right to Privacy," 4 *Harvard Law Review* 193 (1890).

224 *Griswold v. Connecticut*, 381 US 479, 485 (1965).

what happens when a fact is elevated from minimum to strict scrutiny; it seems more than sufficient as an explanation of the perpetually unsettled state of the law. Indeed, pointing out conflict has tended to restrict the process of change — in order to effect a particular change — because, again, it tends to view the law as a machine or some other kind of object needing alteration, instead of as a process. The law may well be static or mechanical, but history suggests that we are too busy struggling, to reach that question; it seems only to be reached by writers on the law. History suggests that we are part of the struggle and can't disentangle ourselves sufficiently to put ourselves — much less the law — outside of it. At most we can ask: what other state-of-the-art legal doctrines await clarification as facts of the individual, or as formulations of the word "every" as Madison used it?

History *seems* to indicate that crises, of varying degrees, lead to the elevation of scrutiny of facts and it seems to be worthwhile to take note of the struggles which have attended the elevation of various facts. The Civil War ended slavery, the Equal Rights Amendment is still not in the Constitution, and in between lies the civil unrest which brought about legal equality.[225] Is that the way it works? Nor will we be finished with eminent domain even if it is restricted as to housing. I have been asked what happens if an individual's business is seized by eminent domain and the business is the individual's sole source of income. Has the maintenance right been violated? What if a business is seized and an employee loses employment? Has the maintenance right been violated? I just don't know. Such questions are bewildering — what they are not, is hypothetical. They are factual situations which exist now, and must somehow be resolved — with vast implications for American life. However, the question does suggest that *formulation* of an individually enforceable right means the process of the *identification* of further facts of the individual, has begun. That would mean that the New Bill of Rights — the bare beginnings of the enforcement of which are traced in this essay — is already in the past, probably in the fairly distant past.[226] And certainly we are long overdue for understanding what, in fact, is maintenance. Our Supreme Court, through its doctrines over two hundred years, has ordered that we remain in ignorance of that fact. We shall see, however, whether its writ still runs.

What does seem clear is that at least two factors are involved in elevating scrutiny for a fact: circumstances which prompt a change in the consensus with respect to a fact, and words which express that change. Certainly in *Kelo* the Court has reiterated its opposition to elevation "in the air." Before it can exalt, you have to tell it the fact you want exalted. The "property rights" movement may not be interested in providing the answer to that question. To change the law, however, that is what the Court requires.

---

225 See Jack M. Balkin, "How Social Movements Change (or Fail to Change) the Constitution: The Case of the New Departure," http://ssrn.com/abstract=847164.

226 That is, strict scrutiny is problematic with respect to a fact of the individual, but also, how was the New Bill of Rights construed so as to undermine the individual and inhibit inquiry into the facts of the individual? Where is evidence of that in this essay?

## THE NEW RIGHT TO HOUSING UNDER THE NEW DUE PROCESS ANALYSIS

The following applies the entirely new Due Process analysis promulgated by the Court in *Lawrence*, an analysis we shall call the "how not why" analysis (under *Lawrence*, Constitutional analysis *in toto* is "how not why").[227] Note that the Court arrives at its new analysis by conflating the Due Process Clauses of the Fifth Amendment and Fourteenth Amendment: "Had those who drew and ratified the Due Process Clauses of the Fifth Amendment [requiring due process for the Federal Government] or the Fourteenth Amendment [requiring due process for the states] known the components of liberty in its manifold possibilities, they might have been more specific. They did not presume to have this insight. They knew times can blind us to certain truths and later generations can see that laws once thought necessary and proper in fact serve only to oppress. As the Constitution endures, persons in every generation can invoke its principles in their own search for greater freedom."[228] Note that one of the indicia of liberty is — not freedom — but rather, "greater" freedom, meaning that liberty is a process.[229] Note that oppression as a "fact" implies that Due Process is a fact. Note also that this new analysis obliges us to state *how*, not *why*, eminent domain over housing violates the Due Process Clauses, or, now, Due Process; the *Lawrence* Court does not tell us why Fifth and Fourteenth Amendment Due Process are conflated — it tells us the result of that conflation. For the Court — echoing John Marshall — that conflation is what the Constitution is.

When the Court conflates Fourteenth Amendment Due Process and Fifth Amendment Due Process, it produces the right to liberty. When it conflates Fourteenth Amendment Due Process and the First Amendment, it produces the right to education.[230] Education and liberty share an indicium, in the view of the

---

227 See also Daniel O. Conkle, "Three Theories of Substantive Due Process," http://ssrn. com/abstract=911628.

228 *Lawrence* at 578-579.

229 It echoes "free" in "free exercise thereof," suggesting that, as in the case of liberty, one of the indicia of freedom of religion is process. For what other facts of the individual is process an indicium — for example, what is the housing process? Is process an indicium for a fact of the individual? What, in fact, is process?

230 *Grutter v. Bollinger*, 539 US 244 (2003). In *Grutter*, diversity supposedly survives strict scrutiny. However, the Court derives that holding from the liberty component of the First Amendment; the liberty component is in the application of the First Amendment to the states through the Due Process Clause of the Fourteenth Amendment. So what is really going on? The Court is establishing a liberty component to the Equal Protection Clause (under which the case is brought) in order to justify its decision. Much as, in *Lawrence*, Justice Kennedy found that privacy goes to liberty, in *Grutter* diversity goes to liberty. *Grutter* doesn't vindicate diversity against strict scrutiny — it elevates liberty out of minimum scrutiny, from an interest to an individually enforceable right. *Grutter* vindicates liberty. What Kennedy complains about in his dissent — and what the commentators note — is that the Court abolishes the scrutiny continuum by ascribing a liberty component to equal protection. Nevertheless, *Grutter* was decided at the same time as *Lawrence*, and equally reflects an intent to abandon the scrutiny continuum. In protest at the notion, the *Grutter* Court says that "[s]trict scrutiny is not 'strict in theory, but fatal in fact.'" (At 326, citation omitted). Whatever that may mean in general, in *Grutter* strict scrutiny does prove fatal — to strict scrutiny. The doctrine enunciated in both *Grutter* and *Lawrence* is

Court. In liberty, it is expressed as a choice to associate. In education, it is expressed as a choice to engage in robust debate.[231] One suspects that, for the Court, this indicium is an indicium of Due Process, and that Due Process is, *inter alia*, *in fact* a process of choice (this was the conclusion in *Roe v. Wade*,[232] which has now been expanded to the entire Constitution). What in *fact* (not in *law*) is Fifth Amendment Due Process? What in *fact* (not in *law*) is Fourteenth Amendment Due Process? The Court no longer sees Due Process as a part of the government machine, or as a tool to be used on that machine — it doesn't see government as a machine at all. Government itself is a fact of the individual.

That is why the Court sees education and liberty — formerly regarded as facts instituted or controlled by, or indeed having at any relation at all to, government — as facts of the individual. Indeed, the Court has reversed itself: it now sees government institution and control (what government proposes to do and does) as indicia of a fact of the individual. Under minimum scrutiny, facts such as liberty and education were perquisites of government; but (and this has not been noticed previously) the *Lawrence* Court abolished minimum scrutiny in every case, and now government is a perquisite of the individual. How has the individual made use of that perquisite? This is an entirely new question, but just as John Marshall suggested was the case, there is no master or servant here, or even any power. There is only the individual. This allows us to ask another new question: what in fact is government? This is a question the Founders have already asked and answered regarding Due Process and the Court has affirmed the answer. With regard to everything else, looking on government as a fact gives us a new perspective on the way the Supreme Court operates: government as a fact enjoys strict scrutiny. In what context? That question compels admission of facts, but that admission is forbidden by minimum scrutiny. This contradiction guarantees opposition, not to the facts, but rather, to the Court. It is a prescription for scofflaws.

In order to show that Due Process protects housing, the *Lawrence* analysis requires a *factual* showing that government treats housing the way it treats free

---

that facts which enjoy strict scrutiny, are facts of the individual and are vindicated in every case.

Under the *Grutter* facts, education now enjoys threshold scrutiny, that is, an involuntary deprivation of education must measurably effect a common government purpose. We now await a case in which, for Constitutional purposes, the facts are identical to those in *Grutter*, with the exception that due process is substituted for liberty. This will elevate education to exclusive scrutiny, that is, an involuntary deprivation of education will have to urgently implement a vital government purpose.
We see now that the Court in *Boyd* did not quite have its hands around the right question: what is the result when the Fourth and Fifth Amendments are conflated? What happens when substantive due process is conflated with the Fifth Amendment takings clause? Nothing related to the clause, apparently, because it is not part of that clause, according to *Lingle v. Chevron*, 544 US ___ (2005).

231  For a discussion of *Grutter* and *Lawrence* as signaling the end of the "minimum scrutiny" regime, see Calvin R. Massey, "The New Formalism: Requiem for Tiered Scrutiny?" http://ssrn.com/abstract=540122.

232  410 US 113 (1973).

speech and freedom of religion. There is no burden of proof as to why the Founders established Due Process — it is there. The false step of "why" is the entire history of "affirmative" rights and their failure before the Court. We move on. The Due Process Clause states that "No person shall...be deprived of life, liberty, or property, without due process of law...."(There is, of course, an identical provision in Article First, Section 8 of the Connecticut Constitution, so abridging housing also violates the Connecticut Constitution.) This provision is covered by James Madison in his famous statement, so it prevents "every assumption of power in the legislative or executive...."

With regard to freedom of religion, the First Amendment says that "Congress shall make no law respecting an establishment of religion, or prohibiting the free exercise thereof...."With regard to free speech, the First Amendment says that "Congress shall make no law...abridging the freedom of speech, or of the press...."These statements re-phrase Madison's statement as prohibitions: every=no.[233] And so the First Amendment prevents "every assumption of power in the executive of legislative...."Therefore, laws which propose to abridge, or abridge, freedom from an establishment of religion or the free exercise of religion, or speech, or the press, are assumptions of power. This is also something which has never been pointed out before.

We can also say that the First Amendment prevents every establishment of religion or prohibition of the free exercise of religion, or abridgment of the freedom of speech, or of the press. From this it follows that every law which proposes to abridge freedom from an establishment of religion or the free exercise of religion, is an assumption of power.[234] Likewise, every law which abridges freedom from an establishment of religion or the free exercise of religion, is an assumption of power. And so every law which proposes to abridge freedom of speech, or of the press, is an assumption of power and every law which abridges freedom of speech, or of the press, is an assumption of power.[235]

These conclusions also apply to joint abridgements: every law which proposes to abridge, or abridges, freedom from an establishment of religion or the free exercise of religion, and proposes to abridge, or abridges, freedom of speech, or of the press, is an assumption of power. As we stated above, every law which proposes an assumption of power, is without due process of law, and every law which establishes an assumption of power, is without due process of law.

Now the eminent domain actions in New London come into focus as violations of Due Process. The actions propose to abridge Susette Kelo's housing, and so are an assumption of power. The actions also abridge her housing, and are an assumption of power. Thus, the actions' proposal to abridge, and their abridgement of, her housing, are an assumption of power. It follows that the actions

---

233 But what, in fact, is freedom of speech? It is moot in any dispute if the parties stipulate what in fact it is, but what if they don't agree? Then we come to know that currently our understanding is pitifully primitive as to what, in fact, freedom of speech is. See Larry Alexander, "Freedom of Expression as a Human Right," http://ssrn.com/abstract=285432.

234 See *Lemon v. Kurtzman*, 403 US 602 (1971).

235 See *Bantam Books v. Sullivan*, 372 US 58 (1963).

propose an assumption of power, and are without due process of law. The actions also establish an assumption of power, and are without due process of law. The actions violate the Due Process Clause of the Fifth Amendment, which was sought to be shown. Involuntary deprivation of housing violates Due Process because it violates a fact of the individual.

This then is the mechanism provided in the Constitution for evaluating facts in the Constitution, and recently affirmed in *Lawrence*. According to the Court in *Lawrence*, there are only three tests on which evidence is admissible in determining whether a fact is vindicated: 1) is the fact in the Constitution? 2) does government propose to abridge the fact? 3) does government abridge the fact? Susette Kelo's housing is "property" in the Fifth Amendment. Government treatment of her housing is the same as government treatment of freedom from an establishment of religion or the free exercise of religion, and freedom of speech, or of the press: government proposes to abridge, and abridges, her housing. The burden, therefore, shifts to government to show that its treatment of housing differs from its treatment of freedom from an establishment of religion or the free exercise of religion, and freedom of speech, or of the press. Government cannot meet that burden.

These facts have certain consequences. No individual is involuntarily deprived of housing because no individual could ever be involuntarily deprived of housing — and that is because there is no fact of government in housing.[236] Government is removed from housing, not through any "process," but rather, by bringing it into the Constitution. This is the process to which James Madison and John Marshall alluded, or, Constitutional Process. For the Court, this replaces all accumulated Constitutional jurisprudence.

In one respect Justice Powell was right: he indicated in *San Antonio* that it is not relevant to inquire *why* protected facts are in the Constitution; it is not the right approach to give those as *reasons* facts are in the Constitution. The question is not, *why* a fact *should be* protected in the Constitution. The Court wants to know *that* a fact *is* protected in the Constitution. Facts in the Constitution are identified by the way government treats them.

The question *why* becomes relevant when legislation on this order is enacted: "Eminent domain shall not be exercised with respect to housing unless it specifically fulfills an overriding government purpose." This creates an exception to unlawful detainer. What does it imply for other exceptions to unlawful detainer of housing? Why? In addition, what does it imply for other facts besides housing? Again, why? Since it implies that a general welfare purpose (subject to minimum scrutiny) does not exist in the case of an eminent domain removal from housing, what other general welfare purposes justifying removals from housing — also subject to minimum scrutiny — must fail? These questions implicate legislative intent with respect to the Constitution. Which brings us around to the beginning of our discussion.

---

236 This is exactly James Madison's argument with respect to the fact of freedom of religion in his "Memorial and Remonstrance Against Religious Assessments," 1785.

It is now time to see how America's muddleheaded political class, bereft of any sense of individual rights, and with corruption breathing down their necks and public opinion in their faces, sought to get ahead of a runaway Constitutional crisis.

# CHAPTER 3. THE NEW BILL OF RIGHTS AS LAW

## THE FATE OF REFORM WITHIN CONFUSION

The journey was tortuous on the way to stalemate, as public opinion and the political system opposed each other over eminent domain and its implications. The reform process had all the characteristics of a diplomatic negotiation between hostile parties. Trying to make sense of proposed reforms was like trying to read a statement through gauze. Public opinion was startled to find its supposed servant, the political system, alienated by the idea of taking facts out of the political system. Public opinion could not look to the political system for assistance, so public opinion's own formulations — reflecting decades of abdication of political responsibility — made it extremely difficult to discern what public opinion wanted. For its part, the political system recognized an enemy in public opinion and determined to make no concessions. The language it offered contained no facts of importance to public opinion, and addressed none of the mechanisms of power which the political system had increasingly placed outside the political process and out of public view.

The response to *Kelo* was an upheaval of established means and ends. The political system couldn't think beyond business as usual and didn't know what public opinion expected of it. For the political system, Federal tax and spend powers and state general welfare powers, meant minimum scrutiny for almost every fact; it was not about to allow public opinion to change that situation. The judiciary struggled to be relevant and had no idea what public opinion or the political system intended the rules should be. Public opinion was mighty, but also, mighty inarticulate — undeveloped and contradictory.

The result was that the ship of state was in uncharted waters.

## THE RESPONSE OF THE POLITICAL SYSTEM

Connecticut, the home of the *Kelo* case, provided the best example of the perfect storm of complications which arose from the idea of the political system making even the slightest change to the eminent domain laws. This revealed how much the political system had relied on eminent domain in order to function smoothly:

> One of [New London's] state representatives blasted a proposed moratorium on eminent domain Tuesday as "a fundamental assault on our constitutional form of government" that would illegally benefit a single group of private citizens, the occupants of the Fort Trumbull neighborhood. Rep. Edward Moukawsher, a Democrat whose district covers parts of Groton and New London, wrote to House Speaker James Amann requesting that the speaker ask Attorney General Richard Blumenthal for an opinion on the legality of a moratorium. Moukawsher made clear that he considered any potential legislative intervention in the Fort Trumbull development project illegal under state law and a violation of both the state and federal constitutions. The letter sharply attacked a potential compromise on the issue of eminent domain reform: a deal that would halt all state seizures of private property for either economic development or blight clearance until either the summer of 2006 or the date legislators agree to revise state laws on government takings. That deal, which was tentatively hashed out but never finalized by House Minority Leader Robert Ward, [Republican]-North Branford, and leading Democrats in the House, would explicitly prohibit the New London Development Corp. from evicting the occupants of the private homes and apartments seized at Fort Trumbull. It also leaves open the possibility that the legislature would vote next year to retroactively declare such takings illegal. Moukawsher said he was concerned that the legislature would vote to ban the economic development justification that underlies the property seizures at Fort Trumbull, a move he said would overstep the legislature's authority. "I believe that it is beyond the power of the legislature to enact legislation to deprive a party of vested rights," Moukawsher wrote. The General Assembly "may, within limits, legislate retroactively," he said, "but the power to act retroactively is proscribed if the legislation deprives a party of substantive rights based on prior law...."Moukawsher also contended that legislative intervention to protect the Fort Trumbull occupants from eviction would violate prohibitions on enacting laws for the benefit of private individuals, and would be an affront to the judiciary's review and approval of the project. "I can think of no instance where the respect that should and must be accorded to the decisions of our highest court and the highest court in the land has been given so little consideration in proposing legislation," Moukawsher wrote. A moratorium is an attractive, if temporary, solution for opponents of eminent domain — and for legislators eager to be seen as protecting property rights in the face of a public outcry over the *Kelo v. New London* decision — but the idea has infuriated Moukawsher and fellow Rep. Ernest Hewett, [Democrat]-New London, who have both supported the Fort Trumbull project. Hewett, when he was a city councilor, voted to approve the municipal development plan, which was developed in consultation with Pfizer Inc., as the drug manufacturer developed its $300 million research complex on an adjacent property. Meanwhile, Rep. Michael

Lawlor, [Democrat]-East Haven, co-chairman of the Judiciary Committee and one of those who has discussed the issue of a moratorium with Ward and others, said there was no concrete plan to pass such a bill in the current special session, and that Amann and Democratic leaders did not expect to discuss the issue at all until after municipal elections next week. "The possibility of a moratorium is being discussed only to buy some time to give everyone the opportunity to understand the issues enough to make a decision on what the state laws should be," said Lawlor, who also noted that he supports the New London project and does not believe the power to condemn properties for economic development projects should be stricken from the statutes, as Ward has recommended. The legislators need time to craft meaningful reform, he said, but simply waiting until the regular session after promising to tackle the issue during the special session is a politically unpalatable alternative. "I'm happy that someone's pushed back, because the defenders of the New London project were silent for a long time," Lawlor said. "The supporters of the project need to be heard...."Lawlor rejected the claim that the state would be overstepping its bounds in telling the city when and how it may proceed. "The municipalities in Connecticut exist only because the state gives them permission to exist," he said. "By state law, we can, in effect, regulate what any municipal government does, and we can certainly tell a municipal government what they can and can't do prospectively. I don't think there's any question that we could tell them not to do something." Moukawsher's letter comes on the heels of other input to state legislators from the city, including some from Director of Law Thomas J. Londregan, who e-mailed a number of lawmakers Tuesday with proposed arguments against a radical overhaul of eminent domain law. According to Londregan's message, the question of whether the NLDC and the city can pursue evictions lies with the judiciary, not the legislature. "If the legislature has this power (then) no court decision is ever final," he wrote. "The losing party can get a legislative fix after the courts have ruled. Surely this is basic legal doctrine. Am I missing something here?"[237]

The time was out of joint — so was the nose of the political system. After all, the housed — evidently content to play the flunkey — and the political system were natural allies. The political system had privileged them — homeowners were even compensated for an eminent domain taking! Now one good turn deserved another — instead, the housed turned on the political system! (The reaction of the homeless to *Kelo* is the subject of detailed studies, which I have overlooked.) This was unfortunate, but not tolerable. The political system hated public opinion, felt public opinion was ungrateful, and would destroy public opinion at every opportunity. Eminent domain over housing was itself evidence of this last, as were proposals to "reform" eminent domain. So was minimum scrutiny.

In spite of their best efforts to conceal it, legislators kept facing a "facts of the individual" analysis which forced its way up through the deliberations. The "reform" efforts[238] kept coming back to three questions:

1. what do you want to protect?
2. from what do you want to protect it?
3. how much do you want to protect it?

---

237 *The Day*, November 2, 2005.

238 On its website, the National Conference of State Legislatures posts the proposed state revisions to eminent domain: www.ncsl.org.

Behind these lay the larger question: could the American political system — self-confessedly caught off guard by the response to *Kelo* — generate meaningful eminent domain reform? The society itself had been deceptively calm, with relatively low unemployment and continuing, if slight, economic growth. Real wages were growing for the most politically important groups, the upper middle class — often identified with homeowners — and above. At least on the surface, the opposition to *Kelo* did not appear to arise from economic despair, or even discontent.

Beneath the surface, however, changes were occurring which the political system should have anticipated, and didn't. The opposition to *Kelo* should have been seen as one more assertion of the power of homeowners in the United States. It was impossible to seriously conclude that they would accept in 2005 the same rights which *West Coast Hotel*, in 1937, had conferred on them with respect to facts. That was no power at all — an absurdity, and doomed. Homeowners were the new power in the land, and even if they didn't know what to do with power when they got it, it should have been clear that they were in the process of removing facts from the discretion of the scrutiny regime; they were in the process of acquiring all the power.

The political class — stupefied and degraded by "minimum scrutiny" regime corruption — resisted this change in power. It had become dominant in the power structure, while probably close on half the population lived at a level which violated the maintenance provision of the New Bill of Rights. The political system — with its undemocratically small Congress, noncompetitive party system and wildly socio-economically unequal states — was ripe for a fatal surprise.[239] Corruption was so thoroughgoing[240] that it was more aptly described as

---

239 The United States Census Bureau released poverty figures on August 30, 2005 (archived at www2.census.gov), and these were endlessly discussed. The Milton S. Eisenhower Foundation is just one of many organizations which maintain online archives of poverty-related studies: www. eisenhowerfoundation.org. Income stratification was also a constant concern. See reports archived at the Center on Budget and Policy Priorities (www.epi.org) and the Economic Policy Institute (www.cbpp.org). What is the effect on poverty or income stratification of the exercise of eminent domain over housing? No one has any idea, because no research has ever been done on the subject.

240 And so perceived by public opinion in polling: "Missteps and misconduct that have reached into all levels of government — from the White House and Congress to governors' offices in Connecticut and Ohio — led 88 percent of those surveyed to say the problem is a serious one." *Chicago Sun-Times*, December 9, 2005 (Chicago, Illinois, archived at www. suntimes.com). An awareness was dawning that legal doctrines (*e.g.*, minimum scrutiny or eminent domain) could simply be inherently corrupt — graft by different names: "Traditionally, national governance and corruption challenges have been seen as: i) particularly daunting in the poorer countries, with the richer world viewed as exemplary; ii) anchored within a legalistic framework and focused on formal institutions, iii) a challenge within public sectors, and, iv) divorced from global governance or security issues — seen as separate fields. Through an empirical approach based on the analysis of the 2004 survey of enterprises by the World Economic Forum, we challenge these notions and portray a more complex reality. We suggest that the undue emphasis on narrow legalism has obscured more subtle yet costly manifestations of misgovernance, which afflict rich countries as well. Emphasis is also given to measurement and analysis of misgovernance when the rules of the game have been captured by the elite through undue influence. We

a lack of direction — part of that corruption was, as we have seen, related to the exercise of eminent domain and so was attributable to the "minimum scrutiny" regime. Consequently, there were few formal guarantees of economic stability in the future for most people — the economy depended on political decisions, even though the power manifestly lay in the preservation of housing. Debt was pervasive, the nature of work was changing, and there was a widespread sense of the contingent nature of survival — the temperature of the economy was taken daily. The greatest security lay in loyalty to the system, but survival was the system's own chief goal. Therefore how stable could the society really be? Most importantly, as the third Constitutional epoch proceeded after 1937, the "minimum scrutiny" regime had progressively corrupted every fact by turning them over to an uncheckable political system. The United States was thoroughly corrupt, but the Supreme Court forbade public opinion to do anything about it. This reduced confidence in the political system to nothing; the entire system was degenerate, a political tinderbox awaiting a spark.

Independent political expression had all but disappeared: issues were channeled through, and disposed of by, the two political parties, which denatured and commodified them. Political groups — above all, the massive body of American homeowners, probably the largest discrete economic force in the world — used (without joining) the two parties to facilitate access to the vast resources commanded by government. In short, the parties were gigantic cartels in which corruption was both means and end. But government itself exercised no independent power. It exercised a monopoly over no fact. Patriotism might be reflexive, but it was hollow; there was no real government power, a realization which shook public opinion as public opinion investigated corruption in the wake of the *Kelo* decision: what to do about it? It was impossible to put faith in government — there was no government in which to put it; at the end of every avenue there was a

---

construct a new set of ethics indices, encompassing forms of (legal) corruption not subject to measurement in conventional (illegal) corruption indicators. It is found that manifestations of legal corruption may be more prevalent than illegal forms, such as outright bribery, and particularly so in richer countries...."Daniel Kaufmann, summarizing his article, "Corruption, Governance and Security: Challenges for the Rich Countries and the World," http://ssrn.com/abstract=605801. "In 2004, 98 percent of US House incumbents kept their seats. Only 5 incumbents lost to challengers — the second-lowest number in our history. Eighty-three percent of the 435 House races were won by landslides. Nearly 90 percent of incumbents were reelected by margins of at least 20 percent. In 14 states, every race was won by a landslide margin of at least 20 percent. Only four states recorded no landslide victories. State legislative races were even less competitive. Nationwide, 40 percent of the more than 7,000 races were uncontested." Ted Rueter, "Non-Competitive Elections Threaten Democracy," archived at www.collegenews.com. Maine, with its 1545 square miles and population of 1.05 million, sends two Senators to the United States Senate; so does California, with its 7734 square miles and population of 34 million. The United Kingdom's House of Commons has 658 members for a population of 60 million; France's Assembly has 577 members for a population of 60.5 million. The United States' House of Representatives has 435 members for a population of 295.7 million. Among other things, these wild discrepancies undermined the democratic foundation of the state, thereby contributing to the furtherance — and the stubbornness — of the "minimum scrutiny" regime.

mirror. And what was public opinion? Undeveloped demands in no shape for a political arena in which ideas died by a thousand small cuts.

This at a time when public opinion felt the need to defend facts against their destruction by corruption: the resistance to *Kelo*. How to eliminate discretion with respect to facts when that situation comprised most policy in the United States? Needless to say, the political system was unprepared for — indeed, was unaware of — the emerging argument that content neutrality (the limit of control of protected speech) was as important a rule in housing as it was in protected speech. This brand new and revolutionary idea, was treated by the political system as an impertinent affront to power, which it is — it is a wild card; the point is, it was being played. A popular bumper sticker said, "Visualize world peace." This one is much more difficult: "Visualize content neutral health and welfare regulation." That staggered even the "property rights" movement, which, after all, advocated the exercise of eminent domain under some circumstances. A "facts of the individual" analysis means depriving government of almost *all* the power it currently exercises (if "exercises" is the proper word for what has gone on). That is why the political system so strenuously opposes it, but that is also why public opinion (for which it is a matter of survival) is stumbling toward it, in time-honored fashion: blinkered selfishness leading to the establishment of a general principle. Discretion — the supposed animating force of the American (indeed, the world) political system — had immobilized the political system; all the political system could do — lumbering toward its collapse — was to bemoan the loss of power while public opinion proceeded to trip it up. Gulliver, tied down, comes to mind.

With the political system accounting for almost all the political activity (the attitude of the military and police was murky at best and kept well out of sight)[241] and the rest of the society economically dependent on it, there should have been no surprise to the system that what was in effect a system of political suppression, should have generated opposition in the extremely indirect fashion of an opposition to a court decision concerning an arcane subject such as eminent domain. But then, if the political system had not been surprised by the opposition to *Kelo*, it would not have been the system it was.

Neither was it unprecedented that the protest was led by the middle class. Two of America's greatest — and most violent — political crises occurred, not only under comparable economic circumstances, but also, at the behest of the middle class: the Revolution and the Civil War. A debate over legal ideas was at the heart of both disputes.

Politicians' comments post-*Kelo* reflected an uneasy awareness of having entered a strange area of apparently familiar territory. The opposition threatened a loss of political control, most immediately in case reform did not prevent forced removals but instead provoked an endless series of physical confrontations in the course of those same removals.

---

241 For a discussion of the private police state within a state, see David A. Sklansky, "The Private Police," 46 *U.C.L.A. Law Review* 1165 (April 1999).

Soon after the *Kelo* decision, an apparently drastic remedy — but one reflecting the confusion surrounding the issue — was proposed in California in the form an initiative, in several sections, to amend the California Constitution. Two provisions demonstrate the erratic response:

> "Private property may be taken or damaged for a stated public use only when just compensation, ascertained by a jury unless waived, has first been paid to, or into court for, the owner. Private property may not be taken or damaged for private use."

It appears the authors meant to tighten up "public use" by mandating that it be "stated." However, any formulation can be developed to satisfy this requirement, without changing the outcome in any eminent domain action. The problem is that no definition of "private use" is provided. In default of that, the courts would be likely to apply the traditional idea: "private" — forbidden — use is eminent domain used in violation of another law or as a result of some criminal violation.

> Private property may be taken by eminent domain only for a stated public use and only upon an independent judicial determination on the evidence that the condemnor has proven that no reasonable alternative exists. Property taken by eminent domain shall be owned and occupied by the condemnor or may be leased only to entities that are regulated by the Public Utilities Commission. All property that is taken by eminent domain shall be used only for the stated public use.[242]

The eye-opener here is "no reasonable alternative." Strict scrutiny says that the government action must be specifically fulfill an overriding government purpose. "Specifically fulfill" is usually taken to mean that there is no reasonable alternative. Under this provision, therefore, it would appear that all eminent domain is subject to strict scrutiny. One wonders whether the authors realize this, and if so, whether they realize the level of opposition likely to develop by governments and private interests which have always used eminent domain under minimum scrutiny. Note that this provision provides strict scrutiny for housing with respect to eminent domain, and so immediately raises the question with respect to housing and other facts, in what other contexts they receive strict scrutiny? In the alternative, what is the likelihood that a pressured court would reconcile "no reasonable alternative" with "public use" to find that "no reasonable alternative" in this proposal, means "rationally related to a legitimate government purpose" — effectively gutting the proposal? Or does this language change the role of the State in the Federal system, making it impossible for the state to legislate for the general welfare?[243] The owner, occupation and leasing provisions seem to be merely more invitations to creative evasion, and not likely to change the outcome of any eminent domain action. Finally, the California legislature passed a series of "process-oriented" eminent domain reforms, simply giving more time to property

---

242 See the full text at http: //www.calredevelop.org/docs/sca_15_bill_20050713_introduced.pdf.

243 This is an increasing concern of the Supreme Court. See Timothy Zick, "Statehood as the New Personhood: The Discovery of Fundamental 'States' Rights," http://ssrn.com/abstract=600142.

owners to contest takings, and unsuccessfully attempting to give meaning to the vague terms "blight" and "public use." The measures reflected the contempt of the political system for public opinion's anxiety about important facts. As we shall see, the response to the new laws was an initiative which went far toward propelling California—the world's sixth largest economy—into the fourth Constitutional epoch.[244]

The Connecticut General Assembly decided to conduct its review of eminent domain law through a specially convened Joint Judiciary and Planning and Development Committee, which began hearings on July 28, 2005.[245] Susette Kelo told the Committee even after she lost the *Kelo* case: "The city has owned my house for years [pursuant to the condemnation order — part of the eminent domain proceedings], it is still my home and I am never going to leave it."[246] But nothing was done to remove her, so Kelo's housing had defeated the state's general welfare powers, under which most facts enjoyed only minimum scrutiny. This meant her housing enjoyed a higher level of scrutiny. The implications followed forthwith from the facts. Above all, for how long? And, how much higher? Under what circumstances? To what extent? Who else's housing enjoyed this higher standard? What other facts enjoyed this higher standard? Her defiance raised the issues of civil disobedience and the entry of the police and the military into politics — it should not be overlooked that this controversy is about the occupation of territory, and what forces will occupy it. Connecticut Governor M. Jodi Rell, somewhat obscurely calling eminent domain "very complicated and very personal," wanly asked whether the *Kelo* redevelopment plan could "co-exist with those houses that are currently there."[247] Predictably, there were discussions of the meaning of "blight," "economic development," and expressions of concerns by planners about changing eminent domain law when so many projects were well advanced based on current law.[248]

The legislatures do not seem to be the arenas in which these issues are being resolved; instead, they are merely part of the ongoing process of sifting concepts and formulations. Alabama's revision of its eminent domain law is a good example. Signing it on August 3, 2005, Governor Robert Riley said: "What our new law does is restore the level of protection that existed prior to the Supreme Court's ruling in June," even though the decision merely ratified previous rulings on eminent domain. The Alabama law purportedly eliminated eminent domain for industrial, commercial, office, retail or residential development, but could be used to construct roads, public buildings and to remove blight; blight included

---

244 *Central Valley Business Times*, September 29, 2006 (Stockton, California, archived at www.centralvalleybusinesstimes.com).

245 The transcript is not yet available, but Connecticut General Assembly committee hearing transcripts are generally available at http://www.cga.ct.gov. Online videotapes of the hearings are available at http://www.ctn.state.ct.us/ondemand.asp?search=eminent.

246 *Greenwich Time*, July 29, 2005 (Greenwich, Connecticut, archived at www.greenwichtime.com).

247 *The Stamford Advocate*, July 30, 2005.

248 *The Stamford Advocate*, July 29, 2005; *The Day*, July 31, 2005.

areas which are obsolete, faulty in arrangement or design, or in danger of becoming blighted. As Dana Berliner, an IJ attorney, said of the blight provision: "All of these are ways of saying we'd like to construct something else here that has a different layout." In a remarkable development, an informal Alabama poll, taken immediately after the legislation was signed, revealed that 85% of respondents felt the legislation would not change outcomes. The governor replied that he was willing to consider changes. This was the sequel, a nuanced revision seemingly tailored to the extreme poverty of Alabama: "[Senator Larry] Dixon, [Republican]-Montgomery, said he will propose a constitutional amendment [to be put to voters] that would prohibit the use of eminent domain to remove blighted neighborhoods. Rep. Gerald Allen, [Republican]-Cottonwood, said he's working on a similar constitutional amendment that will restrict or ban the use of eminent domain in blighted neighborhoods. Both expect opposition from city officials who want to retain the power to clean up declining areas of town. Sen. E.B. McClain, [Democrat]-Midfield, expects city officials to make a powerful argument."[249]

The attraction of restricting eminent domain with respect to blight, was that it seemed to be focusing on facts. However, this was illusory: it merely raised the question, what is the Constitution? Here is a typical attempt to narrow down blight:

> Consider the following definition of blight from Pennsylvania's Urban Redevelopment Law:
>
> *35 Penn. Stat. § 1702:*
>
> *It is hereby determined and declared as a matter of legislative finding —*
>
> *(a) That there exist in urban communities in this Commonwealth areas which have become blighted because of the unsafe, unsanitary, inadequate or over-crowded condition of the dwellings therein, or because of inadequate planning of the area, or excessive land coverage by the buildings thereon, or the lack of proper light and air and open space, or because of the defective design and arrangement of the buildings thereon, or faulty street or lot layout, or economically or socially undesirable land uses.*
>
> *...*
>
> *Therefore, [blight clearance and related redevelopment activities] are declared to be public uses for which public money may be spent and private property may be acquired by the exercise of the power of eminent domain.*
>
> This definition of blight is absurdly overbroad. It allows for eminent domain to be used to take property that falls into *any one* of the laundry list of conditions in paragraph (a). Any of the categories in this list could be subject to abuse, but focus on the last one: "economically or socially undesirable land uses." Here is a translation of that language: "*Kelo*-style economic development takings can be done in Pennsylvania under the guise of blight." To add insult to injury, property owners are held to a high standard in challenging blight designations.
>
> Now consider this definition of blight, from the *same chapter* of the Urban Redevelopment Law:
>
> *35 Penn. Stat. § 1712.1*
>
> *(a) Notwithstanding any other provision of this act, any Redevelopment Authority shall have the power to acquire by purchase, gift, bequest, eminent domain or otherwise, any blighted property as defined in this section*

---

249 January 1, 2006 (archived at www.al.com).

...

*(c) Blighted property shall include:*

*(1) Any premises which because of physical condition or use is regarded as a public nuisance at common law or has been declared a public nuisance in accordance with the local housing, building, plumbing, fire and related codes.*

*(2) Any premises which because of physical condition, use or occupancy is considered an attractive nuisance to children, including but not limited to abandoned wells, shafts, basements, excavations, and unsafe fences or structures.*

*(3) Any dwelling which because it is dilapidated, unsanitary, unsafe, vermin-infested or lacking in the facilities and equipment required by the housing code of the municipality, has been designated by the department responsible for enforcement of the code as unfit for human habitation.*

*(4) Any structure which is a fire hazard, or is otherwise dangerous to the safety of persons or property.*

*(5) Any structure from which the utilities, plumbing, heating, sewerage or other facilities have been disconnected, destroyed, removed, or rendered ineffective so that the property is unfit for its intended use.*

*(6) Any vacant or unimproved lot or parcel of ground in a predominantly built-up neighborhood, which by reason of neglect or lack of maintenance has become a place for accumulation of trash and debris, or a haven for rodents or other vermin.*

*(7) Any unoccupied property which has been tax delinquent for a period of two years prior to the effective date of this act, and those in the future having a two year tax delinquency.*

*(8) Any property which is vacant but not tax delinquent, which has not been rehabilitated within one year of the receipt of notice to rehabilitate from the appropriate code enforcement agency.*

*(9) Any abandoned property. A property shall be considered abandoned if:*

*(i) it is a vacant or unimproved lot or parcel of ground on which a municipal lien for the cost of demolition of any structure located on the property remains unpaid for a period of six months;*

*(ii) it is a vacant property or vacant or unimproved lot or parcel of ground on which the total of municipal liens on the property for tax or any other type of claim of the municipality are in excess of 150% of the fair market value of the property as established by the Board of Revisions of Taxes or other body with legal authority to determine the taxable value of the property; or*

*(iii) the property has been declared abandoned by the owner, including an estate that is in possession of the property.*

Unlike Section 1702, Section 1712.1 is a serious and reasonable attempt to define property that is actually blighted. The contrast between the two contains two related lessons for post-*Kelo* economic domain reform. First, legislators considering reform must take a hard look at all of the definitions of blight in their state. Second, definitions of blight like Section 1702 must systematically be replaced by narrower definitions like Section 1712.1.[250]

---

250 October 12, 2005, Benjamin Barros from his website, http://lawprofessors.typepad.com/property/2005/10/a_tale_of_two_b.html.

The problem here was the same one Justice Stevens had faced in evaluating "economic development" with respect to eminent domain. There, an infinite number of facts fell under the term, "economic development" and raised the issue of the Constitutional status of eminent domain as a fact. Here, an infinite number of terms fall under the fact, "property," and in turn raises the question of *its* Constitutional status. No matter how specific the list of conditions under blight, "property" is always one of them. Narrowing the definition of blight means raising the question of "property." Its definition, then, becomes the central focus — for a while. The "debate" over eminent domain was merely one of terms chasing each other without the Constitutional status of any of them being clarified: eminent domain to economic development to blight to property to eminent domain. They all became bones of contention in the struggle for power. "Property" now found itself in the cross-hairs. Begging questions — such as the level of scrutiny for housing — simply raised issues with which the political system was progressively *less* able to deal.

One unlooked-for result in changing the law of blight was to throw all past government actions into question. What rights vested as a result of such changes? How was all finance implicated — health and welfare regulation, any kind of building, all bonds, taxes and appropriations — by such changes? Loose eminent domain reform left loose ends. The Wisconsin eminent domain reform included a definition of blight as vague as any: "'blighted property' means any property that, by reason of abandonment, dilapidation, deterioration, age or obsolescence, inadequate provisions for ventilation, light, air, or sanitation, high density of population and overcrowding, faulty lot layout in relation to size, adequacy, accessibility, or usefulness, unsanitary or unsafe conditions, deterioration of site or other improvements, or the existence of conditions that endanger life or property by fire or other causes, or any combination of such factors, is detrimental to the public health, safety, or welfare."[251] And yet it seemed to be effective, so eminent domain reforms were about the economics of litigation delay (and the use of that delay to form new plans to thwart the reforms), rather than about whether the reformed terms had any meaning:

> Developers of Landmark Gate announced Tuesday they were abandoning a proposed $25 million mixed use project at [Madison, Wisconsin's] Todd Drive and the Beltline. Mortenson Investment Group [MIG] said the state law, which was passed overwhelmingly by the Legislature and signed by Gov. Jim Doyle in late March, had removed its needed leverage to acquire property for the project....[Developer Brad] Hutter...said the difficulties in acquiring properties along the Beltline — including the controversial Selective Video adult entertainment shop were crippled by the law. MIG had purchased two properties and had contracts with two others but was unable to reach agreement with owners of the Open Pantry convenience store and the Bridge Club sites. The Landmark Gate project was awarded to MIG in August 2005 after the city created a redevelopment district along Todd Drive. Hutter said his group entered into the project fully expecting the city's Community Development Authority would use its powers of eminent domain should property acquisition be financially or

---

251 The entire text of the legislation is online at www.legis.state.wi.us.

legally unreasonable. The project has been nearly five years in the making. It included a four-story building with 429 underground parking stalls and 184 surface stalls for retail customers. The upper three floors of the 135,000 square-foot building would be offices, including a new home for Madison-based NRS Corp., an independent consulting firm specializing in research for the home building industry. The bottom floor would house stores and eateries, such as a coffee shop, deli, dry cleaners and bank.[252]

Post-*Kelo*, even successful eminent domain resistance only raised more problems and set off more alarms in the political system. What about bond indebtedness incurred from past eminent domain seizures which, in the contemplation of this new definition, were wrongful? Should that indebtedness be repudiated, by a lawsuit declaring unconstitutional taxes imposed to pay the bond debt? What about bond indebtedness resulting from duress, that is, sales pursuant to the perceived threat of eminent domain using the former law? What about indebtedness resulting from wrongful zoning under the former law? From wrongful health and welfare regulation under the former law? And what were the wrongs committed pursuant to such regulation? Eminent domain reform was predicated on wrongful past takings and the current and future preservation of property. The implication is that the former wrongful use of eminent domain wrongfully took property. In order to prevent this from ever happening again, does the new blight definition mandate controls on appropriations? Does it mandate rewriting the state's tax code?[253]

Certainly the opponents of eminent domain had no idea what came after success — they were by no means prepared to take power. Thus, another unlooked-for result of reform attempts was the charge that eminent domain reformers were

---

252 *The Capitol Times*, June 21, 2006 (Madison, Wisconsin, archived at www.madison.com).

253 Capture of issuing entities — and the pressure to fund debt between the "capturers" — are just two of the issues leading to a reexamination of sovereign debt and its repudiation. What facts would be sufficient to prompt the Court to find that debt was not fundable or only partially fundable, that is, that the debt was the abrogation of government purpose even under minimum scrutiny? A seeming natural for the "property rights" movement, the issue is complicated by idea of "property rights" in the bond holder. The situation also seems to be complicated if the Court itself has been captured. We have just begun to examine "sovereign debt" using an *ad hoc* "facts of the individual" analysis, much of which is taking place in the context of sovereign debt default. For the "property rights" point of view, see William P. Kittredge and David W. Kreutzer, "We Only Pay the Bills: The Ongoing Effort to Disfranchise [sic] Virginia's Voters," www.virginiainstitute.org/publications. See also Herschel Grossman and John B. Van Huyck, "Sovereign Debt as a Contingent Claim: Excusable Default, Repudiation, and Reputation," 78 *American Economic Review* 5 (December 1988), 1088-97; Mara Faccio, "Politically-Connected Firms: Can They Squeeze the State?" http://ssrn.com/abstract=305099; Constantin Gurdgiev, "Project Contingent Repudiation Risk in the Model of North-South Lending." http://ssrn.com/abstract=683314; Craig A. Depken *et al.*, "Corruption and Creditworthiness: Evidence from Sovereign Credit Ratings," http://ssrn.com/abstract=899414; Michael W. Klein, "Risk, Taxpayers, and the Role of Government in Project Finance," http://ssrn.com/abstract=620626; Robert B. Ahdieh, "Between Mandate and Market: Contract Transition in the Shadow of the International Order,"http://ssrn.com/abstract=576421; Robert K. Rasmussen, "Integrating a Theory of the State into Sovereign Debt Restructuring," http://ssrn.com/abstract=558266.

actually seeking to preserve minimum scrutiny for all facts in the context of eminent domain — but on their own terms; they wanted to take over the political system on *its* terms, but with *them* in charge. How to refute it? Better yet, what to do with the state? The movement had no terms, just as the "minimum scrutiny" regime had no limits. This is consistent with viewing the eminent domain dispute as taking place between power groups lacking ideas, rather than between ideas with some chance of being expressed in reform. It is also consistent with persistent and expanding stalemate, which is what happened. In this case, the properties maintained their identities, but other components of the system — to which the opposition to eminent domain paid no attention — stalled. With what effect?

The apparent exceptions to otherwise forbidden "economic development" are more problematic than the language about blight. In the case of a concept such as "economic development" which, as Justice Stevens pointed out, does not, in the first place, distinguish a different kind of eminent domain, making "exceptions" to "economic development" merely puts the question, what is the Constitution? We are back to square one; the concept of "exceptions" retards, rather than advances, the inquiry into eminent domain.[254]

No matter the restrictions on eminent domain, under some conditions housed individuals could be blight, removing them from housing could be a public purpose: the denigration of human beings was explicit in even the most anti-eminent domain proposals. Formulating the issue in this way clearly reveals the barbarity sanctioned by minimum scrutiny for housing, and shows housing, in the "minimum scrutiny" regime, outside the Constitution. At the same time, the authors of these formulations evade the question, what — if anything — is the Constitution? Apart from the implied denigration of human beings, these curious proposals lead to anomalous formulations, such as the idea that it is necessary to destroy the society in order to preserve the society, to develop the society by destroying parts of it.

On October 26, 2005, the Ohio legislature passed a formal moratorium on eminent domain, but the terms raised more questions than they answered. The bill

> [d]eclares a moratorium until December 31, 2006, during which period public bodies are generally prohibited from using eminent domain to take private property that is without blight when the sole or a primary purpose for the taking is economic development that will ultimately result in ownership of that property being vested in another private person.... "Blighted area" means an area within a county but outside the corporate limits of any municipality, which area by reason of the presence of a substantial number of slum, deteriorated, or deteriorating structures, predominance of defective or inadequate street layout, faulty lot layout in relation to size, adequacy, accessibility, or usefulness, in-

---

254 July 3, 2005 (archived at www.datelinealabama.com). Almost simultaneously, the Texas legislature passed an eminent domain "restriction" which allowed eminent domain to be used for "economic development" as a secondary purpose. It was immediately criticized as an exception which would swallow the rule. See the *Fort Worth Star-Telegram*, August 22, 2005 (Fort Worth, Texas, archived at www.dfw.com). For later commentary, see www.woai.com (September 20, 2005, archived on the site).

sanitary [*sic*] or unsafe conditions, deterioration of site or other improvements, diversity of ownership, tax or special assessment delinquency exceeding the fair value of the land, defective or unusual conditions to title, or the existence of conditions which endanger life or property by fire and other causes, or any combination of such factors, substantially impairs or arrests the sound growth of a county, retards the provision of housing accommodations, or constitutes an economic or social liability and is a menace to the public health, safety, morals, or welfare in its present condition and use....

Considering that the *Kelo* case revolved around housing, it was unclear how — if its application were to be contested by anyone housed — the legislation would be applied to "deteriorating" housing.[255]

The Michigan legislature — stumped by the vagueness of the term "blight" but determined to preserve it and the discretion it conferred — considered increasing the burden of proof for finding a "public use" in connection with "blight":

> SB 693 would amend Michigan law that regulates property acquisition by state agencies and public corporations, and specify that condemnation for public use does not include takings that are 'a pretext to confer a private benefit on a known or unknown entity....' Both the bill and the resolution specify that public use does not include taking private property to transfer to a private entity, for economic development or additional tax revenue....Under the Michigan measures, takings to eradicate blight would still be allowed. But governments condemning blighted property must demonstrate by 'clear and convincing evidence' that the taking is for a public use. That's a higher test than the 'preponderance' of evidence required for a general condemnation of private property.... Robert Campau, vice president of public policy and legal affairs at the Michigan Association of Realtors, said the higher standard is needed because 'blight is a very difficult thing to define' and it's important to prevent abuse of power."[256]

Since this did not make the term "blight" any clearer (or "public use," for that matter), its effect was to raise the level of scrutiny for the facts involved in an eminent domain action for "blight" — and yet no such facts were part of the proposal. Cause and effect had ceased to be related — the authors clearly didn't know what they were doing. Michigan's proposal held out the inviting prospect of trials, and then appeals, and then court decisions which would be all over the map in terms of their rationales. That, in turn, would require the legislature revisiting eminent domain. In the end it was all about raising the level of scrutiny for facts, but no one wanted to face that issue: it cut too close to everyone's prejudices, everyone's interests, everyone's **profound** ignorance. The question was, when would events cut even more closely and force an end to the state of denial on this issue?

The supposed conflict between the levels of government is a product of the hopelessly muddled "minimum scrutiny" regime, which public opinion is now openly resisting. The political system has long sought to implicate these distinctions as a means of preserving and expanding its power. Whatever the courts'

---

255 The legislation also specifically exempted the Norwood facts (*infra*) in the case pending before the Ohio Supreme Court. The above is the legislative analysis, available online at www.legislature.state.oh.us.

256 *Crain's Detroit Business*, November 21, 2005, December 14, 2005 (Detroit, Michigan, archived at www.crainsdetroit.com). As we shall see, he was off by two months.

and states' view of the matter, a contradiction in the "minimum scrutiny" regime is always encountered when a "subordinate" political entity seeks to raise the level of scrutiny for a fact higher than the level the fact enjoys under the "dominant" entity. The political system enjoys trying to create confusion over this — rejiggering process without granting that process is a fact, then throwing the resulting "reform" at society as an incorporation of public opinion — but a "facts of the individual" analysis shows us clearly what is going on. Would it conflict with a state's minimum scrutiny for facts with respect to eminent domain, if a locality granted intermediate or strict scrutiny for a fact with respect to eminent domain? The following report also highlighted the wide range of legal entanglements implicated by local efforts to restrict eminent domain:

> A proposed ordinance to ban Norwalk's [Connecticut] ability to seize private property for economic development is illegal and would "likely expose the city to substantial damages" if passed unchanged, the city's attorney said yesterday. Corporation Counsel Louis Ciccarello's six-page opinion cautioning the Common Council was issued on the eve of tonight's expected vote on the proposed ordinance to restrict use of eminent domain. Democratic Councilman Michael Coffey, author of the ordinance, said Ciccarello's opinion, coming 24 hours before "one of the biggest votes the council will be faced with," is a ploy by opponents to "obstruct a vote" tonight....Coffey's proposal would restrict Norwalk's use of eminent domain to three areas: construction of public facilities, such as schools or roads; preservation of open space; and protection of health or safety. But Ciccarello wrote in his opinion that the ordinance, as approved by the Ordinance Committee, would be illegal because it falls outside the council's power under the city Charter, and "it conflicts with and frustrates existing state statutes." Ciccarello said the ordinance does not make clear whether the local law would apply retroactively to projects now under way that do or could involve eminent domain. "This is critical because the city and the Redevelopment Agency have an existing land disposition agreement (LDA) with the developers for the Reed-Putnam project, and are negotiating LDAs in conjunction with the West Avenue and Wall Street projects," Ciccarello wrote, referring to three plans to allow developers to remake once-blighted parts of Norwalk. If the ordinance applied to those projects, Ciccarello wrote, "then the developers would likely have substantial claims for breach of contract" against the city. Ciccarello said Norwalk is awaiting a ruling from the Connecticut Supreme Court on whether the Redevelopment Agency can seize the Maritime Motors property — a crucial piece of the Reed-Putnam plan located on West Avenue. The ordinance could undermine a decision in favor of the city and lead to "an immediate lawsuit," he said. But Coffey said yesterday the ordinance would not affect projects in which land disposition agreements have been signed. He also said he was "baffled" and "flabbergasted" that he had not heard concerns about the legality of his ordinance sooner, noting that a city attorney, Katherine Lasberg, attends his Ordinance Committee's meetings each month...."There has never been any comment made to me about the legality (or) wording of it," he said....Coffey said that "hundred of municipalities" have passed ordinances restricting takings by eminent domain.[257]

The flip side problem with *not* restricting eminent domain as to facts was *permitting* it as to facts, such as roads, schools and so on. Representative Charles

---

257 *The Stamford Advocate*, October 25, 2005.

Rangel revealed problems with "scrutiny" when he proposed his own addition to Congress' reform of eminent domain laws. He "said the bill should clarify the conditions for eminent domain usage rather than leave the question to courts. He would allow eminent domain if it were used to produce affordable housing, he said. The bill seems to allow for that, though it isn't mentioned specifically in the text, his office said."[258] Did this permit eminent domain with respect to housing in order to construct "affordable" housing? Did it raise the level of scrutiny for housing which was produced under Rangel's proposal? What was the basis for allowing eminent domain with respect to "affordable" housing, but not other facts? What is "affordable" housing, and does the provision put that at issue? What about other facts relating to housing, such as roads and schools?

These concerns, in turn, increased pressure to codify the level of scrutiny for facts as to which eminent domain permission was not granted. Consider the use of "corridors of protection" (transportation corridors) and the concept of "potential public use." Would these negate any restriction of eminent domain as to any fact? Again they raise the question, what is the Constitution?

> The Illinois State Supreme Court this week agreed to consider a lawsuit filed by homeowners on the proposed path of the Prairie Parkway who say the state's efforts to limit development on the highway are unconstitutional. The suit targets the corridor of protection that the Illinois Department of Transportation established in 2002. Property owners are required to notify the state if they intend to change anything that lies inside the corridor, a 400-foot-wide swath of rural land running between Interstate 88 and Interstate 80, in Kane and Kendall counties. IDOT can then either permit the changes or use eminent domain to buy the property. "The benchmark (for state seizure of private property) then becomes what the owner wants to do with the property rather than what the state intends to do with the property," said Tim Dwyer, a St. Charles attorney who is representing the landowners. Eminent domain should be allowed only when the state can demonstrate a public need for property, the suit argues, not to safeguard a potential public need. Of the 196 properties affected by the protected corridor, 56 owners have joined in the lawsuit. The suit was first filed in 2003 in the Kendall County Circuit Court, which dismissed the case three separate times after finding that IDOT has the right to establish the protected corridor and that the corridor did not financially harm the landowners. When Dwyer appealed the court's final decision, the state appellate court upheld the lower court's ruling. The Supreme Court's acceptance coincides with IDOT's announcement this week that it has concluded that a major new freeway will indeed be built on or near the original protected corridor, although the route will be subjected to several years of further study before an exact footprint for the road is determined. IDOT officials said that the protected corridor was necessary to keep at least one potential route for the road from being permanently blocked by private developments, which can be built much faster than a major new road.[259]

---

258 *Crain's New York Business*, November 5, 2005 (New York, New York, archived at www. newyorkbusiness.com).

259 *Aurora Beacon News*, October 6, 2006 (Aurora, Illinois, archived at www.chicagosuburbannews.com).

The bigger the "corridor" — indeed, the bigger the proposed eminent domain taking — the stronger the tendency to collapse legal doctrines, but at the same time, the greater potential for successful resistance. The largest of the transportation corridors is the massive (upwards of $200 billion) Trans-Texas corridor of new highways stretching south and west across Texas. Taking into account the bias of the following description, note the effort to insulate eminent domain use, not only by folding it into an authority, but also, by insulating that authority from further review by the political process. Note that the Trans-Texas Corridor was exempted BY NAME from recently enacted Texas eminent domain reform legislation:

> The Lone Star State ranks 50th in the high school graduation rate, but Texas roads are ranked number one by truckers. The way things look, our legislature would like to continue that "Texas Miracle...."They failed to pass their "number one" goal, school finance reform, but the Texas Department of Transportation got almost everything they wanted, including a big "thumbs up" on the $184 billion Trans-Texas Corridor. The proposed TTC will be a massive network of redundant quarter mile wide toll roads and "ancillary facilities" stretching across the state parallel to existing interstate freeways. "TxDOT [the Texas Department of Transportation] is as happy as can be," gushed Mike Krusee, Chairman of the House Transportation Committee. And why wouldn't they be? A couple of years ago, Governor Perry's political appointees at the Texas Transportation Commission were granted unprecedented powers by the state legislature. TxDOT is a now a kingdom unto itself. TxDOT can negotiate comprehensive development agreements...with foreign corporations. And TxDOT, with the blessing of our good-haired governor, is in the process of creating the biggest special interest pork funnel west of the Potomac. If TxDOT has its way, the first leg of the Trans-Texas Corridor (TTC-35) will be designed, built, and leased by Cintra, a Spanish public works company, for the next 50 to 70 years. The TTC project was pushed by Perry's appointees as the "only" viable solution to problems with urban congestion. This happened after an already completed and approved study for I-35, including rail and truck lanes — no toll roads — was dumped after Perry took office in 2001. That year, $800,000 in campaign contributions from toll road interests [was] dropped into Perry's lap. Around that time, the TTC plan suddenly appeared to our "visionary" governor....The TTC plan was unveiled by Perry in January 2002 and approved by his appointees at TxDOT five months later with NO STUDY. "Once the Governor decided that this is where we needed to head, he wanted to remove it from the political flow of the state, he wanted it to become policy as opposed to politics, and that was one of the reasons he asked us to move so fast, and we've done an admirable job...[," said] Ric Williamson, Texas Transportation Commissioner....By many estimates, [TxDOT] will need to take more than half a million acres of private property to make their whole TTC boondoggle a reality.[260]

This, in turn, has recently been folded into the largest corridor of them all, one dedicated only vaguely to "trade" — in fact, it is dedicated to political unification of the continent: the International Mid-Continent Trade Corridor. Its lobbying group is North America's SuperCorridor Coalition, Inc., which describes its purpose as follows:

---

260 www.transtexascorridor.blogspot.com. See also www.corridorwatch.org.

North America's SuperCorridor Coalition, Inc., is a non-profit organization based in Dallas, Texas, dedicated to developing the world's first international, integrated and secure, multi-modal transportation system along the International Mid-Continent Trade Corridor to improve both the trade competitiveness and quality of life in North America. The NASCO Corridor encompasses Interstate Highways 35, 29 and 94, and the significant connectors to those highways in the United States, Canada and Mexico. The Corridor directly impacts the continental trade flow of North America. Membership includes public and private sector entities along the Corridor in Canada, the United States and Mexico. From the largest border crossing in North America (The Ambassador Bridge in Detroit, Michigan and Windsor, Canada), to the second largest border crossing of Laredo, Texas and Nuevo Laredo, Mexico, and to Manitoba, Canada, the impressive, tri-national NASCO membership truly reflects the international scope of the Corridor and the regions it impacts. NASCO has officially amalgamated with the former North American International Trade Corridor Partnership, which was a non-profit organization in Mexico dedicated to economic development and improving trade relations through the heartland of America to Canada and Mexico. NASCO and the NAITCP have worked together successfully in the past, and now, with the amalgamation, will operate as one organization under the name NASCO, with a shared mission and objectives. The North American Inland Port Network (NAIPN), a sub-committee of NASCO, has been tasked with developing an active inland port network along our corridor to specifically alleviate congestion at maritime ports and our nation's borders. The NAIPN envisions an integrated, efficient and secure network of inland ports specializing in the transportation of containerized cargo in North America. The main guiding principal of the NAIPN is to develop logistics systems that enhance global security, but at the same time do not impede the cost-effective and efficient flow of goods.[261]

Inevitably, government would soon dispense with attempting to shield the collapse of doctrines and branches of government behind the "minimum scrutiny" regime. It was all about power — but broadcasting the fact could not help but bring it to the attention of an alarmed public opinion:

In a rare endorsement, the Texas Department of Transportation is joining the North America's Supercorridor Coalition, Inc., a nonprofit, international organization based in Dallas. The members of Nasco, founded in 1994, aim to develop the highway infrastructure from Canada through the United States to Mexico, particularly the Trans-Texas Corridor, which would widen and expand Interstate 35 into a mega-trade corridor. A press release Wednesday from Nasco and TxDOT said the two will work together to ensure development of the TTC, championed by Gov. Rick Perry. "The Texas Department of Transportation is formalizing its commitment to work closely with Nasco and its local, state and international members as the strongest voice on the continued development of I-35 and Trans-Texas Corridor 35," said Ric Williamson, chairman of the Texas Transportation Commission. "Without question, Nasco has been the single most influential organization, not just in Texas, but the nation, when it comes to the development of I-35," Williamson added. "They also know what it will take to meet the challenges of the next 50 years." TxDOT will market the I-35 and Trans-Texas Corridor 35 with Nasco to state, national and international audiences, as well as work on common federal priorities, said Amadeo Saenz, TxDOT's assistant executive director for engineering operations. Saenz said

---

261 www.nascocorridor.com.

Nasco's leadership has helped TxDOT to understand how a broad transportation corridor benefits all sides. Saenz and Nasco Executive Director Tiffany Melvin will make presentations on I-35 and TTC-35 at the Northeast Mexico-Texas workshop on logistics for regional competitiveness in Monterrey, Nuevo León, Mexico. Nasco has memoranda of understanding with eight US states and one Canadian province for ongoing cooperation in enhancing the I-35/I-29 and I-94 corridors and major connectors to those highways. Nasco also has signed a letter of intent with the Secretariat of Communications and Transportation of Mexico to develop a plan to monitor the operation of commercial cargo vehicles along I-35 using intelligent transportation systems. The 20-member Nasco Board of Directors includes eight Texans representing Webb, Bell, Denton and Tarrant counties, Free Trade Alliance San Antonio, EWI Risk Services, the International Bank of Commerce and the international law firm Strasburger & Price. Nasco's general membership includes Lockheed Martin..., Hillwood Properties/Alliance Texas, Love's Country Stores, the City of Midlothian, the City of Gainesville, GrowthNet Trading, and Franco Eleuteri & Associates.[262]

Conflating branches of government and legal doctrines raises the stakes, not by forcing the justification of the branches of government and legal doctrines, but rather, by forcing facts of the individual to the fore, that is, by provoking confrontations. Note another ostensible method of preventing eminent domain decisions from being challenged: giving authority, by treaty, to an entity outside the United States: "Wal-Mart is supporting a change in the General Agreement on Trade in Services [negotiated through the World Trade Organization] that would make it easier for the retail giant to set up stores anywhere it wants. Wal-Mart officials say it wants to be able to compete better globally....Local officials would not be able to limit the size and height of buildings, locations or operating hours — all of which various US communities have set limits on."[263] However, this transparent and rather feckless gambit 1) does not stop physical confrontations over the facts; and 2) the facts wind up being litigated anyway through the inevitable dispute mechanisms which even "non-partisan," ideologically "neutral" multinational organizations have to establish. Facts are impish — they don't "go away."

Interestingly, we can directly track eminent domain concepts under the New Bill of Rights — again, the facts will out, and if it's sauce for the goose, it's sauce for the gander. A popular mantra of real estate valuation is, "Location, location, location." Is location a fact of the individual? Are the indicia for housing different for eminent domain than for other applications of health and welfare powers? In lieu of agreement on the indicia of a fact, such as housing, it appears that looking to the facts themselves is the method for arriving at a conclusion: among other housing indicia one is, where it is (as it is? when it is?). If an "economic corridor" exists under eminent domain, is there a "housing corridor" under the New Bill of Rights which would trump even voluntary participation in a development scheme? That is, does such a concept alter the idea of "development" *beyond* the ostensible alternative of simply "building around" individuals who choose not

---

262 *Dallas Business Journal*, January 18, 2006 (Dallas, Texas, archived at www.dallas.bizjournals.com).

263 *The Huntsville Times*, December 16, 2005 (Huntsville, Alabama, archived at www.alt.com).

to sell to a developer? Is "building around" that simple? When does a "housing corridor" arise or go out of existence? Does it arise when, as in the example below, some private entity has designated a space as suitable for housing? In short, are the housing development plans below, in fact, housing? When does housing come into existence? What would be the burden of proof vis-à-vis a private entity which is providing housing and a government entity (or a development authority) which has only an (apparently) minimum scrutiny, general welfare purpose in mind for the same land? What if the private entity wins and the housing never gets built? What in *fact* (not in *law*) happens if the government authority condemns and the proposed use is never carried out? What obligations with respect to the housing would the private entity have under the housing provision of the New Bill of Rights? How much discretion does the New Bill of Rights squeeze out of the political system, and in what ways?

An eminent domain battle is heating up between the Effingham County [Georgia] Economic Development Authority (EEDA) and International Paper's real estate division that goes to the core of a recent US Supreme Court decision allowing private property to be seized for economic development. Further, the issue may ultimately test the sincerity of Georgia politicians who have promised curbs on eminent domain for economic development. The Effingham County Economic Development Authority informed IP Realty in a Sept. 30 letter that it would move to condemn 3,200 acres of timberland IP Realty owns in Effingham County known as the research forest tract if IP Realty did not agree to negotiations to sell the property to EEDA. The Authority says the county has run out of available land for uses such as warehouse distribution centers and condemnation is the only option if IP Realty does not sell willingly. IP Realty President L.H. Ronnie Jr. informed EEDA in an Oct. 11 response letter that IP Realty had spent four years developing the property for residential use and that it was not for sale. The order, Ronnie said, has put the company in a contractual bind with potential buyers and threatens to undo years of master planning for development of the forest research tract. "If the IDA (EEDA) is determined to proceed with the condemnation it has threatened, I request that they do so immediately," Ronnie wrote. "We consider the mere threat of condemnation to be an inappropriate use of your condemnation authority intended only to adversely affect the marketability of our property. Because of our commitments to existing purchasers, we will be forced to take whatever actions are necessary to defend our title." Ronnie said IP Realty already has a fully executed contract for the sale of 500 acres, has reached agreements with developers on two more parcels totaling 1,900 acres, and is close to agreements on the remainder of the tract. IP Realty Land Sales Manager Will Burgstiner said the company cannot renege on those agreements. "We've got contracts on the other pods that we could not morally step away from or legally step away from," Burgstiner said. The Effingham County Commission on Sept. 20 approved a general development agreement with IP Realty to provide water and sewer to most of the residences planned for the property. The County rezoned the property in July 2004 from general agricultural to residential. The EEDA wants to use the property for an industrial park. EEDA's intended use for the property goes to the heart of the Supreme Court decision in *Kelo et al vs. the City of New London*, in which the high court ruled that private property could be seized under eminent domain for the purpose of economic development. The ruling gives cities the power to raze homes and businesses to make way for projects that could include shopping malls, hotels and other private developments with the potential to generate higher tax revenue for the local government. Georgia politicians widely condemned the ruling as a threat to private property rights and vowed to strengthen state laws to protect property owners. EEDA's move to condemn the research tract is allowed under *Kelo*, as well as Georgia state law, but that may change when the Georgia General Assembly meets next session. State Senators Eric Johnson of Savannah and Jeff Chapman of Brunswick say that possible actions to limit the use of eminent domain for economic development in Georgia might include stripping local economic development authorities of the power to condemn property for private use. Johnson and Chapman made the remarks during a break in a Sept. 27 hearing before a state Senate panel in Savannah about ways to curb eminent domain in Georgia. The panel, assembled by Johnson and chaired by Chapman, is holding the hearings around the state. "We need to have some ability to limit what is a public purpose, and economic development may not be one of them," said Chapman, a Republican who introduced legislation last session restricting the taking of private property for private enterprise. The legislation passed the Senate and will get House consideration in 2006...."Taking eminent domain power away from development authorities is a possibility because they're not elected officials," Johnson said....As part of its development agreement, IP Realty sold two tracts to the Effingham County Board of Education for two new schools to serve the development. One of those schools, Blandford Elementary school, is under construction and is scheduled to open in the fall of 2006. The County and the state Department of Transportation (DOT) have plans for construction of a $57.8 million Effingham Parkway that will bisect the tract. The County plans to fund its $7.8 million portion of the project through impact fees from new development, including IP's research tract. Construction of the parkway is scheduled to begin in 2007, and it should take about four years to complete the first phase, County spokesperson Karen Robertson said.[264]

What about the very popular and little studied "agricultural security areas?" A closer look reveals the complex issues — of maintenance, environment and development — out of which these "areas" arise:

> Two members of the [California] state Senate agriculture committee held a listening session on Tuesday in Salinas focused on the potential impacts of government use of eminent domain on California agricultural land. The meeting, attended by several growers, cattle ranchers and representatives of the state and county Farm Bureau, follows a decision in the spring by the Supreme Court that gave local governments broad eminent domain power to take private property for private development. Committee member Dennis Hollingsworth, [Republican]-Murrieta, who was at the meeting with chairman Sen. Jeff Denham, [Republican]-Merced, has proposed legislation, SB 1099, that would limit the use of the practice by government agencies to acquire agricultural land.... Farmland, said [Bob Perkins, executive director of the Monterey County Farm Bureau]...is vulnerable to eminent domain transactions because it is relatively inexpensive compared to other land. Between 1991 and 2003, according to Dennis O'Bryant, division chief of the division of land resources protection with the Department of Conservation, more than 25,000 acres of agricultural land protected under the Williamson Act was acquired by public agencies. The Williamson Act, administered by the state's Department of Conservation, provides agricultural landowners with tax breaks in exchange for their promise not to develop the land. More than 16 million acres are now enrolled in Williamson Act contracts. "It is extremely disturbing," said John Gamper, director of land use

---

264 *The Business Report*, October 25, 2005.

and taxation for the California Farm Bureau, of the increase in agricultural lands being acquired by public agencies....[Perkins]...was concerned that there isn't a mechanism between local and state agencies ensuring that agricultural land under Williamson Act isn't scooped up by local entities. "These are all little pieces of the picture. It's not that one is exactly related to the other," he said referring to the Williamson Act and the use of eminent domain. "But the issue is there is a pattern that we believe could lead to that...."Tim Hearne, a South County ranch owner who lives near Long Valley, where the Salinas Valley Solid Waste Authority is considering building a landfill[, said that eighty] percent of the valley, he estimated, is preserved under the Williamson Act. "Eminent domain law does not have enough precautions to prevent public agencies from taking over ag[ricultural] land," Hearne said. "It doesn't seem that the Williamson Act carries any substance at all with these agencies."[265]

Does the "feasible and prudent" standard discussed below, raise the level of scrutiny for maintenance? for other facts? What other contexts are, by extension, subject to review according to this standard?

Interstate Route 81 is a major trucking thoroughfare running through Pennsylvania's prime farmland. With the exception of Thanksgiving and Christmas, eighteen wheelers constantly roll across the area carrying tons of freight in every direction. In late 1988, PennDOT [the state transportation agency] proposed constructing a new Exit 7 interchange along Interstate 81 in the Chambersburg area of Franklin County. This $5.8 million improvement would provide additional access to Chambersburg and relieve traffic congestion on the nearby I-81 interchange and Route 30, which sits about a mile south of the intended location. Lamar and Lois White own a 26-acre farm contiguous to Interstate 81 in Greene and Guilford townships. The farm is in an Agricultural Security Area.... The Agricultural Security Area Act sets up a statewide program designed to conserve, protect, and encourage the development and improvement of Pennsylvania's agricultural lands for the production of food and other agricultural products. To encourage participation in this program, numerous incentives are offered. Landowners receive incentives in exchange for relinquishment of the right to develop the farmland. Compensation is provided by the taxpayers. In June 1994, the Whites received a notice from PennDOT informing them that PennDOT might need to enter their property to conduct surveys and tests for the construction of a new Exit 7 interchange. PennDOT would need to condemn all or a large portion of the White farm to build the proposed exit. Sometime after receiving the notification of possible entry, the Whites refused entry to PennDOT employees. PennDOT made no further attempt to access the Whites' property. In March 1999, PennDOT received approval from the Federal Highway Administration (FHA) to move forward with plans to construct a new Exit 7 interchange. The FHA approval meant that designers could draft final plans, acquire the right-of-way property and construct the interchange as early as Spring 2000. In response to the FHA announcement, the Whites filed a lawsuit against PennDOT in the Commonwealth Court, alleging that PennDOT violated the Agricultural Security Area Law by illegally conducting tests on their land prior to obtaining Agricultural Lands Condemnation Approval Board (ALCAB) permission. PennDOT responded by claiming that they did not need the approval of the ALCAB because they were simply widening an existing road and the ALCAB statute exempted the approval. The lawsuit presented [the question,]... [m]ust the Pennsylvania Department of Transportation have Agricultural Lands

265 *Monterey Herald*, November 2, 2005 (Monterey, California, archived at www. montereyherald.com).

Condemnation Approval Board approval before it files a declaration of taking and condemns Agricultural Security Area farmland? The court began its decision by stating that Pennsylvania Statutes clearly empower PennDOT to condemn land for all transportation purposes. But before condemning agricultural lands that are being used for productive agricultural purposes, PennDOT must request the ALCAB to determine if there is a reasonable and prudent alternative to building the highway on productive farmland. The Agricultural Lands Condemnation Approval Board was created to protect productive agricultural land from condemnation. The board is comprised of six members consisting of the Director of the Office of Policy and Planning, the Secretaries of Agriculture, Environmental Protection, Transportation and two active farmers appointed by the Governor with the advice and consent of a majority of the Senate. The Secretary of Agriculture is the chairman. The board has jurisdiction over land condemned for highway and waste disposal purposes. Once faced with a dispute, the board has sixty days in which to determine whether there is a feasible and prudent alternative to the proposed condemnation. Pennsylvania Department of Transportation argued to the court that the ALCAB has no jurisdiction over PennDOT's power to condemn farmland because the Exit 7 project was simply a widening of an existing road. In section 106(d)(1) of the ALCAB, the statute provides that board jurisdiction does not apply to widening roadways of existing highways, and the elimination of curves or reconstruction on existing highways. According to PennDOT, the Exit 7 project was a simple widening of an existing highway. The court disagreed. It found that the work proposed on Exit 7 was clearly outside the scope of the exception because it involved the addition of an interchange with new ramps and connector roads. The court held that PennDOT must seek ALCAB approval before it can file a declaration of taking.[266]

Are "corridors of protection" and "agricultural security areas" examples of states within a state, areas of power about which we know little, and which we cannot locate within our traditional concepts — examples of discretion run amuck? Assume Susette Kelo accepts the condemnation award and moves out of her house. Is her house still "housing," that is, is it in fact a "housing security area?" Does the state, in fact, exercise "protection" over it?

Recently, the Federal government has established multi-agency-designated "energy corridors" — and even devoted a website to them! It describes the goals and powers of these corridors:

> What Is an Energy Corridor?
>
> ...[A]n energy corridor is defined as a **parcel of land (often linear in character)** that has been identified through the land use planning process as being a **preferred location** for existing and future **utility right-of-ways**, and that is suitable to accommodate one or more rights-of-way which are similar, identical or compatible.
>
> What Are the Components of an Energy Corridor?
>
> Energy corridors may accommodate multiple pipelines (such as for oil, gas, or hydrogen), electricity transmission lines, and related infrastructure, such as access and maintenance roads, compressors, pumping stations, and other structures....

---

266 Jeff Feirick, "Condemnation of Agricultural Security Area Farmland: *White v. Pennsylvania Department of Transportation (PennDOT),*" www.dsl.psu.edu/centers/aglawpubs/ condemnation.cfm+agricultural+security+area+eminent+domain&hl=en.

What Benefits Will Energy Corridor Designation Bring?
- Streamlining and expediting the processing of energy-related permits and projects;
- Providing applicants for individual rights-of-way within designated corridors with a clear set of actions required by each of the Agencies to implement projects in designated corridors;
- Reducing duplicative assessment of generic environmental impacts by focusing further impact assessment on site-specific (on-the-ground) environmental studies to determine route suitability and appropriate mitigation;
- Ensuring needed inter-agency coordination as part of the application process; and
- Encouraging new and innovative technologies to increase corridor capacity.[267]

This very general mandate has aroused the concern of residents of western states, who seem especially affected by such "corridors:"

> The possibility of pipelines and power lines running through private property or even the Bob Marshall Wilderness Areas were a few of the concerns raised during a meeting in Helena [Montana] Thursday, held to discuss the creation of "energy corridors" throughout the West. Other questions raised by some of the 40 people at yesterday's afternoon information session involved whether the corridors will line up when crossing from one jurisdiction to another, and how these energy corridors will mesh with existing public federal and state land management plans. At this point, the answer to many of those questions is unknown. Thursday's meeting is one of 11 being held throughout the West to hear from the public about concerns they want addressed in a Programmatic Environmental Impact Statement that will be developed during the next year. A preliminary EIS should be completed by Jan. 30, 2006, and the corridors must be included in new Bureau of Land Management land-use plans by August 2007. Designating energy corridors is a requirement of the 2005 energy bill signed in August by President Bush. The corridors may provide a route for electrical transmission lines, natural gas or hydrogen pipelines and even fiber optics. No corridors have been designated just yet, although maps are available that show where routes are that are of interest to several energy companies. The point of putting together the EIS — expected to be completed next October — is to have the investigation of the impacts of an energy corridor completed so that when a project is proposed in the future, it can be implemented quickly. The potential routes will only be delineated on public lands, such as those managed by the BLM and US Forest Service, because the federal government has no jurisdiction on private lands. However, concerns have been raised that the corridor could result in the federal government exercising its right of "eminent domain" if private land is needed for the corridor. The lack of specificity as to where the corridors could run, and the probability that they will traverse private property, bothered rancher Bob Marks, who wondered out loud how he could comment on a route when he didn't know where it might lie. "There isn't a blanket of government lands...that doesn't have to cross private land," Marks said. "I think it will be difficult to make a comment on the EIS because we don't know what we are talking about. This is a generic process rather than an intimate process where we can talk about locations. I think that's extremely important." Jim Melton, an environmental consultant in Helena who has worked on EIS documents for 35 years, added that it's important to set some guidelines early on as to the level of

267 www.corridoreis.anl.gov.

detail required in the document, to consider who would be responsible for addressing significant impacts and to have the EIS look at "reasonable, foreseeable impacts" as well as cumulative impacts. In addition, he said that there already are a number of key corridors, "but a lot of the lines on the current plans and past plans do not line up," Melton said. "That's another cut that needs to be made."[268]

There is a proliferation of "corridors," polyglot legal entities only vaguely dedicated to any particular fact, except the fact that eminent domain can be easily exercised through them. Seemingly every road is now a "corridor." There are "blighted business corridors,"[269] "corridors" designated simply by street,[270] areas which threaten to be designated as "corridors," such as "coastal corridors,"[271] "depressed corridors,"[272] "heritage corridors"[273] — even "learning corridors."[274] "Zones" is another term for these entities: there are "redevelopment zones," "enterprise zones," "empowerment zones," "overlay" zones and so on.[275] There are also the districts: "zoning overlay districts," "redevelopment districts," "diking districts," and so on.[276] The "corridors," "zones" and "districts" — the "legal entity" state within a state — saw the crumbling of the Fifth Amendment's "public use" requirement: all was "use," but none of the "legal entities" were government. The law was ceasing to distinguish anything: it was ceasing to exist. The "corridors" and other such clumsy terms, are code words for the covering up of fact, which the political system has learned from the Supreme Court: it is the Supreme Court which is the heart of duplicity. Its policy of lying is at least one precedent everyone has followed. Of course the stupid thing is that, although the "corridors" take advantage of minimum scrutiny with respect to eminent domain, **they do not thereby avoid physical confrontations over the facts.** When all the fuss and bluster are said and done, will law enforcement move in? Will it be successful? When push comes to shove, who will win?

The "corridors" are the clearest evidence yet of the eminent domain state within a state, and are an example of the political system progressively elimi-

---

268 *Helena Independent Record*, October 28, 2005 (Helena, Montana, archived at www.helenair.com).

269 *Dallas Morning News*, July 14, 2005 (Dallas, Texas, archived at www.dallasnews.com).

270 *La Prensa San Diego*, February 25, 2005 (San Diego, California, archived at www.laprensasandiego.org).

271 March 4, 2005 (archived at www.sfgate.com).

272 *Milwaukee Journal Sentinel*, July 15, 2005 (Milwaukee, Wisconsin, archived at www.jsonline.com).

273 October 12, 2003 (archived at www.cleveland.com).

274 September 22, 2005 (archived at www.nolandgrab.org).

275 The Federal government also maintains a website for its "empowerment zones" program: www.acf.hhs.gov. See the "overlay" zone description and legislation for Jacksonville, Florida, at www.coj.net.

276 See the "zoning overlay district" description and legislation for Clark County, Nevada, at www.co.clark.nv.us; see the "redevelopment district" plan of Palm Bay, Florida at www.palmbayflorida.org.; see the "diking district" plan of the State of Washington at www.apps.leg.wa.gov.

nating the jurisdiction of the Constitution. However, the conflation of eminent domain and "corridor" has merely turned controversy into confrontation; it is a further provocation, exacerbating tensions precisely because it is promoted as a substitute for Constitutional debate. In short, facts of the individual push themselves to the fore. These "entities" are neither public nor quasi-public nor private, nor anything along the continuum — they are simply subversions, their end is totalitarian. The "minimum scrutiny" regime was squeezing the Constitution out of existence. Without the "facts of the individual" analysis, it would disappear unmourned, even unnoticed.[277]

In the end, and no matter how vague it seemed, legislation reforming eminent domain had to be applied to ongoing projects involving eminent domain — and this promised an entirely new arena of confrontation. Congress' efforts as they related to a New Jersey project involving several hundred homes, highlighted the confusion. What was the difference, if any, between economic development and redevelopment? What use of Federal funds triggered the eminent domain restriction?

> The US House of Representatives passed a bill last week restricting the use of eminent domain by local governments and there is disagreement over its impact on redevelopment in the city. "It appears that Long Branch would not be affected in any way," said James Aaron about H.R. 4128, the Private Property Protection Act of 2005, that passed by a vote of 376 to 38 in the US House of Representatives on Nov. 3. "The bill will affect commercial development," Aaron explained. "Long Branch is working under a redevelopment statute. The bill says nothing about a redevelopment statute...."But an attorney who has been retained to represent two homeowners in the city's Beachfront North, phase II redevelopment zone, known as MTOTSA (Marine and Ocean Terraces and Seaview Avenues) said the bill is unclear. "If Long Branch has federal funds in the [MTOTSA] project, the city may not be able to go forward with the ac-

---

277  The "corridors" are also chafings under the outdated political arrangement of the United States. Issues involving gerrymandering, interstate commerce, as well as eminent domain, reflect the inability, under the "minimum scrutiny" regime, to reach government as a fact of the individual, which was the premise of *Marbury*. The measure of the inadequacy of state boundaries can be understood interactively by the reader by manipulating the socioeconomic date online at the government's www.nationalatlas.gov. See also Samuel Issacharoff and Pamela S. Karlan, "Where to Draw the Line? *Vieth v. Jubelirer*, *Cox v. Larios*, and Judicial Review of Political Gerrymanders," http://ssrn.com/abstract=568903. As a result, the states themselves now chase increasingly exotic remedies: "Over the last few decades, state and local governments increasingly have adopted tax and other policies to encourage economic development within their borders. These programs have recently come under attack as potentially inconsistent with the U.S. Supreme Court's dormant Commerce Clause jurisprudence. [U.S. Const. Article I, § 8 authorizes Congress to "regulate commerce among the states," and is read by the Supreme Court as forbidding state action which unduly burdens interstate commerce through actions which discriminate against other states.] In an opinion issued in late 2004, the Sixth Circuit Court of Appeals invalidated Ohio's investment tax credit, contending that it discriminates against interstate commerce. The U.S. Supreme Court has granted certiorari in the case. In the meantime, similar litigation is underway in other states. In reaction to these developments, legislation has been introduced in Congress to protect the right of states to provide tax incentives....[T]he interstate economic effects have significance for the Commerce Clause analysis of state tax incentives." Kirk J. Stark and Daniel J. Wilson, summarizing their article, "What Do We Know About the Interstate Economic Effects of State Tax Incentives?" http://ssrn.com/abstract=868692.

quisitions," William J. Ward of Carlin & Ward, Florham Park, said. "But it is confusing. It is not clear if the city has to receive federal funds in general or if it has to receive those funds for the specific redevelopment project," he said.... An attorney with the Institute for Justice (IJ), a nonprofit law firm based in Washington, D.C., that specializes in the protection of private property rights, said the bill could potentially affect all cities in New Jersey if it becomes law. "Cities would have to choose between economic development or economic funds," Dana Berliner, IJ senior attorney said. According to the bill, economic development is defined as "taking private property without the consent of the owner, and conveying or leasing such property from one private person or entity to another private person or entity for commercial enterprise carried on for profit, to increase tax revenue, tax base, employment or general economic health...."[New Jersey Representative Frank] Pallone said he thinks legislation stronger than this bill should be approved to "ensure that we curb all abuses of eminent domain....The Protect Our Homes Act simply states there should be no taking of homes for economic development unless there are rare and exceptional circumstances involving a public health crisis," Pallone said. About one month ago, Pallone introduced his own legislation in the US House of Representatives to prohibit communities from invoking eminent domain, except under extreme circumstances. The legislation would seek to provide federal incentives to encourage municipalities to accomplish the following:

- show that they have explored all necessary alternatives to eminent domain;
- ensure that, in the rare cases where homes are taken, all homeowners receive compensation well beyond the market value to reflect relocation cost and intangible value of a family's home;
- redevelopment plans include affordable housing for families and seniors and an equivalent housing plan in the case of commercial development; and
- provide the residents of a community have the ability to petition their local government to include a referendum on the project.[278]

As it turned out, only a "facts of the individual" analysis could mediate between branches and doctrines of the "minimum scrutiny" regime:

Saying that Groton [Massachusetts] misused its powers to take property, a developer has sued the town for giving selectmen the authority to seize land off Lowell Road by eminent domain at a special Town Meeting last fall. In a lawsuit filed in Middlesex Superior Court last month, Washington Green Development says the eminent domain vote taken at Town Meeting in September was illegal because the town was using the measure to derail the company's 44-unit townhouse development. The Groton Electric Light Commission had said at Town Meeting that it wanted to purchase the property because it was an ideal location for its department offices. The Light Department currently has its headquarters on Station Avenue....Attorney Ray Lyons, who represents Washington Green, said his client...applied for the project under the state's affordable housing law, Chapter 40B. In communities that do not meet the state's threshold for affordable housing, the law allows developers to bypass local zoning if they set aside at least 20 percent of the housing units at below-market prices....The townhouse plan had faced opposition from local officials since last spring, when Washington Green appeared before town boards. Last March, the Zoning Board of Appeals denied the permit on grounds that the housing plan created health and liability risks for the town because it was close to an electric substation.

278 November 11, 2005 (archived at www.atlanticville.gmnews.com).

Washington Green appealed the decision, and in September the Massachusetts Department of Housing and Community Development's Housing Appeals Committee overturned the zoning board's decision, saying the health and liability risk for residents living in the housing was not a sufficient reason to deny the permit, according to the complaint. Gloria Fuccillo, who owns the Lowell Road property, was angered by the Town Meeting vote, saying she had originally offered to sell her 13.5 acres to the Light Department, but had been refused. The Light Department had already taken steps to put its offices on Sandy Pond Road and didn't need her property for its offices, she said she was told. "The only reason [the town] wants it is because of that 40B," said Fuccillo. "I'm definitely rooting for the contractor."[279]

The conflict begins between zoning and eminent domain. Then it goes to a conflict between local and state powers. Then it goes to a conflict between exercises of health and welfare powers. Then we are back to square one, trying to figure out the difference between zoning and eminent domain. Round and round it goes. Recourse can only be had to a "facts of the individual" analysis which harmonizes housing and government through the maintenance concept.

## THE RESPONSE OF THE JUDICIARY

In *Kelo* the Court demanded that public opinion accept the idea that although the Court *could* vindicate for government an abuse of the rights of an individual, that same Court *could not* vindicate for the same individual the same rights against the same government. In the response to *Kelo* public opinion declined any longer to accept that idea.

The response of public opinion to the *Kelo* decision meant that judges had immediately to begin implementing an *ad hoc* direct scrutiny analysis. There was no choice. However, absent elevation of scrutiny for facts, the stability of the judgments was necessarily problematic. That instability had to do with the inability of the courts to indicate *which* facts enjoyed direct scrutiny and which did not: they could not implement direct scrutiny, only foist it on the parties. The clearest evidence of the pressure of public opinion was that the courts simply began to subject eminent domain actions to direct scrutiny with respect to *all* facts. Among other lesser ironies, this was a blind revelation of the lack of faith of the lower judiciary in the United States Supreme Court:

> Eviction notices for landowners on the site of the proposed Washington Nationals baseball stadium won't be issued until Major League Baseball agrees to terms with the city government, a D.C. Superior Court judge said yesterday.... The D.C. government is working to use its eminent domain authority to take possession of 15 parcels of privately held land. Construction is scheduled for completion in 2008. "At the point that I'm satisfied that the baseball deal is going forward, I will sign the orders of possession," Judge Joan Zeldon said in a court hearing. "Don't ask me what happens if [baseball owners] don't agree,

---

279 *The Boston Globe*, February 5, 2006.

because I don't know....."Judge Zeldon said once the bonds are sold she would "promptly sign" the land over to the city.[280]

Note that the Judge not only wants the agreements, she wants the bonds sold first. But why? After all, the Judge makes no distinction between the properties to be seized, and she is not permitted to do so, under *Kelo*. No wonder, then, that she says, "I don't know," regarding the implications of her decision. *Kelo* makes hash of her reasoning. There are no facts (such as "the baseball deal is going forward") which must be found for the government entity to have its right to exercise eminent domain affirmed, *unless the Court doubts there is, in fact, a government purpose*. The decision is itself an indicium of an absence of government purpose. The Judge is saying that the eminent domain action fails under direct scrutiny. Then where is she finding authority for her decision? Not under *Kelo*, but in light of *Kelo*. *Kelo* is that case in which "facts [premising] a constitutional resolution of social controversy had proven to be untrue, and history's demonstration of their untruth not only justified but required the new choice of constitutional principle." The true facts were "facts that the country could understand, or had come to understand already, but which the Court of an earlier day, as its own declarations disclosed, had not been able to perceive...[:] applications of constitutional principle to facts as they had not been seen by the Court before." The facts of *Kelo* were lies. They were false facts, and public opinion knew it. The Supreme Court had not been able to bring itself to do anything about these lies, so it had to promulgate them. Such a situation could not go on. The Judge was forced to adopt new standards to reconcile the Constitution to the true facts. Implementation of the direct scrutiny standard followed inexorably.

The Oklahoma Supreme Court decided to take the bull by the horns, and actually attempt to give some meaning to "economic development" in connection with the following facts and law. The result was an ill-disguised mess in which the Court only further entangled itself trying to prevent the use of eminent domain for "economic development alone":

> [Muskogee] County initiated condemnation proceedings against... [l]andowners for the purpose of acquiring temporary and permanent right-of-way easements for the installation of three water pipelines. Two of the proposed water pipelines (referred to by the parties and hereinafter collectively referred to as "the Eagle Pipeline") would solely serve Energetix, a privately owned electric generation plant, which was proposed for construction in Muskogee County.... Energetix proposed to build the third water pipeline (hereinafter "the Water District Pipeline") on behalf of the Rural Water District No. 5 (hereinafter "Water District") pursuant to a contract [with the County]...which expressly provided for Energetix's agreement to build this pipeline at no cost to the Water District "as part of the consideration to induce certain property owners to grant private easements for the Eagle Pipeline." The Water District Pipeline was intended to serve residents of the Water District who were not currently being served and to enhance current water service to residents of the Water District, who were receiving it. This contract expressly specified that **Energetix's duty to construct the Water District pipeline arises only on the conditions precedent**

---

280 *The Washington Times*, February 25, 2006 (Washington, D.C., archived at www.washingtontimes.com).

that Energetix first succeeds in obtaining all rights-of-way needed to construct the private Eagle Pipeline and Energetix begins construction of the Eagle Pipeline.....The County sought to condemn Landowners' private property pursuant to its general eminent domain power granted by [Oklahoma statute]..., which provides as follows: ["]Any county, city, town, township, school district, or board of education, or any board or official having charge of cemeteries created and existing under the laws of this state, shall have power to condemn lands in like manner as railroad companies, for highways, rights-of-way, building sites, cemeteries, public parks and *other public purposes*....["] (emphasis added). Additionally, we are guided by the applicable general federal constitutional and state constitutional eminent domain provisions, including and perhaps most notably our special [Oklahoma state constitution] provision concerning the taking of private property...: ["]No private property shall be taken or damaged for private use, with or without compensation, unless by consent of the owner, except for private ways of necessity, or for drains and ditches across lands of others for agricultural, mining, or sanitary purposes, in such manner as may be prescribed by law....["] That constitutional provision additionally states "[in] all cases of condemnation of private property for public or private use, the determination of the character of the use shall be a judicial question."

The Court concluded that the easements could not be taken for economic development without a finding of blight. This supposedly distinguished economic development from blight. That seems simple enough. But look at the way Oklahoma law defines blight:

"Blighted conditions" means conditions which, *because of the presence of a majority of the following factors*, substantially impair or arrest the sound development and growth of the municipality or constitute an economic or social liability or are a menace to the public health, safety, morals or welfare in its present condition and use:

1. a substantial number of deteriorated or deteriorating structures,
2. predominance of defective or inadequate street layout,
3. unsanitary or unsafe conditions,
4. deterioration of site improvements,
5. absentee ownership,
6. tax or special assessment delinquency exceeding the fair value of the land,
7. defective or unusual conditions of title,
8. improper subdivision or obsolete platting or land uses,
9. the existence of conditions which endanger life or property by fire and other causes, or
10. conditions which create economic obsolescence, or areas containing obsolete, non-functioning or inappropriately developed structures....

The Court did not address the idea that the purpose of the blight designation was to facilitate development — the argument of the county — and so the elaboration of the criteria for blight was meant to make the finding of blight easier, not harder. It left these criteria alone. The result was the usual hopeless task of defining blight, a dilemma now expanding to embrace another hopeless term, "economic development." Far from providing "property protection to Oklahoma citizens beyond that which is afforded them by the Fifth Amendment to the US

Constitution" (ostensibly a slap at *Kelo*), the decision had the disastrous effect linking government and blight through "economic development" — something which would delight the members of the "property rights" movement — but it also linked property and blight through "economic development," again raising the question, what is property? This was another layer of ambiguity which only sharpened conflict.

Far from restraining the political system, the decision gave the political system food for thought as to new subterfuges in its anomalous struggle with public opinion. Unless government were to be interpreted as having no health and regulatory powers (and the Court goes out of its way to emphasize that it is only putting its restriction on government in the context of eminent domain), the tendency of the Court's thinking was to make it easier, not harder, for government to show blight. "Economic development" opened the door to arguing a single set of facts, either as not rising to the level of development and falling below the level of blight, or as not rising to the level of blight and falling below the level of development. What was the "solely for economic development" test? For example, if government could show, say, three of the criteria, perhaps conditions did not amount to blight, but didn't it also mean that the eminent domain use was not solely for economic development? There was, just as Justice Stevens had implied, no logical distinction between development, economic development and redevelopment. The only thing which seemed to be developing was endless permutation of the word, development. Meaninglessness beckoned. The Oklahoma Court sought to distinguish facts by making meaningless distinctions, but it only drove facts away, putting property owners in jeopardy. The stalemate continued and over the same issues: definitions and concepts.[281]

Like the state legislatures, the judiciary seemed unable to avoid impulsive decisions with increasingly shaky doctrines. *Bailey v. Mesa* was a case in which a business — which provided the maintenance for its owner — was sought to be condemned so more businesses could be built on the site. Again — and as seemed increasingly common — a fact *v.* fact situation was arising: business *v.* business, housing *v.* housing — *Kelo* itself involved both. The Arizona Court of Appeals had to decide whether eminent domain over a business, for the purpose of turning the land over to other businesses, satisfied the State's standard Constitutional requirement of public use. The provision, however, includes this curious language: "Whenever an attempt is made to take private property for a use alleged to be public, the question whether the contemplated use be really public shall be a judicial question, and determined as such without regard to any legislative assertion that the use is public."[282] In effect, this simply adds another layer of minimum scrutiny: the standard for overturning a trial court on appeal is abuse of discretion, *i.e.*, that no reasonable court could have found as the trial court found.

---

281 *Board of County Commissioners of Muskogee County v. Lowery*, 2006 OK 31 (citations omitted, emphasis in original). The text of this opinion is available online at www.oscn.net.

282 *Bailey v. Mesa*, 1 CA-SA-02-0108 (Ct. of App. Div. 1, Ariz.), 2003, 5-6. The text of this opinion is also available online at www.ij.org/pdf_folder/private_property/mesa_decision_10_1_03.pdf.

That is an extraordinarily difficult standard to meet, and basically means that the judicial branch doesn't want to deal with the question anymore. As with Federal law, Arizona law does not state whether "public use" is a fact. Now it has added another term, the factual status of which is unclear: a "really" public use. Nor does Arizona law make clear the considerations out of which the term "really" arises, independent of its use with respect to eminent domain. For the Court, the language meant that "[t]aking one person's property for another person's private use is plainly prohibited...."[283] However, this merely substituted "for" for "really."

The Court then proposed this standard by way of explanation: "anticipated public benefits must substantially outweigh the private character of the end use so that it may truly be said that the taking is for a use that is 'really public.' The constitutional requirement of 'public use' is only satisfied when the public benefits and characteristics of the intended use substantially predominate over the private nature of that use."[284] However, merely repeating the standard did not make it any clearer. Is it intermediate scrutiny, that is, does it require that the government show a substantial furtherance of an important government purpose? Apparently the facts have to be in a closer relationship to the purpose, but no more restriction of the government purpose is indicated. The standard is unclear because no fact is mentioned in it. Instead, the Court is supposed to examine the deal for "public purposes," whether "title to the property [will be] held by a public entity," "end use," and "degree of control" — all standards which invite creative evasion. Nevertheless, in this case the Court did not examine the facts to see if it met all those requirements; instead, it concluded rather summarily that "the intended use of the property is fundamentally for private development" and rejected the eminent domain action.[285] Did this mean that the Court had decided that eminent domain with respect to maintenance shall not be exercised unless it is substantially furthers an important government purpose?

In turn, *Bailey*'s question-begging standard was bound to be a nightmare for the trial courts. One Arizona court tried to apply it to an exercise of eminent domain. The Court found the following facts, but did not lay out its method for arriving at its determination that the facts did not "substantially outweigh" the private benefit. That is because the *Bailey* Court provided no method, only a method for offloading matters onto the trial courts:

> 1. The property will be used for private commercial use, a retail shopping complex. 2. The private parties owning the property ultimately will use it for private profit purposes. 3. No needed public services will be provided by the end use of the property. 4. The City of Tempe, the condemning authority, will exercise only that control it has over other privately owned property within its borders. 5. There are no anticipated public uses of the property. 6. There may be an economic benefit to the community of Tempe from the creation of jobs and some tax revenues. The net economic impact has not been determined. 7. The funds for the redevelopment project are almost exclusively private. 8. Private parties appear to be gaining more financially by the taking of the property

---

283 *Id.*, at 7.

284 *Id.*, at 15.

285 *Id.*, at 16-17.

than the public. 9. The private developer Miravista Holdings and its principals are the driving forces behind this project not the Plaintiff, City of Tempe. 10. Profit, not public improvement, is the motivating force for this redevelopment. 11. The plaintiff wants to improve the 'appearance' of the property within the City of Tempe by removing any heavy industrial activity outside its municipal boundaries. 12. There are some public health and safety issues involved in the taking. The Court refers to the need to mitigate the methane gas concentrations, improve fire protection and resolve the soil subsidence problem. These public safety concerns can be resolved by the exercise of the police powers of the City without taking the property in issue. The only health assessment of the area in question does not support the plaintiff's position. 13. The property being sought does not appear to be a true 'slum' since the owners are providing legitimate and legal commercial services. The conditions that the plaintiff feels threaten the public safety can readily be addressed by exercise of its police powers without resort to taking private property. The anticipated private purposes and benefits outweigh any public benefit or purpose.[286]

This is a perfect example of what happens in an attempt to limit the applicability of an inherently vague term by subjecting it to a test: the prongs of the test proliferate uncontrollably. Why? Because in the first instance the test provides no guidance, because it contains no facts. Predictably, the Arizona Supreme Court refused to hear an appeal of this case.[287] Evidently, the trial courts are not supposed to know what is a "really" public use, but they are expected to know one when they see one. More importantly, this test and its application, resolve nothing. For those seeking to exercise domain, it invites creative evasion. For those seeking to resist eminent domain, it means that ostensible victories can always be revisited and turned into defeats. But the solution was as simple as it was obvious: to amend the Constitutional clause to require that the "use be really, really public." More precision would be attained by requiring that the "use be really, really, really public." Magic would be achieved by requiring that the "use be really, really, **really**" public. And so on, to utopia. To be fair, the original phrase does mean one thing: contempt for the individual.

And now the denouement, in two acts: "The Tempe Marketplace, a luxury development planned for crossroads of the Loop 101 and 202 freeways, apparently will be built. The final roadblock in the way of the 117-acre retail and entertainment complex is gone. Developer Vestar Development Company says it has reached buyout agreements with enough area property owners to go forward with the project. It has been trying for years to get several holdout landowners to sell. The fight landed in court, where the city of Tempe was rebuffed in its attempt to use eminent domain to get the land. The company says it may just build around the two properties whose owners haven't sold. Another option would be for the city to continue its legal fight for the property."[288] Consider the cases

---

286 *Tempe v. Valentine*, September 12, 2005. The opinion is online at www.superiorcourt. maricopa.gov.

287 *East Valley Tribune*, November 30, 2005 (Scottsdale, Arizona, archived at www.eastvalleytribune.com).

288 *The Tempe Republic*, December 21, 2005 (Tempe, Arizona, archived at www.azcentral.com).

and then consider what in fact is "around?" What in law is "around?" What are now the rights of the property owners with respect to "around?" These questions always arise in scenarios which envision building "around" holdouts against purchase offers. We shall see the political system's response to "around" when it came to dealing with Susette Kelo after her defeat. What are the rights of the property owners to revisit the original plan for the development, in order to conform it to Arizona law? Again, minimum scrutiny initiated stalemate — not resolution — of disputes. In addition, under the housing provision of the New Bill of Rights, what right is there to force the reconfiguration of extant "development" plans in order to see that the individual is not involuntarily deprived of housing? Are these questions separate from the question, what, in fact, is housing? Is housing always at issue under the New Bill of Rights? any more or less than protected speech or freedom from an establishment of religion, are always at issue under the old Bill of Rights?

The problematic nature, both of the Arizona law and of the two property-owner victories won under it, became evident when, in act two still *further* eminent domain "restrictions" were proposed in Arizona. However, the concerns and the generalities incorporated in the proposals, generated more heat than light, and were certain to generate more inconclusive litigation: "A legislative committee chairman on Tuesday proposed two amendments to the Arizona Constitution and offered other legislation to bolster private property owners' protections from forced purchase by governments. One of the two resolutions...by Rep. Chuck Gray, [Republican]-Mesa, to put the proposed constitutional changes on the November ballot would create a new right to a jury trial on whether a condemnation is for a public use and therefore allowed under Arizona law. The second resolution would require a government involved in a condemnation to overcome a new legal presumption that the proposed condemnation is for private use and therefore not allowed....During an interview Tuesday, Gray acknowledged that the Arizona Constitution contains stronger protections for property owners than the US Supreme Court says are included in the US Constitution....However, in the wake of the federal court's ruling last year in favor of condemnation for a Connecticut city's redevelopment project Gray said he doesn't want to take the chance that future courts will interpret Arizona's provisions in ways that don't protect property owners. 'If we wait around just sit around hoping that somebody doesn't misinterpret our constitution someday, then I think we're missing an opportunity,' he said....Related bills introduced by Gray, the chairman of the House Committee on Federal Mandates and Property Rights, would require that public bodies disclose the scope and cost of projects involved with eminent domain..., consider eminent domain actions in public...and reimburse private property owners for legal costs in some instances...."[289] The proposal found the legislature even more disposed to act as the judiciary. Did the proposal trump the power of the court? What did the presumption presume? Who knew? And what did the law matter as long as outcomes did not turn into physical confrontations? But if they

---

289 *Tucson Citizen*, December 3, 2006 (Tucson, Arizona, archived at www.tucsoncitizen.com).

did, what then? Disputes drove the law, but the law did not respond by settling the disputes. This tended to conflate the legislative and judicial branches, exactly the situation *Marbury* had suggested accompany involuntary deprivation of a fact of the individual. But neither the legislature nor the judiciary was capable of diagnosing the symptom — they could not understand why they *themselves* were doing what they were doing, or what drove them to do it. There was no awareness on the part of any legislators or judges in the country that *physical confrontation over the facts was relevant to their deliberations*. The "minimum scrutiny" regime had removed them from rationality — but it had not insulated them from it.

> Another judicial response — on firmer legal grounds but apparently also reflecting a more generalized distaste for eminent domain "abuse" — was simply for the court, as the trier of fact, to find that the proposed exercise did not meet the minimum scrutiny standard, that it was not rationally related to a legitimate government purpose because there were no facts to back up the claim of rationality — not that government purpose had failed a factual inquiry. Note the dogged opposition of the political system in the following instance:
>
> Officials in Lodi [New Jersey] have a responsibility to borough residents. But that responsibility encompasses all residents, not just those with a basement. Last week, a Superior Court judge blocked the borough from condemning the Costa and Brown trailer parks. It was an important victory. The US Supreme Court's landmark ruling in *Kelo v. New London* — which sided with a plan by the city of New London, Conn., to take land by eminent domain for private development — emboldened other towns and cities to use eminent domain to seize property. New Jersey courts have not been receptive. Judges in Passaic, Union and Essex counties have dismissed municipal plans to use eminent domain. The Lodi case is a good example of why courts must continue to put the rights of individuals first. The trailer parks may not be the most beautiful residential section of Lodi. But they are not drug-infested, centers of urban blight. They serve a valuable purpose: affordable housing for the elderly and for low-income families. The president of Save our Homes, an organization created to fight the Lodi land grab, says there are 500 people living in the two trailer parks, a not-insignificant number....The judge in his ruling said, "The evidence put forth by the defendants in support of their designation of redevelopment can be summed up as vague criticism of the conditions at the complex upon superficial observations."[290]

Less acceptable was the notion of judges promulgating and enforcing health and welfare regulations — pursuant to *ad hoc* "facts of the individual" analyses — by transforming compensation under eminent domain into punishment:

> An Ingham County [Michigan] judge ordered that five houses at Lake Madison be purchased for more than $1.6 million and removed because of a proposed instrument landing system for the Lenawee County Airport. The homes are involved in an eminent domain lawsuit authorized in July by the Lenawee County Commission to obtain airspace easements for an enlarged runway safety zone needed for an instrument landing system. The proposed landing system has not been installed. Homeowners involved in the lawsuit demanded their entire properties be purchased rather than the air space above them....[One homeowner said that if] an instrument system that will allow landings in poor weather conditions is installed..., "I know it will be less safe...."Airport authorities last year prevented him from building a house on a vacant lot he owns next door, he

---

290 October 13, 2005 (archived at www.northjersey.com).

said. That helped convince him homes on his street will not be as safe as they have been....[The judge ruled that] acquiring only a portion of the five properties needed for the runway protection zone "destroys the practical value or utility of the remainder of the parcel, requiring plaintiff to acquire and pay just compensation for the whole parcel." Other homeowners at Lake Madison whose property is under an enlarged safety zone for the proposed instrument landing system [but not included in the eminent domain lawsuit] might now also seek a government buyout....[291]

This was an obviously unsatisfactory substitute for simply raising the level of scrutiny for housing. A decision on these grounds risked being overturned on appeal on the basis that the decision as to whether taking the entire house was necessary, was essentially a regulatory decision and the court had overstepped the bounds of its authority. What these cases reveal is the grotesque situation of the court scrambling to find a patch for a hole in the law, a patch it uses but will not acknowledge: *sua sponte* it simply goes ahead and raises the level of scrutiny for facts, hoping no one will notice. In short, the courts are engaging in the same sort of conduct which led to the recognition of a need for the right to privacy: imposing patently inappropriate extensions of existing doctrine in order to make room for newly recognized remedies. Some new law is obviously called for.[292]

Finally, juries were also walking away from *Kelo*:

> Jurors awarded $7.7 million yesterday to the former owner of a Gaslamp Quarter [San Diego] cigar store who was forced to move by the city to make way for a new hotel. The verdict in San Diego Superior Court was the latest chapter in the battle of Ahmed Mesdaq and his Gran Havana Cigar and Coffee Lounge. The city used its powers of eminent domain and forced Mesdaq out of the property at Fifth Avenue and J Street so a developer could build a Marriott Renaissance Hotel. The case attracted national attention in the growing debate over the government's power to take private land and hand it over to a private developer in the name of economic development. Vincent Bartolotta Jr., who represented Mesdaq during the two-week trial, called the verdict a "home run" for Mesdaq and important for other property owners. "The message is you've got to play by the rules," Bartolotta said outside court. "You can't take advantage of the little guy because you've got the power." The jury's award covered two aspects relating to the store. The first was the value of the property and the second was the "good will" — the value of a business due to its location, good reputation and other factors. Outside court, Mesdaq welcomed the verdict but said he still would prefer to be in business. "The verdict is what it is," he said. "But I wish we had never had to come this far. I love the Gaslamp. I love San Diego. I just want to work." For two years, he had waged a spirited campaign against the city's attempt to take his land. Exhausted by the legal battle to stop the condemnation, he gave up the fight and vacated the building in June. He now has his business stored in a 400-square-foot storage space as he decides what his next move will be. The trial, over the value of the land and business, pitted Mesdaq against the city. The City Council, acting as the Redevelopment Agency of San Diego, voted in April 2004 to use eminent domain power and condemn the property

---

291 *The Daily Telegram*, January 21, 2006 (Adrian, Michigan, archived at www.lenconnect.com).

292 For more examples of this judicial legerdemain, see Nicole Stelle Garnett, "The Public Use Question as a Takings Problem" http://ssrn.com/abstract=638362.

and others around it for the 334-room hotel. The hotel developer will have to pay the judgment under terms of its agreement with the city. Bruce W. Beach, the attorney who represented the city, said it was unknown whether the verdict would be appealed. "It's too early to say," Beach said. "We are disappointed in the result. There are some legal issues that we need to discuss with the agency first." Bartolotta said the city offered $3 million before the trial. Mesdaq bought the property in 2000 and — combined with renovations he had made — sunk about $2.5 million into the former warehouse. The city long has maintained that Mesdaq knew the hotel proposal was coming when he purchased the land. Mesdaq refused offers to sell and went to court to stop the condemnation. He argued that taking his land and handing it to a private party did not amount to a "public use." That is traditionally why governments have taken property — for public projects such as roads, schools and bridges. In recent years governments have used eminent domain powers for "economic development," arguing that the tax revenue and jobs that private developers bring ultimately benefit the public."[293]

*Kelo* had turned into one of those decisions showing that the Court possesses neither the sword nor the purse: the decision was reviled and not enforced. In addition, the protest against *Kelo* was forcing a "facts of the individual" analysis up through the judiciary through "close calls," situations born of opposition to *Kelo*: eminent domain takings which were being sanctioned by the Court — for traditional reasons and using traditional rules — but yet were somehow making the Court look more closely:

> Yolo [County, California] Superior Court Judge Timothy Fall on Wednesday ruled that Yolo County may acquire the Conaway Ranch through eminent domain proceedings. "The Yolo County Board of Supervisors applauds the court's decision," said Supervisor Helen Thomson of Davis, board chairwoman. "Today's ruling allows us to preserve the most significant remaining open space and agricultural lands in the county for the future of our county by protecting it from private land speculators and developers and keeping our water in Yolo County," she added....Conaway Ranch, east of Davis and Woodland, consists of 17,300 acres of ag[ricultural] land and wetlands habitat and 50,000 acre-feet of valuable water rights....The county argues that the Conaway Ranch offers countywide public interests, including water rights, water supply and water security for Yolo County landowners, residents and businesses; agricultural resources; public health and safety; local and regional flood control alternatives; open space and rural recreation; and the ability to manage natural resources for environmental purposes. Attorney Gary Livaich argued for the defense that the power of the government to take private property was dangerous. Time and again on Wednesday afternoon, Livaich argued that "want" is not the same as "need." "The county wants my client's property — it covets Conaway Ranch," he said. "But there must be a showing of need. There are no facts in the resolution of necessity to support need." The public good was already being served by the current owners, Livaich argued, and speculating on future changes to the property was not sufficient. "Where is the threat?" he asked. "For the county to say: 'I want to take your property and do the same thing you're doing' — there's something wrong with that. That's a dangerous proposition." But the judge ruled otherwise. "Evidence in the administrative record is slim," Fall said. "But that does not mean it falls beneath the standard of substantial evidence. It is

---

293 *San Diego Union-Tribune*, October 29, 2005 (archived at www.signonsandiego.com).

not completely speculative." Fall ruled that the county had met its burden and should be allowed to continue the eminent domain action.[294]

The term "need" is nowhere in California eminent domain law, which uses the same minimum scrutiny standard set in *Kelo*. The County made a standard case to justify the taking: "water rights, water supply and water security for Yolo County landowners, residents and businesses; agricultural resources; public health and safety; local and regional flood control alternatives; open space and rural recreation; and the ability to manage natural resources for environmental purposes." And yet this prompted a notable comment by the Court: it considered the County's justification "slim" and "not completely speculative." "Need" is not the *Kelo* standard, but then, neither is "slim."

Why is the Court even making this comment? Because of the suggestion that the underlying facts are, as in *Kelo*, simply a power grab in which government abrogates government purpose in bald — irrational — exercises of power: "'In the case of Conaway Ranch, eminent domain is being used to take the ranch for an unspecified government use, but I believe it's to get control of the water,' [John Gamper of the California Federation,] said. 'That's the bottom line. They want the 150,000-acre-feet of water rights.' Gamper said that internal county memos discovered through a formal Public Records Request that show the consultant hired by Yolo County to help with the eminent domain action was specifically asked to look into the feasibility of selling water from the ranch outside the county to help finance its acquisition. 'The very purpose they say they want to acquire the ranch for — protecting its water from being sold — is the very thing they're considering doing,' Gamper said."[295] The political system feels that *Kelo* sanctions its hiding its true motives. However, the effect is exactly the opposite: that gambit simply forces more fundamental issues to the surface. Here the Court wants to know if the list is a list of facts or purposes, assumptions or conclusions. What, in *fact*, are "water," "water rights," "water supply" and "water security," "public health and safety," and the other items on the County's list? What is "slim" here, according to the Court, is the justification for the County's assertions, and the Court is wondering whether the County's assertions are facts of the individual. The County may have discretion to make assertions, but does it have discretion not to do a "facts of the individual" analysis with respect to them? Is minimum scrutiny an actual burden of proof, or is it simply an exaltation of form, not over substance, but rather, in lieu of substance, and does minimum scrutiny rob litigants even of the right to require that substance? Are the assertions justified because the County asserts them, or does the County assert them because they are justified? This is the dilemma of minimum scrutiny which opposition to *Kelo* threw back in the Court's face — and the Court knew it. Here is the Court responding simply to power. The Court is moving — the opposition to *Kelo* is moving the Court — toward an *ad hoc* "facts of the individual" analysis. The Court is implying that if the political system can use minimum scrutiny to

---

294 *Davis Enterprise*, December 1, 2005.

295 *AgWeek*, November 16, 2005 (archived at www.cfbf.com).

conflate doctrines and the powers of government, then the Court can conflate the political system and the Constitution. After all, what is the idea that the government's proposal is rationally related to a legitimate government purpose? Assuming legitimacy is rational, then government's purpose is rationally related to what is rational: rational is rational. That tautology is minimum scrutiny. This bleak piece of stupidity was bound to unsettle *both* the political system (including its own judiciary, embarrassingly bound to say that this illusion *is*) *and* public opinion — and it had done so.

The nadir of minimum scrutiny jurisprudence is simply upending Holmes. It is made possible because eminent domain is a generality, and that has produced a power vacuum in the form of a dispute over the point at which a noncompensable health and welfare regulation becomes a compensable taking — the generality issue transferred to another set of terms. The legislative and executive are withdrawn as agents of the political system, which then returns to the judiciary the greater degree of power the judiciary possessed prior to the "minimum scrutiny" regime. Such an assumption of power establishes health and welfare powers *within* the judiciary; the doctrine of such powers, becomes the fact of such powers.

The consequence of this in the eminent domain context, is that even when an eminent domain use is conceded *by the state*, there is nevertheless no compensation. And that is exactly what happened. California Code of Civil Procedure Section 1260.210 says: "(a) The defendant shall present his evidence on the issue of compensation first and shall commence and conclude the argument. (b) Except as otherwise provided by statute, neither the plaintiff nor the defendant has the burden of proof on the issue of compensation." Ostensibly this provision reflects a public policy that "[a]ssignment of the burden of proof in the context of an eminent domain proceeding is not appropriate. The trier of fact generally is presented with conflicting opinions of value and supporting data and is required to fix value based on the weight it gives to the opinions and supporting data.... Absent the production of evidence by one party, the trier of fact will determine compensation solely from the other party's evidence, but neither party should be made to appear to bear some greater burden of persuasion than the other...."[296] The Code sections purport to be *method* of assessing a taking; in fact they are the *law* of taking. When there is no burden of proof, the Constitution disappears — the Court reappears as power (exactly what Madison implied in an assumption of power). That is exactly the role one trial court gave itself.

*Metropolitan Water District of Southern California v. Campus Crusade for Christ* involved a conceded taking of land by the District, compensation for that land, and then an issue over so-called "severance damages" ("damage caused by the taking to the remaining land"[297]). A trial court, newly assigned the case, overturned a *previous* trial court's admission of evidence on the "severance damages" issue

---

296 Quoted in *Metropolitan Water District of Southern California v. Campus Crusade for Christ*, No. E034249 (California Court of Appeal, Fourth Appellate District, Division Two, December 19, 2005), 15. This opinion is available online at www.courtinfo.ca.gov/courts/courtsofappeal/4thDistrictDiv2.

297 *Id.*, at 16.

and, refusing to allow admission of any evidence on the point, refused to award any "severance damages." According to the Court of Appeal, "[t]he question is whether the property owner must prove the existence of severance damages although neither party bears the burden of proof on the issue of compensation"[298] and it found that the second trial court had erred by not allowing the proffer of evidence.

However, the Code section does not distinguish between a taking and "severance damages," even though the Court of Appeal maintains that "[j]ust compensation is the amount that would make the landowner whole for the loss sustained as a result of the taking [and]....includes an award to reimburse the owner for the damage caused by the taking to the remaining land...."[299] This is, in a new guise, the old conflict between noncompensable regulation and a compensable taking — but the Code section resolves it by giving the court health and welfare powers. To be sure, the Court of Appeal sends the matter back to the trial court, for the admission of evidence on "severance damages," on the basis that the Court of Appeal's reading of the Code section imposes the burden on the property owner "of showing his entitlement to compensation for a specific item of severance damages, [although] that...burden is more accurately characterized as a burden of production [a lower burden involving giving the court at least some fact on the basis of which it can go ahead and make its evaluation]."[300]

An embarrassed Court of Appeal is trying to establish what it feels is a right, by expressing it as a burden — but there is no longer any right, and the Court has to mischaracterize law in order to get its result. The Code sections simply conflate fact and law — the assumption of power to which Madison objected. Is this case between a private party and government, or between branches of the government? Is the seizure of power the cause or the effect of the contest for power between the branches? Given the ostensible mutual interest of the branches of government in the survival of the "minimum scrutiny" regime, why can't they agree?[301]

## The Public Responds

Public opinion had balked. It had decided that eminent domain is an effort to make people propertyless. On the issue of eminent domain, the political system and public opinion had ceased to communicate. The California legislature considered a two-year moratorium on eminent domain over housing. A comment by a State Senator reflects a political system blindsided by a change in public opinion: "We're asking for an extraordinary remedy, but do we have an extraordinary problem?....Too often we legislate by hysteria."[302] Note that this echoes the statement — on the other side — by the attorney for the Yolo County landown-

---

298 *Id.*, at 19.

299 *Id.*, at 16.

300 *Id.*, at 19.

301 The utility announced it would appeal. Endless, aimless litigation loomed.

302 *The San Diego Union-Tribune*, August 31, 2005.

ers: "Where is the threat?" And yet the stalemate continued. The breach both created and revealed weakness in the political system.[303] The weakness was the assumption that the economic and political spheres functioned in tandem. In fact, there was no policy "lubricant" to make them function together; there was only an unexamined assumption of identity of interest. Once it was examined, it was found to be empty. Also, there was no policy "reserve" if the synchronism should fail. In short, the society had no articulable rationale. Comments by Thomas Jefferson, John Marshall and Abraham Lincoln suggested that much more intensive thinking needed to be done — but it was never done. Minimum scrutiny was imposed and the Constitution stopped. Not surprisingly, a technique such as eminent domain — previously a matter of common consent — now became a bone of contention, a point of attack on the system. Also not surprisingly — given the Court-imposed ban (minimum scrutiny) on the investigation and discussion of facts — opponents of eminent domain could hardly cope with the complexities their opposition had unleashed. There didn't even seem to be any awareness that the debate was not in the least academic, that slight shifts in sentiment could have major effects when carried into political action.

The complexities erupted abruptly in plans already in an advanced stage of development. Some are so unprecedented they are hardly believable. These new controversies not only constituted tests of will, but also, tests of understanding of the issues involved, and revealed that there were hardly any legal or social tools to handle them:

> Concerns about eminent domain have cast a cloud over an improvement project on a section of Olive Boulevard east of Interstate 270 in Creve Coeur [Missouri] where motorists regularly encounter three traffic jams on weekdays. The Koman Group, the developer involved in the road work, needs a sliver of property from a service station at Olive and CityPlace Drive for the project. It has asked Creve Coeur's City Council to extend by 30 days a deadline to begin the work. The postponement would give the company more time to secure the land. But at a special meeting early Saturday morning, the council instead voted to temporarily delay the use of eminent domain to obtain the property. Some members were upset that neither the station owner nor its operator attended the meeting. Frustrated representatives of the Koman Group later said they are considering whether to halt the project, which also involves a major expansion of the CityPlace office and store complex. A lawyer for Koman, Paul Chesterton, said he doesn't know whether the company should give up or continue. Mayor Harold Dielmann said a new Trader Joe's market is set to open Jan. 1 on the northwest corner of Olive and Craig Road near CityPlace. Its operators expect truck deliveries via a new roadway that is part of the project. Dielmann, who favors the development, said the "domino effect" of the delay imposed by the council could hurt other projects. Koman needs the property now occupied by a BP Amoco station. The corporate owner has signed a letter of intent to sell the property to Koman for $1,050,000, Chesterton said. He said the property is appraised at $350,000. The station operator has the right to buy the property before anyone else and has recently moved to exercise that right. Koman says that if the operator does so, Koman may have to use eminent domain to purchase the en-

---

303 *The Decatur Daily*, August 6, 2005 (Decatur, Alabama, archived at www.decaturdaily. com).

tire property rather than just the small sliver of land along the west side of the service station they want for the development. The company fears that without the ability to use eminent domain, it would have to pay as much for the sliver as for the entire lot, if the station operator could prove he did not have enough land left to operate the station. Chesterton said the corporate owner assured him it wants to sell to Koman. But some on the council wanted to hear from the owner and operator. "It's the Creve Coeur business owner who is missing from this equation," said council member Laura T. Bryant, 4th Ward. Chesterton said four property owners had land needed for the project. He said Koman bought the other properties, including a Denny's restaurant, "at great expense." Council member Michael Barton, 1st Ward, said he saw no reason not to use eminent domain. "This is not someone's house," he said. He called BP Amoco "a large, globally held operator who has negotiated a price they think is fair." He said the station operator, a franchise holder, has fewer rights. Council members voted 5-1 to delay using eminent domain to purchase the entire property, pending further investigation. Barton voted "no."[304]

Inevitably, boycotts accompanied physical confrontation over the facts, but, like the eminent domain reform proposals themselves, these were conceptual loose cannons on deck. They proceed in several ways. One is by identifying "Companies That Use, Attempt to Use, or Support Using Eminent Domain to Steal Land from Private Property Owners," and then involves people providing "a link to story about the use of eminent domain, as well as the company's corporate website and a contact page or email address (when possible) so that we may contact them and let them know we don't intend to do business with them. And try to keep it limited to large (national or regional) companies, not the corner grocery store. And for the sake of simplicity, keep [them] in alphabetical order."[305] For those directly affected by eminent domain actions, the boycott targets businesses involved the particular action.[306] Finally, the action moves up the business ladder to businesses themselves caught up in eminent domain actions. Branch Banking and Trust has, "[s]ince 1989,...completed the acquisition of 58 community banks and thrifts, more than 80 insurance agencies, and 27 non-bank financial services companies....[It has] more than 1,400 branches in 11 states and Washington, D.C.; [it is] the largest mortgage lender in North Carolina and West Virginia....,[is ranked] as the 9th largest financial holding company in the United States, [and has] total assets topping $107 billion [and] manages more than $20 billion in trust assets."[307] Thus, one wonders whether it was aware either of the nature or of the ramifications of the commitment it was making when it, nevertheless, decided it "will make no loans to developers who plan to build commercial projects on land taken from private citizens by the government through the power of eminent domain....'The idea that a citizen's property can be taken by the government solely for private use is extremely misguided, in fact it's just plain wrong,' John Allison, the bank's chairman and chief executive, said in a statement.

304 *St. Louis Post-Dispatch*, October 30, 2005 (St. Louis, Missouri, archived at www.stltoday.com).

305 www.landthieves.wikispaces.com.

306 See, for example, www.freelongbranch.com.

307 www.bbandt.com. .

In an interview, BB&T chief credit officer Ken Chalk said the bank expects to lose only a tiny amount of business, but believes it was obligated to take a stance on the issue. 'It's not even a fraction of a percent,' he said. 'The dollar amount is insignificant.'"[308] This was an invitation to anyone affected by an eminent domain action, to ferret out any connection the bank might have to that action. More importantly, the boycott efforts, since they do not effectively discriminate between eminent domain uses, have the effect of raising the level of all facts in the context of eminent domain. This in turn raises the question, what other facts should enjoy elevated scrutiny in the context of eminent domain, and on what basis? Thus the tendency of the New Bill of Rights and its "facts of the individual" analysis, is not only toward internal cohesion, but also, toward enmeshing the — unthinking — political system.

From this fraught situation we now turn our attention to the way in which, discounting the floundering political system, public opinion established its own dialogue with the Constitution.

---

308 *Houston Chronicle*, January 25, 2006 (Houston, Texas, archived online at www.chron. com).

# Chapter 4. The New Bill of Rights as Fact

## On Stopping the Third Epoch in Its Tracks

> It is a fair summary of history to say that the safeguards of liberty have
> frequently been forged in controversies involving not very nice people.

— Felix Frankfurter, *United States v. Rabinowitz,* 339 US 56, 59 (1950)

Without any formal or other recognition, the stage was now set for these developments: the reexamination of the nature of the Constitution; the emergence of a separate enforcement system; and the reexamination of facts under the New Bill of Rights. Many of the fact situations below involve the "development" process as it is currently practiced. How — if at all — does this process enforce/violate the New Bill of Rights?

### The Reexamination of the Nature of the Constitution

As the debate over eminent domain turned into a debate over the nature of the Constitution, the states and Congress produced mini-constitutional conventions in the form of legislative task forces or joint committees charged with looking into changing eminent domain; these committees looked to be long-term affairs as the range of debate widened. Post-*Kelo*, governmental bodies at all levels continuously revisited eminent domain. For example, the Connecticut committee simply began meeting monthly;[309] as Missouri floated its proposed changes, North Caro-lina and New York began studying the issue (learning nothing, however, from previous efforts, as the Speaker of the House indicated that the purpose of the North Carolina Select Committee on Eminent Domain Powers was to "examine our state laws that protect property rights and make necessary improvements, if needed, to ensure private property is not seized by local governments solely to benefit commercial developers").[310] The drift of legislative discussions was something the Institute for Justice had inadvertently revealed in its Petitioners' brief when it pointed out that eminent domain "conflates the public use clause of the Fifth Amendment with any private taking that could be claimed to benefit the public."[311] The facts kept intruding on the political system: eminent domain was not an action of the state; it undermined the state by repeatedly engendering struggles in which the state was attacked, *both* from the point of view of discre-tion *and* from the point of view of rights — raising the question, what remained of the state? What were the boundaries of the various constitutional provisions? Eminent domain committees began dealing with these problems as if they had never been posed before — and found it difficult to cope with what they found.

Mutually reinforcing problems presented obstacles to winding up the work of these committees: the inarticulate nature of public opinion; stalemated emi-nent domain situations which could only be resolved by a clear statement of the law; legislative indecision produced by the inarticulate nature of public opinion. Legal terms which, previously, had provided enough direction for action, now seemed to provide only confusion leading to *nothing*. This development — or lack thereof — alone should have prompted legislatures to reexamine underlying doc-trines. However it did not; they hoped something easily resolvable, not profound, was at issue. In any event, the struggle with generalities presented the prospect of continually revisiting the very changes which were supposed to resolve the issue. Also, any changes produced ramifications in other areas of law affected by eminent domain, and then these other areas had to be dealt with. Finally, with facts themselves — such as housing (not to speak of individually enforceable rights) — failing to find a prominent place in the debate, the mechanical concept of government prevailed and limited the thinking of those charged with the task of reforming eminent domain. The Missouri legislature's polyglot task force was characterized by

> wide disagreement. The nine-member group includes attorneys, legislators, a developer, the state's public counsel for utility consumers and a representative of the Missouri Farm Bureau. The farm bureau has the most clear-cut position, arguing that eminent domain never should be used for private development. Oth-ers have urged caution, saying that cities need the power to condemn blighted land to clean up urban decay. But what does "blight" mean? Missouri's legal defi-

---

309 *The Day*, August 26, 2005. The Georgia legislature also set up a standing Eminent Domain and Economic Development Committee. *The Business Report*, September 26, 2005.

310 December 7, 2005 (archived at www.myrtlebeachonline.com). December 14, 2005 (New York, archived at www.westchester.com).

311 Petitioner's Brief at 11.

nition is so vague that stable neighborhoods in the path of development in St. Louis County have qualified. "We've had recent examples where we've crossed the line," said task force member Gerard T. Carmody, an attorney from St. Louis. "But there are larger concerns about turning the faucet totally off...."The definition of blight is still the key, some task force members say. Some want to adopt objective, economic criteria to make sure a redevelopment area is truly failing. "I want the task force to come out with a very strong recommendation" to prevent abuse, said state Sen. Chuck Gross, [Republican]-St. Charles, a member of the group. But that will be controversial because the definition of blight also affects other chapters of state law, such as those governing tax increment financing [see below] and tax abatement. One task force member, state Rep. Steve Hobbs, [Republican]-Mexico, said he received a 3-inch-thick analysis from an attorney worried about the unintended consequences. Hobbs concluded that instead of redefining "blight," legislators should "just make it harder to use" by adding procedural safeguards and the opportunity for speedy judicial review. He also wants to prohibit the taking of raw farmland for economic development. Developer Goodson, who lives in Lafayette Square in St. Louis, said government's power to take land should always be used sparingly. But sometimes it is needed, he said. At a recent meeting, Goodson recounted his daily drive, past burned-out homes and vacant lots. "We can either leave and rope it off or take it back," he said. "If we're going to take it back, we've got to have that tool."[312]

When Missouri's task force finally got around to issuing its "recommendations," they guaranteed that the state's political system would be endlessly revisiting eminent domain. Just as in the case of the judiciary, there was no method based on facts, only a method of offloading the issue from the task force. And so, again in the absence of facts, the number of suggestions proliferated meaninglessly and the issues promised to make a never-ending circuit of the legislature, thence to the legislature, thence to an alternately balking and subversive executive branch, and back once more to the legislature. Just as in the case of the judiciary, "decisions" made closer to the front lines of the controversy, were really requests for clarification as to what was desired, with a subtext desiring to proceed with business as usual and not change eminent domain at all:

> A government task force is recommending tougher standards for taking people's property through the use of eminent domain powers, but is leaving it to others to come up with some of the specifics. The group appointed by Gov. Matt Blunt settled Wednesday on 18 recommendations that generally would strengthen the rights of private property owners when governments, utilities and developers want to acquire their land. One recommendation would prohibit private developers from using eminent domain powers to acquire land — reserving that power only for governments and perhaps utilities. Another recommendation would prohibit the use of eminent domain solely for economic development purposes....But the task force recommendations still would allow the use of eminent domain to take abandoned or "blighted" property — even if the result is a transfer of the land to another private entity for improvements.... Task force members, who ranged from city developers to rural property rights advocates, agreed that the current blight definition is sometimes stretched and abused to take land that is not really run down but rather is coveted for big developments such as shopping malls. The task force suggested the current blight standards remain in place for awarding government tax incentives to developers

---

312  *St. Louis Post-Dispatch*, November 30, 2005.

but recommended the Legislature create a higher standard needed to declare land blighted for eminent domain purposes. The panel also recommended that courts be given independent power to review appeals of blight designations, without having to give preference to a condemning authority's determination. But the panel stopped short of suggesting a specific definition for the tougher blight standards — in part, because its members couldn't agree on one. Blunt's general counsel Terry Jarrett, who served as chairman for the task force, said the recommended changes are "light years better than what we have at this point," even without a specific suggestion on the blight definition.[313]

Exceptions — for types of eminent domain, for certain projects, for certain concepts — became the sub-arena of debate. This showed, again, how unprepared was public opinion to deal with the level of Constitutional scrutiny for facts in the eminent domain — or any other — context. This was the most pernicious legacy of the "minimum scrutiny" regime. Although public opinion instinctively understood that opposition to eminent domain raised the level of scrutiny for all facts, it turned out that after two hundred years under the Constitution, public opinion was still uncertain how to proceed and on what doctrinal basis to proceed. So the eminent domain issue could neither be resolved nor avoided. The debate on the report of the Missouri task force bore hardly any relation to the report, and resulted in stalemate:

> Missouri legislators made an attempt to clarify state eminent domain policy last week; however, the debate quickly broke down into a debate over special situations for minority groups, according to the Kansas City Star. Last year the US Supreme Court ruled that state and local governments could use eminent domain to confiscate property for redevelopment. The decision has forced state and local lawmakers to create their own property rights laws. In Missouri, the eminent domain debate quickly spiraled out of control as lawmakers began to propose non-uniform exceptions to the state's right to confiscate property. First, the House unanimously approved legislation to exempt any house of worship from being subject to eminent domain, citing Constitutional protections of religion. After witnessing the success of that legislation, another bill was proposed to exempt gun retailers with the argument that the Second Amendment should protect them. Next, supporters of the health care industry and stem-cell research proposed that research facilities and hospitals should be exempt because they provide care for people with chronic diseases and save lives. The debate continued for five hours before a joint bill to exempt both research facilities and gun retailers was voted down. The spiraling debate over private property is not unexpected. Legal historians point out that the right to private property is so fundamental to the rights defined in the Constitution, that when eminent domain is questioned all other rights are questioned as well.[314]

313  *Kansas City Star*, December 7, 2005.

314  Free-Market News Network, April 20, 2006 (archived at www.freemarketnews.com). In Alabama, a proposed Constitutional amendment referendum — changing the earlier Alabama eminent domain reform — could not get out of the legislature, and "it was minute differences over details that led to the bill's death....The core of each chamber's version would have enshrined into the constitution an explicit prohibition on eminent domain being used to shift property from one private owner to another. Governments and quasi-public entities such as utilities, schools and economic development authorities could take land only for genuine public use. Examples in the bill included public roads, buildings, parks, airports and utility infrastructure....[T]he House made two changes to the version

By October 2006, thirty states had passed some legislative form of eminent domain reform, but the reforms were vague and grudging. Public opinion responded to many of them by placing much more drastic proposals on the ballot for voters in the November 2006 election. We shall examine the implications of some of these initiatives. These initiatives, although bold in some respects, reflected the idea that the fourth Constitutional epoch had inherited the ambiguities of the third epoch. They showed that the eminent domain issue had proved intractable.

## THE EMERGENCE OF A SEPARATE ENFORCEMENT SYSTEM

There was intercommunication between the different state committees and specialists called on to testify, and of course the issues they confronted were always the same. Thus, in spite of the legislatures' determination to address eminent domain in their own time and way, the pressure of circumstance tended to turn the different task forces and special legislative committees into a cohesive body distinct from their legislature-sponsors. Although events were the real leader, eminent domain had become a convention of sorts, with factions and spokespersons. For instance, Scott Bullock, the lead Institute for Justice attorney in the *Kelo* case, spoke at both hearings and conferences and symposia. To the extent cohesive plans emerged in the context of an ongoing and widening debate, this "body" took on characteristics both of a separate governing entity and of a political party. There was, in short, an embryonic parallel bureaucracy operating on new lines and with new issues to consider: a state within a state, counter to the eminent domain state within a state, simply by virtue of dealing with an issue which, previously, the political system had left alone. Any attention paid to the matter by the political system, weakened the political system.

Among the new "policies" were the various informal eminent domain moratoria — established once the Supreme Court decided to take the *Kelo* case — which had now persisted long after the case had been decided. This highly anomalous state of affairs generated its own social situation with its own implications; indeed, the moratoria — like the New Bill of Rights itself — reflected a new organization of society. What about contracts which had been signed and needed to be

---

that had passed the Senate. The House version would have required that a property owner losing his or her land be paid an amount based on the "highest and best use" of the parcel and be compensated for some other costs associated with having to move. The Senate version would have required only the traditional "just compensation" based on current use of the land. The House also expanded an exemption for the Alabama State Port Authority, more clearly spelling out that the state docks' partnerships with private industries would still be permissible....Those changes became deal breakers....Several other House members lambasted [an amendment to change the election date], first because of the low turnout of a primary runoff versus a general election, secondly because the election date was not previously a point of disagreement between the Senate and House....[Some] senators argued that it was important to present the issue to voters at the earliest possible date. Some other members said privately that they wanted the matter off the table before campaigning for re-election in the fall." April 19, 2006 (archived at www.al.com).

performed? What about financing which had been put together?[315] Are taxation, spending, lending and borrowing, all facts of the individual, and so should we analyze those components of the *Kelo* facts in that way? *Lawrence* conflates Fourteenth and Fifth Amendment due process. Are we thereby authorized to conflate Congress' tax and spend powers and the states' general welfare powers? Are we required to do so? Although no scholarly study has been done on the economic effect of the moratoria, even a glance at one city reveals the importance of eminent domain to the political system:

> A little more than a month ago, St. Louis [Missouri] voters removed Alderman Thomas Bauer in a recall election fueled by his support for the use of eminent domain. Bauer supported using the law to clear the way for a gas station near the corner of Manchester and McCausland avenues. Worried about the potential backlash, Creve Coeur officials recently voted to delay authorizing eminent domain for a project on Olive Boulevard. And in Collinsville, public outcry last month caused officials to back down from their plan to redevelop a 27-acre stretch of land off Illinois Route 157. While eminent domain was never threatened in the case, many people worried it would be the next step in the process. "I don't know specifically if that's why people were upset with our project, but this eminent domain thing has a lot of people scared," said Collinsville City Manager Hank Sinda. "Everybody is in an uproar, ever since the Supreme Court decision...."The Supreme Court's [*Kelo*] ruling, while breaking no new ground, did send shock waves across the country. It had a particular significance in the St. Louis area, where residents are facing more than 15 cases of eminent domain, with several more in the works. Already this year, three cities — Maplewood, Ellisville and O'Fallon — have responded to concerns by passing ordinances limiting eminent domain's use for economic development. Creve Coeur is considering similar legislation, as are officials in St. Charles County.... In 2000, Maplewood was facing bankruptcy. Staff members had not received raises in three years, low pay was pushing police officers and firefighters out the door, and broken equipment went unfixed. "We were hemorrhaging badly," said Mayor Mark Langston. "We needed help." Help came by way of Wal-Mart and Sam's Club. Thanks to the use of eminent domain, officials were able to clear the way for a retail center off of Hanley Road. The deal generated an extra $2.5 million a year for the city. "We had to clear about 133 homes and about six of them fought the move," Langston said. "But with that, we have been able to do a lot for the city." Brentwood, like Maplewood, faced some hard times back in 1996. Eminent domain was approved to clear out more than 100 homes in what is now the Brentwood Promenade. Thanks to that deal, said Brentwood Mayor Pat Kelly, the city no longer charges utility or property taxes. "And we are far better prepared for the future," he said. The question some people ask,

---

315  The importance of the smooth operation of eminent domain is highlighted in this remark by Fitch Ratings on November 28, 2005, in assigning its rating to Chicago bonds issued in connection with the O'Hare expansion project. What happens to the finance picture if there is resistance, law enforcement won't go in, and the project can't move forward? "While the airport maintains significant flexibility for the eventual timing of phase two of the OMP [O'Hare Modernization Program], as well as terminal development and other aspects of the overall capital program, Fitch believes the efficient management of this extensive redevelopment program and adherence to the stated budget will be critical to the maintenance of O'Hare's competitive position relative to other hub airports as well as the airport's current rating status in light of the scope of planned borrowings over the next five to 10 years." See www.fitchratings.com.

however, is how can you help everyone when no one is safe. If you live in the St. Louis region, chances are you are close to one or more ongoing cases of eminent domain. And chances are, you've heard the horror stories. For example, there is Jim Butler of Manchester. Butler owns a Saturn dealership off Highway 141. He is the last holdout against a $131.5 million project headed by Pace Properties Inc. Butler has a thriving business and a great location. Moving would probably cost him a lot more in business than any company would pay him for his land. And there are the Sunset Hills citizens, who are still awaiting their money from a protracted buyout drama with the Novus Development Co. Novus was given eminent domain power to secure 254 houses for a proposed $165 million shopping center between Interstate 44 and Watson Road just east of Lindbergh Boulevard. The company was supposed to close on the homes by September but announced at the last minute that it did not have the financing in place to do so. Last month, Novus asked for more time. Meanwhile, the residents, many of whom have already purchased new homes, have been forced to wait....State Rep. Muschany called the meeting in Brentwood last week to prepare for what promises to be one of the hottest topics in the next legislative session. "Eminent domain is a tool, just like a hammer is a tool," Muschany said. "But if you hit someone in the head with a hammer, you can kill them." Terry Jarrett, chairman of the governor's task force, said the group is looking hard at three key areas: definitions of blight, definitions of public use and condemnation procedures. All three are common points of contention in nearly every case of eminent domain. "One thing that seems to be pretty clear is Missouri needs a stronger definition for blight," Jarrett said. "We have heard that over and over." Blight is a designation that often must be met before a developer can be given the power to use eminent domain to force people from their homes. The problem is that over the years, the traditional definition of blight has gone by the wayside. "Today, basically, blight is whatever a local government wants to deem it," said Andrew Glassberg, a member of the Olivette City Council and a professor of public policy with the University of Missouri at St. Louis. "This has been a problem in the state for a long time, and I'm not surprised people are very angry these days...."Maplewood, which owes its financial life to the controversial law, three months ago passed an ordinance restricting use of eminent domain...."Unless you want your city to keep raising property taxes, there have to be ways for the city to generate new streams of revenue," Langston said. "Like it or not, eminent domain is sometimes needed. What we are trying to do is find the right balance. And that's really hard."[316]

The problem with ending the moratoria — or even keeping them from spreading — was the neglected technical-normative-political morass of eminent domain law.

Reports from St. Louis on the effects of the informal moratorium, showed the participants staking out their tentative ideological positions in an unprecedented political situation:

In the fight to save her home from a bulldozer, Kathy Tripp suffered what looked like a major blow in June. In a landmark decision, the US Supreme Court ruled that cities can condemn people's houses for private development. It seemed that a shopping center soon would replace Tripp's Sunset Hills home. Her loss was supposed to be a gain in Florissant [Missouri]. There, a plan to revive some less-than-holy property near the historic St. Ferdinand Shrine hinged on some extra government muscle to buy land. It got some from the Supreme Court. But in just

---

316  *St. Louis Post-Dispatch*, November 1, 2005.

two months, the tables quickly have turned. Fueled by a backlash, the Florissant plan was killed — at least for now. Tripp, meanwhile, says her battle has found new life. Across St. Louis and the nation, the court's controversial June 23 decision initially was viewed as a win for developers and cities — and a crushing blow for small property owners. So far, it hasn't worked out that way. Instead of running rampant, the use of condemnation has stalled. Two such projects in the St. Louis area have failed. In Sunset Hills and other places, opponents of eminent domain are finding new ammunition and support. "The Supreme Court did us a tremendous favor," said Tripp, who has lived 22 years in Sunset Hills. "Before the (court) ruling, this kind of thing went on, but nobody knew about it. Now, people are starting to listen to us, thanks to the Supreme Court." While the trend has been cheered by property rights advocates, it worries others who think that legitimate projects might be shot down and that development will tilt even more away from older urban areas, such as St. Louis. The reversal might be most obvious in Maplewood. Just last year, a new Wal-Mart opened there, thanks to the city's decision to condemn some residents' houses. Then, last month, under pressure from property owners, the Maplewood City Council backed away from a plan to forcibly buy buildings for a redevelopment downtown. "I don't think there's any question about it: Things have changed," said Maplewood City Manager Martin Corcoran. "Our city was more open to using it. Elected officials are now listening to what people are saying...."" "On the face of it, *Kelo* is bad for the little guy — for the small businessman and homeowner," said Stanley J. Wallach, a St. Louis attorney and chair for the eminent domain committee of the Missouri Bar. "But what this ruling did is it kicked the issue into the public dialogue. And it's growing like wildfire...."All of this attention was a key factor in the failure of MLP Investments' $20 million project near St. Ferdinand Shrine, said Florissant Mayor Robert Lowery. "The problem is, developers are worried about the adverse publicity," Lowery said. "There's [sic] been so many abuses, and a lot of people just don't understand that it can be used properly." Lowery pushed for the MLP plan to revive land he calls "a dump," filled with empty buildings and crumbling lots. MLP planned to build condos, apartments and shops. Lowery said the project was stopped when a lone property owner asked for "twice as much as his property was worth." The city considered using eminent domain, but balked because MLP was concerned about negative attention, he said. Florissant hopes to revive the plan with another developer. "In Missouri, on the local level, you're seeing a political firestorm," Wallach said. "Governments have become a little bit more aware of the other side because of this unprecedented level of public attention." For Tripp, that hasn't meant victory, but it has helped her cause gain a second wind. Her house is among more than 200 that Novus Development Co. wants to buy, tear down and replace with a shopping center anchored by a Macy's department store. Most neighborhood residents have accepted buyout checks, but Tripp and a few others don't want to leave. Sunset Hills has sought condemnation on their houses....Novus' project recently stalled when a lender pulled out after residents filed a lawsuit to block the project. The growing backlash worries Richard Ward, senior principal at Development Strategies. He points out that many important St. Louis area projects, including redevelopment of the Delmar Loop, hinged on using eminent domain. "I'm very concerned," said Ward, whose firm advises cities and private companies on development issues. "If we're interested in recycling urban areas, instead of just promoting sprawl, then we need this tool. There's a lot of misunderstanding about it." In the future, unprepared developers certainly will face roadblocks when they seek eminent domain, said Michael Staenberg, president of THF Realty, a development company in Overland. "If you're not prepared financially, or if you're not ready to be honest and fair, it will be difficult," said Staenberg, whose company used eminent domain to build the Maplewood Wal-Mart. "Cities are watching this closely." Cities like Maplewood. Last month, Maplewood officials withdrew a plan to redevelop downtown after residents protested. The plan would have forced small businesses to sell to a developer. The city went a step further, too, pledging to never again give a private developer the right to use eminent domain in Maplewood. Mayor Mark Langston was also in office when THF built Maplewood's Wal-Mart. "At the time, city services were in danger," he said. "We needed development at any cost." Today, Langston's position "has changed a little bit as we've solved our financial problems and we can be more selective about development," he said. "What we're urging" now, he said, "has made development harder in Maplewood."[317]

It is worth taking an extended look at the interface between development, eminent domain and the post-*Kelo* political environment in the context of St. Louis. First, let's take a look at tax increment financing (TIF), which figures in the St. Louis story. Is TIF yet another state within a state — this time nearly a complete government as the evidence mounts of a complete breakdown of the Constitution? It seems to have its three "branches" neatly in place: "redevelopment" is the executive branch, "blight" is the judicial branch and TIF is the legislative branch. Note that a method for making eminent domain use non-contestable — taking it out of the political system — can involve a bar on matching funds or block grants unless TIF is put in place; TIF can only be used if some sort or special redevelopment or other authority is set up and granted eminent domain use. There is no review of decisions within the authority.

> TIF...is a subsidy originally intended to help redevelop areas that are deemed "blighted" or "distressed." TIF has become very common; it is now authorized in 47 states and is most frequently used in California, Colorado, Florida, Wisconsin, Minnesota, Illinois and Indiana. Although TIF is regulated by the state, it is controlled by the city. Here is how it works: a city designates a TIF district for redevelopment. Usually a TIF district is smaller than an enterprise zone, even as small as several blocks. The area has to meet some state-mandated criteria for distress or blight such as property abandonment, building code violations, age of housing stock, or other measures. In some states, it's sufficient to say that the proposed development will encourage development, create jobs or increase the tax base. Since the area in the district is going to be redeveloped, that means property values will probably go up, and therefore property tax revenues will go up, based on higher assessments. When that increase happens, the property tax revenue from the TIF district gets split into two streams. The first stream is pegged to the original property values before the redevelopment; that amount of tax continues to go to the city, county, school district and other taxing bodies as before. The second stream consists of the increase in taxes resulting from the new development and higher property values — the "tax increment." That stream gets paid into a special fund used to subsidize some portion of the redevelopment in the TIF district. This diversion of tax payments continues until the TIF district expires — usually somewhere between 7 to 30 years, depending on state rules. TIF is versatile. Usually, TIF subsidies pay for new infrastructure (such as streets, sewers or parking facilities) or for land acquisition and parceling (including eminent domain)....Because the city receives the tax increment in annual payments (rather than a lump sum up front), it is often used to support the annual debt service on special TIF bonds — hence the phrase "tax incre-

---

317  *St. Louis Post-Dispatch*, August 27, 2005.

ment financing." Sale of the bonds generates the necessary capital up front. TIF was originally justified the same way enterprise zones were: to help revitalize distressed areas. Aging downtowns, older neighborhoods, and rusting factory areas were intended to benefit. But state TIF definitions of "distress" and "blight" have grown so loose, it's hard to say TIF is reducing poverty. In Maine, any area that is 70% zoned commercial-industrial can be TIF'ed, no matter how wealthy or stable it is. In Missouri, residents of rural Hazelwood were shocked to learn that their community had been labeled "blighted" and therefore TIF-able, apparently because most of the local farm homes were more than 35 years old. It is not unusual to read of TIF revenues subsidizing "big box" retail projects in suburbs that are far away from core-area pockets of poverty. Another problem is how to determine if a TIF is necessary. State TIF rules typically require developers to certify that the project would not occur "but for" the TIF. This requirement was originally enacted to make sure a TIF subsidy is actually "leveraging" private reinvestment that would not occur otherwise. But like so many other development subsidies that are captured by special interests, TIF has grown so loose that the "but for" test often means little. One state auditor asked local officials what they meant by the phrase; the officials gave six different answers....Another big problem is that TIF is basically a shell game between different levels of government. When the city creates a TIF district, it gets to divert revenue that would otherwise go to the county and/or the school district. A few states do not allow the school increment to be TIF'ed, or they allow only the operating budget to be TIF'ed, not the capital budget. But more commonly, the state reimburses the school district for at least some of the diverted revenue. That all boils down to the city's diverting tax revenue from the county and the state.[318]

Which rights of the New Bill of Rights are already being enforced by TIF? Which violated? The discussion below shows the role TIF plays in the financing of the eminent domain action in St. Louis. Which rights of the New Bill of Rights are already being enforced by the development plan in conjunction with TIF? Note the tendency for TIF to create the "redevelopment" state within a state. As one commentator notes: "The key to TIF in most states is that the urban renewal agency receives revenue from all property taxes collected within the increment area, regardless of the entity levying the tax or the type of tax levied. TIF typically traps a portion of every property tax dollar generated in the increment area. This is the magic of TIF. As an increment area matures, a substantial amount of tax revenue can be diverted to the urban renewal agency."[319] Note also that under TIF the developer pays taxes to itself; at the same time, if the project goes bankrupt, government is responsible for payments on the bonds. The conflation of these two facts destroys the government purpose in a manner similar to that which we saw in the true facts underlying the *Kelo* case. In the bankruptcy scenario, it also raises the question, whether housed residents of the government entity are involuntarily deprived of their housing? Finally, the conflation of TIF and eminent domain raises the question, what is eminent domain? Ominously, eminent domain is treated as a doctrine in the Fifth Amendment. However, eminent domain emerges from an analysis of the *facts*, shorn of its status as a doctrine and as

318  This is taken from a research paper archived on the website of Good Jobs First (www. goodjobsfirst.org/research/ch6tif.pdf+tax+increment+financing&hl=en).

319  This is Jeff Nave's commentary at www.djc.com/news/co/11149492. html+tax+increment+financing&hl=en.

simply one more fact, one more weapon in the arsenal of the "minimum scrutiny" regime. What now?

When Novus Companies President Jonathan Browne got a commitment from Regions Bank in February to finance his MainStreet at Sunset development, he kicked the project into high gear, figuring he had the money to get the deal done. He figured wrong. Regions had committed to financing the construction of the $185 million project in Sunset Hills, which included $42 million in tax increment financing (TIF), and getting a third-party lender to finance the property acquisition costs. The deal called for a Regions subsidiary, Morgan Keegan & Co., to line up a third-party bank to buy TIF bonds with an interest rate of 4.5 percent. The straight-to-bond deal would have saved the city $3.5 million in costs associated with issuing the notes. That put Regions on the hook for the $108 million in construction costs and the third-party lender was responsible for the $30 million in land acquisition costs. "Regions did not want to be a part of the TIF notes. They may have stated that. I didn't understand," Browne said. The out-of-town third-party lender, which has never been disclosed, set its terms for financing the acquisitions in July. Browne was told he needed to have all 300 properties in the area proposed for development under contract. At the time, Browne had only 91 percent of the properties under contract or ownership and was fighting for the remaining properties through condemnation. For the last 30 days, Browne said he believed he could negotiate a deal with the third-party lender. "We went to Regions with the classic (bond) structure. They wanted to do a new structure. Typically, every deal I've done, whoever your lender is buys the notes. This bank said we don't want to do that. The problem was that we couldn't get to the first stage with the third-party bank. They were unwilling to do anything except what (they presented)," Browne said. "No deal is without compromise. Deals change. I didn't expect this deal to be any different." Browne's time ran out on Aug. 22. Deals that he made with some homeowners in the proposed redevelopment area were set to close, but he didn't have the money to finance the acquisitions. "We've had properties under contract for as long as 18 months, and we had extensions. We were running out of time." Browne also said two lawsuits filed against the city relating to the development made the Aug. 22 deadline for getting all of the projects under contract unrealistic. Regions St. Louis President Mike Ross said Regions Bank has been ready to fund the project since February and has neither pulled funding nor backed out of the original terms of the agreement with Novus. "As soon as the key terms are met, we are going to proceed with the funding of the project." Regions Bank is still committed to financing $108 million for the construction of the development, but it will not change any of the terms of its agreement, Ross said. "There really wasn't any compromise room," Ross said. "We were clear on day one. We certainly think very highly of (Browne). I think he got caught up in a timeline." When Novus notified the city last week about the third-party lender's terms, Sunset Hills' aldermen called a special meeting Aug. 20 to amend its redevelopment agreement with Novus. The new agreement lowered the required percentage of homes under contract to a minimum of 67 percent, down from 100 percent in order for TIF monies to be issued. The change is designed to make the redevelopment more attractive to a new lender. With the biggest TIF in Sunset Hills history and one of the largest property assemblages to date in the St. Louis area at stake, Browne has spent the week scrambling to find another lender to back the buyout. Browne has extended the contracts he has with homeowners for their property for 30 days, he said, but if it takes longer than 60 days, the project will be dead. "We need to find a lender to do it a different way,"

Browne said. "Either we need a real estate savvy lender who believes this is all possible, or a gutsy cash investor or somebody to buy the bonds. Technically, we think we have another 30 days for an extension on (the homeowners') contracts. I'm not going to ask them to go beyond 60 days. I hope it's 30. The shorter, the better." Novus has spent the past two years buying properties and lining up contracts with property owners in the proposed development area, which includes 300 properties on 67 acres bordered by Interstate 44, Lindbergh Boulevard and Watson Road. In July, Novus secured a $42 million TIF for the project and an additional $18 million in Transportation Development District (TDD) funds for road improvements. Sunset Hills has neither increased the amount of the TIF nor has it been asked by Novus to increase the TIF, according to Sunset Hills Mayor James Hobbs. "The TIF has never changed since day one." Novus settled on a formula to offer residents 175 percent of the 2003 St. Louis County property tax appraisal, which Browne estimates averages between $20,000 and $30,000 more than real market value for the homes. The range of offers Novus has made for residences within the area is $81,000 to $450,000. To date, Novus has spent $4.5 million on the project, including $2.2 million to buy a now-closed Bob Evans restaurant. The developer also has a car wash in the area under contract and is negotiating contracts to buy out other commercial property owners. Wehrenberg Theatres has had preliminary discussions with Novus to locate a new theater at MainStreet at Sunset, said Wehrenberg spokesperson Kelly Hoskins. Plans also call for an office building. Browne said he has an anchor tenant lined up for a 200,000-square-foot parcel, but won't disclose who it is. The anchor will pay about $20 million to build out its space in the center, which will bring the development to more than $200 million. There's been an ongoing fight against the development. Sunset Hills' Board of Aldermen voted in favor of granting a TIF for Novus' proposal even though the city's TIF Commission, an advisory body, recommended against approval. Tom Curran, a member of the commission, said the commission based its recommendation in part on some residents' fears they would not be able to relocate in the Lindbergh School District. Some opponents of the Novus' development have rallied against the proposal on the grounds that the city should not use eminent domain in the area. Will Aschinger, spokesman for the group Stop the Sunset Hills Land Grab, said he doubts Novus will be able to get financing for the project. "The most important thing is, they're trying to shift the blame for their inadequacies for getting tenants and financing." Aschinger cited the Supreme Court's June 23 ruling on a Connecticut city's eminent domain powers in *Kelo v. City of New London*, which has sparked a national outrage on eminent domain, as a reason why the financing for the Sunset Hills development did not go through. "Maybe his tenants are dropping off, or the banks don't want to get involved or ruin their reputation," Aschinger said. St. Louis attorney Gerard Carmody is representing plaintiffs in two lawsuits brought against the city in June. "I think it is important for the city to determine the developer's financial wherewithal before giving it rights over such a large portion of the city," Carmody said. Carmody also questioned Novus' ability to bring two major contracts to fruition, given the company's relatively small size. Novus is currently in the midst of condemnation proceedings for two properties in the first phase of a $99 million proposed development at Manchester and Rock Hill roads in Rock Hill. Novus has spent $5.5 million on property acquisition for the first phase of the Rock Hill development. The first phase is slated to be a $34 million development, with a subsequent phase reaching $65 million. "This developer has two huge projects affecting two communities," Carmody said. "How do we know they're not going to go belly up? We've been asking all along who is going to finance (the Sunset Hills project). People moved out, and they may end up in a situation where the whole area will truly become blighted without any certainty that the redevelopment will proceed." Rock Hill Mayor Julie Morgan said she is confident Novus' Rock Hill development will be built. "Things are moving forward," Morgan said. "They have 23 out of 25 homes on the south side and all but one business under contract." The city is in the initial condemnation proceedings for the homes. "I feel Novus and the citizens will meet in the middle," Morgan said. Novus has confirmed it will present a list of tenants for the development on Sept. 6, Morgan said. The city also has started the process of condemnation for the business in the redevelopment area that is not under contract. Sunset Hills Mayor James Hobbs also believes Novus' proposed project in Sunset Hills will be built. "I have confidence in it going forward. No question about it."[320]

Nevertheless,

> Novus Development Co. was unable to complete by 3 p.m. Tuesday a deal to obtain a partner for the $165.2 million shopping center and office complex it wants to build in Sunset Hills. As a result, the city canceled a meeting of the Board of Aldermen on Tuesday night at which the aldermen would have considered approving a change in the project's ownership. Tuesday's developments were a setback for property owners in the Sunset Manor subdivision who had signed contracts to sell their property to Novus. The company was unable to close the purchases in August because it lacked money. It obtained extensions on many of the options, and those expire Friday. Many residents who signed contracts with Novus purchased new houses expecting to use money from the sale of their Sunset Manor property to pay for them. They're stuck owning two houses and making payments on two mortgages. Novus needs to acquire the 254-house subdivision to build its project on 65.6 acres along Lindbergh Boulevard between Interstate 44 and Watson Road. Even if Novus allows the options to expire Friday, the redevelopment agreement governing the project gives the company nine months from May 25 — or until Feb. 25 — to acquire the property. The city cannot remove Novus as developer because of a failure to buy the property until that deadline passes, said the city attorney, Robert C. Jones. Craig Workman, a spokesman for Novus, said the company was considering a plan that calls for another developer to take a controlling stake in the project. Such a plan would require city approval, he said. "It's getting down to the wire, and things were far enough along that it was time to see if the city had an interest in doing this," Workman said. "Novus simply wasn't ready" in time for an aldermanic meeting Tuesday, Workman said. Jane Chickey, a Sunset Manor resident who moved to South County, said a Novus staff member told her last week that the company was getting a partner and that the property sale should close by Friday. "We need money by Oct. 1," she said. "We have two mortgage payments." Workman said Novus would continue talks with several potential partners in an attempt to complete a deal by Friday. "Things have been moving very quickly the past week," he said. "There aren't too many people who want to see this thing fail." But opponents have been vocal, and Sunset Hills faces two lawsuits over the development. One questions the city's power to grant the use of eminent domain to a private developer. The other wants Sunset Hills residents to vote on the project.[321]

Although the informal moratoria are an unsettled situation, two things are clear: where the moratoria extend to housing, government is enforcing the hous-

---

320 *St. Louis Business Journal*, August 26, 2005 (St. Louis, Missouri, archived at www. bizjournals.com).

321 *St. Louis Post-Dispatch*, September 27, 2005.

ing provision of the New Bill of Rights; where the moratoria extend to businesses providing income to their owners, government is enforcing the maintenance provision of the New Bill of Rights. The housing moratorium tends to dissociate the right to possession from the traditional indicia of possession, such as title or contracts.

This provides evidence for the idea that the Constitution is always the individual, the individual is never the Constitution — the gravamen of the New Bill of Rights and, for that matter, of every new fact of the individual. To what extent and in what ways was government also enforcing the maintenance and liberty provisions? Legal action and the threat of legal action, emerged as another expression of eminent domain moratorium. Which, if any, of the provisions of the New Bill of Rights were being enforced in this way? especially in the context of what appeared to be strictly commercial property? To the extent that this new moratorium emerged from opposition to "economic development," how was it provoking a response from the political system that the general welfare powers of the states were being threatened, the roles of the states in the Federal system being attacked? Is this simply force against force, and not a power struggle within the Constitution? Note that the plan discussed below proposes housing in the place of commercial property. Is this, in fact, enforcement of the housing provision of the New Bill of Rights? Is the answer in any way changed if, among the properties proposed to be condemned, there are none involving businesses which provide the maintenance to the business owner? none which provide maintenance except through income from rentals?

[Stamford, Connecticut] Wall Street property owners fearing the city will seize their businesses for economic development have brought in a pair of big guns in eminent domain law. Scott Sawyer, whose firm represented New London homeowners in the controversial *Kelo* case, and John Louizos, who successfully thwarted Stamford's attempts to seize Curley's Diner, confirmed last week they have been retained by some Wall Street property owners concerned about plans for revitalization. Passed by the Common Council in July 2004, [the plan] proposes building 720 residential units, 1,300 parking places and 45,000 square feet of retail space as well as improving the look of the streetscape. The plan also calls for the city to work with developers to acquire about 30 properties in the neighborhood. Sawyer confirmed he represents an unnamed party that owns a building in the neighborhood. "This particular property owner is more than willing to participate in the plan," he said. The owner does not want his or her property taken, Sawyer said. Sawyer said his biggest concern is how the city determined Wall Street is a blighted area. Louizos' clients are Themis Hios and George Papadopoulos, who own about a dozen store fronts at Main and Wall streets. Neither could be reached for comment, but Louizos said his clients have owned the property since 1958 and do not want to sell it. The building is targeted for acquisition either through negotiation or eminent domain as part of the city's Wall Street plan. The properties cover 4.7 acres north and south of the Wall Street bridge on the east side of the Norwalk River. "The plan shows that our client's property is designated to be taken," Louizos said. "(My clients) want to do what they've always been doing — own their property and derive the benefits of leasing it....We want to make sure their property rights are protected." Although the Legislature asked municipalities to respect a voluntary moratorium on eminent domain while officials consider amending Connecticut property seizure laws, DiScala and the Norwalk Redevelopment Agency are moving ahead with obtaining appraisals and formalizing agreements and designs. "We're about to start a friendly dialogue, without attorneys," with some property owners, he said. DiScala said he is not concerned about Louizos' involvement. "I would expect that," he said. "It's fine." But Michael McGuire, another Wall Street property owner, said news that Louizos and Sawyer are involved does not bode well for the Wall Street project. McGuire, who purchased and renovated the top three floors at 64 Wall St. in 2001, has been a booster of the city's effort to revitalize the neighborhood. But he said he has concerns about the reliance on eminent domain, arguing property owners appear to be bracing for "a long-term eminent domain battle that will be costly to taxpayers and drag on the economic revitalization of the Wall Street area. And that's frustrating as a stakeholder and business owner here." Norwalk Redevelopment Director Timothy Sheehan said redevelopment, whether or not it involves property seizure, always has the potential for a legal battle. "Redevelopment by its very nature is fraught with legal challenges and they should be anticipated going into the implementation stages of the plan," Sheehan said.[322]

## THE REEXAMINATION OF FACTS UNDER THE NEW BILL OF RIGHTS

The inevitable questions of which entity has the right of eminent domain and when and, what is housing, began to make their appearance, as did the extension of the housing right to past eminent domain takings. "Facts of the individual" analyses were forcing their way to the surface, but neither side wanted to acknowledge that this meant raising the level of scrutiny for those facts. Thus, the debate was taking place as a subtext in litigation ostensibly over other issues, such as procedural issues, zoning issues, or crime. Any issue, apparently, was a better one than the Constitutional status of the facts:

> The Ohio Supreme Court listened today to arguments for and against demolishing two of the three houses still standing on the site of the planned Rookwood Exchange office-retail-condo development in Norwood. The two property owners, Joy and Carl Gamble Jr. and Joe Horney, are fighting to get their houses back. They want the Ohio Supreme Court to prevent the project developer, Rookwood Partners, from tearing down their houses while they try appeal two lower court decisions supporting Norwood's use of eminent domain to seize the properties. Norwood and the developer wants the court to allow the demolition of the houses so that the $125 million project can be built. Norwood would receive about $2 million in tax revenues from the project. Bert Gall, an attorney representing the two property owners, told the court that state law doesn't allow private developers to be protected from court injunctions delaying or stopping demolitions while an issue is under appeal. Tim Burke, an attorney for Norwood, disagreed, saying state law allows private developers to tear down property that's transferred to them by an entity that has the power of eminent domain, such as Norwood.[323]

The subtext of the argument was that housing is important, but it never found its way into the formal arguments. Instead, the argument tended toward

---

322 *The Advocate*, September 26, 2005.

323 *The Cincinnati Enquirer*, September 27, 2005 (Cincinnati, Ohio, archived at www.news.enquirer.com).

— without ever arriving at — a demand for discovery on the factual issue of government purpose under minimum scrutiny. Since the Institute for Justice represented the Norwood homeowners, the merit brief advanced the same arguments used in *Kelo*, but the *amici* briefs also raised arguments identical to those in the *amici* briefs in *Kelo*. Obviously, the entire litigation strategy was orchestrated by the IJ.[324] The effect of such orchestration was to stifle the development of any new legal theories. In the event this led to losses, as it had in *Kelo*, it tended to foreclose legal avenues and leave resistance as the only option for the opposition — the situation in New London after the *Kelo* decision.

Is "substandard" housing, housing for purposes of the housing provision of the New Bill of Rights? Does "substandard" housing violate that provision? Is it property? A lesser or different property before it became "substandard?" What happened to the facts which cause it to be judged "substandard?" May eminent domain be used to bring that housing "within" the housing provision? Is there "substandard" maintenance for purposes of the maintenance provision? May eminent domain be used to bring that maintenance "within" the provision? These were the questions involved when eminent domain was sought to be used to *maintain* "standards" (an implied maintenance question) but the facts and policies *underlying* those standards were never discussed. Again and again, public opinion was tripped up because it failed to explore the issue:

> The Town of Bristol [Connecticut] finally has teeth it can bare against three property owners who have allowed their downtown properties to become blights. On Wednesday night, two town boards unanimously adopted a new Redevelopment Plan for Downtown Bristol, a 30-page document that gives the town the authority to seize the three properties — most notably the Belvedere Hotel — within a year if their owners do not make clear and significant steps to rehabilitate them. "This is a landmark thing," said Bristol Redevelopment Agency Chairman Peter Calvet just after the vote. "This is big." And, its authors hope, the beginning of a real change in the way downtown Bristol looks. The owners of the properties must take immediate steps to rehabilitate them, and will be subject to regular reviews of their progress by the agency. If agency members determine they are not making sufficient progress, the town can begin seizure proceedings, purchasing the property at fair market value through its powers of eminent domain, then offering it to viable developers. Though the property owners have up to a year to get their acts together, assistant Bristol Town Solicitor Andrew Teitz said the town has the power to seize all three tomorrow if it wishes and will not wait the entire year if it is clear things aren't going well. "But we want to give them a chance," Mr. Calvet told the town council. The key property on the list is the Belvedere Hotel, the dilapidated 1880 hotel that is the centerpiece of a stalled plan to turn it and several surrounding properties into condominiums and storefronts. Ted Barrows, whose Belvedere Developers LLC owns the building, lashed out at the plan before it was approved, saying negative and inaccurate portrayals by the town and the Bristol Phoenix have hurt his chances to develop the property. Though the mortgage holder, Center Development Corp., may auction off the hotel on Nov. 23 to recoup some $3.2 million in unpaid mortgage payments owed by Mr. Barrows' group, the embattled owner said he nevertheless has things under control. "We are moving ahead," he said.

---

324 The briefs are available online at the Institute for Justice website, www.ij.org.

"We have a contractor in place. Negativism like this does not help....[W]e have taken back control of the project." Council and planning board members were not convinced. Councilor David Barboza termed Mr. Barrows' comments "an Alice in Wonderland approach....We've had nothing but lies, cheating, embarrassment and frustration on this project over the years," added planning board chairman James Farley. "We continually get promises that fall flat on their face." The council also had harsh words for Mark Cutler, a contractor hired by one of the other blight owners, Louis A. DeAlmeida, who owns the former Tuplin's Garage at 382 Thames St. Mr. Cutler said he has been hired to help rehabilitate the old garage, which has lost its roof and now houses only weeds and junked cars. He questioned the ethics of a plan that could lead to the seizure of property in a year when, he suggested, the town could be working cooperatively with owners instead. Town officials took issue with that. "I personally sat down with (Mr. DeAlmeida) more than 10 years ago," said Mr. Calvet. "This is not a one-year thing; this is now in its 11th year." The third property on the list is the so-called "Third oldest house," a ramshackle home tucked behind the Bristol House of Pizza. Its address is 55 State St....Under the plan, if no progress is made "it will be acquired and sold for private development."[325]

When eminent domain was used as a simple police tactic, it conflated branches of government and legal concepts, but more importantly it brought directly to the surface the underlying conflicts in public opinion respecting facts. Is the following example — in which housing interacts with crime — an allowable eminent domain use, if the liberty and housing provisions of the New Bill of Rights are enforced or even if the *Lawrence* liberty right is enforced?

Sarah Marley has already purchased new furniture for her future home on Hopkins Street. "You buy a new house, you have to have new furniture," Marley said. Marley was accompanied by her 2-year-old daughter, Dallas Thomas, at the groundbreaking on Wednesday. She is one of two [low-income] homeowners now eligible to purchase these homes in areas of Woodbury [New Jersey] slated for redevelopment. Marley, her two children, and her boyfriend will all be moving into their home once construction is completed early next year. "This has been my dream for years," Marley said of the prospect of owning a new home. Under the proposal, five single-family homes are being built in an area of Hopkins Street and on Barber Avenue. Two will be constructed immediately, the others will follow shortly, officials explained. The city used eminent domain to acquire rundown properties on these streets and demolish them. "We had issues with drugs, we had issues with police calls," Woodbury Mayor Leslie Clark explained, noting much of the problem is now gone. The idea behind the plan is to do away with some of the city's rental properties and replace them with single-family houses that will be occupied by the buyers....The county, Woodbury, the Paulsboro Community Development Center and The Bank have worked together on this redevelopment project. "The goal is to put up as many homes as we can for low and moderate income families," said Dr. A.B. Frazier, president of the Paulsboro Community Development Center. "With renting comes the element of illegal commerce. With home ownership, you don't find that."[326]

In a proposed airport expansion, are access, overpass and other facts sought to be seized by eminent domain part of the housing of those subject to the eminent

---

325 October 28, 2005 (archived at www.eastbayri.com).

326 *Gloucester County Times*, October 27, 2005 (New Jersey, archived at www.nj.com).

domain action? A proposed expansion in Rhode Island brought to the surface a tangle of fact and law issues or, rather, revealed the tangle in public opinion:

> The Rhode Island Airport Corp. is currently under fire in Warwick, where it used eminent domain to take residential properties that it has leased since 1999 to three rental car companies....[Concerns were raised] about whether that constituted appropriate public use of state property. "The issue in *Kelo* is public purpose. I think most people would think an airport is a public purpose," said Richard Licht, attorney for the Rhode Island Airport Corp. It's unlikely that the corporation would seek to profit by allowing a business unrelated to airport use onto its property, Licht said. The Rhode Island Airport Corp. should have the right to expand its property by taking residences by eminent domain if there is a need to expand the rental car operations..., he said. The Rhode Island Airport Corp. has used eminent domain in Westerly to a lesser extent, through navigational easements: restrictions it secures on residential and other private property to allow planes to fly over that land and prevent buildings and trees on the property from creating safety hazards. The Rhode Island Airport Corp. budgeted $302,000 in the current fiscal year to acquire navigational easements off Runway 32 in Westerly, which ends near the Winnapaug Hills Subdivision, and another $1 million for easements on other Westerly properties, Licht said. Tension was evident Wednesday as residents complained of the corporation's easements in the Winnapaug Hills Subdivision, where it owns several lots and has secured the rights to remove the trees on others. "I'm concerned about the easements. I'm concerned about determining the price of an easement and what that easement will eventually be used for," [the local State Representative] said, referring in part to the fact that Warwick residents were compensated at residential rates for land used for commercial purposes.[327]

And what about wrongful former eminent domain takings? Was the Constitutional status of "housing" at issue long after the destruction of any incarnations of housing? "Former" housing of the "past takings"-variety emerges in this fact situation involving the Tennessee Valley Authority:

> Tennessee Valley Authority land managers will recommend trading away to a private developer 578 acres of Nickajack Lake waterfront, some of it obtained decades ago from farmers and other private owners forced to sell to the government. Tom Kunesh, a spokesman for the Sacred Little Cedar Mountain Defense Coalition that contends American Indian cultural properties would be destroyed by the proposed residential and recreational community, said approval would "definitely" mean a court fight. A board agenda released yesterday shows the utility staff intends to recommend Sept. 28 that the two board members, Bill Baxter and Skila Harris, approve a public auction sale of the land in Marion County "for appropriate exchange of land and other compensation." A swap proposed by developer John "Thunder" Thornton would allow him to build hundreds of homes, a golf course and marina in return for him giving TVA about 1,100 acres, including a Tennessee River island. Some American Indian groups say the project about 30 miles west of Chattanooga would destroy land that is sacred to them and historically valuable next to Little Cedar Mountain. Also, some families who lost their property because TVA had eminent domain powers to buy it say it is wrong for the utility to deal the land away to a wealthy developer.[328]

---

327  *The Day*, September 22, 2005.

328  *The Lexington Herald-Leader*, September 22, 2005 (Lexington, Kentucky, archived at www.kentucky.com).

The legal consequences of past conduct arise when the level of scrutiny is raised for a fact. Does this mean there are no facts of the individual?

The fate of property already owned by government — including property not seized pursuant to eminent domain — also emerged in debates about reforming eminent domain. Would it make a difference if individuals were housed on that land? The health and welfare powers of the state again seemed implicated. We also see the debate beginning to encroach on the question of government property as opposed to private property:[329]

> A [New Hampshire] State Senate panel approved legislation Tuesday that would block government from taking land by eminent domain for private development. The Senate Task Force on Eminent Domain unanimously endorsed a proposed bill for the 2006 session that would only allow eminent domain takings for a "public use." The bill would replace language in existing law that allows such takings for a "public purpose," a broader concept that could allow government to take land and sell it to a for-profit entity....Cornish Democratic Sen. Peter Burling asked if this could hamper the ability of city and town officials to improve a blighted area by selling land to housing developers. "Are we setting up a situation where a community could not sell off lots privately?" Burling asked. Former Senate legal counsel Richard Lehmann answered, "Yes, I believe you are." Eminent domain for private development could be used in a limited way if that private use was "incidental" to the total project. Lehmann gave the example of land taken for a municipal airport that had a Dunkin Donuts store inside....Committee members noted that private development could occur if a city or town purchased a property outright from a private owner rather than having to take it by eminent domain. Lehmann said the new law may act as an incentive for government and private owners to negotiate a sale, as that allows the public buyer to have more options.[330]

At the same time, it isn't always easy to identify New Bill of Rights issues. Are there any in the following facts (keeping in mind your previous conclusions re-

---

329 That is, the debate is beginning to question whether the "private property" distinction of the Fifth Amendment implies that there is, under the Constitution, "public" property, or whether this option is foreclosed under a "facts of the individual" analysis. Previously, it was assumed that there is public and private property for purposes of the Fifth Amendment. Instead, is it the case that, under the Fifth Amendment, there is private property and the individual? Is this the point the *Kelo* homeowners' counsel were attempting to make? **Free** exercise, **private** property, **greater** freedom, **public** use: these qualifiers distinguish the Constitution as process. What distinguishes process? the Constitution? What is the Constitution?

Note that the concept of "private" property — dear to the "property rights" movement — is new in the context of eminent domain. Madison's idea in the "public use" clause was that "limits should be imposed on government action" to meet the "danger....[of] the majority against the minority" — he does not provide the indicia of "danger," "majority" or "minority." Nor does "property" seem to have been a due process consideration — the undisputed power to tax seems to have vitiated any idea of rights in "property." His "public use" protection aroused *no enthusiasm*, and had to be attached by the resourceful Madison to the other, much more popular parts of the Fifth Amendment. This is why the "public use" clause seems unrelated to the other parts of the Amendment. Akhil Reed Amar, "The Bill of Rights as a Constitution," in Ronald Hoffman and Peter J. Albert, eds., *The Bill of Rights: Government Proscribed* (The University Press of Virginia 1997), 346, 298 (quoting Madison).

330 *The Nashua Telegraph*, September 28, 2005 (Nashua, New Hampshire, archived at www.nashuatelegraph.com).

garding TIF)? Which of the interests could assert which rights? Where do complications/objections seem likely to occur as plans proceed?

The long boarded-up Burger King fast food restaurant at the northwest corner of Ferry and Main streets in Anoka [Minnesota] could soon be under new ownership — eminent domain and all. The old Burger King site has been considered an eyesore by city leaders, residents and others because it is located at what is considered to be one of the main gateways to Anoka from the south and the west. The condemnation schedule comes just as an update was presented Monday night from Anoka's Economic Development Commission (EDC) that it was a little concerned with the placement of CVS Pharmacy across the street from the competitor, Walgreen's, at the southwest corner of Ferry and Main streets, according to Bonnie Stoll, member of the EDC. The EDC supports "demolishing the building," but has "concern about having two drug stores located so close to each other," according to the Sept. 8 minutes of the committee. Further, according to the EDC minutes, the commission would "support the land use being market driven and that no subsidy be given to potential buyers." The block on which the former Burger King is located, as well as other parcels there in which property owners are interested in selling, has been identified as a Tax Increment Financing (TIF) area. The only portion of the block that would not be obtained using TIF funds would be the Auto Zone parcel and a segment owned by the Minnesota Department of Transportation (MnDOT). "Tax increment revenue from the council TIF district can be used to undertake planning, property acquisition and redevelopment," said Anoka Community Development Director Bob Kirchner in May. Anoka City Manager Tim Cruikshank said Monday night the city would use TIF funding to acquire the Burger King parcel either via a willing seller or by eminent domain proceedings. Hawkins told the council that the owner of the Burger King parcel had discussed the sale of the property to Walgreen's. But he didn't know just how serious Walgreen's was about obtaining the site, Hawkins said. Eminent domain proceedings and the acquisition of the property by the city through other means, he told the council, would allow Anoka to choose what developer it desired to build on the block. Hawkins would not recommend dismissing eminent domain proceedings until a development plan was actually in place, he said. "You can insist there is development on that property that is acceptable to the city," Hawkins said. The Anoka City Council May 16 on a 4-1 vote authorized Hawkins to proceed with eminent domain proceedings against eight parcels on the block bounded by Ferry, Main and Webster, including the Burger King land. Mayor Bjorn Skogquist voted against authorizing eminent domain at the time, presumably because of the effect on other property owners, including homeowner Tom Ward. "(All of these properties) are linked by a complex set of ownership patterns and real estate negotiations at this time," said Kirchner May 16. At the time eminent domain proceedings were authorized by the council, Ward expressed his preference to have CVS purchase all of the properties without any city involvement. But in lieu of that not happening, Skogquist suggested that the city purchase Ward's three parcels on the condition that other parcels are obtained by either eminent domain or negotiation on the part of the city or CVS. "It's a little difficult with so many property owners involved," Ward said at the time. With Anoka's petition for eminent domain against the owner of the Burger King land, according to Hawkins, it is up to Burger King to negotiate the sale of the land or face condemnation by the city in Anoka County District Court commencing Monday with a hearing.[331]

---

[331] *Anoka County Union*, September 23, 2005 (Coon Rapids, Minnesota, archived at www. abcnewspapers.com).

Is there a maintenance issue in the following (highly partisan) account of "dueling developments?" Was Justice Stevens wrong? When the term "economic development" is used, is it being used as a synonym for maintenance?

> "My story is so strange," [Port Chester, New York] village resident Bart Didden wrote in a letter to the US House Judiciary Committee, "that everyone who hears it agrees that I've been robbed." The congressional committee recently convened to hear testimony about eminent domain abuse, and Didden wanted his experience "as a victim of government policies and laws" to be put into the official record. "I am talking about eminent domain," he wrote, "and takings that are planned in backroom negotiations and sweetheart deals made between developers and elected government officials so hungry for renewal development that would do and say anything, including violating my civil rights and the natural laws of our society." Didden, who is married and has two children, has lived in Port Chester for 45 years. Since 1982, he has been president of U.S.A. Central Station Alarm Corp., a firm that employs 60 people. In 1993, he and his business partner, Domenick Bologna, purchased for $300,000 about 35,000 square feet of property in the Port Chester downtown urban renewal area with an eye toward helping the village "come back to what it once was." (A couple of years ago, the town of Rye of which Port Chester is a part, valued the property at $564,000.) Even though he had plans to maximize the use of his property by selling it to CVS Corp., which wants to build a store on the site, Didden discovered that he had fallen victim to a ruthless application of New York's eminent domain law. He found that he had no real right to challenge the seizure of his property by the village and its "preferred developer," G&S of Old Bethpage, Long Island. Didden went ahead and signed a deal with CVS and got planning commission approval to go ahead with the project. At that point, he claims, G&S came to him with an offer: He could keep his property if he paid them $800,000 or let them share in it on a 50-50 basis. Didden told them to get lost. "That's extortion," he said in his letter to Congress and repeated to me in a phone interview yesterday. Last year, the village offered Didden $250,000 for his property — and he rejected the offer for the insult that it was. The village's lawyers said, "Well, tell it to a judge." But the judges in this county have shown they are not on the side of the small property owners. Eminent domain meant taking property to build bridges, highways and other things for the greater "public good." The modern-day interpretation of eminent domain says that property can be transferred into private hands now, and the new public good is the supposed windfall of greater sales and property taxes. Didden sees no logic in this. He pays his ever-rising property taxes like anyone else and he doesn't get a break on the sales tax for construction materials. But he points out that as the preferred developer, G&S does get substantial tax breaks because the village's scheme is to lease the property back to them for 20 years under a fixed rate. So who's getting the benefit here? But here's the best part, according to Didden. Guess what the preferred developer wants to put on Didden's property, where CVS wants to build. A Walgreens. You can't make this stuff up.[332]

It is not clear how the fact of liberty is implicated by the informal moratoria, until one is apprised of further facts: as she indicated above, once there was a condemnation order in Susette Kelo's case, she ceased to be the owner of her house. Pursuant to the injunction enjoining eviction pending appeal, she was charged "rent" (as of August 27, 2005, the amount was over $50,000); she paid none of it.

---

332 *The Journal News*, September 29, 2005 (New York, New York, archived at www.the journal news.com).

The situation changed with the dissolution of the injunction after the Supreme Court's rejection of the petition for rehearing on August 22, 2005. Without the informal moratorium in her state, she was clearly trespassing (no attempt was made to collect the money). With it, government is enforcing a higher level of scrutiny for liberty in the context of trespass where the facts show housing. Or is she not, in fact, housed? Is she housed in law? Is she legally entitled to have the enforcement order voided? entitled to have title to the house returned to her? entitled to damages? If so, on what grounds? Which facts are relevant to those grounds? Do those facts and grounds imply a higher level of scrutiny for liberty in other contexts? The right to privacy seems to have been transitional between the eras of minimum and strict scrutiny for housing. What remains of the law of privacy if we assume enforcement of the New Bill of Rights? Does Kelo have a cause of action for invasion of privacy, or has that been resolved into strict scrutiny for liberty and housing? Events have transformed the liberty hypothetical in my original article, into reality.

The implications of the New Bill of Rights are felt far down the legal "food chain," as shown in this remark from the Novus project developer: "The collapse of the financing for the [shopping mall] project has left a couple of hundred families in a terrible place....A lot of them are already paying the mortgage on their new home, but now they don't have a buyer for the old one. This has to be resolved, and condemning those 25 houses is the way it has to go forward...."On the other side is the leader of the opposition to the project: "The backlash against that decision is the best thing that ever happened to us....No matter what the court says, I don't think cities can get away with this kind of stuff anymore."[333] Which of these two persons is undermining respect for the rule of law? If either, on what grounds?

These developments demonstrate that examining ever more facts — in ever greater detail — helps us to more sensibly rephrase such apparently daunting, previously unheard of, questions as: how can the New Bill of Rights be enforced? Examination of the facts reveals that that question is better put: how is the New Bill of Rights being lived? This is what the resistance to *Kelo* has revealed. Perhaps the most important implications of the New Bill of Rights are the implications for civil discovery.

The elements reinforced each other: considerations arising from the moratoria made the legislative discussions ongoing, which preserved the moratoria, which allowed new considerations to arise. This cycle confirmed one of the unstated assumptions of the Constitution: no one ever knows all the facts. Comments from the pre-New Bill of Rights bureaucracy give us a glimpse into that era. A La Mirada, California, city councilman articulated the disproportionate — hence conflicting — pressures brought to bear on the political system when a fact of the individual does not enjoy strict scrutiny: "It's an absolute contradiction....How can the left hand demand we meet housing requirements and then the right hand

---

333 *The Washington Post*, September 5, 2005 (Washington, D.C., archived online at www. washingtonpost.com).

hinders our ability to do so by taking away a tool?"[334] Note the constant use of "tool" as a description of eminent domain, as if the Constitution is a machine.

Some of the flavor of the issues raised by the prospect of raising the level of scrutiny for housing, is captured in this email exchange between a planner and me on August 1, 2005:

FROM A PLANNER

I am a mere economic development practitioner working for a small urban community in Eastern Connecticut and certainly unqualified to express a legal opinion in the *Kelo* case. I will leave that up to the legal minds of our State and Federal Governments. However, I do have a fair knowledge of the plight of the urban communities within our state having worked in/for three (Norwich, Hartford & Willimantic) and been the owner of a small retail business in another (New London).

Urban centers in our State and I suspect other states, have become the social service centers for their surrounding regions and consequently house an abundance of non-profit, non-tax producing entities. New London and Hartford are two great examples of a minority of taxpayers paying for the majority of property taxes in their community. Both have one common thread: they are small, without room for growth and only about 40% of the property tax base supports the entire community(s). The other commonality...is...that property values, because of high taxes and high crime, have become depressed compared to their suburban neighbors, hence the target of absentee ownership and speculators. Even in New London a majority of those properties in the Fort Trumbull neighborhood are presently owned by speculators.

Those of us in Economic Development are faced with the challenge of trying to reverse those trends and assist the urban centers from continuing their slide into bankruptcy and becoming bastions of poverty and crime. I am sure all of us are equally sympathetic with Ms. Kelo and any other homeowner who is forced to sell his or her home because of a larger development. I lived in the same home in Norwich over looking the Thames River for over 24 years and certainly enjoyed the location and property. However, for me personally, I love family and friends not structures or property. As long as I would be compensated fairly I would certainly be able to enjoy the love and friendship of my family and friends from another residence.

So I guess the dilemma we (economic development professionals) are in, is that although most of us would prefer not to use eminent domain, we wonder how else can the cities remove blight, increase the property values and create more and higher paying jobs in our urban centers without at least the possibility of eminent domain? The alternatives are bussing, mandated low income housing and services in the suburban communities and restructuring of the property tax as the main way to fund local governments. In Minnesota the towns surrounding Minneapolis/St. Paul pay a fee to the urban centers which goes to offset the cost of providing the housing and services to the poor. I have a feeling none of those alternatives would be well received in New England. The real issue is not legal, it is moral. How else do we fulfill our responsibility to those now living in squalor in our urban centers?

---

334 *Whittier Daily News*, August 21, 2005 (Whittier, California, archived at www. whittierdailynews.com).

> *Although my comments do not address the legal questions you posed, they reflect the frustration of those of us committed to our profession.*

## MY RESPONSE

I think the problem planners have is that the law gives them an insufficient number of tools: the society wants you guys to solve EVERY problem. There's no way, for example, planning can address the overall problems of health care, or education, and yet the problems from those areas wind up being things planners are asked to solve.

My article on *Kelo* is really designed for nonlawyers, so you might want to take a look at it. It may interest you to know that not only is there a legal movement dedicated to increased protection for housing, but also, there is a movement dedicated to increased protection for medical care, and a lot of other areas. These areas are also mentioned in the article.

Historically, from time to time people simply change their minds about a fact. For a long time, the vast majority of people thought nothing of slavery: they weren't slaves, and slavery didn't bother them. Then, through education and a lot of other facts, minds changed, and people simply decided they wouldn't allow society to tolerate slavery any more. This also happened with women's rights. Forty years ago, there would not have been a lot of protest over eminent domain being used over housing. But now there is. It means that people have simply changed their minds about housing. They want housing to have as much protection as free speech.

Frankly, I don't think there's anything anyone can do to turn back this change of mind. In the end — to put it in legalese — there is going to be "strict scrutiny" for housing. What can planners do? They can recognize that these changes are coming and planners simply have to cope with them. You wonder how you can deal with blight if you can't sometimes use eminent domain over housing. I would say that you can deal with it by giving as much legal protection to education and medical care as you give to freedom of speech. That way, there wouldn't be the kind of reckless political decision-making which leads to blight in the first place.

But there is no question that, whether you have a law degree or not, planners are going to HAVE to start thinking of dealing with a world in which there is much greater protection for facts such as education and housing, than there has been before.

This planner's lament is bureaucracy's dawning awareness that it will have to include in its future plans, expanded individually enforceable rights. Using the facts given by the planner, and assuming strict scrutiny for housing with respect to eminent domain, would an eminent domain action over housing be sustained? Assuming intermediate scrutiny? Assuming either elevated level of scrutiny for housing with respect to eminent domain, but also assuming the present minimum scrutiny for education, liberty, maintenance and medical care?

In spite of the manifestly complex problems presented by the eminent domain moratoria, there was no recognition whatsoever on the part of "second-tier" players (planners, financial specialists, the legal community) that some long-term accommodation had to be reached between the political system and public opinion. Following are excerpts of two emails sent by me. The first is to attorneys at the Department of Transportation, concerning opposition to the O'Hare airport expansion, which the Department was in part funding and which involved taking about 500 houses:

> I think this scenario [resistance of the kind seen in New London] is also going to play out in Bensenville [the neighborhood in the path of the proposed O'Hare expansion] and you should be aware of it. Although the *Kelo* counsel did not argue to elevate the level of scrutiny for housing...THE INFORMAL EMINENT DOMAIN MORATORIUM HAS BROUGHT ABOUT A DE FACTO INCREASE IN THE LEVEL OF SCRUTINY FOR HOUSING. From studying the in-depth polling, I think people have simply changed their minds about housing, and now want it to have a higher level of scrutiny. Certainly that is true in the context of eminent domain. So far, the political system has not chosen to acknowledge this change, but it is still having to confront it in actual situations.... At a minimum, I think you should go into the Bensenville neighborhood and find out what degree of resistance you are likely to encounter there, and whether the Administration is willing to do what is required to overcome it. It would be a mistake, I think, not to thoroughly evaluate the potential of this volatile situation....Whatever you decide, you should keep in mind that the evidence shows that public opinion is changing with regard to housing. If it is not to be strict scrutiny for housing in all contexts, it certainly looks like public opinion demands at least intermediate scrutiny for housing in the eminent domain context. And it appears homeowners themselves are willing to physically resist removal. More and more, legislation and court decisions regarding eminent domain are being pushed to the side. You should not depend on them for authority. What matters is what happens in the street. I do hope you are, or will become, aware of these facts.

The second email is to bond specialists at the Fitch bond rating firm, which rates bonds tied to revenue from the O'Hare airport. The O'Hare expansion bond issuance was the largest in the history of Chicago:

> [You] should review the potential for resistance to the use of eminent domain in connection with the O'Hare expansion project....I don't know if you are following developments in Bensenville, which is in the path of the O'Hare expansion. That involves several hundred homes and several thousand people....[Proposed] legislative reforms are simply not resolving standoffs....I think — from what I have been able to gather from scientific polls on post-*Kelo* reaction — that public opinion now wants something like what is called "intermediate scrutiny" for housing, at least in the eminent domain context..... I don't think most eminent domain proposals (including the O'Hare project) would survive this increased level of review. And even if it did, I am not sure the people involved would leave, and if they didn't leave, I'm not sure the police would go in to remove them....You should keep an eye on this issue when formulating your ratings.

These emails met with no response. The question of resistance to the expansion was never discussed, and the bonds proved very popular: "The city of Chicago said it closed its largest-ever bond sale of $1.5 billion on Thursday, providing funds for the recently approved makeover of O'Hare International Airport....

Nearly 100 institutional investors bought the securities in strong demand that resulted in a lower-than-expected interest rate for the city, Chief Financial Officer Dana Levenson said. 'Mayor (Richard) Daley's vision of a modernized O'Hare is moving full steam ahead, and this historic bond sale is another important milestone that has been reached as this critical project is implemented,' said Rosemarie Andolino, the program's executive director."[335]

Nevertheless, a short while later, a new Fitch Ratings special report was issued, entitled "Beyond Kelo: Reactions, Responses and Credit Quality."

> The report discusses possible credit implications of efforts to limit eminent domain powers that have followed the US Supreme Court ruling in *Susette Kelo et al., v. City of New London, CT, et al.*..Fitch believes if eminent domain powers are restricted to a significant degree, municipal credit quality could be restrained or negatively affected. However, in the near-term, Fitch does not expect rating downgrades as a result of the legislation restricting the use of eminent domain in most situations. "By impairing a state or local government's efforts towards economic development, such legislation, if enacted, may limit opportunities for credit quality improvement and rating upgrades....Restrictive legislation has the potential to contribute to a diminution of credit quality over a longer term, in that, the proposed laws limit a state or local government's ability to respond to economic blight or weakened conditions...."The report notes the impact of restrictive legislation mostly will affect development-reliant credit types, such as tax allocation bonds, special assessment debt and obligations structured by state-specific structures....However, the longer-term affect of limiting economic development efforts could impact both development-related debt and broader-based securities issued by the municipality, such as general obligation bonds, lease obligations, and utility revenue bonds.[336]

Obviously the report was myopic in the extreme, but then, there is no evidence that the bond market predicted any opposition to the *Kelo* outcome. Or any emerging opposition to zoning. Or any opposition to taxes to pay bonds issued in connection with eminent domain, or zoning. Or any control by public opinion over facts. And yet all health and welfare regulation was caught up in the eminent domain controversy, and yet the report claimed that "[m]uch of the post-*Kelo* discussion and actions focus on the economic development rationale in eminent domain use, questioning whether or not this purpose is a viable reason to force a sale of privately held property."[337] This was the product of laziness and poor research.

Indeed, it was more advocacy than objective, rehearsing the well-worn generalities, the falsity of which the facts had exposed: "State and local governments generally consider eminent domain as a last resort tool and a necessary power to meet their role in providing for citizens and community needs. Eminent domain is used for a variety of governmental purposes, enabling municipalities to acquire sites for vital public facilities such as schools, police and fire stations, water and wastewater treatment plants, and rights of way for roads or transit, as

---

335 *Chicago Sun-Times*, December 22, 2005.

336 See www.fitchratings.com.

337 "Beyond Kelo" at 2. The report is online at www.fitchratings.com.

well as for economic development viewed as benefiting the area overall."[338] And there was an implied threat from this powerful rating company: "As stated previously, Fitch does not expect rating downgrades as an immediate response to legislation restricting eminent domain powers in most cases. Rather, Fitch views the potential for credit quality improvement as possibly limited by such legislation. Also, Fitch is concerned that broad and very restrictive legislation could be enacted that would dramatically reduce eminent domain powers and thereby limit a state's or municipality's ability to meet basic community needs such as public safety, utility services, education, and public health. Also, given the rising interest in private sector participation in public infrastructure projects, such relationships could be impeded since these partnerships can accrue benefits to the private entity."[339] That the bond market found itself at a loss to account for the resistance to *Kelo* — that it had bizarre recourse to threatening government entities, which are its partner — both were indications of deterioration of power in the political system. Among other things, it constituted attempted extortion of homeowners: the attempted extortion from an elephant by a mosquito. From this perspective the gambit was laughable, but it did promise illimitable horizons of political adventurism. It cannot, then, be surprising that public opinion raced from the "minimum scrutiny" regime like children let out of school.

The links between the bond market and government are so many that the two are scarcely distinguishable. A mere glance at the website of the Council of Development Finance Agencies reveals "our partners:" The Bond Market Association, the International Economic Development Council, The National Association of Bond Lawyers, the Government Finance Officers Association.[340] And they were more than alert to the potential of the eminent domain revolt to stop the smooth flow of cash from the bottom all the way to the top of the political system:

> Forest City Enterprises [of Fresno, California] is not going to bring forward plans for the south stadium project while a proposed initiative takes shape that could effect private developers' ability to develop private property. The city council had asked Forest City to submit alternative site plans for their proposed 85-acre mixed-use project in downtown Fresno, in a project area south of the Grizzlies Stadium. Forest City was due to present those plans at the end of this month, but because it appears one initiative will make the state ballot in November, Forest City won't make its next move until after that time, said Marlene Murphey, director of Fresno's Redevelopment Agency. An initiative to amend the California Constitution is being proposed that would bar state and local governments from condemning private property for private projects or uses. The initiative also would limit the government's authority to adopt certain land use, housing, consumer, environmental and workplace regulations, unless "regulations are adopted to preserve public health or safety, or comply with specified land use planning and property rights limits." Supporters will need to gather 598,105 signatures by July 7 in order to place the initiative on the November ballot. State Senator Tom McClintock ([Republican]-Northridge)

---

338 *Id.*, at 2.

339 *Id.*, at 3.

340 www.cdfa.net.

and the Howard Jarvis Taxpayers Association have teamed up for the campaign and have formed a political action committee....Murphey said the uncertainty has put many proposals, such as Forest City's, in question. Dave Spaur, executive director of the Economic Development Corporation serving Fresno County, said that large redevelopment projects are on hold — not just in California, but across the United States. "The International Economic Development Council is following eminent domain very closely," he said. "Nobody has to wait, but developers are putting everything on hold because it's created a huge question mark." Spaur said some of the proposals winding their way through the legislative process may be "bad apples" that have likely spoiled many deals already. "It's just this legislation hanging over people's head," he said. "It's a national story, and then it's a state story, and you have several large redevelopment agencies in the state, [that] have millions tied up in redevelopment." While Spaur said that Fresno has been "fairly prudent" about its redevelopment projects, cities such as Los Angeles, San Jose, San Diego and Anaheim have multiple projects with multi-year timelines.[341]

Obviously, a strategy aimed at destroying the political system would begin by bringing a halt — through resistance and litigation/reform — to economic activities associated with eminent domain, then proceed to tie up activities associated with any kind of land use, thence to activities associated with any kind of health and welfare regulation.

The system was vulnerable. Liberals had to bite their tongues, because issues such as housing, which they claimed to favor, were bound up in the resistance and yet liberals did not advocate increased individually enforceable rights. Hypocrisy could hardly be trotted out as a political platform. From the right, there was no formulation of alternatives to the traditional policies, but then, that was not their goal: the goal was power, and destroying the political system was an exercise of power; plots and conspiracies could hardly be trotted out as a political platform. This is all short-sighted, but so is the profit concept which is the basis of the bond market. Ominously, there was no call from either side for public support for overarching political themes. Everyone knew there was no political consensus; what is more, public opinion was the enemy of both sides.

So, how much money is siphoned off each year in corruption, for private purpose in violation of minimum scrutiny? How *little* money is government purpose? Post-*Kelo*, the answers depend on how much control public opinion exercises over facts; previously, concepts (for example, "public use") had mediated — as myth. Now, no concepts mediated. But the inquiries contest the definition of the economy: smoothly flowing cash and credit. Due to the tendency of the "minimum scrutiny" regime to collapse distinctions, we don't even have an estimate of how much money raised through bond issuance, is proximately related to eminent domain, much less zoning changes — and the issue has never been addressed, of the relationship of the scrutiny regime to the bond market. We are further confused in this inquiry by the intentional lack of conceptual clarity distinguishing, for example, eminent domain from zoning, or regulation from eminent domain. This is because, during the third Constitutional epoch, turf battles relating to these

---

341 *The Business Journal*, June 9, 2006 (Sacramento, California, archived at www.thebusinessjournal.com).

distinctions were between those who fundamentally supported the "minimum scrutiny" regime — and these debaters were the only ones permitted. It was only a question of who got to use the power; labels didn't matter after control had been obtained.

Resolutely facing the past, the bond market was simply being blind to its own interests. The Fitch response — especially when compared to the momentous interactions of the political system and public opinion — was disturbingly shallow and generalized considering that it was about the source of the bond market's money, the "minimum scrutiny" regime. There was no understanding in the report — indeed, no awareness — of the legal issues involved in the resistance to *Kelo*. The report's contempt and condescension provided — to put it generously — little guidance. Power had rendered the bond market blind to reality.[342] It was not clear how the bond market could flourish in an atmosphere in which municipalities felt unable to issue bonds because of high interest rates imposed by lower credit ratings based on municipalities' unwillingness to use eminent domain, or on the fear that lawsuits would contest the constitutionality of taxes to pay for bonds issued in violation of minimum scrutiny. The bond market was sending mixed signals: it both needed and retarded debt issuance relying on eminent domain. The contemporary American economic situation highlighted these tensions:

> The tax-free municipal bond market is facing a supply crunch, even as a crush of income-hungry buyers are lining up for whatever US cities and states can provide....Many US cities and states took advantage of recent low yields and sold tax-exempt bonds on favorable terms. About $400 billion worth of munis were brought out last year alone. Now, higher interest rates have hiked borrowing costs and slowed new issuances — volume so far this year is down 25% to 30% from year-ago levels....The tax-free muni supply could be constrained further as governments focus on the looming problem of underfunded pension and health-care obligations — the same hangover that afflicts many US companies. The bonds that municipalities are likely to issue to cover those debts will by federal law not be tax-exempt and so will not compete with the dwindling new supply of traditional muni bonds....Even as the supply of tax-exempt muni bonds tightens, demand is growing. A deteriorating outlook for US corporate earnings is boosting these bonds' appeal....Moreover, institutions and mutual funds are stepping up purchases, looking to capture fat tax-exempt yields.... Non-US buyers too are fueling a surge in muni trading, hoping to profit from spreads between U.S.-bond yields and foreign-bond yields....In addition to being largely bulletproof in terms of creditworthiness, most muni bonds are backed with just-in-case insurance....[343]

This bizarre situation was further complicated by the idea that, although bonds represented a comparative oasis of stability, eminent domain use was

342 Fitch is hardly the only "voice" of the bond market to lobby actively against any restrictions on eminent domain; the bond market doesn't like it one little bit. The other organizations mentioned above also oppose restrictions on eminent domain. For some insight into the pathology of bond market sensibilities, see Chunchi Wu *et al.*, "Liquidity, Default, Taxes and Yields on Municipal Bonds," http://ssrn.com/abstract=687500; Thorsten Beck *et al.*, "A New Database on Financial Development and Structure," http://ssrn.com/abstract=615009.

343 May 3, 2006 (archived at www.cbsmarketwatch.com).

destabilizing and challenges to it and its bonds were even further destabilizing. Again, a political system was revealed which relied on itself — specifically, through coercion — to both define and maintain stability. In its view, public opinion contributed nothing to its power. However, when the chickens came to roost at the highest level of state, the political system had no policy alternatives to offer the raft of political interests which depended on it for direction. Even a command economy would resolve nothing: what commands?

The bond market found itself in the wrong on both sides of the coercion equation in ordering government not to change its eminent domain laws: it both had to, and could not, issue this order. Its fulminations were a confession of weakness: when the political system changed, the bond market had no alternatives whatsoever to offer. Public opinion had made coercion less possible by breaking coercion down and opposing the front end component of it — obtaining property or issuing debt. Now it looked to be breaking down and opposing the back end of it — obtaining the money to pay on the bonds. It was, in short, the issue of the power component of the economy. *Kelo* had made the bond market aware that the entire coercive mechanism was based on the politically slender reed of the "minimum scrutiny" regime. If that went — because public opinion thwarted the political system — then the question was, whether to continue funding the political system? Would capital flee, once it became clear that public opinion was launching a rolling attack on the status quo? And yet even if there was a will to continue with the system, what system? How much of the political system relied on the idea that the system itself was unself-conscious? What other areas of health and welfare regulation, besides eminent domain, would now see stalling in the bond component of their operations? Education? Road construction? This inquiry went in tandem with the inquiry into the question, what are the facts of the individual? In short, spending priorities were changing. This was one of the things the political system had not anticipated, did not want, and with which it was completely unprepared to deal — witness the bumbling response of the bond market. Beyond the question, what to fund? lay the question, what to do if physical confrontation over the facts proceeded to tax strikes for any tax which public opinion perceived as improper?

Finally, the tensions in this market between issuers and underwriters revealed that bond issuance also had its government purpose problems under minimum scrutiny. It turned out that bonds — quite apart from purpose for which they were used — raised the issue of capture by underwriters. Government officials playing around in the money market, was not minimum scrutiny at work, it was an abrogation of government purpose. The bonds and associated transactions, or taxes imposed to pay for the bonds, could be repudiated on the basis that they were unconstitutional because they violated the government purpose prong of minimum scrutiny. The same grounds could be asserted for a refund of taxes paid for past unconstitutional eminent domain actions. Malfeasance by officials was not separate from malfeasance by government — thus facilitating legal recognition of government's obligation to pay — because abrogation of government purpose meant that there was no government. Quite apart from public opinion's balking at paying as the scope of corruption became apparent, there was no en-tity to do the paying under such circumstances:

> It would be a [good] thing if more municipalities took a closer, critical look at how their bonds were sold, in general, and took a real interest in the process. The [underwriting industry, through which 80% of municipal bonds are sold], welcomes neither scrutiny nor criticism, [and] has adopted a paternalistic "We know best" style. That's probably to be expected. The market has grown more involved over the past two decades, with underwriters pitching issuers "so-phisticated," or at least mathematically complicated, ideas, typically revolving around refinancing and derivative products, designed to save issuers money.... Are these ideas really going to save municipalities money? Or are they designed to earn more fees for the investment bankers who cook them up? Wall Street's business, after all, is to sell you stuff....The municipal market has a big problem right now, and it can be summed up in three words: swaps and derivatives....The Internal Revenue Service has a problem, because it says that swaps and deriva-tives have been used to conceal payments between the parties to these transac-tions, payments that seem to look a lot like bribes, it says. The Municipal Securi-ties Rulemaking Board has a problem with swaps and derivatives. The board has consistently warned that the shenanigans it has outlawed in the market, things like favoritism and pay-to-play, have migrated to the reinvestment-of-proceeds business, which includes swaps and derivatives. The board has no jurisdiction over the swaps market, because, it says, swaps and derivatives aren't, techni-cally speaking, securities....Municipal-bond analysts have a problem with swaps and derivatives. To this day, none of them can provide a definitive figure on how many municipalities have used these products....The taxpayers have a problem with swaps and derivatives. Public officials are buying things they don't under-stand from Wall Street, things that they can't price or evaluate on their own, and things that represent taking a point of view on the future direction of inter-est rates....[This] business [is] conducted almost entirely in secret....[344]

The argument is that if the bonds are found not to be tax exempt, then that is conclusively presumptive that their issuance violates minimum scrutiny, because it is a showing that there is, in fact, no government purpose in their issuance. That, in turn, is grounds for finding unconstitutional the tax to pay them:

> Let's say a municipality sells bonds, and hires an adviser to help it put to-gether a swap [purchasing bonds with bond proceeds in order to take advantage of a better rate]. The municipality pays the adviser, say, $75,000 for his services. The IRS, after a lengthy audit, follows the money, and now informs the munici-pality: You paid him $75,000 — but he also received $2.5 million from the people who provided the swap. Now a lot of people would have a problem right there. Why would the adviser who was responsible for selecting the winner of the business get a big check — from the firm that was selected to get the business? Who is the adviser working for? There is a very practical consequence of this check writing. The IRS says the $2.5 million payment is implicitly embedded in the swap, and produced a higher-than-normal swap rate. After a lot of math-ematical calculations, they tell the municipality that its bonds are no longer tax-exempt because the sale violated tax law.[345]

As the following discussion of a recently enacted audit program emphasizes, the violation of tax exempt status extends to any entities claiming that bond

---

344 "Commentary," May 24 and June 16, 2006 (archived at www.bloomberg.com).

345 "Commentary," April 16, 2006 (archived at www.bloomberg.com).

money received is used for charitable purposes under for IRS Code $501 (c) (3), a very broad category comprising the following purposes: "religious, educational, scientific, literary, testing for public safety, fostering national or international amateur sports competition, and the prevention of cruelty to children or animals. The term charitable is used in its generally accepted legal sense and includes relief of the poor, the distressed, or the underprivileged; advancement of religion; advancement of education or science; erection or maintenance of public buildings, monuments, or works; lessening the burdens of government; lessening of neighborhood tensions; elimination of prejudice and discrimination; defense of human and civil rights secured by law; and combating community deterioration and juvenile delinquency."[346] The IRS decided that

> The audit program will emphasize compliance with the limitations imposed on private business use of bond-financed facilities under the so-called "95/5" test (requiring that throughout the term of the bond issue at least 95 percent of the use of the facilities financed with the proceeds of the tax-exempt bonds be used...exclusively in furtherance of its exempt purposes). Thus, the examinations will analyze whether any "unrelated business" use of the facilities by the borrowers has occurred. Other issues to be reviewed are whether there are leases of portions of the bond-financed facilities to private businesses....The audits will likely highlight the importance of...proper allocation of the bond proceeds to the facilities that were financed....[347]

It turned out that "[t]he [New London Development Corporation, the redevelopment entity which took title to the *Kelo* properties] is a 501(c)(3) non-profit charity. Its latest IRS filing...discloses total revenue of $8,560,308.00. Of that $8.5 million, $7,941,701.00 comes from 'Government Contributions.'"[348]

Thus, the collapse of branches and doctrines under the "minimum scrutiny" regime tended to turn charitable organizations into government entities, and the violations of government purpose came to be vested in those organizations: they were not charitable organizations, they were private organizations. Now their tax-exempt status was in question, too. Private purpose had become government purpose: the circle was complete, and so was the collapse of the branches and doctrines of government. No wonder, then, that political opinion repaired continually to fact: there were no Constitutional doctrines. Without a Constitution, there was no political system (but to what extent was public opinion now generating a concept of social organization which bore no relation to a constitution?). To be sure, it was a client society, but whose client was public opinion? As it turned out, no ones: the political system had no conception of such a large, anomalous mass. Public opinion was now continually wounded in its *amour propre*, to discover how systematically it was excluded from power.

The assault on bonds was merely one of another of those slow cuts or corrosions by public opinion, of the third Constitutional epoch through the frustration of health and welfare regulation under the "minimum scrutiny" regime. The

---

346 This definition is from the Internal Revenue Service website, www.irs.gov/charities.

347 Duane Morris, "IRS to Initiate Tax-Exempt Bond Audit Program," June 16, 2006 (archived at www.martindale.com).

348 June 30, 2005 (archived at www.dansargis.com).

aim was to raise the Constitutional status of facts. However, that the IRS was even broaching the subject of municipal bonds with respect to government purpose, had a chilling effect on the bond market. Although the number of audits was small, the notion raised the possibility of private suits for violations of the government purpose prong of the minimum scrutiny test. Quite distinct from any alleged malfeasance such as fraud or conspiracy, suits against any number of defendants — charitable organizations, bond underwriters, government entities and government officials — brought bond repudiation into play.

> The announcement of an Internal Revenue Service...audit of a variable-rate municipal bond has a negative effect on the cost of financing paid by the bond's issuer....In the case of variable-rate demand obligations..., rates paid by municipal bond issuers rise immediately to near taxable levels upon the announcement of an IRS audit. Since the interest rates on these issues generally vary on a weekly or daily basis, issuers' costs of funds rise immediately and sharply....Turning to long-term, fixed-rate bonds, anecdotal evidence suggest that some issuers have found it difficult to place new issues at reasonable cost after an audit announcement, even though the audit in question relates to bonds which are already outstanding. As a result, state and local issuers have either canceled or delayed new issues or have found other means by which to finance capital needs, according to the Association's report....[Q]ualitative information supports the hypothesis that the announcement of an IRS tax audit leads to a reduction in liquidity for long-term, fixed-rate bonds....[I]n a market that is relatively illiquid to begin, liquidity is all but lost when the news of an audit is announced.[349]

Standing behind bonds was the issue of taxation itself in relation to government purpose, and the relation of taxation to the Constitution in the emerging fourth Constitutional epoch. The implications for the political system were sharpened tremendously by the Kelo substitution of private for government purpose and, above all, by the Supreme Court's connivance in that and related gambits. By no means did these implications originate in or end with that case. But history had come full circle: property and taxes were fundamental issues in the American Revolution.

---

349 August 20, 2002 (archived at www.bondmarkets.com).

# Chapter 5. The Early Days of the New Bill of Rights

## What the Fourth Epoch Inherits

In response to public opinion's concept of possession, the political system finally looked to be coalescing around the concept of order, as resistance impeded the smooth operation of the regime. Could order be used as a method of splitting public opinion and reducing resistance to the point that resistance could be destroyed? Opposition to eminent domain struck at every organizing principle of the "minimum scrutiny" regime: expertise, progress, development, the standard of living, law. Elitist these notions might be, nevertheless they were the source of all paychecks. It might provide a basis on which the police and the military could be ordered into politics.

Events outpaced authority. On July 31, 2005, *The Day* editorialized:

> Ms. Kelo [in her testimony before the legislative committee investigating eminent domain] presented the other side poignantly, what it's like to be forced out of a well-kept home you love....If the legislature is to preserve eminent domain in its toolbox for repairing hurting cities, it must address this human issue in a way that quiets the public outrage over the issue and invites confidence. Doing so may not be as complicated as many suggest, but it also is not as simple as Scott Bullock, the lawyer for the Institute for Justice, told the committees Thursday. Mr. Bullock's solution would be to completely do away with the use of eminent domain for economic development and tightening up the requirements for its use in blighted areas....That would seem to us to be too draconian, and unnecessarily handicap cities....The alternative is to raise the bar for using eminent domain for urban renewal and municipal development plans from what is currently allowed under Connecticut law. One approach to doing this came

out of Thursday's remarkably illuminating proceedings: somehow to establish more rigorous standards for municipalities in cases in which people's homes are at stake, as opposed to businesses." To my knowledge, this was the first time in the debate that it had been proposed to raise the level of scrutiny for housing. That is, here the debate moved from abstractions such as "economic development," to facts, such as housing. It appeared the newspaper was calling for legislation which reflected the two levels of scrutiny above minimum scrutiny, that is, either

> "Eminent domain shall not be exercised with respect to housing unless it substantially furthers an important government purpose"

or

> "Eminent domain shall not be exercised with respect to housing unless it specifically fulfills an overriding government purpose."

The sentiment was echoed a few days later by Connecticut State Representative Michael Lawlor: "Eminent domain is a very powerful tool....When you're talking about taking people's houses, it's like priceless art. It doesn't matter how much you pay, it's the home you grew up in. No amount of money is going to replace that. Because of that, eminent domain should only be used in the most extraordinary situations. The question is, what are those situations?"[350] Focusing on housing, and the opposition to destroying it, provided legislators what seemed to be a revelation of the vast extent of discretion conferred by the use of hopelessly vague terms in connection with eminent domain. A Kansas proposal to restrict eminent domain meant not allowing it to be used with respect to housing: "If it's somebody's home and they are living there, then sorry, you are out of luck because it isn't abandoned," [State Senator Derek] Schmidt said.[351] At the same time, questions necessarily arose: if housing was not "redevelopment," what was, and on what grounds? If housing did not mean that property was "abandoned" or "blighted," what else did not mean it was "abandoned," and again, on what grounds? Senator Schmidt unthinkingly claimed that his proposal "won't stop governments' abilities to take land for traditional uses such as roadways, bridges or libraries." But will it stop them for at least as long as it takes to litigate such questions as whether, under his proposal, housing enjoys a higher level of scrutiny than roadways, bridges or libraries? a lower one? Does it raise the level of scrutiny for all of them? Meantime, will the deal hold together? In fact, he is engaging in an *ad hoc* "facts of the individual" analysis, without quite realizing that in a "facts of the individual" analysis all facts are scrutinized in relation to one another.

Although *The Day*'s position would appear to "sound" in due process, it made no connection to any other right in either the State or Federal Constitutions. What was the argument advanced to justify elevating scrutiny for housing? "The sacredness of one's [*sic*]home is a fundamental American value."[352] This is the sort of argument which lost in, for example, *San Antonio*, and it again raises the ques-

---

350 *The Day*, August 6, 2005.

351 *Winfield Daily Courier*, October 1, 2005 (Winfield, Kansas, archived at www.winfield-courier.com).

352 *The Day*, July 31, 2005.

tion, what is the Constitution? Given that argument as legislative intent for the two formulations above, would Justice Stevens sustain either as one of his "further restrictions on [the State's] exercise of the takings power," or would he void it as an impermissible alteration of the role of the State in the Federal system, on the grounds that it prevents the State from exercising its health and welfare powers? D. Benjamin Barros of the Widener University Law School, was not much clearer in his testimony before the Pennsylvania House Government Committee, which was considering eminent domain reform legislation. The problem seemed to be hesitation, for whatever reason, to adopt an unqualified elevation — *no matter how slight* — of scrutiny for housing. It was perverse:

> [W]hat seems to be at the core of most people's concern is the possibility that their local governments might take their homes to clear land for a private developer, as the town of New London did in the project that gave rise to the *Kelo* litigation. Focusing on homes would be consistent with the common-sense notion that homes are different from other types of property. People become personally attached to their homes. Homes tie people to their communities. Displacement of people from their homes can separate them from family, friends, schools and jobs. I therefore suggest that you consider giving additional protection to homes in the eminent domain context. While restricting economic development takings is at the forefront of people's minds after *Kelo*, you also should consider protecting homes from more traditional exercises of eminent domain. People unhappy about their homes being taken for a shopping mall are likely to be only marginally less unhappy if their homes are taken for something that fits the classic picture of a public use, like a highway. Many other areas of law treat homes differently than other types of property. Most relevant here, the legal system already gives special protection to people's possession of their homes in a number of contexts, such as making it harder for a lender to foreclose on a home than to repossess another type of property. The law also gives special treatment to homes when interests other than possession are at stake. For example, the government is held to a higher standard when it searches a home than when it searches other types of property, like cars or undeveloped land. Recognizing that homes are special does not mean that local governments should be prohibited in all circumstances from taking homes. There are times when taking homes is vital to the public interest. But there are a number of approaches that you could take to give homes additional protection and encourage government entities to take homes only as a last resort. For example:
>
> Responding directly to *Kelo*, you could prohibit the taking of homes for economic development, but allow economic development taking of some other types of property.
>
> You could permit the taking of a home for any type of public use only after a finding, reviewable by a court, that there is no alternative course of action that would serve the same public goal at a reasonable cost.
>
> You could require governments to pay a premium (say 10 percent or 15 percent) over fair market value for a taken home, which would both provide an economic disincentive to take homes when other types of property are available and compensate the homeowners for some of the personal value they placed in their homes.

These approaches — alone or in concert — would help protect homes while maintaining flexibility for local governments to take other types of property. Common sense tells us that homes are different, and deserve special legal treatment in many contexts....[The proposed legislation....prohibits the use of eminent domain to "turn [the taken property] over to a nonpublic interest." My first observation is that while I understand the intent of the language, the litigator in me sees ambiguities in the phrase "nonpublic interest." "Private person or entity" might be preferable language....Using eminent domain to transfer property to a private developer to spur economic development may be objectionable, but what about the use of eminent domain to transfer the property to a privately-owned utility? To a private university to expand its campus? To a not-for-profit museum or symphony? To a privately-owned hospital that is greatly needed by the community? To a sports team for a new stadium?....[L]ocal governments should have the power to take truly blighted property. The difficult task is to come up with a definition that separates blighted property from merely economically depressed...."[353]

If *The Day*'s basis for elevating scrutiny was unclear, the implication of raising it was quite clear. If scrutiny for housing were to be raised with respect to eminent domain, with respect to what other situations would scrutiny for housing necessarily be raised? If housing is "a fundamental American value" with respect to eminent domain, why is it not "a fundamental American value" in other situations, and as deserving of elevated scrutiny in those situations? Strict scrutiny for housing is implied. Viewed in this light, restriction of eminent domain over housing becomes the wedge by means of which strict scrutiny for housing enters the law. That had to be prevented. On every hand, a parallel system of enforcement beckoned, displacing the arrangements of the political system under the scrutiny regime.

Also, and ironically, raising the level of scrutiny with respect to eminent domain "in which people's homes are at stake, as opposed to businesses," implies the very "draconian" restriction of eminent domain sought to be avoided. If scrutiny for housing were to be raised, but not for business, what is the justification? If housing is "a fundamental American value" with respect to scrutiny, in what respects is not business? It implicates maintenance as a fact of the individual. Consider, for example, a business owner for whom the business is the sole source of income. What about these formulations?

> "Eminent domain shall not be exercised unless it is specifically fulfills an overriding government purpose."

> "Eminent domain shall not be exercised with respect to maintenance unless it specifically fulfills an overriding government purpose."

> "Eminent domain shall not be exercised unless it substantially furthers an important government interest and with respect to housing unless it specifically fulfills an overriding government purpose."

---

353 *Pennsylvania Law Weekly*, September 12, 2005 (archived at www.palaweekly.com). This is his summary of his article, "Home as a Legal Concept," http://ssrn.com/abstract=801245.

What do these formulations imply about other government actions with respect to other forms of income? We see that the New Bill of Rights tends toward internal consistency, as opposed to being a mere list of desiderata; consideration of elevating scrutiny with respect to one of its facts, leads to consideration of elevating scrutiny with respect to another of its facts. Its facts seem to be mutually reinforcing, as if this constellation of facts had long lain dormant in the American mind. The argument and qualification of *The Day* also imply that government *only* acts to vindicate the individual and that this means, in very few and very specific ways. This also serves to link together the facts of the New Bill of Rights.

Other proposals directed toward restraining eminent domain in the case of housing, reflected confusion as to means and ends and the uncertain character of opposition to *Kelo*. California State Senator Christine Kehoe proposed a two-year moratorium (to be made permanent by a state constitutional amendment) on eminent domain for housing when the eminent domain action resulted in "private use."[354] This reflected ignorance of the absence of such a concept in the law of eminent domain, as explained above. The Castle Coalition, another "property rights" organization, had trouble distinguishing housing even when, as with its "Hands Off Housing" campaign, it wished to do so. Its campaign seeks to prevent eminent domain with respect to housing, when the eminent domain action is for "private development," again showing a lack of awareness of the legal emptiness of this term.[355]

In the face of this inability of higher levels of the political system to focus on housing, local organizations simply took matters into their own hands. In Bensenville, Illinois, site of the 500 homes to be taken in connection with the O'Hare airport expansion, the village took the remarkable step of officially recommending that its residents not sell their homes. It also suggested that health and welfare regulation — of which eminent domain was one — could be use to thwart eminent domain. In making its recommendation, Bensenville became, so far as is known, the first government entity in the history of the United States to urge resistance to eminent domain:

DO NOT SELL YOUR
HOME TO CHICAGO

*Chicago cannot take your home
and you do not need to sell your home to Chicago.*

The City of Chicago has recently sent you letters stating that the City of Chicago has designated your property "for acquisition" for Chicago's O'Hare expansion program. The purpose of this letter is to urge you to

**NOT sell your home to Chicago!**[356]

---

354 *Los Angeles Daily News*, August 18, 2005 (Los Angeles, California, archived at www2.dailynews.com).

355 Details of the program are available at www.castlecoalition.org.

356 http://www.bensenville.il.us/REIT%20Ltr1%20122005.doc.

Once again, however, not a word was said about any right to housing. Not selling would mean what it had meant in New London: it would bring physical confrontation abruptly nearer by an automatic transfer of title. Nevertheless, it is instructive to note the creativity which was injected into the dispute over eminent domain over housing. The New London government was opposed or neutral to the *Kelo* property owners and so the legal situation stagnated there. The advocacy of the Village of Bensenville meant that it was drawn into new proposed solutions which brought government ever more closely to recognizing and enforcing the housing provision of the New Bill of Rights. The dimensions of its protection were unclear. The Village certainly appeared to be attempting to provide an impenetrable shield for housing and businesses through its status as a government entity, in the first instance by making arrangements to lodge title in the Village to property which owners wished to sell:

> Residents and business owners now have available, through the Village of Bensenville, legal support that will:
>
> 1) Stop future harassment by Chicago representatives
>
> 2) Prevent threats to throw you out of your home or business in 30 days
>
> 3) Permit you and your family to remain in your home
>
> 4) Permit your business to remain at its current location
>
> 5) Provide you with free legal assistance to help you sort through the complicated issues related to negotiating the right price for your home or business
>
> 6) GUARANTEED compensation — participants will be guaranteed to receive financial compensation that is NO LESS than what Chicago is offering including relocation compensation.[357]

Then there was a resort to subterfuge: "Bensenville trustees voted Tuesday to delay the demolition of homes and businesses that stand in the way of Chicago's planned $15 billion expansion of O'Hare International Airport. The trustees approved a 180-day moratorium on demolition permits within a zone targeted for the project. The vote came one week before contractors were expected to raze two homes near the airport, the first of more than 60 properties acquired by Chicago for demolition to make room for new runways. The move will give the village more time to write a plan to address public health and safety issues related to the demolitions, said Bensenville attorney Joseph Karaganis. The village wants more information from the city of Chicago, such as the sequence of proposed demolition and details of contractors' skills in order to plan for traffic safety, hazardous materials disposal and runoff control, Karaganis said."[358] This seemed nothing more than an effort to stave off demolition, with an unconvincing rationale behind it. Bensenville could not help innovating even when it was being disingenuous — its real statement by this action was that, for some reason it did not specify, houses remained housing even when no one was living in them. In this wholly uncharted territory, the Village seemed determined at least to preserve the socioeconomic profile of the community, raising the question, for which

---

357  http://www.bensenville.il.us/feb6meeting.pdf.

358  *Chicago Sun-Times*, March 7, 2006.

facts was it elevating scrutiny? Could it do so against other State law? Nevertheless, here again we see the "minimum scrutiny" regime at work: the Bensenville officials simply couldn't imagine approaching the situation with new thoughts about the Constitution; there were no other thoughts than those guaranteed to bring about defeat in court.

The fruitless maneuverings of Court and counsel provoked the first violence to erupt over eminent domain since the *Kelo* decision, and this violence was the ultimate failure of Court and counsel. It was no joke opposing the political machine of Chicago Mayor Richard Daley: "The fight over O'Hare expansion has prompted stepped up security in suburban Bensenville, NBC5 reported on Monday. There have been several incidents of vandalism. In August, the home of Bensenville Village President John Geils was sprayed with graffiti. Geils has opposed expanding O'Hare. His prized 1968 Mustang was also severely damaged by vandals. It was the latest in a string of incidents, including anonymous phone threats against the Geils family. As a result, two security consultants have been hired to investigate."[359] Here we see the beginnings of a new adjunct to the moratorium ministate: separate enforcement establishments. How much larger will these grow? And then this: "Some homeowners near O'Hare airport say they are being harassed. It's happening in Bensenville where many residents have held out, choosing not to sell to the city so the airport can expand. But now some homeowners that have decided to sell say they are being attacked by those who don't want the homes to be sold. One family says their home was egged and a window was shot out. They have hired a security company to watch over their home. Mayor Daley Saturday warned that harassment is a federal violation and will not be tolerated. 'No one should be harassed. There's fed money involved in this. Anybody who is doing any harassment of anybody selling a home in regards to any public project is in federal violation and they better be careful,' Daley said. The homeowners claiming to be harassed say they are moving out next week. Meantime, the O'Hare expansion construction continues as scheduled."[360] And then this:

> Another round was fired in the suburban war against the O'Hare expansion project. CBS 2's Mike Parker reports, leaders in Bensenville now accuse the city of Chicago of spreading hysteria, scaring people into selling their homes. To grease the skids for the O'Hare Airport expansion, the city of Chicago is offering the 500 or so targeted Bensenville residents fair market value for their homes, plus $20,000 for relocation expenses. Tim and Patti Taylor, who want to sell their house, say that extra money is enticing. "We want the best for our family and this is going to put us in a better position for buying a house," Patti Taylor said. But Bensenville village officials Monday claimed the offer of extra money is a cruel hoax designed to spread hysteria. "It wants to buy as many homes as possible, demolish [them], scare the neighborhoods and make sure that this panic peddling continues until there's nothing left of the community," said Bensenville Village President John Geils. "Those are all incorrect statements. Those are all false," said Rosemarie Andolino with the O'Hare Modernization

---

359  October 31, 2005 (archived at www.nbc5.com).

360  November 5, 2005 (archived at www.abclocal.go.com).

Program. She says the city simply wants to help impacted residents get on with their lives. There are signs of more trouble ahead when the city of Chicago starts tearing down the homes being bought. Bensenville village officials are promising a battle over demolition permits. Getting those permits, it is clear, won't be easy. Leaders in Bensenville also deny they harassed the first people to sell for the airport. The village president called the claims a public relations stunt by the city of Chicago.[361]

Finally, compounding confusion, the Illinois legislature was on the verge of passing eminent domain legislation:

> Key to the agreement [between houses of the Illinois legislature] is a guarantee that Chicago city officials can continue their expansion of O'Hare International Airport under the current laws, which give them sweeping powers to condemn private property in suburban communities bordering the airfield. Nearly 1,000 special redevelopment districts now active around the state could also continue operating under the old rules....But the vast majority of private property owners in Illinois would get stronger protections in cases where government officials want to take their land for use by the community. The bill would put a greater burden on government officials to show why they want to condemn a piece of property. It also would increase the amount of money they have to pay if they succeed....The Illinois legislation would put the burden on public officials to justify in court the need to condemn private property. Current law generally puts the responsibility on the private property owner to prove that the government's condemnation plan is unjustified. The legislation would raise the bar even higher in some cases where local officials want to take private land for private development. In those instances, the bill would also require that government officials meet the civil court system's standard of "clear and convincing" evidence that the condemnation is necessary. If the condemnation were needed to clean up blight, however, the higher standard wouldn't apply, even in cases where the land was being seized for private development.[362]

This proposal was ripe for litigation, mainly because, although it purported to exempt the O'Hare expansion and other supposedly done deals, it did not settle any levels of scrutiny for facts. Therefore, it could be contested — by opponents even of exempted projects. What did "exemption" mean in the context of due process or, for that matter, in the context of any legal term? Is it Constitutionally allowable on due process grounds to permit the O'Hare project to avoid a review on the new "higher standard?" By attempting to restrict to eminent domain with respect to time (approved projects), the legislation merely raised timeless, or doctrinal, issues. Nor did it prevent an inquiry — even with respect to approved projects — into whether there had in fact been a public purpose in those approved projects, or whether there had been a substitution of private for government purpose, thereby violating the minimum scrutiny by which those approved projects had passed muster in the first place. Indeed, by imposing a "higher standard," the legislation invited review of previously approved projects. Nothing could avoid the inquiry into the level of scrutiny for facts, which public

---

361 November 7, 2005 (archived at www.cbs2chicago.com).

362 *Chicago Tribune*, April 20, 2006.

opinion — in its incoherent way — was now demanding. More litigation delay loomed for the O'Hare expansion project.

The challenge to health and welfare or tax and spend powers had broadened to include valuation, and threatened to spill over from eminent domain to regulation of any kind. This occurred in the midst of the ongoing debate over the point at which government regulation — requiring no compensation to an owner although it may lessen the value of property — becomes an eminent domain-like taking requiring compensation. Are valuation and regulation, doctrines or facts?

A [Georgia] Senate study committee has held the last of four hearings on a proposed law intended to protect property owners from overzealous land regulations. Sen. Chip Pearson, a Dawsonville Republican, said Senate Bill 30 would give the public more leverage to fight "inverse condemnation," property devaluation due to government land-use decisions....Under condemnation law, governments pay a private property owner for land seized for public use. A special master, a lawyer or judge, is appointed to determine the fair market value. Pearson wants to expand the use of the special master process to inverse condemnation. He said the government should pay for property it renders useless by regulation, just like it pays for seized property. Popular at the grassroots level, the bill's supporters say it protects individual property rights....Voters in Oregon amended the state constitution last year to include a similar measure and others are popping up in legislatures nationwide. The bill's opponents, including locally elected officials statewide, say the law would make it financially impossible for governments to uphold necessary land regulations. The Association County Commissioners of Georgia has called the bill "the most dangerous legislation affecting local and state governments introduced in recent years...."State rules forbid landowners along Yahoola Creek in Lumpkin County from building within 150 feet of its banks. The regulation intends to prevent pollution in the stream, but Pearson said the buffer zone prevents owners from using land on which they still have to pay taxes. "People are pretty well adamant that they want something done to stop it," Pearson said. But in Hall County and Gainesville, officials are afraid the bill will weaken their ability to protect the public and the environment. "I see this as an attack on land-use regulations. And some of these land-use regulations are beneficial to citizens," Gainesville Mayor George Wangemann said. Government officials must weigh the rights of private property owners and the good of the general public, West Hall Commissioner Billy Powell said. "Sometimes the overall good outweighs the individual," Powell said. Landowners now turn to superior courts to sue government for damages caused by "over-regulation," said County Attorney Bill Blalock. But Pearson wants a streamlined approach with a special master. "I do not see the necessity for a quick, emergency proceeding for inverse condemnation," Blalock said. "If every property owner had the opportunity to drag into court the city or state...you'd have a whole lot of waste of time and money, it seems to me," he added. The county would have to hire more legal staff and raise taxes to pay for it, Powell said. If land-use regulations are reasonable, the counties shouldn't be targeted, Pearson said. "I think the counties are in a very secure position as long as they abide by what's been the standard practice that's been upheld by the courts," Pearson said. But who determines what is reasonable? A special master merely determines fair market value. The bill does not answer that question. And Pearson said he purposefully did not define inverse condemnation in the bill because it should be decided on a case-by-case basis. "In North Georgia what may be reasonable may not be reasonable in South Georgia. "You may have a 150-foot buffer in South Georgia on a 50-acre tract that may not necessarily mean you would lose the value of the property, because that may not be the only thing you can develop," Pearson said.[363]

In the absence of public opinion demanding an increased level of scrutiny for facts, the political system had enjoyed vast discretion in its decisions regarding these facts. But it had overlooked the necessity for developing a rationale for its decisions, against the day when public opinion did start to change. Thus, when opposition developed to the decisions of the political system, the system had only the vaguest defenses for its own actions and, crucially, *no alternate laws*. The political system had, perhaps, precise regulations, but no precise rationale. Whatever the concepts of general welfare and health and safety had done for the Founders and the states, they were proving astonishingly weak defenses now, and were worthless on the offensive.

But did the law matter? The question was: what would public opinion tolerate? That is, even though polls showed broad-based opposition to *Kelo*, what were the legal dimensions of the opposition, and would the opposition last? The reforms proposed or adopted demonstrated lack of understanding of the issue, but as time went on the element of flat-out political resistance also surfaced. It first appeared in the California moratorium legislation which emerged from the committees; they refused to extend the moratorium to businesses, even where the business was the owner's sole source of maintenance — there was testimony from business owners on behalf of this extension.[364]

Then differing moratorium proposals could not get support on the floor. "We just did not have a critical mass on either side. We bowed to reality," said one legislator.

> The Legislature's response may be developed under pressure from an initiative campaign threatened by conservatives who want to restrict eminent domain to only public uses, such as schools or freeways. Sticking points include whether to protect commercial as well as private property, how to impose a moratorium without delaying ongoing projects, assessing a fair purchase price and whether to make it harder to declare land blighted — a requirement before condemnation. Kehoe blamed Republicans for holding up progress, noting how they voted against the bills in committee. However, Democrats hold majorities in both houses and could have easily passed either measure — or both — on to the gov-

---

363  *The Gainesville Times*, November 3, 2005 (Gainesville, Georgia, archived at www.gainesvilletimes.com). As Polly Price indicates, "[t]he question of the legitimate role of government with respect to private property has defied easy resolution throughout U.S. history. Although the basic proposition that government takings of private property must be compensated was settled at the founding of the United States, no historical consensus has ever been reached on the extent to which compensation is required for other government actions, short of outright appropriations under eminent domain, that affect private property.... What constitutional protection of private property has meant in the courts has changed since the founding era." This is her summary of her *Property Rights: Rights and Liberties Under the Law* (ABC-CLIO 2003), http://papers.ssrn.com/sol3/papers.cfm?abstract_id=447961.

364  *The San Diego Union Tribune*, August 31, 2005.

ernor if the issue had been a top priority, say some of those who had worked on the legislation.[365]

As long as no forced removals took place — as long as the informal moratoria held — it obviously would not matter what the law said. In addition, as we have seen, where there was sufficient local opposition some deals involving the use of eminent domain simply didn't come together.

But time worked against Susette Kelo. As reform deliberations proceeded in Connecticut, it had become clear that coherent legislation could not emerge where no interest opposed eminent domain with respect to facts — was any coherent legislation intended to emerge? The meaninglessness of restrictions expressed in generalities — which raised more questions than they answered and against which Justice Stevens had warned — led to a circus of policies, goals and formulations, in which there was not even consensus as to which proposals changed outcomes and which changed nothing.

The bickering was particularly amusing in light of the fact that the Institute for Justice and the political system are natural allies in the cause of maintaining minimum scrutiny for housing; in fact, they wished to maintain minimum scrutiny for all facts — it was merely a question of who should exercise the discretion provided by the regime. In their greed to manipulate a change in public opinion, but also in their ignorance and stupidity, it never occurred to them to unite on a formula as a basis for sending in law enforcement (the basis of their power), rather than let the initiative pass to property owners who knew only one rule: possession. Crucially at the outset of the crisis, the political system had failed to grasp the importance of what was clear to an otherwise inchoate public opinion: possession. This was why the political system miserably failed to resolve the crisis — and thought it had done so — by maneuvers such as browbeating, sleights of hand involving title and nonsensical "reform" legislation. None of these restored the political system's lifeblood: possession. Possession was the forcible — as opposed to political — entry of public opinion into the political system. How to get it out? The Connecticut situation deteriorated from proposals and counter-proposals, to charges and counter-charges:

> The General Assembly is going to alter the government's right to seize private property. The lawmakers leading the effort to review eminent domain statutes were sure of at least that much. But on Thursday, after a six-hour public hearing on five conflicting reform proposals set before the Judiciary Committee, disagreement seemed as deep as ever between those who consider the taking of a home as the deepest abrogation of American ideals and those who find in the power to do so an impoverished city's final hope to save itself. "I think there's a general willingness to do an eminent domain bill as soon as there's agreement on what needs to be done," said Rep. Michael Lawlor, [Democrat]-East Haven, the committee's co-chairman, in a brief interview in his office. But notwithstanding the furor of eminent domain opponents after the US Supreme Court upheld New London's seizure of homes on the Fort Trumbull peninsula for an economic development project, or the political payback those same opponents have prom-

---

365 *The Daily Breeze*, September 8, 2005 (Los Angeles, California, archived at www.dailybreeze.com).

ised at the polls, Lawlor said convening a special session might be pointless now. After all, he noted, no one has agreed on what to do. After Gov. M. Jodi Rell ordered the New London Development Corp. to reverse its decision to begin the process of eviction last month, Lawlor said, the state's "voluntary moratorium" on eminent domain use appears to be working, giving the legislators time to deliberate on changing the law. "I don't see how doing it now versus doing it in March makes a big difference," he said. House Minority Leader Robert Ward, [Republican]-North Branford, disagrees. On Thursday he repeated his call to convene a special session, formalize the moratorium, and eventually strip the use of eminent domain for private economic development entirely out of state statutes. That was just one in a diverse group of bills reviewed Thursday, which varied from Ward's to a careful rewriting of that section of the law that would require municipalities to more explicitly declare the public benefits and necessities of such takings, but would preserve them as a proper use of eminent domain. Attorneys for the nonprofit Institute for Justice, the law firm that represented lead plaintiff Susette Kelo and the other Fort Trumbull property owners in their unsuccessful Supreme Court challenge, proposed banning condemnations for private commercial development unless property owners consent to the action, and prohibiting development agencies like the NLDC from acquiring property by eminent domain. Meanwhile, the Connecticut Conference of Municipalities, which filed a friend of the court brief supporting the New London project, proposed a substantially different change — requiring a municipality to specifically approve its development agency's takings, parcel by parcel, and to require that owners of condemned property be paid at least 125 percent of fair market value in compensation. Not surprisingly, neither side thought very highly of the other's ideas. Scott Bullock, a senior attorney at the Institute for Justice, lit into one bill, proposed by the committee leadership, saying it "does not make any substantive changes to Connecticut eminent domain law whatsoever." The committee proposal would "simply require that local governments and planning bodies produce more paperwork about a plan and its supposed economic benefits," he said. "The bill might be subtitled the Full Employment for Planners Act. Better planning is no solution and it will not prevent the use of eminent domain for private commercial development and in practice it will probably encourage more abuse." Bullock got as good as he gave, however, particularly from Lawlor's co-chairman, Sen. Andrew McDonald, [Democrat]-Stamford, who peppered Bullock with a series of hypothetical private development projects — a stadium, a college, a hospital, a nursing home — that he said might be driven by a need for economic stimulus, but were no less worthy uses of eminent domain power. "What I'm driving at here is you try to paint the world as black and white, and it's not so black and white," McDonald said. Meanwhile, New London opponents of the project seemed eager to alert the legislators — many of whom voted for some of the $73 million worth of state bonds that have funded virtually all of the work at Fort Trumbull — to the current state of affairs on the largely vacant peninsula. "The municipal development plan is a shambles," said Neil Oldham, co-chairman of the Coalition to Save the Fort Trumbull Neighborhood. "The designated developer is fighting with the NLDC. The NLDC is fighting with the City Council. And the state officials are dithering. It's a royal mess."[366]

And it stayed that way.

Continued possession was not the only means of combating eminent domain. Another was to combat intimidation:

---

366 *The Day*, October 7, 2005.

"Enough is enough." That's the message some Bensenville officials say they want to convey to the city of Chicago and others they say have been threatening and harassing them since 2001. Village President John Geils said Monday that the village has hired two private security advisers to investigate claims of vandalism, property damage and intimidation by people he believes disagree with the village's actions against the expansion of O'Hare International Airport....According to police reports in mid-August, vandals broke into Geils' garage, damaged the windows on his wife's 1968 Mustang and spray-painted profanity on his home. According to Geils and police reports, his father also received a threatening telephone call late on the night before the April 1 municipal election. In recent years, he said, bricks have been launched through the front window of his home on York Road. "Those that are behind this plan (O'Hare expansion) are set out to intimidate me and the rest of us that see the project for the boondoggle that it is," Geils said....All village board members were contacted Monday about Geils' security concerns except Trustee Jeff Williams, who could not be reached. The others said they supported Geils' stance, but only one, Hank Mandziara, said he also has been a victim. His car stereo was stolen last November, his vehicle followed during April's election cycle, and suspicious vehicles sat in front of his home at all hours, he said. "I believe these people are (Chicago Mayor Richard) Daley's minion of cowards who attempt to use intimidation and gross misinformation in order to cause all of us to cease our fight to protect our community from Daley's improper, immoral and illegal taking of our homes, businesses and resources," Mandziara said.[367]

In lieu of a more principled opposition to eminent domain, the property owners' opposition boiled down to a "hunker down" strategy which seemed to prevent removal but meant a future spent in political and legal limbo. The Castle Coalition, a "property rights" group, suggested in its eminent domain "Survival Manual" that people "Get Information, Consult with a Local Lawyer, Detect False Promises, Meet Deadlines and Dates, Plan Your Grassroots Campaign, Organized with Your Allies, Make Noise, Work with the Media, Reform Eminent Domain Laws."[368] However, neither it nor any of the other "property rights" groups had any advice as to what should be done when all legal remedies had been exhausted, the writs of possession had been issued, and law enforcement was coming up the road to enforce them. What then? The opposition to eminent domain was an opposition with no leader and no principled or coordinated ideas, its weapons only possession and the fear (but also loathing) this inspires in the political system. Neither side gave any quarter. None of the players in this drama could forget their roles, which forgetfulnees is made possible only by paying attention to the facts. The biggest failure of the *Kelo* property owners was the failure to relitigate based on the revelation that New London had simply lied and substituted Pfizer's purpose for a government purpose, especially now that that has been analyzed and we know the code words, strategies and signals which tell us that the branches are government are trading lies to hide this substitution. That would have brought the property owners direct scrutiny, and an end to the New

---

367 *Daily Herald*, November 18, 2005 (Chicago, Illinois, archived at www.dailyherald. com).

368 Available online at www.castlecoalition.org.

London project, and would have resulted in return of title to their property. Why didn't they do it? Because they themselves accept the "minimum scrutiny" regime. Fundamentally, they don't want to change the rules, they just want to win by them. They want power, not rights. Here we see the most important success of the regime — it deforms the ability to formulate new ideas which might allow people to escape from it; no one thinks there is any other way to think. Above all, there is no power in ideas.

In response, the political system had informally and provisionally begun to develop a method for dealing with resistance to eminent domain, short of calling in law enforcement (assuming law enforcement is not involved in the acts complained of in connection with the O'Hare expansion): 1) above all concede nothing and change nothing, but rather rely on the minimum scrutiny legal regime, in which litigants argue against themselves; 2) continue to charge "rent;" 3) maintain title in the government entity; and 3) make no changes in plans for the use of eminent domain, including tactics such as pressuring people to leave by threatening eminent domain, and undermining areas by announcing that eminent domain might be invoked or by reducing enforcement of laws. The latter was claimed in connection with perhaps the largest eminent domain action of all, the removal of 6000 residents in Riviera Beach, Florida, in order to make way for upscale housing: "The owners of [businesses] in Riviera Beach's downtown accuse local leaders of not enforcing city codes in order to produce the decay that redevelopment is supposed to remedy. 'They want to leave everything in a dilapidated condition so it seems to everybody and to the government like it's blighted,' said Mike Mahoney, who runs Dee's T-Shirts."[369] Here was the ultimate expression of minimum scrutiny: destruction prompts destruction. Literally, nothing exists except power. As the stalemate continued, the political system began to realize that public opinion had changed fundamentally with respect to facts, and so something had to be done about public opinion — not to accommodate it, but rather to change it:

> Missouri voters probably will see an initiative next year on eminent domain, according to a presentation the Economic Development Corp. of Kansas City's board heard Friday. Spencer Thomson, a member of a state-appointed task force on eminent domain, said the property rights issue has become inflammatory. Property rights advocates, led by the Institute for Justice in Washington, are "exaggerating facts" and "playing to emotions," Thomson said. Thomson, a lawyer...in Kansas City, said the institute has targeted Missouri. He predicted that a ballot measure on eminent domain could be slotted in August or November....EDC board member Peter Yelorda said that lobbying needs to extend to labor unions, construction companies and other groups that sway public opinion. "We can't win this with the dialogue we usually have," said Yelorda, who also chairs the Tax Increment Financing Commission of Kansas City. "We need to have the public understand our position...."Gary Sage, chairman of the EDC's legislative committee, said he expects unprecedented heat next year in Jefferson City [Missouri] on eminent domain and tax increment financing. "This spring

---

369 *Chicago Tribune*, December 2, 2005.

will be the most dramatic shift in economic development priorities in the last 20 years," Sage said.[370]

TIF was not forgotten in the strategy to preserve eminent domain:

> Just as the resurgence of downtown Kansas City became an indisputable fact, a confluence of events totally unrelated to downtown has caused a stampede in the Missouri General Assembly to file legislation diluting the two most important development assistance tools involved in downtown's revival. Legislators from both parties and all parts of the state are planning to introduce bills during the next session of the General Assembly to significantly curtail the use of eminent domain and tax increment financing....[M]embers of both the Missouri Senate and the House of Representatives have called for the elimination of eminent domain for economic development purposes and, in the case of the rural Democratic caucus, the total elimination of eminent domain....Just as cries for elimination of eminent domain have reached a fever pitch, the recurring drum beat of proposals to curtail tax increment financing has been renewed....With the support of some school districts, these legislators are calling for tax increment financing 'reform' which would exclude the use of TIF for retail projects, residential development and greatly curtail the definition of 'blight' within the statute....Abolishing the use of tax increment financing for retail projects would have prevented the entertainment district and will prevent other restaurant, entertainment and retail development in the city as well as the suburbs (consequently eliminating suburban projects which shore up the Missouri tax base and prevent the out-migration of retail sales to Kansas...). [G]reatly limiting the definition of property which is considered blighted under the tax increment financing statute will create tremendous confusion by changing a definition that has been on the statute books since the passage of the Land Clearance for Redevelopment Act in the 1950's. The history of the use and judicial interpretation of the concept of blight in Missouri makes it possible to assess the appropriateness and viability of proposed projects. Changing the definition will be an invitation to litigation which will curtail development downtown as well as elsewhere on the Missouri side of the state line. Now is the time for the community to come together and express its support for TIF and eminent domain to members of the Missouri General Assembly. Without these tools, the City of Kansas City will be virtually defenseless in competition across the state line and with other communities throughout the United States....[371]

In the meantime, the political system moved as quickly as possible to secure the power of eminent domain, hoping that this might have some effect against public opinion, legislation or moratoria. It was not clear, however, how formal approval of eminent domain powers was supposed to prevent physical confrontation:

> Officials here [Long Branch, New Jersey] could be ready to sign a developer's agreement with K. Hovnanian for the redevelopment of Beachfront South by next week, which will trigger more than $10 million in developer's contributions to the city. But the agreement also will result in the taking of homes, either through negotiation or eminent domain, and while the Beachfront South project

---

370 *Kansas City Business Journal*, December 16, 2005.

371 Dick King, "The Missouri General Assembly Has Downtown Progress in its Crosshairs," November 2005 (archived at www.kinghershey.com/newsDetail. asp%3FarticleID%3D33+tax+increment+financing+eminent+domain&hl=en).

has not generated the kind of opposition that manifested itself in the second phase of Beachfront North, it still has its critics. Officials this week scheduled a special meeting for 5:30 p.m. Dec. 21 to review final plans by K. Hovnanian Shore Acquisitions for the redevelopment sector known as Beachfront South and Council President Anthony Giordano said they could sign the redeveloper's agreement then. "I'm very distressed that you have scheduled a special meeting not at a regular time," said Michelle Bobrow, who along with her husband Harold splits her time between homes in Beachfront South and Maplewood. "It is four days before Christmas and Hanukkah and I know what happened with Beachfront North Phase 2 two days before Thanksgiving" when several property owners got court notices, Bobrow said. "I certainly hope you are not going to spoil our holiday...."Lori Ann Vendetti, who owns homes on Ocean Terrace and in Newark and is among the property owners from the Marine Terrace Ocean Terrace Seaview Avenue Alliance who received pre-Thanksgiving Day court notices from the city, also objected to the timing of the Beachfront South meeting. She noted the council has a tendency to conduct redevelopment business on holidays such as its decision last Jan. 1 to hire an appraiser for her section, at a meeting that was sparsely attended. "It kind of looks like you don't want the public's participation," Vendetti said of the Dec. 21 meeting. Vendetti asked why the business couldn't be conducted at a regular meeting, and Mayor Adam Schneider said it was because the redeveloper's agreement has to be signed this calendar year. Another resident, Diane Multare of North Bath Avenue, a critic of eminent domain, shouted at the council when she was not permitted a second turn at the microphone. Under new rules for public participation, each speaker gets only one chance at the microphone, although once there, their time is not limited. "Why do they want to" sign the agreement now? she asked the audience. "On Jan. 8, the governor is going to slap a moratorium on eminent domain projects. Why do they want to beat that deadline?" The state Office of Legislative Services determined earlier this year that the governor does not have the authority to declare a moratorium on the use of eminent domain. Gov.-elect Jon S. Corzine will take office Jan. 17.[372]

Officials in Long Branch simply steeled themselves and moved ahead with eminent domain heedless of opposition:

> Residents who will lose their homes as a result of the city of Long Branch's decade-long redevelopment plan told the council last week they will fight the taking of their properties through eminent domain — and win. It was standing room only at city hall on Wednesday of last week when the City Council unanimously authorized a $300 million project in the Beachfront South Redevelopment zone...."I stand before you sickened," said William Giordano, who is fighting to save his home on Ocean Terrace in the Beachfront North Phase II redevelopment zone from eminent domain. You call this economic development, I call it social discrimination...." Catherine Choras...who is 82 years old, said that when the city began discussing redevelopment a decade ago she remembers plans calling for condemnation to be used sparingly. "We discovered soon after that you were going to take our homes," she said. "We were told, 'Don't fix up your homes.' Consequently, we did not do improvements because redevelopment was hanging over our heads...."The meeting attracted not only city residents who were opposed to the project, but also concerned citizens from neighboring towns. "You are putting people who have good houses out on the street," said Fair Haven resident Margaret Rice-Moir. "I think it is unconscionable." A group of workers from Local 1456 of the Dock Builders Union attended

---

372 *Asbury Park Press*, December 19, 2005.

the meeting in support of the project and the jobs it may offer. "We need projects to feed our families," said Bill Lee, Second Avenue. "My union brothers need projects; [I am] proud to be involved with a jewel in the rough. We are looking forward to working with K. Hovnanian." Harold Bobrow who has a home on Ocean Boulevard in Beachfront South, addressed the union workers. "[The city] is taking homes [from people] like yourselves to move rich people in," Bobrow said to the union members at the meeting. "Remember, us today, you tomorrow. I am not against eminent domain used correctly....I am against eminent domain abuse, which this is. This is Robin Hood in the reverse — you are taking homes from the poor and giving them to the rich."[373]

Neither side was clear with respect to the facts or the law, and so fell back on girding themselves for endless litigation in a legal wilderness: "People unwilling to sell properties to the city for redevelopment could wind up wrangling with lawyers who specialize in eminent domain. The city's [Port Orange, Florida] redevelopment committee approved hiring two attorneys to handle eminent domain cases, namely in the areas declared blighted around east Dunlawton Avenue. City officials said they were arming themselves for possible legal battles with resistant residents."[374] On the other side, "For landowners, fighting city hall may become a way of life, say farmers in the Shenandoah Valley. Producers in the Valley expect the issue of eminent domain to surface over the next several months, especially when farmers discuss key interests with newly elected legislators. A seminar Tuesday at the Virginia Farm Bureau's state convention about eminent domain — the right of a government to take private land for public projects — drew more than 200 producers. The clinic, titled 'Eminent Domain: What Landowners Need To Know Now,' was a featured focus on the second day of the bureau's 80th annual convention. A panel formed for talks on landowners' rights addressed ways property owners can combat businesses that seek to have such property condemned for the purpose of development."[375]

Squaring off against each other, had landed both sides in a shadow world half "legal" half "illegal" — the Supreme Court-created world of minimum scrutiny. The Court often referred to the necessity of litigants making their own arguments respecting the Constitution, but to what extent was it rulings from the Court itself which made this impossible? The Court didn't understand the Constitution, so it assumed no one else could, either. The shadow world of minimum scrutiny was not so much outside the Court or outside the Constitution, as it was simply outside the law. In that world a different logic applied: there, the notion of the Court's jurisdiction was simply a contradiction in terms.

More pointedly in the context of housing, minimum scrutiny for housing with respect to eminent domain, implied a violation of the separation of powers. All terms — including those used to define the three branches — collapsed under

---

373 *The Hub*, December 29, 2005 (Red Bank, New Jersey, archived at www.hub.gmnews. com).

374 *News-Journal*, November 18, 2005 (Daytona Beach, Florida, archived at www.news-journalonline.com).

375 *Shenandoah Valley Herald*, November 30, 2005 (Norfolk, Virginia, archived at www. dnronline.).

minimum scrutiny; the Court would not examine the notion of the separation of powers under the "minimum scrutiny" regime. Is a violation of the separation of powers indicative of a fact of the individual, and should it be added to the list of tests for such a fact? Is the separation of powers a fact of the individual? Are the three branches facts of the individual? Given apparently parallel powers outside the Constitution, are those powers best described as judicial, executive and legislative, or are those terms inapposite, and simply three more shields behind which the Court maintains its power? How does the Court itself describe them as *facts* (not as *law*) when vindicating them? The Court's escape from the Constitution means that a "facts of the individual" analysis is law as *fact*.

The most important aspect of the resistance of public opinion to eminent domain, was simply public opinion articulating its own position, finding its own voice. What was that voice saying? The political question was, whether this public opinion could make the law coherent? Suddenly there was a need to find out, in great detail, what this new expression was, and what it portended. The first in-depth study was done, in which one could see public opinion — out of a welter of conflicting considerations — nevertheless writing the new dimensions of the facts of the individual. It was, indeed, the very voice of the individual: selfish, insightful, passive, ignorant, brilliant, pathological, aggressive, stupid, idealistic, informed, robust. Human.

> While many [New Jersey] residents believe that there are situations when using eminent domain is acceptable, these instances are very limited. New Jerseyans would like to see a statewide standard on the definition of "blight" before property can be taken and support a temporary moratorium on eminent domain until its use can be examined....[A]bout 6-in-10 New Jerseyans have been following the issue of eminent domain, with about half that number (29%) paying a lot of attention to it. As may be expected, homeowners (68%) and residents age 50 and older (68%) are the most likely to be tuned in to this issue. New Jerseyans are somewhat more likely to agree (47%) rather than disagree (39%) that there are times when it is alright to use eminent domain to rebuild an area. But they are divided on whether New Jersey towns have been using this power judiciously. While 37 percent say that eminent domain has been used too much in the state, a similar number say that eminent domain use is either at about the right amount (24%) or too little (11%). However, among those most aware of the issue, a decided majority or 55 percent feel that the eminent domain has been used excessively by Garden State municipalities....A large majority of New Jerseyans, though, would like to see a standard statewide definition of what constitutes blight — 67 percent support this whereas only 24 percent would continue to let towns make this determination. Similarly, two-thirds of residents (66%) would support a temporary moratorium on all eminent domain powers in the state until appropriate uses can be decided upon. Only 22 percent oppose this. Most New Jerseyans believe that when eminent domain is used to take private property for another use, local communities as well as the property owners themselves tend to come up with the short end of the stick. Nearly 2-in-3 New Jerseyans (65%) believe that people who have their homes or businesses taken through eminent domain are not fairly compensated for their asset loss. And an overwhelming 3-in-4 residents (76%) believe that private developers have benefited more than the community by recent uses of eminent domain in their own area. Only 15 percent feel that the public good of their local communities

has come out on top in these cases....Nearly 9-in-10 residents (88%) agree with a town taking vacant or run-down properties in order to build a school. Nearly two-thirds (65%) feel that taking land from a developer to preserve it as open space is an acceptable use. More than half (55%) also say the same about taking vacant or run-down buildings in order to build a shopping center. Residents are divided on using eminent domain to take land from a business to keep it from expanding to prevent noise and traffic in their area. While 43 percent find this use acceptable, slightly more (48%) say it is not OK to use eminent domain for this purpose. Only about 1-in-3 New Jerseyans would give the nod to taking an active business that is surrounded by run-down buildings in order to build newer businesses (36%) or taking low value homes from people in order to build a school (33%). And only a handful of residents would give their approval to taking low value homes from people in order to build either higher value homes (7%) or a shopping center (4%). Across all the questions asked in this poll, residents who have read or heard a lot about eminent domain are more negative toward its current application and more supportive of restrictions on its use. On the other hand, there is very little difference in the opinions of residents who live in different type of community environments — whether urban, older towns and suburbs, or newer growth areas of the state — even though these communities have experienced eminent domain use to varying extents.[376]

This meager, embryonic expression was nevertheless the manifesto of the fourth Constitutional epoch. How surprised the flunkeys of the third epoch would have been to have it described to them this way! But to hear such a description requires a third, divinatory ear. They did not have it. Public opinion had rejected a single standard — minimum scrutiny — with respect to facts. The political system, on the other hand, was accustomed to ruling with complete discretion in a vast range of highly detailed arrangements; it resisted — and certainly resisted others giving it — fact-specific orders. Now this was all upset. To the horror of the political system, public opinion not only relayed its desire to restrict eminent domain in the case of housing; it *also* restricted eminent domain with respect to a broad range of facts *and* to the relation *between* those facts. This was too much. It suggested unending resistance every step of the way in enforcing health and welfare regulation under the "minimum scrutiny" regime.

Striking in these polling results is the total lack of support for untrammeled eminent domain as promulgated by the Supreme Court; unalloyed, it is felt to be inherently abusive. This brought the "minimum scrutiny" regime under suspicion. The underlying conclusion was: minimum scrutiny = corruption. *Kelo* had proved the tipping point at which the political system was too stupid to be harmless. Minimum scrutiny was supposed to permit tax and spend and general welfare purposes; instead, it was seen to displace them. With respect to *all* facts, eminent domain had shown itself to have *no* rational relation to *any* legitimate purpose. It had no future. Now public opinion was turning the system upside down by demanding that the Supreme Court prove its case: the Court had become the defendant.

It is equally striking that not *one* governmental body charged with investigating reform of eminent domain laws, thought to do a thorough poll, querying

376 Monmouth University Polling Institute, October 5, 2005 (archived at www.monmouth.edu/polling/reports.asp).

public opinion in detail on both facts and doctrine. Why not? Because the political system presumed that it already embodied public opinion — that's how it got into power. Anecdotal evidence would suffice. The political system knew best. Neither did those who backed the political system, demand such polling; the bond market, for example, was content to look down its collective nose. Indeed, it never occurred to *anyone* in authority that decades of sponsorship of home ownership had nurtured a non-negotiable demand for possession, a demand which, moreover, looked to be taking center stage of *all* American politics, law, government and power. Such a demand was, by definition, incorruptible, which is why the political system didn't know what to do.

For its part, public opinion wanted to be housed without housing; to be medically cared for without medical care; to be liberated without liberty; to be maintained without maintenance; to be educated without education. Just as in the case of homeowners, the Court, the "property rights" movement, the political system and all the other interests, public opinion wanted power without knowing why. To vindicate individual rights? For power's sake? To survive? Is there such a thing as a culpable people? If so, what then? Understandably, the political system responded to public opinion: you figure it out, but in the meantime don't interfere. These irresolvable dilemmas could not in fact produce results; in law, they could only produce uncertainty. Public opinion was on its own.

What public opinion found is a new world of fact to be explored — and no compass. The change in public opinion with respect to housing could be seen in the choices made post-*Kelo* in spite of the law, which did not mandate those choices:

> Gladys Avakian, who has lived all her 68 years in a house her father designed near Butler Avenue and 10th Street, vows she'll be the last hold-out and the biggest obstacle Fresno [California] Unified could have if the school district tries to tear down her neighborhood to build an elementary school. "Over at that other school site, they still have one old lady in her house. That will be Gladys if they do this here," said Avakian, referring to the Olmos Elementary School site off Chestnut Avenue, just north of Kings Canyon Road in southeast Fresno. Dixie Navarette's house is the last standing at the Olmos school site because the 65-year-old woman dug in at her three-bedroom home on East Inyo Street and refused to move for more than 14 months after a neighborhood evacuation deadline for families in 35 houses. The opening date of Olmos was pushed back a year to August 2007 while the school district negotiated with Navarette and a few other homeowners who went to court to fight eminent domain proceedings that forced the sale of their land. Navarette said she plans to move out before Christmas to a Clovis house she bought with her district settlement in May 2004 and that Fresno Unified is now remodeling to meet her medical needs. Demolition crews are standing by to clear the way for construction, said Ruth Quinto, the school district's chief financial officer. Rather than repeat what happened with the Olmos site, Fresno Unified is rethinking tearing down a neighborhood of 39 single-family homes at Butler Avenue and 10th Street to build an elementary school. A citizens committee — the Choosing our Futures Operational Strategies Task Force — suggested to the school board last month that it consider another 8-acre parcel just to the south at Cedar and Hamilton avenues, adjacent to Sequoia Middle School. The alternative site has fewer single-family homes, more low-income rentals, and some vacant lots. The California Department of

Education has given initial approval to that Cedar and Hamilton site, Quinto said. Now the district must do further study on whether the land meets Fresno Unified and state safety and environmental regulations and provides safe walking routes for children, she said. Quinto said the Butler and 10th site is still under consideration, but administrators are looking at the alternative site at the request of some school board members. At a previous board meeting, trustee Manuel Nunez chastised staff: "What you should've learned from the Olmos site is the expense and time it takes to buy out and move people." Quinto agreed. "Before we tear down a neighborhood, we better make darn sure we have exhausted all viable alternatives. And in the process we might actually find an alternative that wouldn't require displacing 39 single-family homeowners...." Avakian said the alternate site proposed at Cedar and East Hamilton was on a list of properties with "more rickety buildings" that she gave district officials at a June school board meeting.[377]

Note the lack of analysis of the relationship of education to housing. Given what we have seen of the complex interconnections of the New Bill of Rights, we can say at this point that housing is getting a very primitive "facts of the individual" analysis in this example. The analysis is wretched: full of contradictions, fang-baring instead of principle, unexamined assumptions — the whole messy situation accompanying the death of one society and the birth of another.

Even as the debate focused in on housing, it revealed how seriously the "minimum scrutiny" regime had deformed public opinion. Housing could as yet only be discussed in other terms: schools, roads, development, even fairness — it could be discussed as anything but fact, because public opinion did not know what to make of the fact. "Why thousands more should be denied benefits so [Riviera Beach homeowners] can continue living comfortably near the waterfront is the redevelopment plan's politically incorrect question," was one formulation of the issue in the Florida eminent domain controversy.[378] And on the other side: "[W]hy does Riviera Beach focus on more grandiose mansions and condos at the expense of affordable housing...? If 5,000 people are going to be displaced by this 'redevelopment' project, where are they going to go or find reasonably priced housing? That is *not* a good thing to do."[379] Nevertheless, public opinion was beginning to take charge of concepts which previously had been the prerogative of the political system. This appeared to be a crucial step on the way to filling in the gaps in the process, discussed earlier, by which scrutiny for a fact is elevated. What are the "civil rights" mentioned below? Note the emergence of the lawyer as cautioning intermediary.

A battle over the future of Princeton Junction [New Jersey] comes to a head this evening with a hearing and possible vote on whether to designate 350 acres encompassing the crossroads as a redevelopment area....[A] week ago, Princeton attorney Bill Potter gave a lecture for the Princeton Junction Neighborhood Coalition emphasizing the powers the municipal government would gain. Those, he said, include taking property by eminent domain, bonding without a public

377 *Fresno Bee*, December 11, 2005 (Fresno, California, archived at www.fresnobee.com).

378 *The Palm Beach Post*, December 17, 2005 (Palm Beach, Florida, archived at www.palmbeachpost.com).

379 *The Palm Beach Post*, December 15, 2005.

referendum, choosing a developer without competitive bidding, granting tax abatements and superseding the master plan and zoning procedures already in place. He said these decisions could be made without public oversight and input. Now, residents like Susan Conlon of the Neighborhood Coalition feel they're being asked to give up their right to participate in government in exchange for a transit village that hasn't even been planned. "We want the improvements, but we're in a dilemma. The next step in the redevelopment plan is the suppression of our civil rights," she said. Before giving up any right to participate in the decision-making process, the affected residents and business owners want to see the actual plan showing what the finished redevelopment would look like, and how it would affect property taxes, school enrollment, the natural environment and traffic congestion....Earlier this month, Connie Pascale of Legal Services of New Jersey urged affordable housing advocates to be skeptical of redevelopment powers, including the taking of property by eminent domain, at the sixth annual meeting of the Anti-Poverty Network of New Jersey. Often such projects displace residents and replace affordable dwellings with luxury ones that mostly benefit the developers who build them, he said. The term "smart growth" is used to sell redevelopment plans, but the clustering of dense development around existing infrastructure should be practiced regionally, not individually by neighboring municipalities. Otherwise, the end result is to push the poor over the boundary into the next municipality, he said....Meanwhile, a member of the Neighborhood Coalition, Farrell Delman, said he's also wary of [Mayor Shing-Fu] Hsueh's repeated assertions that eminent domain will only be used as a last resort. "Every time the mayor says he's not going to use a power (afforded under the redevelopment legislation) I say, 'Then why do you want it?'" Delman said....Delman would like to see the redevelopment plan before giving the township government such broad powers to execute the plan, but is angry the administration has viewed his skepticism as an opposition to change or progress. "I love the idea of a transit village [the concept for which the city seeks eminent domain authority],' he said. "But I don't want a process that hands over all this power for a plan that I might not greet with a job-well-done." The principles in the resolution to be considered tonight call for an open process, taking the residents' and business owners' concerns into consideration, minimizing any negative impacts on the surrounding area, performing a thorough traffic analysis, remediating contaminated sites within the designated area and through the use of private capital. Other provisions say "the power of eminent domain shall not be exercised unless it can be demonstrated that there is no other alternative to fulfill the public purposes of the redevelopment plan," that developers be chosen by open competition, and that tax abatements or payments-in-lieu of taxation be granted only on the basis of financial agreements enacted by ordinance at public hearings.[380]

What is moving — and tells us that we are living in a new society in its early stage of formation — is that in these examples housing is getting a "facts of the individual" analysis. It is all the more moving that the participants are unaware they are making that analysis. We are overhearing them form a new Constitution — without the assistance of learned counsel and despite a Supreme Court which doesn't want them to do what they are doing. For this is not Founder intent, government, democracy, litigation, legislating and so on — our ragbag of concepts and doctrines. It is simply fact.

---

380 *The Times*, December 19, 2005 (Trenton, New Jersey, archived at www.nj.com).

We see public opinion doing what everyone else was doing post-*Kelo*: carrying out its own *ad hoc* "facts of the individual" analysis. But note that it was a breakdown in government which required public opinion to undertake this analysis. Thanks to a culpable judiciary, this was the voice which minimum scrutiny for housing would not permit the political system to hear. And that was why the political system could not understand or obey it. The Court had stifled the dialogue between public opinion and the political system. Public opinion suffered too: "schools" were approved as uses for eminent domain without any thought that the students in them must come from somewhere, just as "roads" seemed a generally approved use without any thought that they come from somewhere, pass over something and go somewhere — and those considerations have consequences. It was not hard to find lacunae and contradictions in public opinion.

But that is public opinion as filtered through a poll. Here it is in raw form, in a report to me of people testifying before the Connecticut legislative committee studying eminent domain reform (along with my response):

> We broke a few eggs, and let them know that any attempts to screw us on ED reform were DOA. I think they finally got the message. By the end of the hearing (at around 10:00PM) even Lew Wallace, co-chair of the committee, was trying to save face and saying the only reason they had just gone with bills 39 & 40 was for whatever, but that HE was personally opposed to ED for economic benefit. We let them have it on blight too. They are now perfectly clear that this will not be a rollover. People were pissed, and let them know that we know they are crooked. We were also blessed with a particularly good mix of the committee members who were present: bipartisan good guys with 3 evil Democrats, it made for a nice meeting all in all. The consensus was that we had finally worn them down, not vice versa. They also won the bad timing award:
>
> - That morning the legislature memorialized Rosa Parks, who refused to yield her seat and sparked a revolution, and I pointed out that Susette refused to yield her home, and will spark an even bigger revolution because homes are a lot more important to people than seats they don't even own.
> - Ellef [a Connecticut official charged with corruption] pleaded guilty that morning....
>
> There were only 2 of us there from NL, but the rest of the CT citizens were all on the same page, and everyone did a superb job. I told them that if Hartford Mayor Eddie Perez (who spoke) testifies one more time about how wonderful ED is, we are going to find some of his ED victims and get the real story and go up there and pull his campaign finance reports and see who is funding him. I also made it very clear that we are going to be starting to name names of who benefited from *Kelo*, and went into the 2 questions which have to be answered before we reform the laws:
>
> - Quo bono? [to what good?]
> - Quis custodiet ipsos custodes — *who will guard the guardians?*
>
> Nothing scares the shit out of legislators more than when you use Latin on them.

The Utah Ombudsman spoke, and did a phenomenal job of convincing everyone that such a position would be valuable. I suggested it be made a state-wide elective office.

Robert Young, who spoke last, really knocked it out of the park: he showed up with a printout of 2250 ED cases in the CT courts, and discussed how these have grown exponentially just in the past couple of years. He did the math about what this is costing ALL CT taxpayers, not just for the court costs but also for the hundreds of millions suburban taxpayers have to pump into the cities to pay for all this. We have a urban/suburban dichotomy in CT politics, and we are going to follow up on this too. And this ties in to a point Rep. Steve Mikutel repeatedly...that the urban legislators are not going to be our friends on ED reform. But these urban legislators do so at their peril, because their constituents are equally as outraged over *Kelo* as everybody else. Or even more so, because they are always the victims, not the suburban voters.

But if I had to sum up the most important thing to come out of yesterday's hearing, it is that some of the honest Democrats now appear willing to break ranks from their leadership and associate with us.

*But I don't see anything about what they WANT. Generalities can all be gotten around, so no matter how tight they make the blight restriction, there's always a way around it. No matter how tight they make the economic development restriction, there's always a way around it. No matter how tight they make the public ownership restriction, there's always a way around it.*

*These people should start reading about the changes which have already been passed or are about to be passed. None of them work. I've read all the Connecticut proposals, and none of them will change anything. Do these people really think a tighter definition of blight will change anything? It's ridiculous. If they want to restrict eminent domain totally, there's only one formula which will do it. Ask any lawyer, and he or she will tell you that this would stop almost all eminent domain:*

> *Eminent domain shall not be exercised unless it specifically fulfills an overriding government purpose.*

*That is strict scrutiny for ALL facts in the eminent domain context. Why doesn't that group ever have a lawyer sit down and tell them what will work and what will not work? It's a shame, because even as I read the [report], I can tell that the politicians are giving these people the runaround, and when it comes down to it, the legislation passed — if any — will allow these people to do exactly what they're doing now.*

*I really don't think the place eminent domain is going to be restricted is the legislature. I think it will be simply people like Kelo, who refuse to move. And look how they're trying to wear her down — charging her rent, not giving her her title, waiting for her to die or to want to move. That's the main power government has: time. She won't live forever. Government will. Government can afford to wait, and in the meantime, it will use every underhanded trick to wear her down.*

*I don't think your folks realize what a struggle this is going to be, especially since they don't seem to have any idea how to make the law work for them. Oh well, I guess they'll have to learn the hard way.*

John, I understand your rationale and I am not as happy with the crew from New London as I would like to be. My analysis and rationale is to expose the Legislature for doling out the State-Wide-Taxpayer monies to New London, New Haven, Hartford, etc., in hopes the communities in between will take notice and gang up on the legislature cutting off the supply of money to the cities. That's my objective! It's the money! Cut the money out of the equation and the cities can not do eminent domain! That forces them to go to the bank or wallstreet [*sic*] and both of these places do not give the money away, they want repayment. Cities do not like these types of arrangements.

By way of contrast, here is the raw — and clearly outraged — voice of the political system, wounded and betrayed by a change in public opinion. It comes from Connecticut lawyer Peter Costas, former president of the Connecticut state bar association. This *ancien régime* outburst is the political system on its way out — indeed, forcing itself out:

> The current clamor for suspending the Fort Trumbull redevelopment project could, if successful, continue New London's financial and job losses. Moreover, any suspension and subsequent effort to redesign the project would damage the city's efforts to increase tourism and instill community pride in a new maritime center with public access to a riverfront walkway. Until a series of press releases and stories stirred sympathy for the plaintiffs in the *Kelo* case after the final decision in the court battle, there was little opposition to the project. In fact, Gov. M. Jodi Rell on Oct. 23, 2004, urged New London to "recommit ourselves to fulfilling the vision that we outlined for the Fort Trumbull peninsula" and further stated: "There's too much at stake to let this project stumble. Together we've invested far too much money and effort to see it fall apart now. With the help of our congressional delegation we won a major victory in becoming the home of the planned Coast Guard Museum, but unless we move forward we could lose that project, too." Since then, nothing other than the public clamor has justified any effort to delay or modify the development plan adopted by the city, the state and the federal governments. Unfortunately, the truth and fact have been buried in misplaced sympathy for the six remaining holdouts and no real attention has been given to the consequences of further delay.[381]

The sanctimonious tone of this comment revealed a dangerous underlying message: a political system too corrupt to be aware of its own abuses. Putting the Costas comment and the poll results side by side, produces a gap: the political system and public opinion had ceased to communicate on the eminent domain issue. The two sides might just as well have been living on different planets. "Roads and schools" was public opinion's meaningless nod to the political system; it was a lie which said, "I'm not leaving my housing." "Private property rights" was the political system's meaningless nod to public opinion; it was a lie which said, "We want the money." Never had the gross stupidity of American law stood so clearly revealed; ominously, only a breach had revealed it, and the breach was widening. Forty years of a political reaction had so deformed the political system that, six months after the *Kelo* decision, there was still no awareness whatever of any connection between the Constitution and the facts of the *Kelo* case. Discussion of the case at a University of Connecticut Law School panel had an eerily unworldly tone:

---

381 *The Day*, November 6, 2005..

Some, like Richard O. Brooks, a professor of law and founding director of the Environmental Law Center at Vermont Law School, blamed lingering unrest about the case on press reports, which he said had unfairly favored the cause of the plaintiffs and the nonprofit Institute for Justice. Others, including three reporters in an afternoon panel on press coverage, said they thought the public interest had been stimulated by the presence of a compelling group of plaintiffs, by the passionate arguments of critics of the decision who said it would put all private property at risk of seizure by the government, and by the reticence of NLDC and city officials in speaking to the press after the decision was announced....Months after the *Kelo* case was decided, the project that initiated it remains at an awkward standstill, with Kelo and her fellow plaintiffs retaining control over properties that the city has technically owned since 2000....[Kate] Moran [a reporter for *The Day*] said much of the local opposition has questioned the specific project planned for the Fort Trumbull neighborhood, and whether it would really reinvigorate the city as the NLDC, the state and Pfizer hoped it would. "It seemed hard to believe from the ground that this was truly going to be the renaissance coming to the city of New London," she said. "It seemed a lot more murky than that."[382]

Not a word was said about housing.

A proposal by New London — backed by a threat of removal — was designed to induce Susette Kelo to settle:

> Mayor Beth Sabilia wants to let four of the six remaining plaintiffs who sued the city after their homes were taken through the use of eminent domain stay in their homes for the rest of their lives....Sabilia's plan would move the homes of the plaintiffs who lived in their homes when the NLDC exercised eminent domain in 2000. It would include moving two houses, occupied by Byron Athenian and Pasquale and Margherita Cristofaro onto a block formed by East, Trumbull, Walbach and Smith streets known as Parcel 4A. Susette Kelo's and Charles and Wilhelmina Dery's homes already lie within that parcel, although their homes may have to slightly moved to make room for roadwork consistent with the municipal development plan, Sabilia said. Under the plan, the city would maintain ownership of the properties, but the former homeowners would be allowed to live out their days in their homes while paying a life tenancy fee. Whether that fee would be paid instead of taxes or, in effect, act as a rent remained unclear Sunday. The homeowners would also likely be responsible for uncollected taxes on the properties that accrued during the court disputes, Sabilia said. The proposal comes at a crucial time during the overall plan to develop the peninsula. The NLDC is currently in intense negotiations with the Coast Guard to bring a national museum and a research and development center to the peninsula, along with going through with plans to build a hotel and high-end apartments there.... The mayor said she had discussed her proposal with Deputy Mayor Jane Glover. According to the agenda for the Monday council meeting, Glover plans to request that the former homeowners begin paying use and occupancy fees — in effect, rents — on the properties to the NLDC. [Late Monday night, the council voted 4-2 to instruct the NLDC to start collecting rents from the Fort Trumbull property owners....]Michael Cristofaro, who manages his parents' house at 53 Goshen St., said he would likely not support a proposal that made his family a lifelong tenant in a house they had lived in for the past 35 years. "I would have to see what the exact proposal is, but no, I'm not going to go for life tenancy and pay rent to the city for a house that I own," he said. "I suggested moving those

382 *The Day*, December 6, 2005.

properties five years ago," he continued. "I want to see the houses moved, the titles returned to the property owners and we be left alone...." It is still unclear if the proposal will affect the other two plaintiffs. Pataya Construction Limited Partnership, which is managed by Richard Beyer, owns two homes on Goshen Street but Beyer does not live in either house. William von Winkle, who owns three properties on Smith Street within Parcel 4A, did not live there when the NLDC exercised eminent domain in 2000. He moved into 31 Smith St. before the Supreme Court rendered its decision in June 2005. ["The ongoing battle of the last eight years has not been to allow us to live in our homes and pay rent to the city of New London until we die," Kelo said. "To me its kind of morbid to kind of wait for the landowners to pass away just to go and steal the land again," Cristofaro said. Kelo asked the council to also consider moving the properties of plaintiffs Richard Beyer and William von Winkle onto Parcel 4A. Sabilia initially excluded the two because Beyer does not live in Fort Trumbull and von Winkle moved into 31 Smith St. after the court battle began. Sabilia told the council she has received no word from Gov. M. Jodi Rell about whether the plaintiffs would be responsible for back rent, taxes and utility fees accrued during the five-year court case.][383]

The irony was that at the same time New London was moving Susette Kelo, and Connecticut itself was refusing to enact any eminent domain reform, in Florida the legislature was rescuing, for a time, homeowners from the massive Riviera Beach eminent domain use while at the same time presenting a ludicrous spectacle in which public opinion was capable of stopping a large eminent domain use, but not a comparatively small one such as that in New London.

To be sure, Florida passed a reform as vague as that which the Connecticut legislature refused to enact. In Florida's case, it was a "private owner" restriction as opposed to a taxation restriction. Title could still be lodged in the public entity while spinning off all ownership rights to developers. No one asked about the tax implications. No one asked about the implications for the bond rating. Worse, Florida's new law preserved an exception "for public projects, including roads. Such 'traditional' uses of eminent domain are preserved...."[384] This compound vagueness guaranteed endless litigation and gained homeowners time. The potential developer threatened to simply walking away, citing increased costs:

> The [Florida] legislature may have dealt a fatal blow to Riviera Beach's $2.6 billion redevelopment plan when the Senate refused to exempt the plan from a bill that would restrict eminent domain powers in Florida. Immediately following the decision, a lobbyist for the city's likely master developer said it might pull out of the project because of the massive increase in costs it will face without the power of eminent domain. Robert Healy, chairman of Viking Inlet Harbor, has not yet signed a contract with the city to become its master developer. But he has traveled to Tallahassee frequently in recent months to warn legislators that a lack of eminent domain powers would allow speculators to swoop in, purchase properties and force his company to pay exorbitant amounts for them....[The bill] would prohibit governments from taking a home or business and handing it over to a private developer with very few exceptions.

---

383 *The Day*, February 6, 7, 2006.

384 *Miami Herald*, May 4, 2006.

Government agencies would still be able to use eminent domain for traditionally accepted purposes, such as parks, schools, roads and other public utilities.[385]

Yet another factor had emerged to enmesh the political system: individuals similarly situated with respect to an eminent domain use for an identical reason, were now to be treated differently according to the public entity under which they chanced to find themselves and the characteristics of the proposed eminent domain use — number/type of properties subject to the use, degree of resistance or of publicity and so on. The democratic process — unthinkingly relied on by Justice Stevens and commentators to sort through eminent domain issues — had merely produced a variety of routes to stalemate. And so the democratic process now duly came into the crosshairs of the "minimum scrutiny" regime.

* * *

All the actors having assembled on the stage of history, another in the unending sequence of American political melodramas was about to be played.

The denouement of the New London story was the concerted degradation of a political consciousness — Susette Kelo's. It proved to be a case study in the deformation of the ability to articulate individually enforceable rights. Initially, four of the remaining six *Kelo* property owners made deals and agreed to surrender possession. Kelo did not, but she still did not base her claim to possession on *any* right to housing: "'I would like to think the City Council could show some human kindness and just give us back our deeds,'" Kelo said. But the City Council would not.[386]

At the same time, undaunted by Florida's new eminent domain legislation, the mayor of Riviera Beach, Michael Brown — who had given developers all they had requested — vowed to fight for the eminent domain use even after passage of the Florida legislation. His attitude to the homeowners likely to be affected by this had always been, "For all those who don't like it, tough."[387] This horrible hack not only tried — and failed — to gain an exemption for the Riviera Beach development from the new law.[388] After the passage of the eminent domain law, but before its signature by Governor Jeb Bush, Brown also had the City Council push

> ahead with a contract for a massive redevelopment project that could displace more than 5,000 residents. Council members on Wednesday approved a contract with the project's developer, Viking Inlet Harbor Properties, that they hope will protect the city's right to build the $2.4 billion waterfront redevelopment, even if the use of eminent domain is necessary. The move will likely now pit the city against state lawmakers who stripped municipalities like Riviera Beach from using its eminent domain powers to seize personal property to hand over to private developers. 'We know our enemy is now the Legislature,' said...Brown, who insists the project will benefit all residents in this downtrodden town, even those who may be displaced....Riviera Beach officials claim that the Legislature's

---

385 *The Palm Beach Post*, May 3, 2006.

386 *The Day*, June 1, 2, 2006.

387 *The Sun-Herald*, May 7, 2006 (Biloxi, Mississippi, archived at www.sunherald.com).

388 *The Palm Beach Post*, May 4, 2006.

actions now violate their constitutional right under a clause that lawmakers cannot interfere with an existing contract, and that they should be exempted from the restrictive bill.[389]

At which point Governor Jeb Bush indicated that the city had not complied with procedural rules in connection with signing the contract, residents potentially affected by project sued on this basis to void the contract, and the developer withdrew pending purchase offers.[390]

The Mayor was not deterred by lawsuits. A faithful lackey of the regime, he called such actions "shameful" and said, "If they think they can stop us from rescuing this community, they just might get ready for the legal fight of their lives...."[391] Redevelopment seems pure theft, but its practitioners — however corrupt they may also be — are not devoid of belief in its social utility. The developer turned around and threatened to sue the *state*: "Now I'm stuck with these properties but can't develop them because I can't fill in the puzzle pieces....The city spent millions of dollars putting together its comprehensive plan, and we spent well over $1 million in engineering, architectural and planning fees. Our plan now becomes virtually worthless. We're certainly considering joining with other developers and perhaps a group of municipalities about the changing of the rules in midstream," Clark added.[392] This was the argument come full circle: restrictions on eminent domain were themselves takings. This was the argument that the scrutiny regime included the doctrine that the scrutiny regime itself could not be changed. The "argument" that "power is power" was coming into focus. Who in the regime would emerge as its champion? All these actions made it certain that the struggle would be grim, long lasting and ice cold, with no quarter requested or given.

The Mayor need not have fretted himself. If it showed nothing else, the *Kelo* case and its aftermath demonstrated the political system's tenacity and creativity in pursuing and protecting an unconstitutional gain. The Riviera Beach land remained extremely valuable, and the homeowners sitting on it remained poor. Thus the dynamics still tended toward some corruption of democracy — manipulation of the public ownership and "traditionally accepted purposes" exceptions to Florida's new eminent domain law, along with such chicanery as control of public services and regulatory control could provide — in order to slowly wear down the homeowners. Time is clearly on government's side when it comes to breaking down a neighborhood, whatever the law says. What is more, the Mayor and the developer could take comfort in the idea that, whatever hurdles were presented by the eminent domain reform, a right to housing was *not*, even at this late date, among them.

---

389 *The Sun-Sentinel*, May 11, 2006 (Ft. Lauderdale, Florida, archived at www.sun-sentinel.com).

390 *The Gainesville Sun*, June 3, 2006 (Gainesville, Florida, archived at www.gainesville.com); *The Ledger*, June 7, 2006 (Lakeland, Florida, archived at www.theledger.com).

391 *The Palm Beach Post*, June 13, 2006.

392 *The Herald-Tribune*, October 18, 2006 (Sarasota, Florida, archived at www.heraldtribune.com).

Take a look at minimum scrutiny in 2006:

> Riviera Beach has fielded a series of blows, including a backlash from Bush, two lawsuits by residents and the withdrawal of all offers to buy land in the 400-acre waterfront area by the master developer. In addition, the two attorneys contracted to advise the community redevelopment agency abruptly resigned two weeks ago....While the redevelopment appears to be on the ropes, the mayor and city council stand by their strategy. Ultimately, a judge will decide whether the decision to rush the deal with Viking was the best way to jump-start the project. Brown, also an attorney who practices eminent domain law, believes the courts will look favorably on the city's position. The May 10 special meeting was a continuation of Viking's relationship with the city, which began in September when the council selected the company as master developer, he said. "For the governor and the state legislature to pull the rug out from under us...there's got to be relief in the court system that we can get," Brown said....[A] 30-day deadline to finalize the agreement with Viking has passed, raising the question of whether the May 10 deal is still valid. Tied also to the deadline is Viking's pledge to pay off $8 million in bonds that the [redevelopment agency] borrowed to operate in 2003. With no deal, the council voted last week to have the city put up the money on behalf of the [redevelopment agency] to cover the bonds, which come due July 5....Bob Healey, Viking's chairman, said the recent opposition, including the lawsuits, has forced developers to rethink their plans. Viking isn't abandoning the project, Healey said, but the idea of the project being tied up in court isn't a pleasant thought....Despite the slowdown, Viking is still in the driver's seat: It has acquired $50 million in land throughout the city, Healey said....Miami attorney Toby Price Brigham, whose law firm represents some residents of the redevelopment area,....contends that the city's deal with Viking is flawed because it left it up to the developer to pick the properties to be targeted by eminent domain. Since those properties weren't listed as part of Viking's agreement, the courts may find that the city must operate under Florida's new eminent domain law, he said....Samuel Goren, a Fort Lauderdale attorney whose firm represents [redevelopment agencies] in Delray Beach, Lake Worth and Oakland Park,....said cities like Riviera Beach could try to persuade state lawmakers that the eminent domain reforms are overreaching and require tweaking in the next year.[393]

This was a political landscape littered with the refuse of the "minimum scrutiny" regime. But note the landscape itself. Justice Stevens had been right in saying that there was no way to distinguish use of eminent domain for economic development, from any other use. But legislatures plowed ahead and did it anyway. The result was that the political landscape comprised all facts: the law could not distinguish one from another.

In Chicago, reality was overtaking the O'Hare expansion project:

> With runway construction at O'Hare International Airport falling behind schedule and hikes in oil prices and inflation driving up costs, officials are questioning the timetable and even the viability of the $15 billion airport expansion project. The Federal Aviation Administration says it doesn't know when the city will begin work on two runways. And Chicago aviation officials this spring announced a one-year delay in building another runway on the north end of the airport. The major airlines are voicing support for some variant of the ambitious

---

393 *The Palm Beach Post*, June 25, 2006.

parallel-runway configuration that Mayor Richard Daley unveiled in 2001. But the carriers acknowledge they are in no better position today than they were then to help pay for Chicago's O'Hare overhaul....Despite its crisscrossing runways, the existing airport is working well for United and American, which operate more than 85 percent of O'Hare flights. The nation's two largest carriers have even stopped grousing about government-imposed O'Hare flight caps because they provide stability in an industry mired in turmoil. Making O'Hare operate more efficiently — the cornerstone of Daley's plan — is already happening. The FAA says flight delays are down 30 percent since the caps were imposed, saving the airlines millions of dollars in fuel and labor costs. The big carriers are cutting back on O'Hare flights in a strategy to boost ticket prices. They can do so because the flight caps mean there's no room for a discount airline like Jet-Blue Airways to compete in the Chicago market....Amid signals that the scope of O'Hare expansion may be changing, Hartsfield-Jackson International Airport in Atlanta [Georgia] commissioned its fifth runway on Tuesday. At a cost of only $1.3 billion, the new runway is expected to reduce departure delays by 50 percent at Hartsfield, which has surpassed O'Hare as the world's busiest airport....[O'Hare's air traffic controllers who participated in a simulation test of a modernized O'Hare] said the simulations revealed excessive taxiing times — as long as 4 miles and 45 minutes for planes to reach their gates after landing — and a very congested airport bordering on gridlock conditions. "It was just an ugly situation, so bad that controllers were yelling at each other and we had to stop the simulation," said Craig Burzych, local president of the controllers union at O'Hare tower. "It just didn't work, and it's going to be a nightmare if this expansion plan goes through." The controllers blamed many of the problems on the city's new airfield layout, saying there aren't enough taxiways going around the north side of the terminals. The result is a bottleneck at the intersection of two key taxiways...on the southeast side of the airfield....Chicago's airport expansion chief...said city officials anticipated that the taxiway intersection might become a choke point, and they are considering adding a circular taxiway to reroute United planes, which account for more than 40 percent of O'Hare operations. But building the new taxiway would require relocating an existing runway farther north....The city has failed to identify funding for the [new] taxiway, which the FAA says is critical to making the new runways work efficiently. The airlines have balked at city requests to provide the funding....[T]he reduction in delays as a result of the first new runway will be negligible — from 16 minutes of delay per plane to 15 1/2 minutes, FAA computer modeling has shown. The real benefits come later, if the project can be completed.[394]

The point about eminent domain here was that it was a hustle which had to work as all hustles do: quickly, before all the ramifications of the deal become clear to all the players. Delays in eminent domain — brought about by a refusal to surrender possession — allowed other real and potential hazards to come into consideration. These, in turn, jeopardized the deal.

This was the flip side of maintenance: the "minimum scrutiny" regime — which putatively turned questions of fact over to one process or another for resolution — meant streamlining or eliminating process. The regime's job, as we saw in the actions of its Supreme Court flunkeys during the *Kelo* oral argument, was to facilitate the hustle by brushing aside pesky individual rights issues. Therefore, process — delay — became a point of attack by public opinion on the po-

---

394 *Chicago Tribune*, May 17, 2006.

litical system. And where did this all show up? Take a guess, before reading the following:

> About $3.5 billion of O'Hare International Airport bonds are vulnerable to a credit rating downgrade because of the airport's rising costs and possible cut-backs by United Airlines and American Airlines, Merrill Lynch & Co. said in a report. In December, Chicago sold $1.5 billion of the tax-exempt debt to kick off a $7.5 billion expansion and renovation at O'Hare. The $3.5 billion of debt, known as third-lien general airport revenue bonds, has an underlying rating of A from Fitch Ratings, fifth-lowest of 10 investment grades. Moody's Investors Service has a comparable A2 rating, while Standard & Poor's has the debt rated one level lower, at A-minus. "The single-A rating is vulnerable to the downside," said Merrill analyst Philip Villaluz, who wrote the May 16 report. Villaluz said O'Hare could be squeezed in the future as increasing debt from the expansion will drive its cost per enplaned passenger to $16 by 2014 from $9. He also wrote that the number of gates to be retained by United, O'Hare's largest carrier, re-mains unknown because of legal issues that surround United's leases.[395]

Now who would buy O'Hare bonds? Now where was the smugness of the bond market? More importantly, the complex of facts brought to light by the O'Hare eminent domain use, suggests that not only does eminent domain violate individual rights, but also, that eminent domain is used in response to a complex of individual rights violations — it doesn't remedy sociopathology, it is an indi-cium of sociopathology. But who among the players in the eminent domain crisis had any insight into this? They were distracted by these same crisis roles. Did the bond market study the opposition to eminent domain, to determine the role of the bond market in the new regime? No. This was irresponsible. Did the opponents of eminent domain ever give a thought to the role of the bond market in such a regime? No. This was also irresponsible. If corruption characterized the pro-ponents of eminent domain, thoughtlessness characterized its opponents. There was more than enough blame to go around, for the stalemate which ensued.

Perhaps the ugliest, saddest and most revealing battlefield in the twilight of the third Constitutional epoch, was located in St. Louis. As so often with the phony show of the "minimum scrutiny" regime, the entire affair unwound as melodrama, leaving only debris behind. The financing couldn't be finalized when opposition continued, so the other property purchases could not take place, even though owners had gone ahead and purchased new housing. That made them liable for two mortgages. They sued. Litigation wound up voiding the authori-zation for tax increment financing, and then authorization for the project itself. What was left was the housing the owners no longer occupied, but which some-how had to be kept up:

> Officials have acted to make sure that houses in the Sunset Manor subdivi-sion meet city housing and nuisance code requirements. After inspections in the neighborhood on June 12, the city staff sent out notices ordering owners of 35 properties to begin repairs within 21 days. The 254-house subdivision on the east side of Lindbergh Boulevard just south of Interstate 44 would have become the major part of a 65-acre shopping center and office complex. That project collapsed after Novus Development Co., the developer, failed to receive financ-

---

395 *Chicago Tribune*, May 18, 2006.

ing. Novus had obtained options to buy most of the property. Anticipating that sales would go through, some homeowners gutted their houses as they prepared to move to new homes elsewhere. Because Novus could not raise money to purchase the properties, the sales fell through. The inspection notices targeted issues such as painting, and boarded-up doors and windows, City Engineer Ron Williams told aldermen on Tuesday. If the problems are not resolved, the city has authority to make repairs so the houses meet code requirements and put a lien on the properties to get reimbursed for the cost. The city also ordered other property owners to cut grass and remove junk and trash. Aldermen also authorized the staff to complete the paperwork so Sunset Hills could obtain about $25,000 from the federal community development block grant program. The aldermen from 1st Ward, which includes Sunset Manor, want that money targeted to their area. The funds could help pay for renovation of about five houses.[396]

The set — the housing — was still there, but it housed no rogues, fools or buffoons. It housed no one at all. Was it still housing?

Missouri finally passed an eminent domain law, but it had all the earmarks of another piece of ambiguous, confusing eminent domain legislation. Compounding the difficulty was the continuing viability of the notion that "economic development" had some logical content. Even a lay commentator could see that it was a craven, inept concoction which resolved nothing:

> The legislative mandate states, "No condemning authority shall acquire private property through the process of eminent domain for solely economic development purposes" and, at first blush, all seems well. But...why is the word "solely" used if the legislative intent is to truly prevent government entities from taking the property of residents and business owners through the use of eminent domain for economic development purposes? In that context, why not use a more restrictive word such as "primarily" rather than "solely?" The difference is dramatic. Using "solely" as the criteria if there is any other purpose involved, the use of eminent domain for the purposes of economic development would be legal regardless of the degree of the other use. On the other hand if a more restrictive word such as "primarily" had been used and the evidence showed that the primary purpose of the eminent domain was for economic development its use would not be authorized. Why didn't the legislature use a more restrictive term? Could it be because they wanted to permit the most flexibility for land to be taken by cities using the power of eminent domain for economic development while appearing to restrict its use? Unfortunately, the bad news gets even worse. The legislation specifically defines the term "economic development" as the "use of a specific piece of property or properties which would provide an increase in the tax base, tax revenues, employment, and general economic health." If only it stopped there but it does not; it goes on to exclude from the definition, among other things, "the elimination of blighted, substandard, or unsanitary conditions." Interestingly enough, the new legislation does not contain a definition of "blighted." Instead, in a move reminiscent of the old bean under the shell trick, the legislation states that the blight determination in eminent domain cases will be determined "with regard to whether the property meets the relevant statutory definition of blight."[397]

---

396 *St. Louis Post-Dispatch,* June 29, 2006.

397 *Branson Courier,* May 4, 2006 (Branson, Missouri, archived at www.bransoncourier.com).

Nor was this the end. Deep dissatisfaction with the work of the legislature led to a ballot initiative, which read in part: "In addition to any right of compensation provided in the aforementioned provisions of this section, if the right to use, possess, sell or improve any private property is impaired by any land use regulation or statute enacted after October 7, 2006 and the date upon which the owner acquires their record title in the property, and such law or regulation reduces the fair market value of the property, the owner shall be entitled to just compensation for the reduction in the fair market value of such property under this section as a regulatory taking." This initiative, in turn, was not permitted on the ballot "because the order of petition pages turned in were not in sequence, which made the petitions containing over 220,000 signatures invalid." Such technical reasons were used to deny access to the ballot to eminent domain initiatives in several states, which in turn evoked the fury and renewed determination of their supporters.[398] The stalemating and revisiting of the eminent domain issue, continued. This was a sore which — perpetually irritated — would never heal, and the political actors serving as irritants could not understand the reason: the controversy was symptomatic of the third epoch's declining powers. It was over, but no one wanted to say it was over, because no one knew where to turn next.

\* \* \*

As of June 29, 2006, the city of Chicago had purchased about 200 of the approximately 600 homes scheduled to be torn down to make way for the O'Hare airport expansion. "'Well, most people don't like the way they're doing it, but Daley gets his way most of the time,' said Robert Garland, whose townhouse is in the O'Hare Expansion area. The city argues that it has legal authority now to start demolishing the properties it has bought, but has so far refrained. Officials will not say when they will fire up the bulldozers. 'We are very confident we can work with the village and we will continue to make the best effort to again minimize impacts to the community (and) folks living in the community,' said Rosie Andolino, O'Hare Modernization Program director."[399]

The opposition to *Kelo* spread outward from eminent domain: to zoning, to all health and welfare regulation, to the "minimum scrutiny" regime, to government as a fact. What sort of fact? Every step of the way the political system met the opposition with grudging concessions, granted uncomprehendingly — a creeping paralysis of the political system in which power went right back to the streets. In this situation, there was no "law." And the third branch of government? It lay in the street — and was derided. *Kelo* is a strange case — it presents its absence. The Court had lost the crisis of legitimacy. Opponents of "affirmative rights" had claimed that such rights would turn judges into executives with all power, to the mighty peril of the Constitution. In the event precisely the opposite occurred;

---

398  *St. Louis Post-Dispatch*, October 4, 2006. The text of this and other initiatives proposed in response to state eminent domain reform legislation, is available at the website of the American Planning Association, *www.planning.org*. For a sunnier view of Missouri's new eminent domain law, and the process by which it was achieved, see Dale Whitman, "Eminent Domain Reform in Missouri: A Legislative Memoir," http://ssrn.com/abstract=932077.

399  Archived at www.abclocal.go.com.

*Kelo* abrogated the Court — it had *no* power. Much to everyone's surprise, the Court was eliminated by a political system which did *not* do what the Court said it *could* do, rather than — as had for so long been feared — by a political system which *did* do what the Court said it could *not* do. Ironically, where there was *no* law there was no *Court* — just the state of affairs the elaborate scrutiny continuum had intended to ward off. This in turn was because government, as a fact, had changed its nature. Reality had its own syllogism, undreamed of in our legal theory — and sprung it. The Court? The Constitution? *Kelo*? None was fact. This was the New Bill of Rights as *coup de grâce*. The housing right? Under certain circumstances. The other rights of the New Bill of Rights? To a certain degree. New facts of the individual? We must ask ourselves. These ambiguities were the inheritance of the fourth epoch of the Constitution.

The Ohio Supreme Court's decision in the *Norwood* case, summed up the dilemma of the judiciary one year after *Kelo*. It provides a glimpse into the emerging jurisprudence of the fourth Constitutional epoch as the judiciary struggles with the new, ambiguous role assigned to it by public opinion.

The Court, unanimously forbidding the planned taking of housing for a shopping center, patched together pieces of the "minimum scrutiny" regime with the New Bill of Rights and the "facts of the individual" analysis:

1. The Court explicitly referred to the relationship between government and the individual posited by the "facts of the individual" analysis, saying that eminent domain "is fraught with great economic, social, and legal implications for the individual and the community."[400] The Court even explicitly referred to housing in the context of eminent domain: "For the individual property owner, the appropriation is not simply the seizure of a house. It is the taking of a home — the place where ancestors toiled, where families were raised, where memories were made;"[401]

2. Although stated in somewhat fuzzy terms, the Court held that "property rights" (although not property) are indicia of democracy and liberty, and confirmed that constitutional analysis — following the "facts of the individual" analysis — is speculative, not normative: "property rights are integral aspects of our theory of democracy and notions of liberty....The right of private property is an *original* and *fundamental* right, existing anterior to the formation of the government itself; the civil rights, privileges and immunities authorized by law, are *derivative* — *mere incidents* to the political institutions of the country, conferred with a view to the public welfare..."[402] From this ambiguous wording, the Court concluded that "property" is a "fundamental right" which is "strongly" protected.[403]

But "strongly" in what sense, and on what basis? The homeowners had wanted to contest the taking before having to leave (Ohio law provided that posses-

---

400 *Norwood v. Horney*, ___ Ohio St.3d ___, 2006-Ohio-3799 (2006) at 3. The opinion is available online at www.sconet.state.oh.us.

401 *Id.*, at 3.

402 Quoted in *id.*, at 13, 14 (emphases in original, citations omitted).

403 *Id.*, at 15.

sion could be obtained when the taking compensation was deposited in Court, and no intervening process was allowed). This the Court found to be an unconstitutional violation of the separation of powers, depriving the Court of its role in determining substantive issues. However, the Court did not find that this *Marbury* abrogation of government lifted the facts out of minimum scrutiny in the context of eminent domain. Neither was the Norwood chronology contested — that is, government purpose was not contested on the grounds that there had been a substitution of private for public purpose — so facts were not lifted out of minimum scrutiny due to that abrogation of government theory, either.

What seemed to move the facts above minimum scrutiny was the Norwood municipal code itself, which allowed for the taking of property in "deteriorating" condition, and the determination of Norwood to prevent this by taking them for "economic development." The Court found that the property could not be taken for "economic development" — a meaningless term which the Court did not define: "economic development by itself is not a sufficient public use to satisfy a taking. Although economic benefit can be considered as a factor among others in determining whether there is a sufficient public use and benefit in a taking, it cannot serve as the sole basis for finding such benefit."[404] The Court found the aspect of the Norwood municipal code which justified the eminent domain use — that the neighborhood was "deteriorating" — unconstitutionally vague because it involved speculation, that is, a determination made in the absence of fact. In connection with this part of the decision, the Court appeared to establish strict scrutiny as the level of review for eminent domain: "We hold that when a court reviews an eminent-domain statute or regulation under the void-for-vagueness doctrine, the court shall utilize the heightened standard of review employed for a statute or regulation that implicates a First Amendment or other fundamental constitutional right."[405] This seemed to raise the level of all facts to strict scrutiny in the context of eminent domain. But all was not as it seemed.

Supposedly, the Court got around having to apply this new test to "economic development" itself, but the implication is clear that the Court found that "economic development" was not void for vagueness. So from the outset — in the same opinion in which the Court established the new test — the Court violated the test. The contradiction became immediately clear. Why was "deterioration" amenable to adjudication under the new standard, if "economic development" was not? Supposedly, "economic development" had factual content, but apparently it could never be the basis for eminent domain; all facts enjoyed absolute protection — even beyond strict scrutiny — with respect to eminent domain in the context of economic development. Fair enough. And yet, "deterioration," which the Court found devoid of factual content (a "standardless standard," the Court called it),[406] could survive strict scrutiny. So a term which had factual context could not survive strict scrutiny, whereas a factually empty term could.

---

404 *Id.*, at 36.

405 *Id.*, at 39-40.

406 *Id.*, at 42.

Norwood substituted a holdingless holding for a standardless standard. The tantalizing prospect of strict scrutiny in the context of eminent domain, fell apart. If anything, the Court seemed to hold out an alternative prospect — strict scrutiny for property in the context of eminent domain: "we hold that government does not have the authority to appropriate private property based on mere belief, supposition or speculation that the property may pose such a threat in the future....To permit a taking of private property based solely on a finding that the property is deteriorating or in danger of deteriorating would grant an impermissible, unfettered power to the government."[407] But what is property? All the Court would say on this subject was that eminent domain use must include an "inquiry on the property's condition at the time of the proposed taking."[408] This was an embryonic expression of direct scrutiny and incorporated *Euclid*'s concept of maintenance, and yet *Euclid* — initially an Ohio case — was never mentioned for the maintenance proposition.

Why didn't the Court examine "economic development" under its new vagueness eminent domain standard? Because the Institute for Justice did not ask the Court to do so. How could it? The IJ felt that "economic development" had logical content, even though the *Kelo* Court — upholding the use of eminent domain — had held that it had none (the Ohio Court had nothing to say about this part of the *Kelo* opinion). Above all, *Norwood* stands for the same proposition as the Arizona *Bailey* case: developing a test which says, "Don't come back to us with more of these cases" — in short, offloading the issue onto the trial courts. This was another prescription for stalemate and confrontation. But the Norwood residents got to keep their housing. For now. And the Court put off the day of a parallel enforcement system based on a new Constitutional epoch.

There were two schools of thought as to *Norwood*. Thomas Merrill of Columbia University said that "[t]he judiciary would be blind to reality if they didn't acknowledge that level of discomfort people have with eminent domain and property rights" — *Norwood* was red meat thrown to public opinion. On the other hand, "'It's a complete vindication ... of the rights of every home and business owner in the state of Ohio,' said Dana Berliner, an attorney with the Institute for Justice, a Washington-based law firm that represented the plaintiffs in the case."[409] And well might the IJ exult: it had convinced the Court to sign off on a concept which had no meaning.

In the real world, however, this meant that the Court had to dissemble. The Court's failure to come up with a sensible, comprehensive decision — because it was attempting to apply the outmoded "minimum scrutiny" regime to a new Constitutional fact situation — left the fourth epoch another St. Louis-style desolate, confusing Constitutional war zone. There were manifest gaps in the opinion:

> Property rights advocates hailed Wednesday's Ohio Supreme Court ruling...as a victory for property owners in Norwood, in Ohio and across the nation.

---

407 *Id.*, at 44.

408 *Id.*, at 44.

409 *The Cincinnati Enquirer*, July 27, 2006.

But the three Norwood property owners who took their case to the state's highest court may have won the war but lost the battle. Joseph P. Horney, the lead plaintiff in the landmark Supreme Court case, triumphantly forced open the temporary fencing Wednesday that surrounds what's left of the neighborhood, an 11-acre site. Once inside, he looked around and said, "It's painful to see the neighborhood. There's not much left of it...."[What the property owners fought for]...seems almost uninhabitable, surrounded by a desolate field of weeds and the drone of highway traffic. In ruling that Ohio cities cannot take property by eminent domain solely for economic development, the seven Ohio Supreme Court justices upended a developer's plans to build a $125 million shopping center and office complex on what used to be a residential neighborhood.... Closer to home, the impact of the decision wasn't as clear....Norwood officials speculated the developer could alter plans, beginning construction on part of the property while waiting out the three holdouts. But Anderson's partner in the Rookwood Exchange project, the Miller-Valentine Group, has previously dismissed that idea because the plans called for an integrated, mixed-use complex in which design changes at one end of the property could affect the entire project....While the Ohio Supreme Court gave the property owners a clear legal victory, the practical consequences of the decision could leave lower courts in a quandary. The houses of the three plaintiffs in the case are still standing, under a Supreme Court injunction blocking their demolition. They are the only homes left in what used to be a densely packed working- to middle-class neighborhood. They've been fenced off, salvaged for parts and neglected for more than a year. The titles are held by Rookwood Partners, which has paid for the properties and paid taxes on them for a year. Lawyers for the city will try to get the developer and the property owners to reach a settlement for the three remaining properties, said Timothy M. Burke, Norwood's attorney in the case. If they're unable to reach an agreement, a judge will have to order the three properties transferred back to their original owners and make them whole. But the Supreme Court gave no guidance about how to make that happen.[410]

How was anything to be done with the property, now that "economic development" had been ruled out as rationale? The banning of the concept implied that nothing had been done to the property. And yet, in the ultimate irony of this dizzy affair, had it not "deteriorated" as a result of unconstitutional government conduct? The problem was that, under the Court's formulations, "blight" existed, but was not caused by "deterioration" and could not be ameliorated by "economic development."

To compound the confusion, the Court had not a word to say in criticism either of Norwood's standard — and vague — definition of blight, or of zoning. Both apparently passed "heightened scrutiny when reviewing statutes that regulate the use of eminent-domain powers."[411] But what about the unconstitutional acts which had produced the condition of the property inherited by the Norwood "victors," a condition the product of unconstitutional acts with respect to which — since the Court did not say that Norwood did not in *fact* have a government purpose — the owners still enjoyed only minimum scrutiny? What new causes of action did the property owners have, considering their plight had been caused by unconstitutional conduct? Who could deny that this unanimous Court had just

---

410 *Id.*

411 *Norwood* at 2.

handed the property owners a RICO lawsuit? And what about the previous owners, who had sold under what was now, clearly, duress? How could a new use of
the property be sanctioned by Norwood if at the same time it was the subject of
suits aimed at its prior unconstitutional conduct with respect to the same property? And then there are the other Ohio eminent domain uses, which owners had
lost prior to *Norwood*, but now seemed to have "won." What exactly did they win
in each of the following situations?

> Depending on how one looks at it, the Ohio Supreme Court's ruling on emi-
> nent domain Thursday came too late for Emma Dimasi — or just in time. The
> Ohio First District Court of Appeals ruled this month that Cincinnati could take
> the home of the 80-year-old Clifton widow for the $4 million Dixmyth Avenue
> road-widening project. The city tore down the house last week. While the deci-
> sion came too late to save the home, it could be just in time to save the appeal.
> Within hours of the Supreme Court decision, Dimasi's son and lawyer, Vincent
> A. Dimasi, asked the appeals court to reconsider. The Supreme Court's decision
> criticized lower courts for "an artificial judicial deference" to states and cities,
> Dimasi said. That might give him another chance to make his argument that the
> city's action was driven by economic benefits — the $122 million expansion of
> Good Samaritan Hospital — rather than transportation improvements. If the
> Dimasis prevail on appeal, it's unclear what they would win. They could theo-
> retically get the land back — without the house but with a road. But since no
> Ohio court has ever had to "undo" an eminent-domain case, no one knows how
> that would work. All over the state, lawyers for property owners are prepared
> to make similar arguments:

> In Clifton Heights, the city of Cincinnati took 20 properties and small busi-
> nesses to replace them with a new university-driven development plan. That
> case is now before the Ohio First District Court of Appeals, where lawyers for
> the property owners say Thursday's decision bolsters their case. Specifically,
> the court ruled that "deteriorating" conditions can't be used as a justification
> for eminent domain. "In this case, the city employee that did the review decided
> that anything less than 100 percent new was deteriorated — even down to a
> single piece of chipped paint," said Matthew W. Fellerhoff, the attorney for the
> owners.

> In Cleveland, the port authority is using its eminent-domain powers to
> muscle out small-time developers in the Flats District along the Cuyahoga River
> in favor of a big-time developer who needs parking to build a $230 million shop-
> ping and housing complex. "It seems like to me it's a very good decision," said
> Paul Shaia, one of the owners who operates a parking lot at the site. "It's absurd.
> They want to take a public parking lot to give to a developer to make it a public
> parking lot."[412]

The questions we examined earlier, were popping up in the fourth Constitutional epoch: were roads sacrosanct government purpose? did education trump
housing? did eminent domain necessarily collapse the doctrines and branches
of government? The complex ramifications of *Norwood* in these actions, afforded
a glimpse of the parallel bureaucracy — the third epoch's attempt to cope with
the response to *Kelo* — giving way to its replacement phenomenon: maintenance.
Public opinion — at the same time it was removing facts from the political system

---

412  *The Cincinnati Enquirer*, July 27, 2006.

— was inserting itself in the political system where those facts had been. Among other things, this was a reminder that the concept of the individual is indeterminate, and so all political arrangements — no matter of how long standing — are provisional. More importantly, victory in eminent domain actions meant that the prevailing facts of the cases now had to be maintained, and public opinion had to maintain them. The demands of a parallel enforcement system began to press: should a bond be floated to rebuild the neighborhood? Was that, indeed, mandated by the case? Maintenance had seemed to be the least definable of the rights of the New Bill of Rights — problems defining it had been among the reasons for leaving maintenance to the political process. But the property owners in *Norwood* had maintained housing. What now? Maintenance turned out to be paramount among the facts pulled out of the political system in the fourth Constitutional epoch, just as the Court's persistent invocation of it — across Constitutional epochs with opposed views of the Constitution — seems to have predicted. It was up to public opinion to decide what path was marked out for it to follow after *Norwood*. Public opinion hadn't a clue.

Like every other epoch, the fourth Constitutional epoch had to deal, not only with the new policies it wished to implement, but also, with a legacy produced under rules over which it had had no control. Public opinion had inherited a power system about which it knew little. Was "legacy" — or "heritage" or "consequences" or some other formulation — now a fact of the individual? It was a pressing issue in every one of these new Ohio eminent domain situations. What is the political system of the fourth Constitutional epoch? Judiciary, executive, legislative, Constitution, law — do these concepts have a different, or any, meaning in this new epoch? The fourth epoch's problem was the same as that which had confronted every other Constitutional epoch: it had to come up with results. *Norwood* may have been a *victory*, but as a *result*, it was a stalemate, as all the litigants realized. This was the reality the fourth epoch had to face.

The Court was a continuing problem. The feebleness of its reasoning was suspicious — just as with the Court in *Kelo*, the *Norwood* Court was dissembling, conniving, laying traps again, and producing substantially the opinion Justice Stevens contemplated in saying that states were free to restrict the use of eminent domain. That alone was suspicious, and the result bore out the suspicion, for the freedom in *Norwood* amounted to concurring in *Kelo* — and reaching a different result. What kind of freedom was that? What part of the *Norwood* Court's reasoning said to government, "Go ahead and do what you want, but do it in a way which will make public opinion *go away*"?

*Norwood* was a Trojan horse, in which the Court was attempting to give the "minimum scrutiny" regime viability in the new epoch. The Court was exercising its "corruption reflex," its understanding that the "minimum scrutiny" regime was synonymous with corruption — otherwise that regime simply could not have functioned. The Court automatically assumed that such would be the case in any new regime, and so it was playing its *West Coast Hotel* role of providing the political system with discretion in which corruption could flourish. Is it correct in its assumption? Nor was it clear that public opinion was unwilling to admit that Trojan horse into the new epoch. The fourth epoch inevitably had to deal with legacy government: what to do with a judiciary which — in medieval fashion — viscerally connived? And once public opinion found out that the judiciary was *still* conniving, *still* mendacious, what would be the response in the new epoch? What was the fourth epoch's notion, if any, of the judiciary?

So much for the ambiguities and dissembling at the outset of the fourth Constitutional epoch. What is not ambiguous is that the anti-eminent domain movement sought to end health and welfare regulation under the "minimum scrutiny" regime. This was dramatically revealed in an otherwise typically confusing anti-eminent domain initiative forbidding public-to-private property transfers in connection with the use of eminent domain. The initiative included this shot across the bow in section 8: "Government actions which result in substantial economic loss to private property shall require the payment of just compensation. Examples of such substantial economic loss, include, but are not limited to, the down zoning of private property, the elimination of any access to private property, and limiting the use of private air space."[413] Does this provision maintain property? Is that a "yes or no" question?

The Nevada Supreme Court struck the section from the initiative on "single subject" severability grounds, but its reasoning revealed its loyalty to the scrutiny regime. The Court immediately understood that "this section is extremely broad and concerns any government action that causes substantial loss." So what was the problem with it in connection with a provision restricting eminent domain? Although the Court noted that it itself had found that inverse condemnation cases were the "constitutional equivalent to eminent domain," it did not provide an internally consistent distinction between inverse condemnation and eminent domain — the problem which had always plagued this doctrinal dispute. Thus it simply assumed that "'government actions' related to construction projects, public transportation routes, and the denial of requested zoning changes or special use permits are in no way 'functionally related' or 'germane' [the test for determining if one section of an initiative constitutes a "single subject" in connection with another] to eminent domain, and this section clearly fails to provide sufficient notice of the wide array of subjects address in section 8 or the interests likely to be affected by it." Section 8 was simply broader than the explicit eminent domain provision of the initiative, in which case it is not clear why the Court did not strike the eminent domain provision and not section 8. But it was clear that the "minimum scrutiny" regime was in the crosshairs of the anti-eminent domain movement. Nor did the Court find that section 8 could not validly be the subject of initiative, only that it had to be supported as an independent proposition.[414] The anti-eminent domain movement was pushing the courts toward the world of facts. However, the movement was too stupid, ignorant and self-obsessed to see that it was pushing the courts in a direction it would never have wanted the courts to go: toward the fourth Constitutional epoch's doctrine

---

413  Quoted in *Nevadans for the Protection of Property Rights v. Heller*, No. 47825 Nevada Supreme Court (September 8, 2006), 5-6 (archived online at www.nvsupremecourt.us).

414  Id., at 20-21.

of maintaining important facts. At the same time, the courts had not yet articulated the doctrine.

New York City Mayor Michael Bloomberg has said that if eminent domain were to be restricted, "Every big city would have all construction come to a screeching halt....In the real world you can't say, 'Well, it's just school or just hospitals.' The economics are what pays for those schools...."[415] This is the canonical "minimum scrutiny" litany, the same one recited by the Justices of the Supreme Court. It is a picture of reality, and Bloomberg — incapable of conceiving of another — is proselytizing. For Bloomberg too is obdurate — and he has had quite enough of the pretensions of public opinion!

> In recent weeks, Mr. Bloomberg has traveled to Washington to meet with members of Congress on [eminent domain reform]. He also convened a group of 100 Manhattan-based political donors for a lunch at which he handed out a wallet card of priorities, including "Eminent Domain — Oppose legislation that would cripple affordable housing and responsible re-development (like Times Square)...."While Mr. Bloomberg has already made it known that he supports the use of eminent domain for private development when a neighborhood is "blighted," his comments yesterday were his most forceful to date and signal that he is readying for a fight on eminent domain in much the same way he has entered national political debates on gun control and abortion....The issue put Mr. Bloomberg in the center of yet another national dbate. A professor of public policy at Baruch College, Douglas Muzzio, called Mr. Bloomberg the "mayoral Robert Moses" and said eminent domain is a powerful tool that the mayor doesn't want to give up. "There are those of us who remember the carnage of...slum clearance," he said.[416]

Why does Bloomberg — this doughty knight (Don Quixote) of the "minimum scrutiny" regime — persist? Because the political system includes one important duty which is not often noted. Public opinion has to be reminded that public opinion is not part of the "minimum scrutiny" regime. So browbeating public opinion is part of the job. However, where public opinion proves resistant, Bloomberg is setting terms of unending confrontation. That was fine with him. Just as the Supreme Court justices had dropped their masks, the other actors in the political system were now abandoning their claim to be political.

Now it was about force and the order maintained by force. Feeble efforts in Congress to restrict eminent domain, meant that Congress had to be marched back into line, just as Justice Ginsburg had marched New London's counsel back into line: weaker members of the cabal had to be disciplined by stronger members. Bloomberg went on to push a resolution through the 2006 US Conference of Mayors which tended to confirm the power of eminent domain as a state within a state. Just as arguments in favor of states' rights with respect to slavery, had ignored the implications of facts for rights, so now the mayors sought to protect state and local "rights" — by implication, simply, power. It was a piece of buffoonery, of course — justifying eminent domain as a force for building housing when eminent domain was used to destroy housing. But the point of the mayors

415  March 8, 2006 (archived at www.nyl.com).

416  *New York Sun*, May 3, 2006 (archived online at www.nysun.com).

was clear enough: to try to ensure that no power was exercised except their own by dressing this up in the language of rights:

> WHEREAS, eminent domain is a fundamental and necessary power of government, and

> WHEREAS, the purpose of eminent domain is to allow governments to undertake projects that benefit the whole community, while providing just compensation to property owners for the value of their property, and

> WHEREAS, throughout American history, federal, state and local governments, have used eminent domain to promote the Nation's social and economic welfare with the construction of such essential projects as roads, bridges and schools, and

> WHEREAS, eminent domain is also critically important for municipalities to promote sensible land use, revitalize distressed communities, clean up polluted land, build new infrastructure, and alleviate the problems of unemployment and economic distress by fostering economic development, and

> WHEREAS, economic development, which provides jobs and opportunity to communities, is a fundamental duty of local governments, and

> WHEREAS, one of the biggest obstacles to the revitalization of our metropolitan areas, which include center cities and older inner-ring suburbs where more than 80 percent of the nation's population resides, is the difficulty of assembling parcels of land of sufficient size to allow for new economic development, and the creation of affordable housing, and

> WHEREAS, the absence of appropriate sites often limits opportunities to foster economic development and create affordable housing in places where needs are most significant, and

> WHEREAS, the United States Supreme Court's decision in KELO v. New London has resulted in the examination of the use of eminent domain for economic development at the local, state and Federal levels, and

> WHEREAS, governments should only exercise the power of the eminent domain to achieve important public development objectives that benefit the community, and

> WHEREAS, most private property acquisitions by the government are voluntary, and

> WHEREAS, powers of eminent domain are rarely exercised and are only used by the government as a tool of last resort, and

> WHEREAS state and local laws should address protections to individuals regarding the use of eminent domain, and

> WHEREAS, there are a number of tax benefits often desired by property owners under the threat of eminent domain, and

> WHEREAS, the Congress has limited the use of some federal funds in connection with state and local economic development projects involving eminent domain and provided for a study by the Government Accountability Office on the use of eminent domain,

NOW THEREFORE BE IT RESOLVED, that under our federal system the use of eminent domain by state and local governments is fundamentally a state and local matter and should be addressed by state and local political processes that respond to distinctly local needs and conditions, and

BE IT FURTHER RESOLVED, that the Federal government should not take any additional action to alter the rules governing the use of eminent domain until it has received the Government Accountability Office report and held comprehensive hearings.[417]

The bond market expressed itself forcefully through political actors. Arizona's eminent domain saga looked to continue as the Governor rejected even an anomalous eminent domain reform bill:

> Gov. Janet Napolitano has rejected a measure she says would keep cities from rejuvenating older, more rundown areas of town. Napolitano vetoed a bill Tuesday that would have kept local governments from condemning property to make room for other types of development. The bill made it harder to declare eminent domain, unless there was a clear public need for things such as roads or parks. It also would have forced cities to give a slum or blight designation to individual properties, instead of large swaths of land. And property owners would have had a chance to make improvements before the government forced a land sale. But the governor said the bill went too far by severely limiting the ability of cities to deal with urban blight. She argued that local governments need to balance the rights of private property owners with the need to redevelop rundown areas. 'Without such a balance, slum areas can go unabated and become epicenters of criminal and gang activity,' Napolitano said.[418]

This clown also tripped over herself in urging the use of eminent domain to improve neighborhoods since, again, eminent domain was used to destroy housing. However, that was not inconsistent in this slave of the bond market:

> **Alumnus Magazine:** Let's talk about bonding. Can the state bond? There's a lot of sentiment in Arizona about not allowing the state to go into debt.
>
> **Napolitano.** We absolutely can bond and we should. Let me give you an example. Do you have a mortgage on your home? Of course. The reason you have a mortgage is because you are going to live in your home for many years. It's a long-term asset. Rather than not being able to pay for basic expenses the year you buy your home, you take out a mortgage. That's what people do. That's what bonding is at a public level. Right now, we're involved in a billion dollars worth of school construction projects. We should be bonding for that. Particularly at today's interest rates, it's really dumb not to be in the market right now.[419]

Like Napolitano, Governor Tom Vilsack genuflected before the "minimum scrutiny" regime in rejecting Iowa's weak eminent domain reform bill:

---

417 The resolution is online at the website of the U.S. Conference of Mayors, www.us-mayors.org.

418 *East Valley Tribune*, June 7, 2006 (Phoenix, Arizona, archived at www.eastvalleytribune.com).

419 *Alumnus Magazine*, Spring 2003 (archived at www.uagrad.org).

[He] has decided to veto legislation intended to curb the ability to local governments to take private property for development. The bill, approved by broad bipartisan majorities in the House and Senate, dealt with local governments' eminent domain powers, banning the seizure of private property for economic development. The bill included several exceptions, such as allowing cities to forcibly acquire private property in severely blighted areas....Vilsack expressed concerns that the bill could hurt local job-creation efforts...."You have an interesting balance between job growth, which everybody supports, and restricting the power of government, which a lot of people support," he said.[420]

The "minimum scrutiny" regime permits no new legal concepts; it holds every legal concept hostage to it by holding each legal concept hostage to all the others (the same goes for regime actors). No new legal concepts enter the regime, and when extant legal concepts threaten to change, other legal concepts of the regime are arrayed against the change. We have heard the pronouncement of the Choir of Mayors and Governors: the scrutiny regime means, no change. Scrutiny means, prevailing in physical confrontations over the facts. As a result, for the regime, legal ideas are indicia of criminal law and procedure; these latter are at every point subordinate to the concept of scrutiny. Force — not facts — rules all.

\* \* \*

At this point, history intervened to bring us around to our initial examination of the role of the Federal Government in eminent domain, in the Poletown example. The Federal Government embroiled itself in the meaninglessness of "economic development," adopting a similar concept of the "economic interest of private parties." On June 23, 2006, President Bush issued the following Executive Order:

It is the policy of the United States to protect the rights of Americans to their private property, including by limiting the taking of private property by the Federal Government to situations in which the taking is for public use, with just compensation, and for the purpose of benefiting the general public and not merely for the purpose of advancing the economic interest of private parties to be given ownership or use of the property taken.....Nothing in this order shall be construed to prohibit a taking of private property by the Federal Government, that otherwise complies with applicable law, for the purpose of:

(a) public ownership or exclusive use of the property by the public, such as for a public medical facility, roadway, park, forest, governmental office building, or military reservation;

(b) projects designated for public, common carrier, public transportation, or public utility use, including those for which a fee is assessed, that serve the general public and are subject to regulation by a governmental entity;

(c) conveying the property to a nongovernmental entity, such as a telecommunications or transportation common carrier, that makes the property available for use by the general public as of right;

---

420 *Sioux City Journal*, June 2, 2006 (Sioux City, Iowa, archived at www.siouxcityjournal.com).

(d) preventing or mitigating a harmful use of land that constitutes a threat to public health, safety, or the environment;

(e) acquiring abandoned property;

(f) quieting title to real property;

(g) acquiring ownership or use by a public utility;

(h) facilitating the disposal or exchange of Federal property; or

(i) meeting military, law enforcement, public safety, public transportation, or public health emergencies....

This order is not intended to, and does not, create any right or benefit, substantive or procedural, enforceable at law or in equity against the United States, its departments, agencies, entities, officers, employees, or agents, or any other person.[421]

This self-imposed restriction — not mandated by any legislation or court decision — was a signal that new facts were moving out of the political system. Which ones, to what extent, and in which contexts? Note that the forbidden activity relates not only to "ownership," but also to "use." What causes of action, in what parties, would this Order have created had it existed at the time of the Poletown taking? Can this Order be restricted to eminent domain takings, or does "use" extend it to regulations promulgated by the Federal Government? Is this a permissible restriction of the powers of the Federal Government? To the preservation of which facts does this Order commit the Federal Government?

Whatever the Government's putative immunity under the Order, now that it had entered the fray in which facts and their implications were contested, could it any longer isolate facts or powers which could not be contested, or had it begun to give up that power regardless of the reservations it seemed to make? Whatever reserved powers the Administration claimed for the Federal Government with respect to eminent domain, these began to be eroded from the *inside* — from legislators attempting to protect constituents locally from eminent domain exercised on the national level:

Congresswoman Sue Kelly introduced legislation in Congress Tuesday that would close a loophole in national energy law and proactively preempt New York Regional Interconnect from invoking eminent domain to carry out its power-line project that would run from Oneida County to Eastern Orange County. "Eminent domain is a tool that will likely be sought to advance this widely-opposed plan," said Kelly on the floor of the House. In an effort to block that, Kelly introduced the "Protecting Communities from Power Line Abuse Act." The proposed legislation would rescind a provision in the Energy Policy Act that allows permit holders to petition the US District Court for a right-of-way to construct power lines via eminent domain. Kelly voted against the Energy Bill when it passed Congress in 2005, and she also opposed the legislation during attempts to pass it into law in 2003-2004. "This gives eminent domain power not to an accountable government entity, but rather to private companies," Kelly said on the House floor. She noted that until this provision is repealed, local residents as

---

421 The complete text is online at www.whitehouse.gov.

well as their local and federal governments are powerless in preventing a permit holder from seeking eminent domain to build power lines. NYRI is applying to construct a 1,200-megawatt electric transmission line across a 200-mile span of New York. The route proposed by NYRI will travel through the federally protected Upper Delaware Scenic and Recreational River — an area which is part of the National Park Service's National Wild and Scenic Rivers System.[422]

If this Federal use of eminent domain could be stopped, what other Federal exercises of eminent domain could be stopped? And then what other tax and spend powers could be restricted? What implications did this have for the Federal debt market? And yet what was the principle underlying the opposition to this eminent domain use? Kelly herself — like proponents of eminent domain — also regards it as a "tool" and indicates only that the plan is "widely-opposed." No importance is given to the protection of specific facts, much less the level of Constitutional scrutiny at which that protection operates. The Administration had sought a general prohibition regarding a general rule, but the opposition to *Kelo* was about facts, not about generalities. The Government could no longer rule through generalities because there was no longer a consensus regarding generalities. How could the Federal Government not be forced, sooner or later, to commit itself to factual indicia of "advancing the economic interest of private parties?" What then? The Federal Government had admitted facts into its area of discretion. Did it even know what it was doing?

The New Bill of Rights originated in public opinion's sense, not that doctrinal boundaries had been crossed, but rather, that **facts** had been violated. In *Kelo* the Court demanded that public opinion accept the idea that although the Court *could* vindicate for government an abuse of the rights of an individual, that same Court *could not* vindicate for the same individual the same rights against the same government. In the response to *Kelo* public opinion declined any longer to accept that idea. The combination of hazy rationale and sharp perception accompanying the New Bill of Rights on its odyssey of enforcement, is remarkably similar to the motivation accompanying the French Declaration of Rights. As one historian has noted:

> [The French] believed...that all misgovernment and all public ills were due to a failure to recognize the rights of man. They did not need Locke or Hobbes, Mably or Rousseau, to teach them this truth. They did not much care whether rights had existed before the state, or the state before rights. They only knew that for centuries Frenchman had been forced to do this and prevented from doing that by their landlords and their kings. The Declaration was neither the manifesto of a new nation...nor a revolutionary class program. It was a Bill of Rights, reasserting liberties which had been overruled, establishing rights which had been obscured by wrongs.[423]

To which we must add a — somewhat melancholy — word describing the crisis attending the decline of the Roman Republic, a period similar to that attending the birth of the fourth Constitutional epoch in that the crisis of the Re-

---

422 July 18, 2006 (archived at www.midhudsonnews.com).

423 J. M. Thompson, *The French Revolution* (Sutton Publishing 2001) at 85-86.

public was also characterized by an inability to find an ideological footing after the collapse of the doctrinal basis of the era:

> This does not imply that in the crisis there was any dearth of "alternatives" — that is to say, different courses that might be adopted as the situation changed — or that it was impossible to introduce this or that reform....Yet one thing could not be done: no new force could be created that was capable of placing the absolute and largely ineffectual inherited order on a new footing. As long as this remained impossible, even reforms tended only to prolong the crisis....An order usually fails when the community is no longer able, with its help, to perform its tasks more or less satisfactorily, or at least without causing major damage.[424]

Across the United States, both sides now awaited the first serious clash over the question, what are the facts of the individual? The question was to be answered using one of three methods: the new scrutiny continuum, the New Bill of Rights, or the "facts of the individual" analysis. But one or another of them had to be used. Why?

---

424 Meier at 491.

# Conclusion

As we have seen, the anti-eminent domain movement both formed part of, and contributed to, the breakdown of the scrutiny regime. It is part of a vast change in Constitutional interpretation, and needs to be seen in that light. The origin of the change was public opinion's conclusion that its security — certain facts — had been stolen by the political system. Public opinion now demanded these facts be removed from the political system. The political system had failed public opinion.

The removal process began with a sense of the abuse of facts of human importance. Then it moved to identify government as the abuser, and to limit the most sensational techniques of abuse. From there it inquired into similar powers to abuse, and into other facts, generated complaints with respect to those facts, and then imposed even more limitations on governmental powers. Power by power and fact by fact, the scrutiny regime was broken down. The movement seemed at times inarticulate and inconsistent — and it inherited immemorial dilemmas of power — but the source was clear enough: a sea change in public opinion that was not to be denied. The tenacious but inept response of the scrutiny regime did not prevail against it.

From these developments emerged the political component, the supreme doctrine of the fourth Constitutional epoch: every law maintains an important fact. However much the old issues and anomalies asserted themselves in this new doctrine, they were sorted by a new set of inquiries, into the terms, every, maintain and important. The cases we have examined show us both continuity between the Constitutional epochs, and change from one to another.

We have seen the pervasive importance of maintenance in the Supreme Court's jurisprudence. It is one of those terms which was carried over from the pre-scrutiny days into the scrutiny regime, forming part of an informal Supreme Court jurisprudence which would inevitably assert itself as doctrine and now, in the fourth Constitutional epoch, has done so. Maintenance was vital to the outcome in Village of *Euclid, Ohio v. Ambler Realty Co.*, which established both the constitutionality of zoning and housing as an indicium of maintenance. For the Court, not only did zoning have a role in maintaining housing, it also had a role in creating it. That concern survived in *Kelo v. New London*, when Justice Kennedy insisted — in his tests for government purpose — that that purpose involve an inquiry into the past, into that which exists, before government proposes to change it. This is the death of discretion.

Even the terms of *Euclid* marched across the epochs. It was not enough for the Euclid Court that there be a "rational relation" between the facts and the government purpose. It proceeded to define the term as involving an examination into policy results.

The Court's concern with results was subordinated when the scrutiny regime took over in *West Coast Hotel*. Nevertheless, maintenance survived within the scrutiny regime, even in *West Coast Hotel*. For that Court, the importance of minimum wage laws was not that they vindicated the role of the legislature in the political system. The laws were important because they were an indicium of maintenance. Wages were an important fact with respect to maintenance, and wage laws needed to be upheld because maintenance had to be vindicated. Maintenance was an unchanging fact of human experience — tested over time — and from the scrutiny regime, and earlier, it made its way into the New Bill of Rights.

That the *West Coast Hotel* Court did not explicitly give primacy to the maintenance concept was merely one of the faults of *West Coast Hotel* which undermined the third Constitutional epoch from its very outset. In its subordination of liberty, the Court skipped over many important questions regarding the indicia of liberty and the factual relationship of liberty to the facts of *West Coast Hotel*. Opposition to the scrutiny came to form around concepts to which the Court had paid insufficient attention. It is now a commonplace to say that it was a poor choice to link liberty to minimum wage laws, and such a link had not been advanced by the State of Washington, which had passed the minimum wage law. How poor that choice was came to be seen in *Lawrence v. Texas*, which found sodomy laws unconstitutional. Nevertheless, *West Coast Hotel* became the foundation for what later emerged as the three levels of scrutiny: minimum scrutiny, in which laws are found Constitutional if they are rationally related to a legitimate government purpose; intermediate scrutiny, in which laws are found Constitutional if they substantially further an important government purpose; and strict scrutiny, in which laws are found Constitutional if they specifically fulfill an overriding government purpose. As these levels were examined more carefully, they provided opportunities for opposition.

The consensus is that the bases and tenets of the scrutiny regime were overthrown in *Lawrence*, but previous cases had clearly prepared the way for what the

Court now found. The Court found that, in certain cases, sodomy was liberty, and found the law banning it in these cases unconstitutional because the law "furthers no legitimate government interest."[425] Whatever the factual relationship between sodomy and liberty, the Court's analysis turned this test into a mandate of maintenance. Regarded as a scrutiny regime case, *Lawrence* took "furthers" from intermediate scrutiny and "legitimate" from minimum scrutiny. How could it do so? By substituting liberty as a fact for liberty as a goal (the latter being the *West Coast Hotel* innovation). The *Lawrence* Court said that if liberty is sustained, then it is maintained. Government was no longer free to "dream" or "fantasize." The facts kept it on a short leash.

The Court never uses "maintain" or "maintenance" in *Lawrence*. How, then, do we know that the Court is interested in reading "government purpose" out of the Constitution? By a line of cases which gave increased prominence to "government purpose" as a factual test. The Court moved, in Midkiff, Romer, Virginia and Kelo, from a position of virtually dispensing with facts in considering "government purpose," to articulating careful steps for factual discovery of "government purpose." These tests were the death of "government purpose" because they revealed that "government purpose" was a stalemate with respect to both normative and speculative concerns. The scrutiny regime was supposed to neatly resolve things. Instead, it proved to be its own death sentence. The impetus behind eminent domain reform, and the broadening base of opposition to *Kelo*, showed that clearly.

The new test said that not only must there in fact be a "government purpose," but also, that purpose must have a relation to other facts predating the institution of the policy. The Court was interested in seeing that the state had maintained important facts — a survival of Euclid. This accorded with the gravamen of the complaint of the opposition to Kelo itself: the scrutiny regime had allowed government to ignore what is, in favor of what might be. The political system had to be awakened from its dream, otherwise known as discretion.

Justice Kennedy said that the Court needs to know if, in fact, there is a government purpose and he said that the Court can only do so after the Court has seen facts relating to specific criteria. He adduced a huge number of terms for civil discovery: plausible, impermissible, private, benefit, businesses, incidental, depressed, economic, validity, concern, substantial, commitment, before, review, variety, chose, particular, project, unknown, space, build. Every one was a corpus of case law. But they could be reduced to this: there had to be facts in need of a policy; otherwise, law is the maintenance of facts, and there is no government purpose. This was training a political system which had no intention of being trained.

I had written to the group Develop Don't Destroy Brooklyn, which included property owners whose properties were subject to eminent domain for a projected massive development in Brooklyn, New York. The "Atlantic Yards" project is a gargantuan skyscraper + stadium, seven-block proposed construction project. I wrote to remind them: "I don't think it will take a genius to find out that private purpose has been substituted for government purpose in the Atlan-

---

425 *Lawrence* at 560.

tic Yards case. There is already so much evidence of it in the press that it seems impossible that a judge would not grant an injunction — even at this relatively early stage — against the project on the basis that it violates minimum scrutiny because there is no government purpose, only private purpose. However, when attorneys defending the Atlantic Yards residents go into court to make that motion, they had better be prepared to show that they have done their homework: they had better take the depositions and subpoena the documents implied by Justice Kennedy's remarks. Attorneys have become so lazy under the former hazy definition of government purpose, that they don't do their work. The Atlantic Yards residents should bring heavy pressure on their attorneys to do the work Justice Kennedy demands."[426] The argument of the ensuing complaint was that private purpose had been substituted for government purpose: "In order to meet the Constitutional requirements of the Takings Clause, government may seize private property through the power of eminent domain only if the taking is for public use. The taking of plaintiffs' properties here violates that stricture because the [project] itself was conceived by [developer Bruce Ratner], and is being driven by his needs, motives and vision, not those of the public at large. Far from emerging from a legitimate democratic process where the public interest is identified and articulated by its elective representatives,...here the project is a product of a developer's dream — and a conscious effort to bypass City procedures mandating meaningful local review, planning, democratic oversight and community input. By the summer of 2002, FCRF [Forest City Ratner Companies, the developer] had developed plans for the [Brooklyn] project — plans which centered on several huge commercial and residential buildings and an indoor sports arena — and were ready to quietly approach City officials for support. Support came, virtually immediately; by the end of that summer, Mayor Bloomberg, and his deputy for economic development, Daniel Doctoroff, were on board." Government processes involved in establishing government purpose, were a "sham," the resulting government formulations a "pretext."[427] This was the story of the *Kelo*

---

426 August 3, 2006, at www.nolandgrab.com.

427 The complaint is online at http://dddb.net/php/reading/legal/eminentdomain. I sent the lawyers these comments on the complaint: "1. Look into the 501(c) (3) status of the EDC and the ESDC [the two non-profit development corporations designated to handle the Atlantic Yards project]. You may want to talk to a tax attorney about this. Basically, for these entities to enjoy tax exempt status, their actions must have a government purpose. That is, I think it is the same test for governments themselves—there must be a government purpose for their actions. If so, you might want to inform the IRS, and you may want to contest the use of any monies they may have gathered or dispensed. As you know, it's about the money, so you may as well track down every cent. Were any bonds issued yet in connection with this fiasco? That's where you want to attack this as well. That activity must also comply with 501 regulations—the bonds must have a government purpose. Make sure those bonds do NOT get issued or are cancelled. Stop the flow of that money....2. Consider civil RICO. In connection with that, I notice that although you allege conspiracy, you don't allege fraud. There are undoubtedly many fraudulent statements made officially by these people in using government processes as a pretext for this taking. 3. Your equal protection argument is, perhaps, not as clear as it could be. Even when, for equal protection purposes, facts do not enjoy a higher level of scrutiny with respect to a targeted group, that targeted group has nevertheless suffered an equal protection injury if

taking, all over again. However, when it distinguished *Atlantic Yards* from *Kelo*, the IJ misrepresented the chronology, and its own role in advancing an incorrect chronology: "In *Kelo*...the city had followed a specific process, and did not have a developer when it conceived of the project."[428] Much more important was the idea that, as lawyers challenged the absence of government purpose, they were bringing into enforcement what was, in fact, government purpose: maintaining important facts. Thus the Constitution had come full circle. However, in the process the scrutiny regime had been eliminated.

The drive beyond restriction of eminent domain use finally produced a property right amendment. Unnoticed by either its opponents or, apparently, its proponents, California's Proposition 90 struck back at the weak eminent domain reform passed by the California legislature. The Proposition even went far beyond the usual anti-*Kelo* eminent domain reforms which restrict when eminent domain may be used. It even went beyond "*Kelo* plus" initiatives, which demand compensation not only for eminent domain takings but also for land use regulations which reduce the value of real property.[429] Proposition 90 overthrew the

---

policy involving the facts with respect to the targeted group, doesn't have a government purpose. That is how you get equal protection for groups which don't fall into the usual suspect classes [race and sex]. It doesn't matter if the Court is unwilling to extend suspect class status to new groups. Since government purpose is an issue of fact for the trier of fact, all you need to show is the targeted group, injury and private, as opposed to government, purpose, and you have made out an equal protection case. It's not our doing that the Court made government purpose an issue of fact in *Romer v. Evans* and *U.S. v. Virginia*, and then articulated it in the context of eminent domain in Kennedy's *Kelo* concurrence. The Court has done so—let them live with it. The point is that government purpose operates as an issue of fact for the trier of fact, with respect to EACH and EVERY part of the Constitution. Everything done by government in the United States, must in FACT have a government purpose. Thus, I don't think you should have used 'no rational purpose' in your equal protection claim. That means, 'no facts.' And that is certainly true here, but not perhaps precisely the point. The point is that there are NO facts to show government purpose, and there ARE facts to show private purpose. This means there was no government purpose."

428 *New York Law Journal*, October 27, 2006 (archived at www.law.com).

429 For a brief introduction to the other initiatives, see *The Thicket*, September 27, 2006 (archived online at *www.ncsl.typepad.com*). The "Kelo plus" initiatives may be considered the flip side of so-called TABOR (taxpayer bill of rights) initiatives, which put a cap on state spending/taxing based on a formula measuring inflation and population growth—an attack on "government purpose" tax and spend power under minimum scrutiny, and an embryonic attempt to formulate factual indicia of both government and maintenance. The TABOR proposals have come in for much polemical—but not much scholarly—commentary. See a bibliography at *www.legis.state.wi.us/lrb/pubs/tapthepower.htm*. Colorado has been wrestling with the effects of its TABOR law for over a decade. See a summary at *http://www.ncsl.org/programs/fiscal/taborpts.htm*. Needless to say, the bond market was not amused by Colorado's TABOR law, and lowered its credit rating. See Dennis Hoffman and Timothy Hogan, "The Taxpayer's Bill of Rights: Evidence from Colorado and Implications for Arizona," *http://wpcarey.asu.edu/seidman/reports/tabor.pdf*. See also Iris J. Lav and Karen Lyons, "Maine's 'Taxpayer Bill of Rights' Proposal Fails to Fix Flaws of Colorado's TABOR," 40 *State Tax Notes* No. 2 (April 10, 2006); Therese J. McGuire and Kim S. Rueben, "The Colorado Revenue Limit: The Economic Effect of TABOR," 40 *State Tax Notes* No. 6 (May 8, 2006); Andrew Reschovsky, "The Taxpayer Bill of Rights (TSBO): A Solution to Wisconsin's

scrutiny regime and established the doctrine of the fourth epoch: every law maintains an important fact.

Proposition 90 did not mention land use regulation, or regulation at all — it cast its net very widely: "government action." Section 3, Paragraph 8 of the initiative stated: "Except when taken to protect public health and safety, 'damage' to private property includes government actions that result in substantial economic loss to private property. Examples of substantial economic loss include, but are not limited to, the downzoning of private property, the elimination of any access to private property, and limitations on the use of private air space. 'Government action' shall mean any statute, charter provision, ordinance, resolution, law, rule or regulation."[430] The examples provided guidance if the government action relates to real property. But what if it didn't? Proposition 90 related to "private property," not merely to real property. The broadest concept of property in American law is known as the "property interest," and under the Fourteenth Amendment its reach is extensive.[431] For example: "Beyond employment the [Supreme] Court [has] found 'legitimate entitlements' in a variety of situations....[S]tudents [are accorded] some due process hearing rights prior to suspending them, even for such a short period as ten days....[A cause of action for discrimination is] a property interest....Beyond statutory entitlements, the Court has looked to state decisional law to find that private utilities may not terminate service at will but only for cause, for nonpayment of charges, so that when there was a dispute about payment or the accuracy of charges, due process required the utility to follow procedures to resolve the dispute prior to terminating service."[432] If government lowered unemployment compensation — or ended it — was that compensable under Proposition 90? Was an electricity rate increase? Was "education" a property interest, such that suspension was compensable? Was lack of health insurance compensable under Proposition 90? Housing eviction? Suddenly the academic debate we reviewed earlier regarding facts as rights had entered the Constitutional arena.

The scrutiny regime reacted peevishly to "regulatory takings" initiatives such as Proposition 90. For the regime, these initiatives were neither logical extensions of eminent domain reform proposals nor did they reflect public opinion's decision to eliminate the scrutiny regime. Instead they were underhanded attempts to insert such initiatives in eminent domain reform proposals, and public opinion could not have the last word with respect to them: "[T]he best hope for an orderly and governable California future will be for some courageous judge to step in and limit Proposition 90's effect to the eminent domain seizures that are the focus of its appeal. For when voters are deceived by an inaccurately titled and

---

Fiscal Problems or a Prescription for Future Fiscal Crises?" 33 *State Tax Notes* No. 4 (July 26, 2004).

430 The text and analysis of the Legislative Analyst are online at *www.ss.ca.gov/elections*.

431 *Board of Regents v. Roth*, 408 US 564 (1972).

432 This summary is provided at *www.law.cornell.edu*. Citations omitted.

deceptively hyped ballot measure, they need some educated backup."[433] And yet Oregon's similar Measure 37 had been upheld by the Oregon Supreme Court,[434] and "regulatory takings" laws were consistent with the scrutiny regime. The basis of opposition to "regulatory takings" initiatives was that it was an inherent feature of the regime that the regime could not be changed—a baseless, not to mention provocative, contention which showed a regime fatally out of touch with the facts.

Washington's Initiative 933 made it crystal clear that its compensation provision reached as far as the concept of property, to any type of regulation, and to a much higher level of scrutiny than minimum scrutiny. Indeed, it was a maintenance right to property: "To avoid damaging the use or value of private property, prior to enacting or adopting any ordinance, regulation, or rule which may damage the use or value of private property, an agency must consider and document: (a) The private property that will be affected by the action; (b) The existence and extent of any legitimate governmental purpose for the action; (c) The existence and extent of any nexus or link between any legitimate government interest and the action; (d) The extent to which the regulation's restrictions are proportional to any impact of a particular property on any legitimate government interest, in light of the impact of other properties on the same governmental interests; (e) The extent to which the action deprives property owners of economically viable uses of the property; (f) The extent to which the action derogates or takes away a fundamental attribute of property ownership, including, but not limited to, the right to exclude others, to possess, to beneficial use, to enjoyment, or to dispose of property; (g) The extent to which the action enhances or creates a publicly owned right in property; (h) Estimated compensation that may need to be paid under this act; and (i) Alternative means which are less restrictive on private property and which may accomplish the legitimate governmental purpose for the regulation, including, but not limited to, voluntary conservation or cooperative programs with willing property owners, or other nonregulatory actions....For purposes of this act, the following definitions apply: 'Private property' includes all real and personal property interests protected by the fifth amendment to the United States Constitution or Article I, section 16 of the state Constitution[435]

---

433  *The Daily Breeze*, October 17, 2006 (archived at www.dailybreeze.com).

434  *MacPherson v. Department of Administrative Services*, Oregon Supreme Court No. S52875 (February 21, 2006), online at http://www.publications.ojd.state.or.us/S52875.htm.

435  "Private property shall not be taken for private use, except for private ways of necessity, and for drains, flumes, or ditches on or across the lands of others for agricultural, domestic, or sanitary purposes. No private property shall be taken or damaged for public or private use without just compensation having been first made, or paid into court for the owner, and no right-of-way shall be appropriated to the use of any corporation other than municipal until full compensation therefor be first made in money, or ascertained and paid into court for the owner, irrespective of any benefit from any improvement proposed by such corporation, which compensation shall be ascertained by a jury, unless a jury be waived, as in other civil cases in courts of record, in the manner prescribed by law. Whenever an attempt is made to take private property for a use alleged to be public, the question whether the contemplated use be really public shall be a judicial question, and determined as such, without regard to any legislative assertion that the use is public:

owned by a nongovernmental entity, including, but not limited to, any interest in land, buildings, crops, livestock, and mineral and water rights."[436] The implications of this section were that maintenance of property is the mandated initial goal, and that the question of government with respect to property, is rarely if ever reached.

But now there was no scrutiny regime to answer the question, what in fact is property? by referring it to the political system—the procedure of the scrutiny regime. Thus, the initiatives now inherited the immemorial ambiguity of the facts. The doctrine was explicit, but the facts were just as murky as ever. Nor was there any indication that public opinion would share the definition of property — whatever that was — which had motivated those who had drafted laws in the name of public opinion. Nor was there any indication that the drafters' restrictions were the extent of what public opinion demanded with respect to the facts. Were the advocates of these propositions, ready to govern?

In any event, on the basis of these propositions it is possible to formulate a property right which captures the trend of the initiatives: "Eminent domain or regulation of any property interest shall not be exercised unless it specifically fulfills an overriding government purpose, and shall be compensated at the full value of such exercise." Note, however, that this is not legally equivalent to, "No individual shall be involuntarily deprived of property." For the "property rights" movement, property was an indicium of power, not an indicium of the individual. There was no consensus that property is a fact of the individual.

Public opinion had begun the work of removing facts from the political system. And that is the perspective in which we must in the end see the opposition to *Kelo*. *Kelo* itself — while purporting to vindicate the scrutiny regime — undermined it, both in its own terms and in the reaction it generated. Public opinion had become aware that everything about the scrutiny regime undermined the regime. This meant that the regime could not command the support of public opinion: the third Constitutional epoch had lost the mandate to govern. It could not, and did not, survive that loss, no matter how many cases proceeded to uphold — or seem to uphold — the remnants of the regime.

No doctrine could survive public opinion, if survival — as here — was in question. There had to be no question, or there could be no survival. This is consonant with the view that Constitutional epochs succeed each other simply on the basis of perceived political needs. Such a conclusion seems to call in question the putative internal consistency of the doctrines of the Constitutional epochs. That, however, in turn assumes — perhaps fancifully — that internal consistency has to do with the emergence, dominance and decline of these epochs whereas its presence, as we have seen, is only intermittently traceable. As for the scrutiny regime, the only law it seemed to have established was that corruption is inversely proportional to the size of the middle class. In the event the fourth Constitutional epoch came rapidly to be characterized by struggle for mastery of the terms

---

*Provided,* That the taking of private property by the state for land reclamation and settlement purposes is hereby declared to be for public use."

436  The text is online at www.secstate.wa.gov/elections/initiatives/text/i933.pdf.

"every," "maintain" and "important." But the working out of those struggles is yet to come. Our story of the birth of the new epoch is finished.

*Sauve qui peut.*

# Bibliography

NOTE: The fourth Constitutional epoch and its concerns are too new to have found their way into monographs. The scholarly work so far is confined—if that is the term for the copious production—to essays, as is this bibliography. It is not intended to be comprehensive, merely suggestive of the lines of argument currently carried out in the periodical literature.

## Constitution and Rights

Avi Ben-Bassat and Momi Dahan, "Social Rights in the Constitution and in Practice," http://ssrn.com/abstraction=407260.

Avinash Ashutosh Bhagwat, "The Test That Ate Everything: Intermediate Scrutiny in First Amendment Jurisprudence," http://ssrn.com/abstract=887566.

Reynaud Neil Daniels, "Counter-Majoritarian Difficulty in South African Constitutional Law," http://law.bepress.com/expresso/eps/1363.

Michael Steven Green, "Legal Revolutions: Six Mistakes about Discontinuity in the Legal Order," http://ssrn.com/abstract=881073.

Steven J. Heyman, "Ideological Conflict and the First Amendment," http://ssrn.com/abstract=436985.

Kurt Lash, summarizing his article, "The Constitutional Convention of 1937: The Original Meaning of the New Jurisprudential Deal," http://ssrn.com/abstract=264214.

David D. Meyer, "Lochner Redeemed: Family Privacy After Troxel and Carhart," http://ssrn.com/abstract=288816.

Charles A. Sullivan, "Re-reviving Disparate Impact," http://ssrn.com/abstract=581503.

Neil Walker, "Legal Theory and the European Union," http://ssrn.com/abstract=891032.

G. Edward White, "Historicizing Judicial Scrutiny," http://law.bepress.com/uvalwps/uva publiclaw/art31.

Adam Winkler, "Fatal in Theory and Strict in Fact: An Empirical Analysis of Strict Scrutiny in the Federal Courts," http://ssrn.com/abstract=897360.

## Democracy and Government

Matthew D. Adler and Chris William Sanchirico, "Inequality and Uncertainty: Theory and Legal Applications," http://ssrn.com/abstract=886571.

Jeffrey C. O'Neill, "Everything that can be Counted Does not Necessarily Count: The Right to Vote and the Choice of a Voting System," http://ssrn.com/abstract=889466.

Michael J. Perry, "Protecting Human Rights in a Democracy: What Role for the Courts?" http://ssrn.com/abstract=380283.

## Education

Michael Heise, "Educational Adequacy as Legal Theory: Implications from Equal Educational Opportunity Doctrine," http://ssrn.com/abstract=815665.

Yoram Rabin, "Deconstructing the Constitutional Right to Education," http://ssrn.com/abstract=896519.

## Eminent Domain

Hanoch Dagan, "Takings and Distributive Justice," http://ssrn.com/abstract=158194.

William Fischel, "The Political Economy of Public Use in Poletown," 2004 Michigan State Law Review 929 (Winter 2004).

Howard C. Klemme, "Takings and the Regulatory Roles of Government (Introduction and Overview)," http://ssrn.com/abstract=348400.

## Housing

Nestor M. Davidson, "'Housing First' for the Chronically Homeless: Challenges of a New Service Model," http://ssrn.com/abstract=898259.

Richard K. Green and Susan M. Wachter, "The American Mortgage in Historical and International Context," http://ssrn.com/abstract=908976.

## Judiciary

Edward K. Cheng, "Independent Judicial Research in the Daubert Age," http://ssrn.com/abstract=885387.

Helen J. Knowles, "From a Value to a Right: The Supreme Court's Oh-So-Conscious Move from 'Privacy' to 'Liberty,'" http://ssrn.com/abstract=921916.

Lawrence B. Solum, "Procedural Justice," http://ssrn.com/abstract=508282.

## LIBERTY

Catherine L. Carpenter, "On Statutory Rape, Strict Liability, and the Public Welfare Offense Model," http://ssrn.com/abstract=907682.

Thomas L. Hafemeister, "Parameters and Implementation of a Right to Mental Health Treatment of Juvenile Offenders," 12 Virginia Journal of Social Policy and the Law No. 1 (2004).

Eric S. Janus and Wayne A. Logan, "Substantive Due Process and the Involuntary Confinement of Sexually Violent Predators," 35 Connecticut Law Review No. 2 (Winter 2003).

## MAINTENANCE

Bruno Amable et al., "Welfare State Retrenchment: The Partisan Effect Revisited," http://ssrn.com/abstract=889041.

James W. Ely, "'To Pursue any Lawful Trade or Avocation:' The Evolution of Unenumerated Economic Rights in the Nineteenth Century," http://ssrn.com/abstract=881833.

## MEDICAL CARE

Michael Patrick Allen, "The Constitution at the Threshold of Life and Death: A Suggested Approach to Accommodate an Interest in Life and a Right to Die," http://ssrn.com/abstract=595763.

Scott C. Burris, "From Security to Health," http://ssrn.com/abstract=890425.

Mark A. Hall, "The History and Future of Health Care Law: An Essentialist View," http://www.law.wfu.edu/x2083.xml.

Marshall Kapp, "Geriatric Depression: Do Older Persons Have a Right to be Unhappy?" http://ssrn.com/abstract=310581.

Abhik Majumdar, "The Right to Die: The Indian Experience," http://ssrn.com/abstract=902875. .

Diana Hassel, "Sex and Death: Lawrence's Liberty and Physician-Assisted Suicide," http://ssrn.com/abstract=902429.

## PRIVACY

Lois L. Shepherd, "Looking Forward With The Right Of Privacy," http://ssrn.com/abstract=225040.

Daniel J. Solove, "A Taxonomy of Privacy," http://ssrn.com/abstract=667622 .

## PROPERTY

William L. Andreen, "The Evolving Contours of Water Law in the United States: Bridging the Gap between Water Rights, Land Use and the Protection of the Aquatic Environment," http://ssrn.com/abstract=889744.

Gregory S. Alexander, "Property As a Fundamental Right? The German Example," http://ssrn.com/abstract=384161.

Laurence R. Helfer, "Toward a Human Rights Framework for Intellectual Property," http://ssrn.com/abstract=891303.

Marca Weinberg, "Assessing a Policy Grab Bag: Federal Water Policy Reform," http://ssrn.com/abstract=320420.

## RELIGION

Steven Douglas Smith, "Barnette's Big Blunder," http://ssrn.com/abstract=417480.

## SPEECH

Larry Alexander, "Freedom of Expression as a Human Right," http://ssrn.com/abstract=285432.

Clifford G. Holderness, Michael C. Jensen and William H. Meckling, "The Logic of the First Amendment," http://ssrn.com/abstract=215468.

## TAXATION

Dennis Hoffman and Timothy Hogan, "The Taxpayer's Bill of Rights: Evidence from Colorado and Implications for Arizona," http://wpcarey.asu.edu/seidman/reports/tabor.pdf.

Iris J. Lav and Karen Lyons, "Maine's 'Taxpayer Bill of Rights' Proposal Fails to Fix Flaws of Colorado's TABOR," 40 State Tax Notes No. 2 (April 10, 2006).

Robert W. McGee, "Taxation and Public Finance: A Philosophical and Ethical Approach," http://ssrn.com/abstract=461340.

Therese J. McGuire and Kim S. Rueben, "The Colorado Revenue Limit: The Economic Effect of TABOR," 40 State Tax Notes No. 6 (May 8, 2006).

Andrew Reschovsky, "The Taxpayer Bill of Rights (TSBO): A Solution to Wisconsin's Fiscal Problems or a Prescription for Future Fiscal Crises?" 33 State Tax Notes No. 4 (July 26, 2004).

# INDEX